# Trade and Employment

From Myths to Facts

# Trade and Employment
## From Myths to Facts

*Editors: Marion Jansen, Ralf Peters, José Manuel Salazar-Xirinachs*

INTERNATIONAL LABOUR OFFICE • GENEVA

Trade and employment: from myths to facts / International Labour Office. - Geneva: ILO, 2011
International Labour Office

ISBN: 978-92-2-125320-4 (print)
ISBN: 978-92-2-125321-1 (web pdf)

trade / trade liberalization / employment / employment policy / gender equality / informal economy / developed countries / developing countries
1 v.
09.05.1

*ILO Cataloguing in Publication Data*

This publication has been produced with the assistance of the European Union. The contents of this publication are the sole responsibility of the authors and can in no way be taken to reflect the views of the European Union or the International Labour Organization.

Photocomposed in Switzerland                                                    SCR
Printed in Switzerland                                                          ATA

# PREFACE

Trade negotiations –bilateral, regional or multilateral – routinely lead to debates on the implications for employment. There are promises of new and better jobs as well as concerns over job losses and pressure on wages and labour rights. Factual assessments of the employment and distributional impacts of trade agreements are, however, too often missing.

This edited volume tries to address this disconnect between the trade-and-employment linkages in public debates and the relative absence of factual assessments of the employment and distributional implications of trade. The publication is an outcome of a joint project of the European Commission and the International Labour Office on "Assessing and addressing the employment effects of trade".

This publication has three objectives: First, to fill knowledge gaps by taking stock of the existing evidence on trade and employment with a focus on work using recent methodologies and datasets and on work that pays special attention to the functioning of labour markets. Second, to contribute to the design of tools that governments, social partners and experts can use to evaluate the employment effects of trade. And third, to contribute to the design of policy mixes that promote open markets whilst at the same time promoting quality jobs with adequate levels of protection.

We are confident this publication will contribute to strengthening the evidence base for trade and employment policies. Ultimately, we hope that it will facilitate the design of new generations of coherent policies that ensure the economic and social sustainability of globalization.

María Angélica Ducci
Executive Director
Office of the Director General
International Labour Office

Fokion Fotiadis
Director General
Directorate-General for Development
and Cooperation - EuropeAid
European Commission

# CONTENTS

# EDITORS AND CONTRIBUTORS

## EDITORS

Marion Jansen, Coordinator, Trade and Employment Programme, International Labour Organization (ILO).

Ralf Peters, Economic Affairs Officer, Trade Negotiations and Commercial Diplomacy Branch, Division on International Trade, United Nations Conference on Trade and Development (UNCTAD).

José Manuel Salazar-Xirinachs, Executive Director, Employment Sector, International Labour Organization (ILO).

## CONTRIBUTORS

Günseli Berik, Associate Professor of Economics, University of Utah.

Olivier Cadot, Senior Economist, The World Bank; Professor, University of Lausanne; and Fellow, Centre for Economic Policy Research (CEPR).

Céline Carrère, Associate Professor, University of Geneva and Fellow, Fondation pour les Études et Recherches sur le Développement International (FERDI).

Joseph Francois, Professor of Economics, Johannes Kepler University; Director of the European Trade Study Group (ETSG); Board Member of the Global Trade Analysis Project (GTAP); and Research Fellow at the Center for Economic Policy Research (CEPR).

Bill Gibson, Professor of Economics, University of Vermont.

Margaret McMillan, Associate Professor of Economics, Tufts University; Deputy Division Director, Development Strategy and Governance Division, International Food Policy Research Institute (IFPRI); and Research Associate, National Bureau of Economic Research (NBER).

Anushree Sinha, Senior Fellow, National Council of Applied Economic Research (NCAER).

Vanessa Strauss-Kahn, Associate Professor of Economics, ESCP Europe and Research Affiliate, Centre for Economic Policy Research (CEPR).

Íñigo Verduzco, Research Analyst, International Food Policy Research Institute (IFPRI).

# ACKNOWLEDGEMENTS

The editors wish to thank Erik von Uexkull and David Cheong for their continuous support to this book project. They also want to thank Azita Berar Awad, Sara Elder, Frédéric Lapeyre, Naoko Otobe and Simonetta Zarrilli for their comments on earlier versions of this manuscript. Acknowledgements also go to the participants of the Expert Meeting on "Assessing and addressing the effects of trade on employment" in December 2009, in particular to the discussants Marc Bacchetta, Marco Fugazza, David Kucera, Jörg Mayer, Scott McDonald and Pierella Paci.

# INTRODUCTION: TOWARDS A COHERENT TRADE AND EMPLOYMENT POLICY

1

*by Marion Jansen, Ralf Peters[1] and José Manuel Salazar-Xirinachs*

In the era of globalization, most economists and policy-makers have asserted that trade liberalization has a strong potential to contribute to growth and that those effects will be beneficial for employment. This belief has strongly influenced the liberalization policies of the last 25 years, in multilateral, regional and bilateral settings. Yet survey evidence illustrates that negative perceptions of the labour market effects of trade are frequent and persistent among the population, particularly in the industrialized world but increasingly also in developing countries. Recent surveys show an increasing concern about income and job security (Milberg and Winkler, 2011). In the United States, 40 per cent of respondents to a recent survey expected that the next generation will have lower standards of living (Anderson and Gascon, 2007). Some 62 per cent said job security had declined; and 59 per cent said that they were having to work harder to earn a decent living. Surveys also show that concern about job security and job quality is often linked to increases in trade and foreign direct investment (FDI) in the perception of the public. Approximately 75 per cent of US respondents replied that "outsourcing overseas hurts American workers". Another survey shows that about half of North Americans and Europeans think that "freer trade" results in more job destruction than job creation (German Marshall Fund, 2007).

Those numbers, however, do not indicate that interviewees have an entirely negative perception of globalization. Indeed, evidence based on surveys that make a distinction between growth and employment impacts of globalization reveals

---

[1] Ralf Peters contributed to this publication during his stay at the International Labour Office (ILO) as the chief technical advisor for the EU-financed project "Assessing and Adressing the Effects of Trade on Employment" that has provided funding for this publication. The opinions expressed in this chapter can in no way be taken to reflect the views of the EU, the ILO or the UNCTAD.

that a majority of respondents in industrialized countries believes in the positive growth effects of globalization that are so often emphasized in the public debate. But they appear to doubt that growth effects also positively affect the majority of citizens. Indeed, recent survey evidence in European countries (Eurobarometer) indicates that in all but one of the 43 countries surveyed, the majority of respondents believed that globalization provides opportunities for economic growth but increases social inequalities. In all countries surveyed, the majority of respondents agreed with the statement that globalization is profitable only for large companies, not for citizens.

Also in developing countries, there is concern about the distribution of gains from trade. Relevant survey evidence is rare, but those conducting country-level work easily become aware of such concerns. This has also been the case in the context of the field work conducted for the European Union (EU)-funded project that has financed the publication of this edited volume. Workers and employers in Indonesia express concern about the effect of competition from cheap Chinese imports.[2] In Bangladesh, textile workers demonstrated in December 2010 because they had been denied payment of the legal minimum wage by their employers, which included powerful multinational companies.[3] In Guatemala, working conditions – including pay – in the exporting agricultural sector have been a subject of controversy for many years. Even in emerging economies with booming exports and strong growth figures, such as China and India, there is concern that trade does not deliver the expected miracle in terms of jobs. In China, the share in manufacturing employment has remained rather stable for the past ten years (Chen and Hou, 2009), notwithstanding massive annual increases in manufacturing exports, which have reached an average of 20 per cent growth per year in the period from 2000 to 2007 (WTO, 2008).

The Great Recession has increased concern among policy-makers that the crisis experience may strengthen negative perceptions of globalization. Indeed, concern about a possible backlash against globalization has risen and dominates part of the debate in the trade community. In an attempt to avoid such a backlash and to gather sufficient public support for further multi-lateral and regional trade liberalization, policy-makers are looking for answers to the question of why the employment and distributional effects of globalization have persistently been perceived as much less positive than the growth effects. During the period in which this chapter was written, there have been a multitude of statements and initiatives related to trade and employment linkages, including a statement by the Director-General of the World Trade Organization, Pascal Lamy, emphasizing the relevance of the employment impact of trade flows.[4]

---

[2] See *The Jakarta Post*, 21 Jan. 2010 and 23 Apr. 2011. In the latter, the Chamber of Commerce calls for renegotiating AFCTA.

[3] See *Financial Times*, Asia Pacific Edition, 12 December 2010.

[4] *Neue Zürcher Zeitung*, 1 Dec. 2010.

The ongoing public debate reflects an effort to base arguments and statements on existing theoretical and empirical evidence on trade and employment linkages; however, that evidence suffers from a number of important shortcomings:

- First, the theoretical and empirical literature on the benefits of trade and trade liberalization has for a long time been geared towards analysing its growth and overall welfare effects. This is particularly true for quantitative work using simulation methods (e.g. computable general equilibrium (CGE) models), work that is often used as a point of reference for trade negotiators as it allows them to evaluate the economic effects of the negotiation positions they take. On the other hand, quantitative work focusing on the employment effects of trade is relatively scarce.

- Second, the public debate on trade and employment linkages generally clumps together the different channels or links without distinguishing clearly between such different aspects of "trade" as: trade liberalization measured by changes in the trade policy regime (reflected, for instance, in changes in the level of industrial or agricultural tariffs); trade integration measured by volume of exports or imports; trade openness measured by value of exports plus imports over gross domestic product (GDP); or the value of outsourcing or total flows of FDI. Yet all of these are quite different aspects of "trade". While the theoretical and empirical literature usually makes careful distinctions on the variables to measure these different aspects of trade policy or trade and investment flows, these distinctions are not successfully channelled into the public debate.

- Third – and reflected in the discussion in the paragraphs above – the existing evidence is still dominated by the labour market effects of trade in industrialized countries. As data availability improves, an increasing number of studies focus on developing countries; but data limitations remain severe for the poorest among them.

- Fourth, until recently, most of the theoretical and empirical trade work ignored major trade-related realities, such as the existence of trade costs and the role of individual firms in trade performance. This has dramatically changed with the arrival of the so-called new-new trade theory and empirical evidence based on firm-level data. There is a growing body of academic literature linking those new theoretical and empirical approaches to labour markets and to employment, but it is still in its infancy.

- Fifth, the existing work that links trade and labour markets tends to be based on strong simplifying assumptions concerning the functioning of the labour market. This is most strikingly reflected in the fact that most relevant work totally ignores the existence of an informal economy, although this often represents the majority of economic activity in developing countries. There is again a growing body of literature that tries to address this situation by building more sophisticated labour market structures into theoretical and empirical models, but so far the existing evidence does not allow for general conclusions.

- Sixth, both the political debate and the analytical work systematically struggle with the fact that trade tends to affect different aspects of labour markets in parallel. In particular, trade tends to have an effect on both the quantity and the quality of employment, where the latter can take the form of wage effects or effects on labour conditions such as those regarding occupational safety and health. Arguably, citizens are interested in the combined effect on the labour market, but economists continue to struggle with the question on how to assess this combined effect.

- Seventh, evidence on how different combinations of trade and social protection and labour-market policies affect employment outcomes is scarce, if not absent. The popular debate on the need to design "coherent" policies is therefore largely based on an analytical and empirical void. The renewed interest in the positive role of government intervention – triggered by the Great Recession and a number of success stories in emerging economies – has led to a new wave of policy-related research that, however, so far does not provide clear guidance on what "coherent trade and labour policies" may look like. The one exception to this rule may be the emerging consensus that open economies should be characterized by strong social protection systems (ILO, OECD, World Bank and WTO, 2010; Jansen and von Uexkull, 2010; Paci, Revenga and Rijkers, 2009).

With evidence incomplete and scattered, experts nevertheless agree on one thing: trade-employment linkages depend on the specific trade channel considered and take different forms in different countries. Policy-makers who wish to design policies to optimize the benefits for their country should therefore ideally be able to base their decisions on country-specific evidence or – as a second best alternative – on evidence based on the experiences of similar countries.

In the light of the knowledge gaps discussed above and the consensus that policy advice should ideally be based on country-specific evidence, the chapter themes in this volume and their content have been designed with a threefold objective in mind. First, the book tries to contribute to filling some of the gaps discussed above by taking stock of the existing evidence on trade and employment with a focus on work using recent methodologies and datasets and on work that pays special attention to the functioning of labour markets. Much of the material discussed is based on country-specific studies and emphasis is put on a number of themes that receive relatively little attention in the mainstream trade and employment literature, such as the question of the gender aspects of trade or the link between trade and the informal sector. Second, the book tries to contribute to the design of tools that governments and experts – even in environments of poor data availability – can use to evaluate the employment effects of trade. Third, the book aims to contribute to the debate on coherent labour and trade policies.

This edited volume contains six chapters focusing on different themes. Chapter 2, authored by Margaret McMillan and Íñigo Verduzco, provides an overview of the most recent literature on trade and employment. It is followed by a chapter on the methodologies used to assess the employment effects of trade, which is authored by Bill Gibson. Chapter 4, by Anushree Sinha, focuses on the relationship between trade and the informal economy; the chapter contains an overview of existing evidence on this relationship and a discussion of different approaches and methods to assess the employment effects of trade in countries characterized by a large informal economy. In Chapter 5, Günseli Berik discusses the mechanisms through which trade may affect women and men differently, and provides an overview of the existing evidence on the gender-specific employment effects of trade. Chapters 6 and 7 deal with two different challenges frequently associated with trade liberalization. In Chapter 6, Joseph Francois, Marion Jansen and Ralf Peters provide a discussion of the adjustment processes following trade reform, with a particular focus on adjustments in the labour markets; measures to assess adjustment costs related to labour churning are presented and policies to address adjustment concerns are discussed. Last but not least, Céline Carrère, Vanessa Strauss-Kahn and Oliver Cadot examine the relationship between trade reform and the diversification of imports and exports; with poor countries being – on average – characterized by undiversified exports, their analysis of the drivers and impacts of diversification provides new food for thought on the possible role of governments in enhancing the growth and employment effects of trade.

Jointly, the six themed chapters in this volume contain a wealth of country-specific evidence – notably for developing countries – on trade and employment linkages. Individually, each of them provides useful contributions to the three objectives pursued by this book project. In the following section, we summarize some of the main insights that arise from a careful reading of the six chapters.

## 1.1    FROM MYTHS TO FACTS: FILLING KNOWLEDGE GAPS WITH NEW EVIDENCE

- Allocative efficiency depends on institutional settings

Trade reform is typically expected to lead to the reshuffling of production factors – such as labour and capital – from activities that have become uncompetitive to activities that have remained or have become competitive. In traditional trade theory, this reshuffling would take the form of a shuffling across sectors. In the new-new trade theory, it is competitive firms that absorb the production factors liberated by uncompetitive firms and this transition may take place between firms within the same sector (Melitz, 2003). A third alternative is that laid-off production factors end up being employed in the non-tradable sector.

Much of the welfare gains from trade are expected to emerge as an outcome of this reshuffling process as factors end up being allocated to activities where they are more efficient. McMillan and Verduzco argue in Chapter 2 of this book that allocative efficiency depends to a large extent on national institutional settings, an argument that has also been made in Haltiwanger (2011). Haltiwanger describes how well-functioning economies are characterized by a constant reshuffling of resources due to the fact that firms are constantly forced to adjust and adapt to changing economic circumstances. Such well-functioning markets are more likely to be found in developed countries and are – in theory – characterized by full employment. In such smooth markets, those that adapt well will survive and grow, while those that adapt and adjust poorly shrink and exit. In good economic times, and in well-functioning economies, this process – although associated with lay-offs of workers – typically does not result in long unemployment spells and instead tends to lead to increased earnings. In such a situation, globalization has the potential to lead to improved market selection, higher productivity growth and higher earnings growth for workers. Yet Haltiwanger (2011) also emphasizes that many things can go wrong in this reallocative process if economies are distorted, for instance if transportation or communication infrastructure are not sufficiently developed, if ineffective (or non-existent) competition policy does not prevent large firms from abusing their market power, or if financial markets are not sufficiently developed to fund new and expanding businesses. Haltiwanger argues that reallocation has little chance to be productivity enhancing in such distorted economic environments and that – in extreme cases – "de-coupling" may take place, i.e. cases in which policy reforms induce downsizing and exit of some firms but do not lead to the expansion of other firms. Long unemployment spells of workers may be the end result. Another result may be that the relative size of the productive segment of the economy shrinks rather than expands, as illustrated by McMillan and Rodrik (2011).

The theme of changes in factor allocation is also discussed in the sixth chapter of this book that is specifically dedicated to the adjustment process following trade liberalization. While most of the literature discussed in that chapter assumes that impediments to the adjustment process only temporarily create problems with resulting economic losses, already early contributions to the literature (Mussa, 1978) highlighted how the existence of adjustment costs may prevent production factors from being allocated to their intended activities. In economic terms, this would imply that the expected long-run equilibrium is never reached. Mussa's model, together with other contributions to the literature discussed in Chapter 6, therefore imply that the existence of market frictions or other adjustment costs can have significant welfare implications in the long run.

While most of the literature surveyed in Chapter 6 concludes that adjustment costs are minor compared to the long-run welfare gains from trade reform, new evidence discussed in McMillan and Verduzco (Chapter 2) and some of the models discussed by Francois, Jansen and Peters (Chapter 6) give reason to believe that adjustment costs should not be ignored and that there may be a role for governments in facilitating economic transition following trade reform. Labour market structures appear to be very important. Davidson and Matusz (2000) have shown that certain structures can lead to adjustment costs that offset gains to a significant extent. In the context of changing global trade patterns following the Great Recession, the question also arises whether governments may have a role in assisting the economy to adjust to the new global equilibrium.

Most of the discussion on allocative efficiency is predicated on the assumption of advanced economies where, under initial conditions, productive structures are relatively highly diversified and most of the labour force is employed. Under such conditions, the main challenge is the reshuffling between sectors or enterprises and related adjustment costs. While there are important insights in this literature, that apply to the formal sectors of all economies, this assumption does not correspond to the realities of productive structures and labour markets of most developing countries.

- Job creation in the exporting sector may be disappointing

In the past, economists tended to believe that workers displaced from activities that have become unprofitable after trade reform would be absorbed by the exporting sector where they would often end up receiving better pay. New empirical evidence indicates that the picture may be somewhat different. Two recent studies from Latin America show that job destruction may be higher than job creation, at least for several years after liberalization. Casacuberta and Gandelman (2010) and Muendler (2010) show that trade opening in Uruguay and Brazil resulted in higher job destruction than job creation. Displaced workers were not absorbed by the most competitive industries, but moved into non-trading sectors or out of formal employment. A reason why companies in expanding sectors do not increase their workforce is likely to be the increase of the average productivity in these sectors. Some supporting evidence has been found, by Menezhes-Filho and Muendler (2007) in the case of Brazil.

The study by Ebenstein et al. (2009) discussed in McMillan and Verduzco's chapter in this volume also indicates that absorption in exporting manufacturing sectors may be disappointing. In a study of the United States (US), they find significant employment reallocation in response to import competition and off-shoring with both phenomena being associated with a reduction of employment in manufacturing. Consistent with Kletzer (2001), they find that workers who leave manufacturing to take jobs in the services sector suffer from a wage decline of between 6 and 22 per cent. In other words, workers displaced by trade or offshoring end up in less well-paid services jobs.

- The informal economy cannot be ignored

The evidence discussed in Chapter 4, written by Anushree Sinha, indicates that there is likely to be a two-way relationship between trade and informality[5]. On the one hand, trade reform is likely to have an effect on the size and the performance of the informal economy; while on the other hand, the existence of an informal economy is likely to affect an economy's supply response to trade reform. Sinha's overview of quantitative work analysing the first link – i.e. the impact

---

[5] See also the joint ILO-WTO publication by Bacchetta, Ernst and Bustamante (2009) on this theme.

of trade reform on the informal economy – provides examples in which trade has contributed to increasing the formal economy as well as examples in which the opposite took place. The mechanism behind the first result is that open markets lead to increased opportunities for firms in the formal economy with a resulting expansion of that segment of the economy. Conversely, the informal economy may increase, if trade leads to increased competition for formal firms, forcing them to become informal or to rely on informal production factors or suppliers in order to remain competitive. In her chapter, Sinha also describes the mechanisms through which the existence of a large informal economy may hamper the supply response to trade reform in developing economies. Lack of access to credit and skilled workers, together with inefficiencies due to the small size of firms that is typical in the informal economy, are among the most important factors that limit the possibilities of the informal economy from taking advantage of the opportunities of openness. Addressing informality may thus be a crucial element of strategies to increase the supply response to trade reform in developing countries, particularly in the least developed countries (LDCs).

- Trade does not necessarily reduce gender discrimination and may even reinforce it

In Chapter 5 of this book, Günseli Berik describes how trade expansion has brought a substantial increase in employment for women workers in developing countries in labour-intensive export-oriented industries since the mid-1970s. While these jobs have contributed to women's economic autonomy and status in the household, the conditions of work in these industries have been poor, marked by persistent low wages, gender wage inequalities, extremely long hours and job in-stability. In many poorer developing countries, employment opportunities created in these sectors have been the only formal jobs that many women could access and are perceived to be better than the alternatives of unemployment or work in subsistence agriculture. Despite narrowing gender wage gaps – due to increasing education levels – women appear unable to reap the full benefits of their rising education levels as the discriminatory part of the gender wage gap is persistent, or has even increased in some developing countries where trade has expanded. A possible explanation suggested in Chapter 5 for these wage trends is that trade liberalization is accompanied by other policies, and global processes, that under-mine women workers' bargaining position in wage setting – even as women increase their schooling level relative to men. Decentralization of global production, in-creased corporate buyer and investor mobility, and increasing competition from other low-cost countries may adversely affect wage growth for workers who are concentrated in export sectors.

Berik describes that, after the initial benefits from trade expansion, women have been struggling in countries that have managed to combine strong export performance with significant growth rates. In East and South-East Asian countries that moved up the technology ladder and diversified exports, women's relative employment opportunities have declined. This outcome may be, just like the gains in the first place, partly linked to sectoral effects, as women may have limited job-specific skills in the new sectors. Another argument made by Berik is that these skill deficits interact with gender norms and stereotypes about women's weaker commitment to the workforce and lower need for income to shape employer hiring and placement decisions. Thus, the initial benefits for women from international trade may not be persistent without additional targeted policies and changing perceptions of gender division of labour in households.

- Country specifics determine how and to what extent trade liberalization contributes to increased diversification

The debate on export diversification is intimately linked to the debate on the growth effects of trade. In their seminal article on "stages of diversification", Imbs and Wacziarg (2003) showed that economies diversify as they grow until they reach an advanced level of income, at which point they start specializing again. The authors of Chapter 7 (Cadot, Carrère and Strauss-Kahn, 2011) in this volume have shown that a similar relationship holds for export diversification and income. In other words, wealthier economies tend to be characterized by higher levels of export diversification until they reach a certain level of income. In their chapter in this volume, the authors show that trade liberalization is typically followed by an increase in export diversification. But this effect is stronger in middle-income countries than in low-income countries. Thus, trade liberalization appears to support diversification but, in terms of diversification, countries with higher capabilities appear to benefit relatively more than those with lower levels.

The authors also find that, in middle-income countries, trade liberalization facilitates the consolidation of export positions in that it contributes to growth at the intensive margin (more exports of already-existing export products). In low-income countries, it instead contributes to growth at the extensive margin, i.e. the exports of new products. Indeed – and as pointed out by the authors – the poorest countries are often highly concentrated, and trade liberalization is therefore unlikely to contribute to increasing exports in sectors in which they already specialize (often natural resources).

There is, in fact, evidence that trade liberalization in poor country settings has led to loss of production and jobs in manufacturing (de-industrialization) as well as agriculture (Kwame Sundaram and von Arnim, 2008; Chang, 2009).

## 1.2 GENERATING FACTS: PROVIDING TOOLS TO GENERATE MORE EVIDENCE

Several of the chapters in this book contain detailed discussions on quantitative and qualitative methods to assess the employment effects of trade. In addition, the book dedicates one chapter especially to assessment methods. Chapter 3, authored by Bill Gibson, provides an exhaustive discussion of econometric and simulation methods that have been used in the economic literature to assess the employment impact of trade. The structure of the discussion allows readers to evaluate the quality and comprehensiveness of the employment-related information provided by assessment methods of different levels of sophistication. Gibson's chapter also contains information on data, software and modelling-skill requirements needed to implement the different methods. As such, the chapter aims to provide the reader with information on the different trade-offs at stake when choosing one method rather than another. The chapter provides useful information for policy-makers and national experts who wish to assess the employment impacts of trade in their own country.

- Using economy-wide rather than partial equilibrium methods

On the basis of his discussion, Gibson concludes that it is preferable to use economy-wide rather than partial equilibrium methods to evaluate the employment effects of trade. By focusing on a subset of sectors, partial equilibrium analysis carries the risk of painting an overly positive or overly negative picture of the employment effects of trade. The former may lead to too much complacency regarding the need for government policies to prepare economies for the challenges and opportunities inherent to trade reform; McMillan and Verduzco warn in their chapter against such complacency. An overly negative picture, instead, may lead to an anti-trade bias.

Sinha also argues in Chapter 4 in favour of the use of quantitative general equilibrium approaches to measure the employment effects of trade reform on informality. Though the informal sector is typically associated with the production of non-tradable goods, the various links between the formal and the informal sectors that are discussed in Chapter 4 imply that trade policy changes are typically not limited to one sector.

- Getting the micro-foundations right is important

Gibson also argues in favour of sound micro-foundations of models used to evaluate employment effects of trade. Countries differ in their labour market and other characteristics that are crucial in order for the benefits from trade to materialize. These characteristics should be reflected in models used to evaluate the employment impacts of trade and thus lead to country-specific evaluation exercises. Models not reflecting the economy at hand may produce wrong predictions. Getting the micro-foundations right is also important for the design of government policies. Like other economists, Gibson argues in favour of policies that act at the micro-level and directly address the incentives of individual economic actors. In order for such policies to be designed correctly, the incentive structure of individual actors needs to be thoroughly understood.

Gibson's chapter provides an overview of the different labour market assumptions that have been used in quantitative work, in particular in CGE models. The discussion in that chapter creates the impression that much more can be done to include more realistic labour market assumptions in simulations. One aspect that is crucial for developing countries is dealt with in detail in Anushree Sinha's chapter on trade and the informal economy.

- Modelling the informal economy

Due to the sheer size of the informal economy, assessments of the impact of trade on employment in developing countries should take the specific characteristics of this sector into account. Case studies are helpful to understand the links between the formal and the informal sectors. However, Sinha argues in Chapter 4 that it may be difficult to draw general conclusions from case studies and argues thus in favour of quantitative approaches. The development of CGE models that can be used as a tool for trade policy analysis is described in the annex of Chapter 4. In order to take into account the existence of an informal economy within such approaches, it is typically assumed that a formal economy and an informal economy co-exist, but that they differ in one or several aspects. In her chapter, Sinha presents and discusses different ways of modelling the behaviour of the informal economy within general equilibrium approaches. The informal economy may, for instance, be assumed to produce different products or to use different production factors than the formal economy. Production technologies may also be assumed to differ and the informal economy is typically assumed not to generate any tax income for the government. Ideally, the assumptions made regarding the behaviour of the informal economy should be adjusted to the country that is the object of the analysis.

- Assessing labour market adjustment following trade reform

Adjustment is the focus of Chapter 6, by Francois et al.; the discussion in that chapter reveals that there is a growing theoretical literature on adjustments in labour markets following trade reform. This literature has notably benefited from numerous contributions by Davidson and Matusz, assembled in their recent book titled "International trade with equilibrium unemployment" (Davidson and Matusz, 2010). Unfortunately, the insights from their work have – to our knowledge – not yet found their way into CGE exercises.

Nevertheless, standard CGE simulations generate information that can be useful for policy-makers concerned about adjustment costs of trade reform. As described in Chapter 6 of this volume, it is straightforward to generate information on the structure of employment, for instance in terms of sectoral allocation, before and after trade reform. This allows policy-makers to identify the sectors in which the most important adjustments take place. In addition, it is possible to generate estimates for the share of the workforce that is likely to have to change jobs as a consequence of trade reform. It is straightforward to generate those estimates with standard CGE approaches. Different options for generating the relevant values are presented in Chapter 6. The chapter also presents an overview of existing estimates based on those methods and for different preferential trade liberalization scenarios involving Latin American countries. Estimated values range from a displacement of less than 1 per cent of the labour force to as much as 17 per cent. While adjustment in labour markets may not be a concern in the first case, the second scenario certainly deserves policy-makers' attention. These findings also support

11

the idea that estimates of labour market-related adjustment costs should become a standard element of CGE exercises, which simulate the economic effects of trade reform.

- Assessments should focus on the occupational rather than the industry level.

In Chapter 2 of this volume, McMillan and Verduzco make the point that when studying the impact of trade or offshoring on wages and employment, the industry level may be the wrong unit of analysis. If most of the downward pressure on wages occurs in general equilibrium, whereby wages equilibrate across manufacturing sectors very quickly, but not necessarily across larger aggregates, then industry-level analyses miss the most relevant effects of international trade on wages. In a recent paper, Ebenstein et al. (2009) find almost no industry-level wage effects; however, they do find significant employment reallocation in response to import competition and smaller employment responses to offshoring, while import penetration and offshoring are both associated with job losses in manufacturing.

To estimate the general equilibrium effects of trade and offshoring on wages, Ebenstein et al. (2009) calculate occupation-specific measures of offshoring, import competition and export activity. If labour market rigidities do not work through frictions in the reallocation of workers within manufacturing but – instead – between occupations (for example, if they are more likely to remain in the same occupation when they switch jobs), then occupation-specific measures of international competition are more appropriate for capturing the effects of trade and offshoring on wages. Their results suggest that this is indeed the case, and that international trade has had large, significant effects on occupation-specific wages. They find that, in the case of the US, a 1 percentage-point increase in occupation-specific import competition is associated with a 0.25 percentage-point decline in real wages. While some occupations have experienced no increase in import competition (such as teachers), import competition in some occupations (such as shoe manufacturing) has increased by as much as 40 percentage points with accordingly significant negative effects on wages. In line with other recent contributions to the offshoring literature, these findings therefore emphasize the need to work with occupation-specific data when evaluating the employment effects of trade and offshoring. Increased efforts should also be put into the systematic collection of relevant data.

## 1.3   COHERENT AND EVIDENCE-BASED POLICY-MAKING

- In most cases, strong social protection systems are preferable to targeted adjustment assistance

Labour appears to bear the bulk of the costs from the adjustment processes following trade reform. Trade reforms do not appear to have strong negative effects on unemployment rates, but costs for unlucky individuals can be substantial. Although trade competition does not target particular types of workers, evidence suggests that trade-displaced workers tend to be slightly older, have more tenure and higher earnings in their lost job. There is no strong evidence, though, of trade-induced unemployment being very different from unemployment caused by other shocks.

A further contributing reason to the evidence that the characteristics and unemployment spells of trade-displaced workers are similar to those losing their job for other reasons could be that trade liberalization does not necessarily cause entire non-competitive sectors to shrink and others to expand, but also causes labour churning within sectors. The authors of Chapter 6, therefore, develop indices measuring intra-sectoral employment movements.

Adjustment assistance, i.e. policy measures to mitigate the costs of adjustment from trade, can be designed to redistribute income or to increase efficiency, depending on the political goals. From an economic perspective, generally-available adjustment measures should be preferred over targeted trade adjustment assistance. Apart from the moral concerns as to why those affected by trade liberalization should be treated differently than those affected by other shocks, including those stemming from globalization as a whole, targeted assistance appears to have had rather mixed success in facilitating structural adjustment. It addition, it is nearly impossible to identify all workers adversely affected by trade liberalization.

The political economy argument – that there is more support for liberalization if adjustment assistance exists – is important, but may be less relevant if a strong social security system for the general public is in place. Very concentrated structural changes, such as mass lay-offs or regional concentration, may however justify specific trade adjustment assistance.

- Infrastructure and education are the foundation of economies' diversification potential

Econometric work presented in Chapter 7 by Carrère, Strauss-Kahn and Cadot provides interesting insights into the main drivers of export diversification. Not surprisingly, and consistent with other literature, they find that remoteness leads to higher export concentration, i.e. lower diversification. They also find that preferential market access positively contributes to export diversification, along both the intensive and extensive margins. Also, this result confirms findings in other related papers. Net inflows of FDI, on the other hand, appear to lead to stronger export concentration at the intensive margin.

A very important finding is that the quality of infrastructure and education levels are strongly correlated with export diversification. Given the public-good character of infrastructure and education, the authors of Chapter 7 therefore emphasize the key role of government-supported supply-side measures for trade and employment outcomes.

- Governments have a role in helping firms to survive or to grow …

Their analysis, in Chapter 7, of diversification patterns along the intensive or extensive margins, respectively, provides interesting information for those governments who consider targeting policy intervention towards specific sectors or subsectors. Export growth at the intensive margin – i.e. export growth in terms of higher sales of existing export products – contributes more strongly to overall export growth than growth at the extensive margin – i.e. export growth in terms of sales of new products. Thus, if governments are interested in export (and employment) growth, they should consider using policies that foster growth at the intensive margin, according to the authors. Export promotion can play a useful role in this, in particular if it is targeted towards overcoming collective action problems and assists firms in reaping the benefits of agglomeration externalities that appear to be inherent to exports. Bacchetta and Jansen (2003) and WTO (2006) provide useful insights into how export promotion policies can be designed that are in line with WTO commitments.

- … in particular, in the case of informal firms

Informal firms are disadvantaged, since trade tends to benefit larger and more productive firms, while informal firms are usually small and less productive. Since a high share of employment is in the informal economy, an average of 80 per cent in low-income countries and 40 per cent in middle-income countries, it can be beneficial to enable informal firms to benefit from trade. In Chapter 4, Sinha identifies capital mobility between the formal and informal sector as an essential factor. Wages in the informal economy are likely to increase with trade opening if capital is mobile, while they may decrease if capital is not mobile. Thus, policies facilitating access to capital for informal firms would have a positive impact on their productivity. Governments can also support small-scale informal entrepreneurial activities through training and marketing support, as well as by promoting better linkages between flagship exporting firms and local suppliers in the value chains. A major objective is to support formalization of informal firms, for instance, by addressing administrative and other barriers.

- Gender aspects of trade to be addressed through gender equity policies

A more equitable distribution of benefits from trade expansion can only be achieved if gender differences in employment are low with respect to the distribution among sectors, occupations and skill levels. If women are stuck in low-skilled low-paying jobs, the impact of trade will inevitably be different for men and women. An important policy recommendation for governments made in Chapter 5 is, therefore, to pursue general gender equity policies with the objectives to increase women's employment options through education, childcare provision and alleviation of unpaid workload, in order to improve the quality of jobs that are created through strong enforcement of labour standards, organizational adjustments in the workplace and infrastructure investments.

- Education and skills policies prepare the ground for the development of new export products

Intervening at the extensive margin is notoriously difficult, and the question of corresponding policies is often falsely associated with the question of whether governments are, or are not, well-placed to "pick winners". Since governments cannot pick winners with any certainty, the point is rather to set in place a process of self-discovery based on collaboration between public institutions and the private sector that can accelerate the accumulation of capabilities while providing feedback to correct mistakes and minimize their costs (Salazar-Xirinachs, 2010). The econometric analysis presented in Chapter 7 indicates that trade liberalization at the right stage of development can be another factor contributing to development of new exports in low-income countries, i.e. diversification at the extensive margin. Nevertheless, in many low-income countries, particularly numerous LDCs, exports have remained highly concentrated notwithstanding trade liberalization. To those countries who consider actively supporting the development of specific (sub-)sectors in this context, the authors signal that policies pursuing "little pushes" may prove to be more fruitful than attempts to land "big hits". They also warn that technology choice is crucial; in particular, they argue that the successful adoption of new technologies and production methods requires the availability of capabilities to master tacit knowledge needed to apply more sophisticated approaches.[6] Here again, supply-side interventions in the form of appropriate education and skills policies can make all the difference in terms of the actual trade outcomes of trade liberalization policies.

Training and education are also important if countries want to limit the widening of the skill premium that is caused by trade. McMillan and Verduzco argue in Chapter 2 of this volume that trade has been shown to increase wages of high-skilled workers relatively more than those of the low skilled. This is the case in both developed and developing countries, and governments that want to reduce this effect may work to increase the supply of skilled workers.

Woessman (2011) emphasizes in an ILO-WTO co-publication the important role of cognitive skills for long-run growth. Cognitive skills are the basic mental abilities we use to think, study and learn. They include a wide variety of mental processes used to analyse sounds and images, recall information from memory, make associations between different pieces of information, and maintain concentration on particular tasks. While cognitive skills can be strengthened at any stage of life, evidence presented in Woessman (2011) suggests that investments in early childhood education are likely to be particularly beneficial. This is the case, because education gained at one stage is an input into the learning process of the next stage, and the productivity with which investments at one stage of education are transformed into valuable skills is positively affected by the level of skills that a person has already obtained in the previous stages. Woessman (2011) also emphasizes that strong cognitive skills learned during school years facilitate lifelong learning in the sense of a constant adjustment to new technologies, and to change more generally. So-called soft skills are also important for employability (King, 2009). Many employers complain that the following skills are lacking: problem-solving skills; learning skills;

---

[6] See also the finding in Acharya and Keller (2007) that countries and enterprises with a higher absorptive capacity benefit more from foreign technology than those countries where a large proportion of firms is uncompetitive or in an infantile stage, and where absorptive capacities of new technologies are low because of weak human and financial resources.

communication skills; interpersonal skills; social skills, such as teamwork and also the sense of responsibility and devotion to work.

Governments also have a role in supporting the constant adaptation of the economy, and particularly of the workforce, to changes in the economic environment and new technological challenges. This can be done by developing policies and mechanisms that facilitate the matching between demand for and supply of skills, as outlined in ILO (2008) and in the G-20 training strategy developed by the ILO (ILO, 2010). Evidence indeed shows that successful economies have tended to be characterized by institutions and services that help workers and enterprises to adjust to change and by institutions and policies that anticipate and meet future labour market demand for skills.

## 1.4 PUBLIC PERCEPTIONS VERSUS POLICY-MAKERS' DECISIONS CONCERNING GLOBALIZATION

We started this chapter describing the discrepancy between public perceptions of globalization and policy-makers' action in this domain. Policy-makers' decisions in the domain of trade and FDI have led to impressive increases in trade and capital flows in the decades preceding the Great Recession. Preferential trade agreements and bilateral investment agreements were mushrooming in the years preceding the crisis. In the same period, however, surveys and media coverage provided evidence of rising concerns in civil society about the social effects of globalization.

The Great Recession has interrupted the pattern of continuous growth in trade and capital flows. It has also led to increases in protectionist sentiments and calls for more control of capital flows. In the industrialized world, the bailouts of banks followed by surges in unemployment and cuts in government spending are likely to have strengthened previously existing negative perceptions of globalization.

Policy-makers seem to have three options in this context. They can continue to do "business as usual" and continue to support trade liberalization strategies together with strategies that support global capital flows. Alternatively, they may succumb to protectionist pressures, i.e. stop supporting liberalization strategies or even raise new barriers to trade. A third alternative would be to opt for policy mixes that maintain open markets but are likely to generate broader benefits and stronger public support. Of the three alternatives, the third one is, in our view, the right one, but also probably the most challenging one, because it requires a more complex and balanced response from policy-makers and a more sophisticated understanding from the general public.

The experience during the Great Depression showed clearly that increased protectionism is a highly undesirable reaction to the recent crisis and to public discontent. Yet the recent crisis is unlikely to have been an ordinary hiccup of an otherwise healthy global system, and returning to "business as usual" may therefore not be a viable alternative either. Indeed, the contributions to this book provide plenty of evidence indicating that public concerns about globalization are unlikely to be purely based on misperceptions. McMillan and Verduzco's chapter provides evidence of trade liberalization leading to wage decreases in industrialized countries or misallocation of resources in developing countries. Berik's chapter provides examples of trade liberalization worsening the situation of female workers, and Sinha provides examples of countries where trade reform led to increases in informal employment. Francois et al. report evidence of cases where trade reform led to significant labour reallocation in individual economies. Each of those chapters also provides numerous examples of positive labour market outcomes of trade reform. Yet the examples of less-positive or even negative outcomes are – in our opinion – frequent enough to explain much of the discontent expressed by the public in opinion surveys or public debates.

The two easy alternatives – protectionism and "business as usual" – excluded, the third alternative remains. It is admittedly the one that is most challenging to implement, but it should not come as a surprise that acting in complex global markets and international relations requires sophisticated answers. Indeed, the recent failure of the financial sector illustrates the mistake of a simple market-driven solution and the complexity inherent in balancing public regulations and supervision when acting in a global and fast-changing environment. This may therefore be a good moment to pause, carefully think through what a coherent policy mix – delivering outcomes acceptable to majorities of voters – would look like, and rebalance policy approaches.

Policy rebalancing seems to be imperative in a situation where national public opinion and private sector players are struggling to adjust to the changes in global balances resulting from the crisis. Policy-makers need to develop more balanced packages of trade policies that recognize that one-size-fits-all solutions are not appropriate, and that sequencing and timing issues as well as relationships with complementary structural policies and conditions – such as education and skills – are fundamental.

The individual chapters in this book provide plenty of inputs for fresh thinking about appropriate policy mixes, and possible elements of such mixes have been outlined in the previous section of this introduction. A coherent set of policies should, in our opinion, pursue three objectives: (1) it should encourage structural change in a direction that is conducive to the creation of better jobs, and does not push large cohorts of the workforce into low-productivity jobs; (2) it should provide appropriate levels of protection to those going through particular hardship during adjustment phases; and (3) it should guarantee an appropriate distribution of the gains from trade.

The word "appropriate" already indicates that levels of protection and redistribution will probably end up being different across countries. It is quite straightforward to show in a median voter model that voters end up opposing trade liberalization if the gains from trade are distributed too unevenly (Boix, 2011). In a recent IMF paper, Kumhof and Rancière (2010) show that income inequality can represent a source of financial crisis. These are the types of situation that policy-makers should try to avoid. If ongoing waves of globalization and technological change contribute to an increasingly skewed distribution of incomes, this is a situation that should be addressed, as expressed in objective three. Reversing globalization and stopping technological change are not appropriate or even feasible answers. With an increasing amount of evidence that globalization weakens the bargaining power of workers (McMillan and Verduzco in this volume; Baccaro, 2008), redistribution without explicit government intervention is arguably increasingly unlikely. On the other hand, the redistribution tools at the disposal of governments may be limited in the context of global capital mobility and increasingly powerful global private players. The question, therefore, arises whether cross-border dialogue and a public-private sector debate on the question of redistribution are necessary to find solutions to this dilemma.

Strong and broadly targeted social protection systems appear to represent the answer to meet objective two. Evidence collected during the Great Recession is rather unanimous in its findings that countries with well-functioning social protection systems in place fared better during the crisis (Jansen and von Uexkull, 2010; Paci, Revenga and Rijkers, 2009). Such systems would also provide appropriate protection for the needy during adjustment processes following trade reform. Extensive research conducted in the 1990s and the early 2000s provides plenty of insights into the design of systems that provide protection while maintaining incentives to adjust. Social protection systems could be accompanied by special safeguards in trade agreements that allow economies breathing space when exposed to unexpected and significant changes in trade flows. Such safeguards do already exist in multilateral agreements (Bacchetta and Jansen, 2003) and similar provisions could be included in forthcoming multilateral, regional or other preferential arrangements. Governments may also consider choosing carefully the timing of trade liberalization. Trade reform in the context of economic depression may make adjustment processes unnecessarily harsh or lead to decoupling, as mentioned above. It may also unnecessarily raise public discontent against liberalization, as suffering induced by the business cycle may be attributed to the government's trade policies.[7]

The role of governments in directing structural change and promoting productive transformation (objective one) is the subject of the traditionally controversial debate around industrial policy that is currently enjoying a revival, albeit sometimes under different names (e.g. promoting competitiveness, new industrial policy, structural transformation, economic diversification). Findings presented in this volume support the idea of a role for the government in terms of providing public goods like infrastructure and education. But when it comes to implementation, financially restricted governments will automatically have to set priorities regarding which types of infrastructure and where, and regarding which types of education and how. Such priority setting is likely to result in favouring the development of certain sectors or regions over others. It is also very likely that priority setting in one domain (e.g. ed-

---

[7] As happened in Canada in the context of NAFTA, according to Gaston and Trefler (1997).

ucation) will only bring significant spin-offs if it coincides with matching developments in other areas (e.g. technology). Examples of coordination failures in the domain of skills and technology are numerous, as illustrated by the co-existence of skilled unemployment and vacancies for skilled workers in numerous countries. The fact that imported technologies need to find a matching capacity base in order to trigger growth has been mentioned above. This conclusion finds support in the observation that successful globalizers, such as China, Costa Rica, the Republic of Korea and Viet Nam, have invested in expanded access to education and vocational training while at the same time linking those policies with their trade and sectoral support strategies. Skills and education policies that support broad access to education and are imbedded in a system that facilitates the matching of demand for and support of skills are therefore likely to be key elements of modern versions of industrial policy.

# REFERENCES

Acharya, R.C.; Keller, W. 2007. "Technology transfer through imports", *NBER Working Paper* No. 13086.

Anderson, R.G; Gascon, C.S. 2007. "The perils of globalization: Offshoring and economic security of the American worker", *Working Paper* No. 2007-004A (Federal Reserve Bank of St. Louis).

Bacchetta, M; Ernst, E.; Bustamante, J.P. 2009. *Globalization and Informal Jobs in Developing Countries*, ILO-WTO Co-publication, Geneva.

Bacchetta, M.; Jansen, M. 2003. "Adjusting to trade liberalization: The role of policy, institutions and WTO disciplines", *WTO Special Study 7* (Geneva, WTO).

Baccaro, L. 2008. "Labour, globalization and inequality: Are trade unions still redistributive?", *IILS Discussion Paper* DP/192/2008 (International Institute for Labour Studies).

Boix, C. 2011. "Redistribution policies in a globalized world", in M. Bacchetta; M. Jansen (eds): *Making globalization socially sustainable* (Geneva, ILO-WTO co-publication, forthcoming).

Cadot, O.; Carrère, C.; Strauss-Kahn, V. 2011. "Export diversification: What's behind the hump?", in *Review of Economics and Statistics*, Vol. 93, No. 2, pp. 590-605, May.

Casacuberta, C.; Gandelman, N. 2010. "Reallocation and adjustment in the manufacturing sector in Uruguay", in G. Porto; B.M. Hoekman (eds): *Trade adjustment costs in developing countries: Impacts, determinants and policy responses* (World Bank and CEPR).

Chang, H-J. 2009. "Rethinking public policy in agriculture: Lessons from history, distant and recent", in *The Journal of Peasant Studies*, Vol. 36, No. 3, pp. 477-515, July.

Chen, L.; Hou, B. 2009. "China: Economic transition, employment flexibility and security", in S. Lee; F. Eyraud (eds): *Globalization, flexibilization and working conditions in Asia and the Pacific* (ILO).

Davidson, C.; Matusz, S.J. 2000. "Globalization and labour market adjustment: How fast and at what cost?", in *Oxford Review of Economic Policy*, Vol. 16, No. 3, pp. 42- 56.

Davidson, C.; Matusz, S.J. 2010. *International trade with equilibrium unemployment* (Princeton University Press).

Ebenstein, A. et al. 2009. "Estimating the impact of trade and offshoring on American workers using the current population surveys", *NBER Working Paper* No. 15107.

German Marshall Fund. 2007. "Perspectives on trade and poverty reduction: A survey of public opinion", *Key Findings Report*.

Haltiwanger, J. 2011. "Globalization and economic volatility", in M. Bacchetta; M. Jansen (eds): *Making globalization socially sustainable* (Geneva, ILO-WTO co-publication, forthcoming).

ILO. 2008. *Conclusions on skills for improved productivity, employment growth and development*, International Labour Conference 2008.

ILO. 2010. *A skilled workforce for strong, sustainable and balanaced growth: A G20 training strategy.*

Imbs, J.; Wacziarg, R. 2003. "Stages of diversification", in *American Economic Review*, Vol. 93, No. 1, pp. 63-86.

Jansen, M.; von Uexkull, E. 2010. *Trade and employment in the global crisis* (ILO).

King, K. 2009. "A technical and vocational education and training strategy for UNESCO: A background paper". Available at: http://recoup.educ.cam.ac.uk/news/tvetstrategyforunesco.pdf (accessed 31 May 2011).

Kletzer, L.G. 2001. *Job loss from imports: Measuring the costs* (Washington, DC, Institute for International Economics).

Kumhof, M.; Rancière, R. 2010. "Inequality, leverage and crises", *IMF Working Paper* WP/10/268.

Kwame Sundaram, J.; von Arnim, R. 2008. "Economic liberalization and contraints to development in Sub-Saharan Africa", *DESA Working Paper* No. 67.

McMillan, M.; Rodrik, D. 2011. "Trade, employment structure and structural transformation", in M. Bacchetta; M. Jansen (eds): *Making globalization socially sustainable* (Geneva, ILO-WTO co-publication, forthcoming).

Melitz, M.J. 2003. "The impact of trade on intra-industry reallocations and aggregate industry productivity", in *Econometrica*, Vol. 71, No. 6, pp. 1695-1725, Nov.

Menezes-Filho, N.A.; Muendler, M.A. 2007. "Labor reallocation in response to trade reform", *CESifo Working Paper* No. 1936.

Milberg, W.; Winkler, D. 2011. "Offshoring and economic insecurity: Worker perceptions and labor market realities", in M. Bacchetta; M. Jansen (eds): *Making globalization socially sustainable* (Geneva, ILO-WTO co-publication, forthcoming).

Muendler, M.A. 2010. "Trade reform, employment allocation and worker flows", in G. Porto; B.M. Hoekman (eds): *Trade adjustment costs in developing countries: Impacts, determinants and policy responses* (World Bank and CEPR).

Mussa, M. 1978. "Dynamic adjustment in the Heckscher-Ohlin-Samuelson model", in *Journal of Political Economy*, Vol. 86, No. 5, pp. 775-791.

Gaston, N.; Trefler, D. 1997. "The labour market consequences of the Canada-US free trade agreement", in *Canadian Journal of Economics*, Vol. 30, No. 1, pp. 18-41.

OECD; ILO; World Bank; WTO. 2010. *Seizing the benefits of trade for employment and growth*, Final report prepared for submission to the G-20 summit meeting, Seoul (Korea), 11-12 Nov. 2010.

Paci, P.; Revenga, A.; Rijkers B. 2009. "Coping with crises: Why and how to protect employment and earnings", *World Bank Policy Research Working Paper* No. 5094.

Salazar-Xirinachs, J.M. comments on: Cimoli, M.; Dosi, G.; Stiglitz, J.E. 2010. "*Industrial policy and development: The political economy of capabilities accumulation*", 22 Feb. 2010 at South Centre, Geneva.

Woessmann, L. 2011. "Education policies to make globalization more inclusive", in M. Bacchetta; M. Jansen (eds): *Making globalization socially sustainable* (Geneva, ILO-WTO co-publication, forthcoming).

WTO. 2006. *World Trade Report 2006: Exploring the links between subsidies, trade and the WTO.*

WTO. 2008. *International Trade Statistics 2008.*

# NEW EVIDENCE ON TRADE AND EMPLOYMENT: AN OVERVIEW

# 2

*By Margaret McMillan[1] and Íñigo Verduzco*

## 2.1    INTRODUCTION

In 1983, Anne O. Krueger, completed three volumes titled *Trade and Employment in Developing Countries* for the National Bureau of Economic Research. In Volume 3, "Synthesis and Conclusions", she writes:

> "Everyone agrees that unemployment is a 'problem' and that increased employment opportunities are an 'objective' in most LDCs. Employment and employment growth are major points of concern in virtually all of them. There is less agreement, however, on the nature and cause of the 'problem' and on why employment creation is desirable."

Strip away the dates from these volumes and one would be hard pressed to guess whether the volumes were written today or 30 years ago. For example, the *official* unemployment rates presented in table 2.1 indicate that unemployment in developing countries is much higher today than it was in the 1980s. Moreover, the numbers in table 2.1 almost certainly understate unemployment in these countries since they typically do not include those who choose not to participate in the workforce.[2]

---

[1] The authors would like to thank Dani Rodrik, Bill Gibson, and the editors of this book for comments and suggestions. We would also like to thank participants in the Expert Meeting on Assessing and Addressing the Effects of Trade on Employment organized by the EU and ILO for their comments.

[2] For example, the World Bank's report "Economic Growth, Employment Generation and Poverty Reduction in Nigeria" 2009 points out that a common problem in the African context is that all those who do not seek work because they feel that there is no work available are likely to be classified as economically inactive. As a result, official unemployment numbers are sometimes quite low.

Table 2.1: Global unemployment rates, by region

| Region | Unemployment rate in | | |
|---|---|---|---|
| | **1986** | **1994** | **2007** |
| | **%** | **%** | **%** |
| East Asia and the Pacific | 2.31 | 2.94 | 10.69 |
| Europe and Central Asia | – | 9.41 | 15.02 |
| Latin America and the Caribbean | 5.46 | 7.24* | 10.17 |
| Middle East and North Africa | | 12.81** | 20.83 |
| South Asia | – | 3.9 | 16.88 |
| Sub-Saharan Africa | – | – | 28.77 |
| High income: non-OECD | – | – | 7.74 |
| High income: OECD | 7.68 | 7.63 | 5.75 |

\* Average (1993, 1995). \*\* Earliest available (1991)
Source: Authors' calculations using data from CIA World Factbook 2007 and WOI (2010), see:
http://www.photius.com/rankings/economy/unemployment_rate_2007_0.html.

Today, one of the most commonly cited reasons for unemployment in both developed and developing countries is increased trade and offshoring. In developed countries, the fear is that jobs are being exported to low-wage countries. In developing countries, the primary concern is that trade liberalization is wiping out entire sectors that cannot compete with cheaper imports from China or more sophisticated products from developed countries. Despite the prominence of these concerns in the public debate, there has been remarkably little theoretical or empirical work on this issue.[3] Part of the reason for this is that the standard Heckscher-Ohlin-Samuelson (HOS) trade model assumes full employment, which has tended to shift the discussion of the effects of trade away from labour market outcomes. Additionally, unlike unemployment in developing countries, unemployment in many developed countries has been relatively low for several decades, making the assumption of full employment seem reasonable to many economists primarily focused on developed countries.

As Krueger (1983) noted, the standard HOS model is not a satisfactory analytical framework within which to study problems of unemployment in developing countries. For the purposes of her volumes, she relied heavily on extensions of the HOS framework that emphasized the importance of factor and product market distortions. More recent theoretical advances in the trade literature incorporate firm heterogeneity (Melitz, 2003), search frictions and equilibrium unemployment (Davidson and Matusz, 2009),[4] firm heterogeneity and bargaining between workers and employers (Egger and Kreickemeier, 2009), and all of the above plus idiosyncratic match quality (Helpman, Itsknoki and Redding, 2009). These recent studies have given more

---

[3] See Goldberg and Pavcnik (2007).

[4] This reference is to the recent book by Davidson and Matusz (2009), which synthesizes the work these two authors have done incorporating labour market frictions into trade models. According to Matusz, this work began in the 1980s when he was a graduate student at Michigan.

attention to the employment effects of trade liberalization and have moved away from the HOS assumption of full employment.

In addition to these developments, there has been a significant change in focus in the trade literature or, as Feenstra (2007) and Grossman and Rossi-Hansberg (2008) would call it: a change in paradigm. Feenstra (2007) argues that trade theories and the empirical evidence can be reconciled with the findings from the empirical literature – although not "traditional" trade theories such as the Heckscher-Ohlin model – if we "... adopt a new paradigm which emphasizes how tasks or activities can be sent across borders."[5] Instead of viewing trade – in goods and services – as an exchange of material goods,[6] an increasing number of papers have approached the study of trade as the exchange of specific tasks that form the value chain.[7]

These theoretical advances have important implications for policy-makers in developing countries. The three most important implications are: (1) the extent of the gains in allocative efficiency associated with trade liberalization depends critically on the institutional setting; (2) exposure to international trade can have an impact on aggregate employment and therefore the rate of unemployment; and (3) exposure to international trade can increase wage inequality in both rich and poor countries. This means that governments can and should play a role in shaping the relationship between trade and employment.

With this in mind, this paper builds on recent literature surveys on trade, employment and inequality (Hoekman and Winters, 2005; Goldberg and Pavcnik, 2004 and 2007) to discuss the most recent theoretical and empirical findings in this field. The paper is organized around what we consider to be some of the most important features of developing country labour markets not sufficiently emphasized in the recent trade literature.[8] First and foremost is the importance of the agricultural and informal sectors in most poor countries. Even though most of the new theoretical work is general equilibrium in nature, the focus of these models is still primarily on activity in the industrial sector. This is because most trade theorists believe that industrialization is the key to growth and that growth will automatically lead to job creation. Nevertheless, by focusing only on outcomes in the industrial sector, these studies leave out the majority of the population of most developing countries. Detecting the general equilibrium effects of trade and offshoring on labour markets in developing countries is complicated because of the large informal-sector presence

---

[5] See Feenstra (2007).

[6] By material goods we mean physical units of either finished or intermediate manufactured goods.

[7] In this sense, a task can be anything from the assembly of a chair to data analysis or the design of an airplane wing.

[8] For example, in a review of the work on globalization and employment, Lee (2005) notes the importance of taking into account movements in and out of the formal sector in developing countries. He argues that the narrow scope of papers that focus primarily on the manufacturing sector leave out the informal and non-manufacturing sectors of the economy, which is where most employment takes place in low-income countries. As Lee notes, he is not the first to point this out. Greenaway (1993), Collier (1993), and Agenor and Aizenman (1996) have all challenged the view that trade liberalization leads to an increase in employment. Lee (2005) also notes that the effects of globalization on employment vary greatly depending on regional and institutional factors and that the effects of trade liberalization on employment should be analysed on a case-by-case basis.

in both traded and non-traded goods in many of these countries (see table 2.2). But, to really understand the effects of trade on labour market outcomes in developing countries, workers in the informal and agricultural sectors must be included in distributional analyses. Related to this is the question of rural-urban linkages and the extent to which job creation in the industrial sector can reduce unemployment. As Harris and Todaro (1970) pointed out, simply increasing the number of jobs in the urban sector can actually increase urban unemployment because the increase in the number of jobs could increase rural-urban migration, thereby increasing the number of jobseekers in the urban sector. Other issues we address include: asymmetric bargaining power between labour and capital; the importance of initial conditions; the quality of jobs; information sharing and its potential to reduce unemployment; and the implications of trade in tasks for employment in developing countries.

We begin this review in section 2.2 with a description of trends in trade policy and employment in the industrial sectors across countries over the period 1980–2006. The reason for studying the industrial sector is that the promise of trade liberalization lay in its ability to stimulate manufacturing exports. The goal of this section is simply to document broad trends in manufacturing employment and wages over time and across countries, and to relate these trends to the trends in trade policy. Section 2.3 reviews the recent empirical evidence on trade and employment that takes into account the concerns raised above. In section 2.4 we turn our attention to the role that government policy can play in ensuring that trade and foreign direct investment (FDI) create jobs in developing countries. Section 2.5 concludes with a synthesis of the empirical results and directions for future research.

Table 2.2: Employment in the informal sector

| Region | Year | Employment in the informal sector as percentage of total employment (%) | Female share in total employment in the informal sector (%) |
|---|---|---|---|
| East Asia and the Pacific | 2000 | 71.00 | 44.99 |
| Europe and Central Asia | 2004 | 3.85 | 39.23 |
| Latin America and the Caribbean | 2006 | 55.27 | 43.59 |
| Middle East and North Africa | 2003 | 30.25 | 12.10 |
| South Asia | 2004 | 39.80 | 9.11 |
| Sub-Saharan Africa | 2004 | 27.55 | 51.51 |
| High income: non-OECD | 1999 | 7.36 | 38.94 |
| High income: OECD | 1999 | 23.00 | 23.67 |

Note: Table shows data for the latest available year.

Source: Authors' calculations using ILO's KILMnet data.

## 2.2  TRADE AND EMPLOYMENT: AGGREGATE TRENDS

The goal of this section is to present some stylized facts about trade, wages and industrial employment that can be used to stimulate further discussion about the employment effects of trade liberalization. In addition, we focus here primarily on developing countries because that is where the most dramatic changes occurred. We find that: (1) developing countries have significantly reduced industrial tariffs over the past decade; (2) two-thirds of industrial employment is now located in developing countries, and that China drives this trend; and (3) at least in the aggregate, trade liberalization is not correlated with changes in real wages or industrial employment. We cannot and do not wish to imply that our results say anything about causality between changes in trade liberalization and labour market outcomes, but they do show the general pattern of correlation between these variables.

Our data come from UNIDO's *INDSTAT2 2009* and the *Economic Freedom of the World: 2009 Annual Report* database.[9] One of the nicest features of these datasets is that they span a 26-year time-horizon for a large number of countries. Thus, we are able to document long-term trends in the data.[10] As noted by Krugman (2008) and others, researchers have disputed the validity of the Stolper-Samuelson theorem based on evidence or data that spans only a short period.[11] According to Krugman, the adjustment process that starts as a result of trade within the Stolper-Samuelson framework takes some time, so analysing data over short periods of time might reflect disequilibria more than a finalized effect. So, Krugman notes, the Stolper-Samuelson framework "should not be taken too seriously when interpreting data over short periods, say, five years"[12]. A limitation of our data is that it is aggregate in nature and it only covers the industrial sector.

### 2.2.1  Trends in openness, real wages and employment

Table 2.3 shows the dramatic percentage point declines in tariffs in the developing world between 1980 and 2005 by region. Figure 2.1 shows the strong upward trend in developing country exports as a share of GDP between 1980 and 2006. By 2006, exports as a share of GDP in developing countries averaged around 32 per cent, surpassing the average for developed countries of 27 per cent.

---

[9] Indicative tariff rates for each country in this database are obtained by using unweighted means for each country's tariff rates. The ultimate data sources are various issues of the WTO, ITC, UNCTAD *World Tariff Profiles*.

[10] By short-term we mean a five-year time-frame. On the other hand, long-term refers to a time-frame greater than five years, where relocation and disequilibria effects tend to disappear.

[11] The Stolper-Samuelson theorem states that under a particular set of assumptions (e.g. constant returns to scale, perfect competition) a rise in the relative price of a good will lead to a rise in the return to that factor which is used most intensively in the production of the good, while a fall in the relative price of a good will lead to a fall in the return to that factor which is used most intensively in the production of the good. In the context of trade, opening to trade is expected to increase the relative price of the good which uses the relatively abundant factor in an economy and, in this way, increase the relative returns to that factor.

[12] Krugman (2008).

Table 2.3: Changes in tariff by region

| Region | Mean tariffs (%) | | | | | | Change (1980–2005) percentage points |
|---|---|---|---|---|---|---|---|
| | **1980** | **1985** | **1990** | **1995** | **2000** | **2005** | |
| East Asia and the Pacific | 31.9 | 24.3 | 25.2 | 24.8 | 13.2 | 9.0 | −22.8 |
| Europe and Central Asia | 44.0 | 26.0 | 18.2 | 18.2 | 8.8 | 6.2 | −37.8 |
| Latin American and the Caribbean | 37.9 | 35.6 | 23.6 | 23.6 | 10.6 | 8.0 | −30.0 |
| Middle East and North Africa | 25.1 | 20.5 | 22.9 | 22.9 | 22.4 | 11.7 | −13.4 |
| South Asia | 63.0 | 62.9 | 57.9 | 57.9 | 25.1 | 14.9 | −48.2 |
| Sub-Saharan Africa* | 28.3 | 28.7 | 25.2 | 25.2 | 14.1 | 12.7 | −15.6 |
| **All developing, average** | 38.4 | 33.0 | 28.8 | 28.8 | 15.7 | 10.4 | −28.0 |
| Non-OECD, non-developing | 18.2 | 11.2 | 13.2 | 13.2 | 9.6 | 7.3 | −10.9 |
| OECD, non-developing | 9.2 | 7.9 | 7.8 | 7.8 | 3.7 | 3.5 | −5.7 |
| **All non-developing, average** | 13.7 | 9.5 | 10.5 | 10.5 | 6.7 | 5.4 | −8.3 |

Source: Authors' calculations based on data from Economic Freedom of the World (2009).

Note: Madagascar was excluded from the sample due to inconsistencies in the data.

Figure 2.1: Evolution of export share in GDP by income level

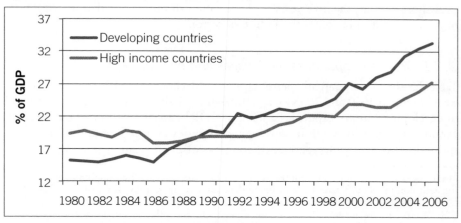

Source: Authors' calculations with data from the World Bank's World Development Indicator database, 2009.

Table 2.4 shows average annual percentage point changes in real industrial wages and employment by region and income level. For all of the developing regions of the world, real wages measured in United States dollars (US$) have fallen, with the largest declines in the Middle East, North Africa and sub-Saharan Africa. Part of the reason for this is that real wages are reported in US$. A number of countries

Table 2.4: Annualized changes in real wages and employment, by region and income group (1980–2005)

| Region | Annualized percentage change in real wages (per employee) | Annualized percentage change in employment |
|---|---|---|
| Developed Economies | 0.33 | –0.51 |
| East Asia and the Pacific* | –1.56 | 3.87 |
| Europe and Central Asia | –2.88 | 4.35 |
| Latin America and the Caribbean | –1.27 | –0.07 |
| Middle East and North Africa | –4.39 | –0.42 |
| South Asia | –0.27 | 0.16 |
| Sub-Saharan Africa** | –3.55 | –0.84 |
| **World** | **0.01** | **1.36** |

| Income group | Annualized percentage change in real wages (per employee) | Annualized percentage change in employment |
|---|---|---|
| High Income: OECD | 0.49 | –0.51 |
| High Incom e: nonOECD | 0.00 | –0.46 |
| Low Income | –6.79 | –0.56 ? |
| Lower Middle Income*** | –4.18 | 2.67 |
| Upper Middle Income**** | –1.95 | 1.54 |

* The numbers are –2.02% and 5.80%, respectively, if China is excluded from the sample.

** The numbers are –9.40% and –1.34%, respectively, if South Africa and Mauritius are excluded from the sample.

*** The numbers are –4.31% and –0.27%, respectively, if China is excluded from the sample.

**** The numbers are –2.20% and 1.68%, respectively, if South Africa is excluded from the sample.

? Excludes Viet Nam due to lack of data for the country before 2000. The 2000–05 rate when Viet Nam is included is 8.4%.

Source: Authors' calculations based on UNIDO INDSTAT2 data. Time period covered is 1980-2005.

have experienced significant declines in the value of their currency. However, we note that these trends are consistent with the findings of the World Bank (1995), which showed a divergence in real wages between developed and developing regions of the world. The report warned of a substantial risk that inequality between rich and poor countries could grow over the coming decades. The numbers in table 2.4

are also consistent with what we know about the industrialized world. Industrial employment is contracting, while real wages for those who remain employed in the industrial sector have increased. For a recent discussion of these stylized facts regarding wages and employment in the industrial sector of the United States, see Ebenstein et al. (2009).

Table 2.4 also shows that average annual employment growth in the industrial sector of developing countries has been mixed. Average annual growth in industrial employment in East Asia and the Pacific was 3.87 per cent. When China is excluded from the sample, the annualized percentage point increase in industrial employment is even higher, at 5.8 per cent, reflecting the tremendous success of Viet Nam in particular. In Latin America and the Caribbean, the average annual percentage point change in industrial employment was -0.07; in the Middle East and North Africa (-0.42 percentage points) and sub-Saharan Africa (-0.84 percentage points) average annual growth in industrial employment has been negative. If one excludes South Africa and Mauritius from the sample, average annual growth in industrial employment in sub-Saharan Africa has been -1.34 percentage points. This means that industrial employment in sub-Saharan African contracted by more than 25 percentage points over the period 1980-2005.

Table 2.5 shows total employment of industrial workers by region. In 1980, more than half of all industrial employment was located in the developed world. By 2005, more than two-thirds of industrial employment was located in the developing world, with China accounting for roughly 65 per cent of the total employment of industrial workers in the developing world. Also notable is the 26 percentage point increase in industrial employment in China between 2000 and 2005 – the period following the Chinese Government's official "go global" policy, which became effective in 1999. This policy was designed to encourage Chinese private and state-owned enterprises to expand overseas. The period 2000-05 also coincides with a decline in industrial employment for all other regions of the world, both developed and developing, with the exception of a modest increase in industrial employment in Latin America and the Caribbean, which occurred mainly in Brazil.

### 2.2.2 Correlations between tariffs, employment and real wages

We now turn to an analysis of the correlations between trade liberalization and wage and employment outcomes. Figures 2.2.a and 2.2.b show correlations between five-year changes in industrial employment and five-year changes in tariffs[13] lagged by one five-year period. Figure 2.2.a includes China, while figure 2.2.b excludes China. We used lagged changes in tariffs for two reasons. First, using lags partially helps us to get around the endogeneity problems associated with examining the relationship between trade liberalization and labour market outcomes. Second, using the lagged five-year change in tariffs also, in part, helps us to address the fact that labour markets

---

[13] A negative number indicates a reduction in tariffs, i.e. a more liberalized stance with respect to international trade.

Table 2.5: Total employment per region and year

| Region | Employment ('000 workers) | | | | | |
|---|---|---|---|---|---|---|
| | **1980** | **1985** | **1990** | **1995** | **2000** | **2005** |
| **East Asia and the Pacific** | 26'844 | 32'592 | 59'487 | 64'792 | 55'200 | 69'400 |
| China | 24'400 | 29'700 | 53'000 | 58'300 | 44'900 | 59'400 |
| Rest | 2'444 | 2'892 | 6'487 | 6'492 | 10'300 | 10'000 |
| **Europe and Central Asia** | 6'067 | 5'678 | 11'100 | 24'200 | 21'000 | 17'600 |
| **Latin America and the Caribbean** | 9'605 | 10'400 | 8'297 | 7'525 | 8'598 | 9'438 |
| **Middle East and North Africa** | 2'363 | 2'526 | 2'749 | 3'273 | 2'250 | 2'125 |
| **Sub-Saharan Africa** | 2'706 | 2'558 | 2'796 | 2'915 | 2'822 | 2'190 |
| South Africa and Mauritius | 1'435 | 1'497 | 1'640 | 1'551 | 1'422 | 1'275 |
| Rest of SSA | 1'271 | 1'061 | 1'156 | 1'364 | 1'401 | 916 |
| No. countries in rest of SSA | 21 | 17 | 16 | 15 | 11 | 5 |
| **South Asia** | **7'866** | **7'671** | **9'236** | **11'000** | **8'928** | **8'180** |
| India | 6'801 | 6'469 | 7'184 | 8'777 | 7'754 | 8'180 |
| Rest of South Asia | 1'065 | 1'202 | 2'052 | 2'209 | 1'174 | na |
| **Total developing** | 54'180 | 60'363 | 92'508 | 112' 341 | 97'397 | 108'018 |
| **Non-OECD, non-developing** | 1'844 | 2'058 | 2'636 | 2'178 | 1'902 | 1'642 |
| **OECD, non-developing** | 59'400 | 54'400 | 56'600 | 58'700 | 60'700 | 52'300 |
| **Total non-developing** | **61'244** | **56'458** | **59'236** | **60'878** | **62'602** | **53'942** |

Source: Authors' calculations based on data from UNIDO's INDSTAT2 2009.
Note: Data for South Asia in 2005 is not available; data for 2004 is used instead.

might adjust slowly to changes in trade policy. Figure 2.2.a shows that, in the aggregate, the correlation between lagged five-year changes in tariffs and five-year changes in industrial employment is close to zero, with the exception of China.[14] When we exclude China, we get a more nuanced story. On average, the correlation between changes in tariffs and changes in employment is zero, but the large number of points both above and below the regression line highlight the heterogeneity of experiences across countries and the need for more country-specific research to shed light on the various experiences.

---

[14] While the slope is negative, this relationship is not statistically significant.

Figure 2.2.a: Short-run association between lagged trade liberalization and employment, developing countries

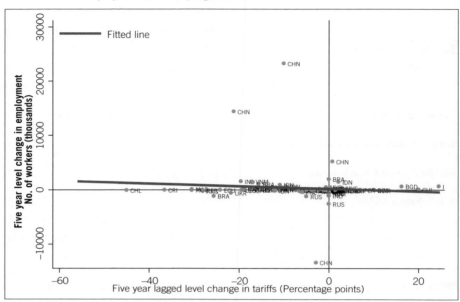

Source: UNIDO INDSTAT2 (2009); *Economic Freedom of the World* (2009).

Figure 2.2.b: Short-run association between lagged trade liberalization and employment, developing countries (excluding China)

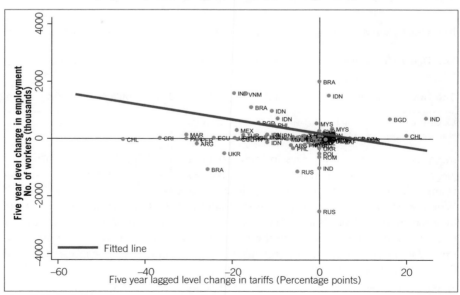

Source: UNIDO INDSTAT2 (2009); *Economic Freedom of the World* (2009).

Figures 2.3.a and 2.3.b repeat this exercise using long differences. For example, figure 2.3.a shows that, between 1980 and 2005, China reduced its industrial tariffs by 40 percentage points and increased the number of workers employed in the industrial sector by a little under 40 million. When China is excluded from the sample, the long-run correlation between tariffs and employment is statistically significant and negative indicating that a reduction in tariffs is positively correlated with industrial employment. However, the R-squared on this regression is only 0.05 and figure 2.3.b reveals once again a lot of heterogeneity in experiences across countries.

In figures 2.4.a and 2.4.b we examine the relationship between tariffs and real industrial wages. Both figures reveal a tremendous amount of variation in changes in tariffs with very little variation in real wages. The negative intercept of the regression line in figure 2.4.b is consistent with the trends shown in table 2.4: on average, real industrial wages in developing countries have fallen.

It is important to keep in mind that the revealed correlations do not rule out strong effects on individual countries. To the contrary, these figures raise a number of interesting avenues for further research. For example, China and India both experienced similar reductions in tariffs of around 40 percentage points over the long run. Why did industrial employment in China boom while in India, one of the most aggressive liberalizers of all, industrial employment only increased modestly?

Figure 2.3.a:  Long-run association between trade liberalization and employment, developing countries

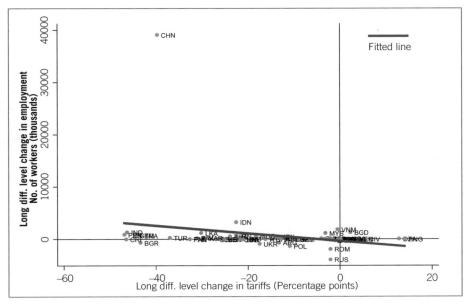

Source: UNIDO INDSTAT2 (2009); *Economic Freedom of the World* (2009).

Figure 2.3.b: Long-run association between trade liberalization and employment, developing countries (excluding China)

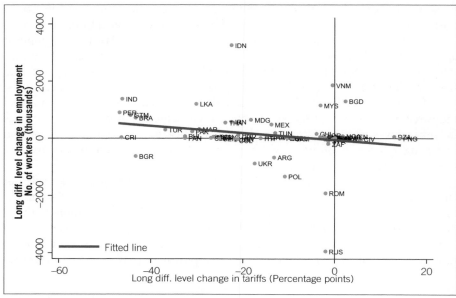

Source: UNIDO INDSTAT2 (2009); *Economic Freedom of the World* (2009).

Figure 2.4.a: Short-run association between trade liberalization and real wages, developing countries

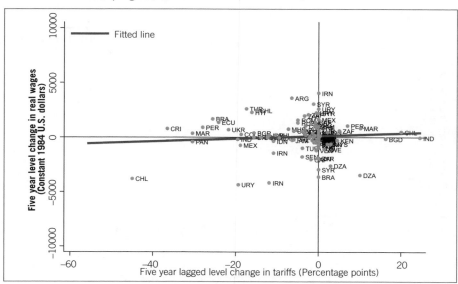

Source: UNIDO INDSTAT2 (2009); *Economic Freedom of the World* (2009).
Note: Wages refers to total annual compensation received by workers as defined by UNIDO's INDSTAT2 database

Figure 2.4.b: Long-run association between trade liberalization and real wages, developing countries

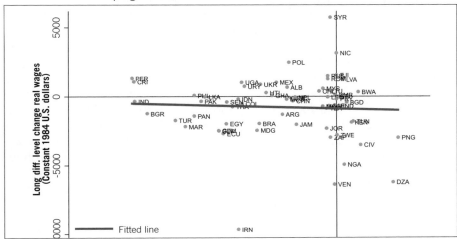

Source: UNIDO INDSTAT2 (2009); *Economic Freedom of the World* (2009).

Note: Wages refers to total annual compensation received by workers as defined by UNIDO's INDSTAT2 database.

Figure 2.5: Import penetration and import penetration from low-wage countries to the United States, 1979-2002

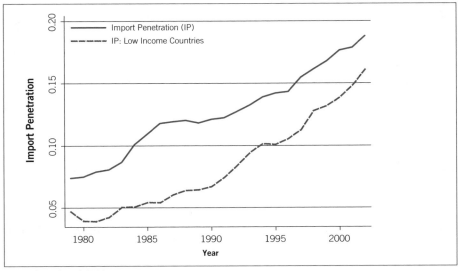

Source: Ebenstein et al. (2009).

Note: Import penetration and import penetration from low-wage countries come from Bernard, Bradford Jensen and Schott (2006). We aggregate the industry-level data to an annual number using employment weights calculated from the Current Population Survey's Outgoing Rotation Groups 1979-2002.

We hope that our discussion of these figures will help stimulate additional research at the country level designed to explain some of these puzzles.

Finally, as noted by Harrison and McMillan (2009) the revealed declines in real wages in developing countries partially help to explain the trends in offshoring. For US firms that invest offshore and for those that import intermediate inputs from abroad, it is primarily the US$ value of these wages that are important. Figure 2.5, borrowed from Ebenstein et al. (2009), reveals that import penetration into the United States from developing countries jumped from only 1 per cent in 1980 to a little over 15 per cent in 2002. Trends presented in Grossman and Rossi-Hansberg (2008) reveal the high degree of correlation between imports and imported inter- mediate inputs, or what is commonly referred to as offshore outsourcing. Figure 2.6 from Ebenstein et al. (2009) shows that practically all of the increase in offshore employment between 1980 and 2005 occurred in low-income (low-wage) countries. However, they also note that almost all of the increase in employment occurred in two countries: Mexico and China.

Figure 2.6: Offshoring by US-based multinationals

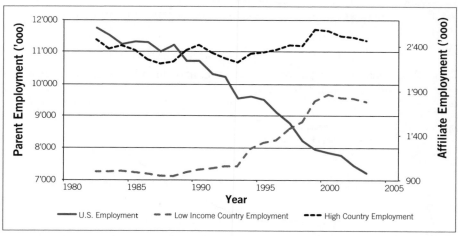

Source: Ebenstein et al. (2009).

Note: Authors' calculations based on the most comprehensive available data and based on firm-level surveys on US direct investment abroad, collected each year by the Bureau of Economic Analysis (BEA) of the US Department of Commerce. Using these data, we compute the number of employees hired abroad by country by year and the aggregate of these numbers by low- (high-) income countries according to World Bank classifications.

## 2.3 TRADE AND EMPLOYMENT: FIVE LESSONS FROM RECENT EMPIRICAL WORK

In this section, we review some of the most recent and innovative country studies that examine the relationship between trade and employment. To make this section more reader friendly, we have grouped the evidence by the broad sub-themes mentioned in the introduction: trade and employment in general equilibrium; asymmetric bargaining power; trade liberalization when unemployment is already high; the quality of jobs; and trade in tasks.

## 2.3.1 The general equilibrium effects of trade on employment are significant

In a study of the South African economy, Rodrik (2006) notes that South Africa's unemployment rate (between 24 and 40 per cent) is one of the highest in the world. Many observers blame the unions for excessively high wages and thus unemployment. However, Rodrik finds that the root cause of high unemployment in South Africa is not the unions but the shrinkage of the manufacturing sector since the early 1990s. According to Rodrik, the weak performance of the export-oriented manufacturing sector has deprived South Africa of job creation at the relatively low end of the skill distribution. Econometrically, Rodrik shows that import penetration is one of the key factors behind weak performance of the export-oriented manufacturing sector.

In a study of the Brazilian economy, Menezes-Filho and Muendler (2007) combine insights from the Melitz (2003) model with worker heterogeneity providing a compelling empirical example of the importance of some of the more recent theoretical breakthroughs. These authors link worker-level panel data with firm-level data and industry-level data to obtain a rich dataset that allows them to test many implications of the most advanced trade models (for example, heterogeneous-firm models that incorporate heterogeneous labour) for Brazil. By doing this, the authors are able to assess the impact of Brazil's trade liberalization during the 1990s on jobs, while controlling for a number of worker-specific, firm-specific, industry-specific, and economy-wide structural reforms. Their dataset allows them to follow workers throughout the liberalization period and observe the path of their employment history in greater detail than previous studies. They are particularly interested in the effects of trade liberalization on employment status, type of employment (formal or informal), and job reallocations.

Their results show that firms in industries with a "comparative-advantage"[15] and exporting firms[16] shed workers more frequently. Moreover, firms with comparative advantage and exporting firms also hire workers less frequently than the average firm. Thus, on net, trade liberalization leads to net employment losses in these firms. This is surprising given the standard predictions of international trade models that would indicate that these sectors and firms would potentially hire more workers when liberalization occurs. Furthermore, they also show that tariff reductions and increased import penetration are associated with an increase in the likelihood of a

---

[15] Those industries where Brazil has a comparative advantage with respect to the rest of the world. The authors use UN COMTRADE data from 1986–98 to calculate sectoral-level comparative advantage measures following Balassa (1965).

[16] Which may or may not be firms in industries with a sectoral comparative advantage.

worker transitioning into informality and unemployment, as well as a lower probability of a transition from informality back to formal employment. They also find
that trade liberalization in Brazil has been associated with longer reallocation times
for workers moving from a formal-sector job to another formal-sector job. Their results are robust to different levels of exposure to trade, firm-level productivity and
worker heterogeneity, as well as other general trends that occurred in the country
during the period studied, such as skill-biased technological change and labour market
reforms.

The findings by Menezes-Filho and Muendler (2007) are important given the
rise in informal employment that has been observed in the recent decades and that,
to a large extent, seems to have coincided with broad trade liberalization around
the world. Moreover, they also point to important institutional and structural aspects
of labour markets and the way in which these respond to trade liberalizations.
However, it is difficult for the authors of this paper to provide insights on the relative
importance of labour market rigidities since they focus on only one country, Brazil.

In a study of the United States, Ebenstein et al. (2009) make the point that
when studying the impact of trade or offshoring on wages and employment, the
industry level may be the wrong unit of analysis. If most of the downward pressure
on wages occurs in general equilibrium, whereby wages equilibrate across manufacturing sectors very quickly but not necessarily across aggregate sectors (i.e. agriculture,
industry and services), then industry-level analyses miss the most relevant effects of
international trade on wages. This finding is particularly relevant for developing
countries where much of the economic activity takes place outside of the formal
sector. In fact, Ebenstein et al. (2009) find almost no industry-level wage effects.
However, they do find significant employment reallocation in response to import
competition and smaller employment responses to offshoring: import penetration
and offshoring are both associated with job losses in manufacturing. Consistent with
Kletzer (2001), they also find that workers who leave manufacturing to take jobs
in the services sector experience average wage declines of between 6 and
22 percentage points.

To estimate the general equilibrium effects of trade and offshoring on wages,
Ebenstein et al. (2009) calculate occupation-specific measures of offshoring, import
competition and export activity. If labour market rigidities do not work through
frictions in the reallocation of workers within manufacturing but, instead, between
occupations (for example, if workers are more likely to remain in the same occupation
when they switch jobs), then occupation-specific measures of international competition are more appropriate for capturing the effects of trade and offshoring on
wages. Their results suggest that this is indeed the case, and that international trade
has had large, significant effects on occupation-specific wages. This is an important
result, and this kind of analysis has rarely been used when studying the effects of
trade or offshoring on labour market outcomes.

If, as in the case presented by Ebenstein et al. (2009), labour market frictions
operate more strongly through rigidities in changing occupations rather than industries or sectors, this could offer a plausible explanation as to why we observed little

association between trade liberalization and labour market outcomes at the industry level. This is an indication that, within the industrial sector, labour rigidities are not too strong and, thus, labour can relocate within manufacturing relatively easily. Ebenstein et al. (2009) go on to show that labour is not as mobile across occupations. Their results suggest, at least for the United States, that a 1 percentage point increase in occupation-specific import competition is associated with a 0.25 percentage point decline in real wages. While some occupations have experienced no increase in import competition (such as teachers), import competition in some occupations (such as shoe manufacturing) has increased by as much as 40 percentage points. The downward pressure on wages due to import competition has been commonly over-looked in the literature because it operates between and not within industries.

The magnitudes of the effects appear to be important. The authors report that total employment in manufacturing fell from 22 million to 17 million, with the steepest declines in the early 1980s. Total employment for the least-skilled workers (with a high-school diploma or less), declined over the entire period, while employment for workers with at least a college degree increased in all but the last three years of the sample. Additionally, real hourly wages fell for workers with a high-school education or less, while manufacturing workers with at least a college degree realized the largest wage gains. In terms of offshoring trends, offshore employment as a percentage of total employment of US multinational firms increased from 28 per cent in 1982 to 36 per cent in 2002; these increases occurred concurrent to a reduction in the US workforce for these firms, from 12 million workers in 1982 to 7 million in 2002. The authors find significant relocation of workers across industries due to import competition and smaller responses of employment to offshoring. Finally, the authors find that a 1 percentage point increase in import penetration is associated with a 0.6 percentage point decrease in manufacturing employment in the United States; they observe an increase of nearly 8 percentage point in import penetration for this country, which would explain almost 5 per cent of the reduction of employment in manufacturing. They also note that this effect has been felt more strongly by workers with a high-school education or less.

## 2.3.2 Labour has lost bargaining power relative to capital

Numerous reports in the popular press describe the decline in labour's share of income as an outcome of a struggle between capital and labour, with owners of capital winning at the expense of labour. These accounts typically present owners of capital as having greater bargaining power compared to labour, ostensibly because capital is footloose and can quickly relocate to wherever it can find the highest returns. For example, *The New York Times* quotes Stephen Roach of Morgan Stanley, who points out that "… the share of national income going to the owners of capital through corporate profits is surging. The share going to labour compensation is falling. This is not the way a democracy is supposed to work …". Rodrik (1997) describes a similar type of bargaining game between capital and labour. Some observers have even suggested that this increase in capital mobility has made workers in both receiving and sending countries worse off. As Kanbur (2001) points out, if instead of receiving a competitive return, capital and labour bargain over wages and employment, an increase in capital mobility is akin to increasing the bargaining power of capital in *both* labour markets. Despite these claims, however, there have been very few efforts to test the relationship between increased capital mobility and labour's share of income.

Work by the US Bureau of Economic Analysis (BEA) confirms that the foreign operations of US multinational corporations (MNCs) continue to grow at a rapid pace. One explanation offered by the BEA for the increase in overseas investment is the privatization of electric utilities and telephone companies as well as the liberalization of direct investment policies in foreign host countries. Harrison and McMillan (2004) show that expansion abroad has also been associated with an increase in the return to capital abroad relative to its return at home. In 1977, the return on capital[17] for affiliates in developing countries, 8.84 per cent, was virtually indistinguishable from the return for parent firms, 8.82 per cent. However, between 1977 and 1999, the return to capital increased by 4.5 percentage points for parent companies while it increased by 55.7 percentage points for developing country affiliates. During this same period, real wages in these developing country affiliates fell by over 20 percentage points for both production and non-production workers. The divergence in returns to capital and labour in these developing country affiliates is striking. Furthermore, research by the BEA shows that the average return on capital for overseas affiliates has been consistently much higher than the return for similar US corporations without overseas affiliates (Mataloni, 1999). One outcome is likely to be upward pressure on returns to capital in the United States as firms shift real capital abroad; these increasing returns to capital are documented using aggregate US data in Poterba (1997).

Harrison and McMillan (2004) explore this issue in an econometric framework using confidential, firm-level data from the BEA, which collects detailed information on US multinationals and their affiliates abroad. Data are collected on employment, labour compensation, sales and other variables. What is unique about these data is that they include detailed information on the activities of the US affiliates located in other countries and their parent companies operating in the United States. With this information, supplemented by additional data on the operations of US firms operating in the United States, it is possible to test whether relocation by US firms abroad reduces wages for remaining workers in the US parent plant.

With these data, they also address whether US workers in *other* plants are being threatened by plant relocation. They call this the "neighbour" effect. For example, they test whether workers in US auto plants are forced to accept lower wages when other US plants relocate some of their auto operations abroad. Thus, they are able to distinguish between the threat effect of affiliate activity in Europe, where wages are comparable, with activity in Mexico or other developing countries. They hy-

---

[17] Calculations of the return on capital and labour's share include net income, which may reflect the practice of transfer pricing. If firms report higher profits abroad for tax purposes, then net income will be measured with error. Harrison and McMillan (2004) find similar trends in horizontally- and vertically-integrated firms and conclude that transfer pricing is not driving these trends.

pothesize that firm relocation to developing countries is more likely to put downward pressure on US wages than relocation to other industrialized countries.

The framework for this research is based on a model of imperfect competition, where firms receive excess profits and firms and workers bargain over those profits. If firms find it easier to relocate to regions with lower labour costs, this gives them a bargaining advantage, resulting in lower wages for workers remaining in the United States. The theoretical framework leads to a set of estimating equations where they look at the determinants of labour compensation as a function of several variables. Those variables include factors such as fixed costs to plants of relocating abroad, and the number of other plants relocating in the same sector (the so-called "threat" effect). This research then leads naturally to a focus on the determinants of labour demand as a function of international factors. Their framework is consistemnt with Blanchflower, Oswald and Sanfey (1996) who find empirical evidence of rent sharing between labour and capital in the US manufacturing industry.

Their preliminary findings based on the operations of US multinationals in the manufacturing sector suggest that increased capital mobility may indeed be associated with negative labour market outcomes. Over the period 1977–99, multinational manufacturing firms shed close to 2 million jobs in the United States.[18] They also document that labour's share of income has fallen dramatically and real wages have remained flat. The loss of jobs in the United States has been partially offset by an increase in the number of jobs overseas. Although Brainard and Riker (1997a, 1997b) claim that these offsetting forces do not occur within the same firm, there is still the possibility that employment at home is being replaced by employment abroad through substitution across firms. Harrison and McMillan's preliminary analysis suggests that substitution occurs as some parent firms reduce employment in the United States and other US parent firms increase employment abroad through the establishment and expansion of their affiliates. This kind of substitution is likely to be overlooked if researchers focus purely on within-firm effects.

This evidence is consistent with work by Bertrand (2004) who finds that import competition changes the nature of the employment relationship. Bertrand argues that wages are negotiated at the time a worker enters a firm and are thereafter shielded from external labour markets. Employers have an incentive to shield workers from external competition for three reasons: (1) it is an optimal way for risk-neutral firms to insure risk-averse workers against cyclical fluctuations; (2) previous studies have validated the relevance of such wage-setting arrangements; and (3) the empirical relevance of such arrangements is relatively easy to test. According to Bertrand, a low elasticity of wages to labour market conditions is an indication that such agreements persist. Because of the endogeneity between local labour market conditions and wage-setting practices, Bertrand focuses on foreign competition to identify the impact of product market competition on wage-setting practices. She shows that an increase in import penetration reduces the elasticity of current wages to the unemployment rate that was prevailing at the time the employee was hired.

---

[18] See table 1 of Harrison and McMillan (2004).

### 2.3.3 Trade liberalization's efficiency gains can be cancelled out by unemployment

The experience in Mozambique's liberalization of its cashew industry shows a different side of the story. McMillan, Rodrik and Welch (2003) study the liberalization of Mozambique's cashew trade in the early 1990s, and explore how the drastic series of reforms had negative economic effects. Reform occurred in 1991–92, with the replacement of the export ban by export taxes, which were gradually lowered, and the privatization of the state trading company and the holding company of processing plants. In their empirical work, the authors establish a model whereby welfare changes (on all parties involved in the process) from changes in export taxes and other reforms are separated into export-quantity effects, terms-of-trade effects, unemployment effects, and traders' margin effects. They found that farmers did earn more and output rose, but nowhere near the magnitude estimated in previous studies. The surplus generated by cashew reform is estimated at US$11.48 million, but the average increase for farmers amounted to US$5.13 per household per year, or less than four days' average wage in Mozambique. Additionally, cashew processors were net losers from these reforms, incurring an average annual loss of US$7.3 million, while traders and exporters of raw cashew benefited the most. The authors note that the closing of the processing plants caused large numbers of unemployed workers, who remained unemployed long after the closing of the plants. They mention that nearly 90 per cent of the displaced workers were still unemployed in 2001.

---

**Box 2.1: Information sharing can reduce unemployment**

Anirudh Krishna (2007) found that many poor Indians in dead-end jobs remain in poverty, not because there are no better jobs but because they lack the connections to find them. Any Bangalorean could confirm the observation: the city teems with labourers desperate for work, and yet wealthy software entrepreneurs complain endlessly about a shortage of maids and cooks.

Inspired by this paper, Sean Blagsvedt created a village-level LinkedIn, the professional networking site so popular in the United States. Blagsvedt quit Microsoft and, with his stepfather, Ira Weise, and a former Microsoft colleague, built a social-networking site to connect Bangalore's white-collar workers with blue-collar workers. To reach workers earning US$2 to US$3 a day presented special challenges. The workers would be unfamiliar with computers. The wealthy potential employers would be reluctant to let random applicants tend their gardens or their newborns. To deal with the connectivity problem, Babajob pays anyone, from charities to Internet cafe owners, who find job-seekers and register them online. Babajob covers its costs through employers' advertisements. Instead of creating an anonymous job bazaar, Babajob replicates online the process by which Indians hire in real life: through chains of personal connections.

The exact number of jobs created by Babajob and the impact this has had on the lives of the poor is not yet known. But Blagsvedt is exploring the possibility of working with collaborators to get answers to these questions. In the meantime, Blagsvedt has kept himself busy opening another such project in Indonesia.

---

McMillan, Rodrik and Welch (2003) hypothesize that the diminished magnitude of gains, particularly for farmers, is due to market asymmetries, specifically imperfect competition. For example, the number of unlicensed cashew traders increased after liberalization, and cashew-exporting firms that were created after reforms were few and thus had considerable power regarding the purchase of raw nuts and the prices that they demanded. Another factor that the authors suggest was involved in the disappointing results from Mozambique's liberalization was the regulated and protected cashew industry in India. After the export ban was removed, India was able to buy raw cashews for an average of US$0.79 per kilogram from Mozambique, and earn an average of US$1.79 per kilogram selling processed cashews in its protected sector. This implies a terms-of-trade loss for Mozambique. The authors conclude by discussing two additional disappointments: the costs of unemployment resulting from losses to Mozambique's processed cashew export sector and the lack of supply response among cashew growers to higher prices for their product and the ability to export raw cashews. In reference to the latter point, lack of credibility of government reforms and high sunk costs of planting cashews did not lead to a quick or substantial growth in planting and harvesting cashew trees. If the Government of Mozambique had sought to increase the credibility of its reforms, this would have mitigated the loss of jobs in cashew processing in relation to increased activity in growing of raw cashew, but supply did not increase since government policy was not seen as credible, and uncertainty in future cashew policies and prices persisted.

One important lesson that can be drawn from this case study is that in order to predict the impact of trade liberalization, it is imperative to understand the initial conditions. If Mozambique had full employment, then the efficiency gains from trade liberalization – small as they were – would not have been wiped out by the cost of unemployment. Additionally, if policy-makers had understood that farmers consume the majority of the cashew nuts that they grow, they would have realized that liberalization of the cashew sector would not have had a big impact on household income.

## 2.3.4 Trade can have an impact on the quality of jobs

Job quality is difficult to define. Broad definitions typically include wages, job security, hours worked and number of accidents on the job. More qualitative measures are available on a case-by-case basis but are difficult to quantify and compare across countries (Robertson, Brown and Le Borgne Pierre, 2009). The evidence on trade and the quality of jobs is mixed. If trade liberalization leads to a downsizing of the labour force in the industrial sector and if these workers take lower paid jobs in other sectors, then trade liberalization is likely to lead to a lower "average" quality of jobs even though the quality of the jobs for workers who remain in the industrial sector may increase. Additionally, if increased trade increases the options of capital relative to labour and/or increases the rate of job churning, then exposure to trade is also likely to lead to a reduction in the average job quality in the affected country.

However, as Artuç and McLaren (2010) point out, exposure to trade can actually raise the workers' option value, thereby increasing the quality of jobs in the long run. In what follows, we review some of the most recent evidence on this topic.

Robertson, Brown and Le Borgne Pierre (2009) provide a nice overview of the issues surrounding trade and the quality of jobs. The countries included are: Cambodia, El Salvador, Honduras, Indonesia and Madagascar. The primary focus of the country studies is the textile and garment industries. In all five country case studies, the authors show that exposure to international trade and investment in the textile and garment sectors is correlated with an expansion of the number of jobs in the industrial sector and a contraction of employment in the agricultural sector. Because working conditions in the textile and garment industries are generally better than those in agriculture, the case-study authors conclude that the movement of workers from agriculture to apparel is likely to have improved overall working conditions in these countries.

In addition, recent developments call into question the effectiveness of relying on textile and garment manufacturing as a first step towards industrialization. The chapter on Madagascar raises the important point that while increased exports in the textile and garment industry did raise wages and employment for a period of time, the final dismantling of the multi-fibre arrangement (MFA) customs quotas on 1 January 2005 put an abrupt end to these positive developments. Since 2005, exports have stagnated and wages and employment have declined. The chapter on Madagascar concludes on a disconcerting note, claiming that the success of Madagascar's export processing zone "added fuel to the idea that using EPZs to develop a productive manufacturing base and promote employment was a positive development path for African governments. This chapter shows that this strategy is no longer sustainable, as a result of the end of the MFA. Yet, no alternative growth model has been designed." A similar situation occurred in Indonesia as a result of the Asian financial crisis. Employment and wage growth in the textile and garment industries were reversed while employment in the agricultural sector increased. It has been argued, however, that the jobs in that sector generated through trade in developing countries are not lost for that country group and that they may have positive externalities such as the empowerment of women, even if they are temporary (see Chapter 5 in this volume).

Harrison and Scorse (2010) ask whether outsiders can influence the quality of jobs in developing countries. They analyse the impact of anti-sweatshop activity by US activists on wage and employment outcomes in Indonesia. They compare the wage growth of unskilled workers in foreign-owned and exporting firms in the textiles, footwear and apparel sectors before and after the initiation of anti-sweatshop campaigns. They find that anti-sweatshop activity in the United States induced large real wage increases in targeted enterprises. However, they also find that there were costs associated with this activity including reduced investment, falling profits and increased probability of closure for smaller plants. They find no significant effect on employment.

Much of the media has focused its attention on the exploitation of children by multinationals and their abysmal working conditions.[19] According to Edmonds and Pavcnik (2005a, 2005b), the ILO estimates the proportion of children who work at 18 per cent, with the majority clustered in low-income countries, mostly Asia and sub-Saharan Africa. However, less than 3 per cent of children aged 4-15 work outside the home, so child workers are typically engaged in the economic activities of their parents, usually related to agriculture. Additionally, although working children devote considerable time to employment, an average of 16 hours per week, many still attend school. However, working has consequences for total completed schooling, and longer hours worked in particular leads to dramatic decreases in total educational attainment. In two related papers, Edmonds and Pavcnik (2005a, 2005b) and Edmonds, Pavcnik and Topalova (2008) find that poverty is the primary determinant of child labour. The implication is that if trade liberalization can reduce poverty, then trade liberalization can also reduce the incidence of child labour. Edmonds and Pavcnik (2005a, 2005b) show that because most households in Viet Nam are net exporters of rice, the liberalization of the rice sector that increased the price of rice increased household income and reduced child labour. To conclude, the authors emphasize the importance of the negative relationship between living standards and child labour.

Until very recently, the bulk of offshoring has been led by developed economies. In a chapter on trade and foreign direct investment, Harrison and Rodríguez-Clare (2010) review the literature on the impact of FDI on factor markets in developing countries. They report that almost all studies find that workers in foreign firms are paid higher wages, presumably because labour markets in developing countries are not perfectly competitive and because foreign firms tend to be more productive. Before controlling for firm and worker characteristics, the wage gap tends to be large. For example, Martins and Esteves (2007) report a wage gap of 50 per cent for Brazil, and Earle and Telegdy (2007) report a wage gap of 40 per cent for Hungary.

However, these wage gaps can be due to other factors. For example, if foreign firms attract more productive workers, then it would be reasonable to expect that these workers would demand higher wages to compensate for their higher productivity. In that case, the wage gap between wages in foreign and domestic firms would be explained by differences in the characteristics of the type of workers they hire. This seems to be the case; after controlling for firm and worker characteristics, the wage premium paid by foreign firms drops significantly. For example, Martins and Esteves (2007) follow workers who move to or leave foreign enterprises using a matched worker and firm panel data set for Brazil for the period 1995-99. They find that workers moving from foreign to domestic firms typically take wage cuts, while those that move from domestic to foreign firms experience wage gains. However, the wage differences are relatively small ranging from 3 to 7 per cent.

---

[19] See, for example, the 2009 article by CNN's Olivia Sterns, available at: http://edition.cnn.com/2009/HEALTH/09/25/child.tobacco.picking/index.html.

The authors conclude that their results support a positive view of the role of foreign investment on labour market outcomes in Brazil.

Harrison and Rodríguez-Clare (2009) conclude that there is no evidence to support the view that foreign firms unfairly exploit foreign workers by paying them below what their domestic counterparts would pay. Further evidence supporting this view comes from Harrison and Scorse (2010) who find evidence that foreign firms are more susceptible to pressure from labour advocacy groups, leading them to exhibit greater compliance with minimum wages and labour standards. They find that foreign firms in Indonesia were much more likely than domestic enterprises to raise wages and adhere to minimum wage requirements as a result of anti-sweatshop campaigns. They also find that the employment costs of anti-sweatshop campaigns were minimal, as garment and footwear subcontractors were able to reduce profits to pay the additional wage costs without reducing the number of workers.

## 2.3.5 Trade in tasks has ambiguous implications for employment

Trade in tasks is commonly referred to as offshoring. The term "offshoring", as used by Grossman and Rossi-Hansberg (2008), encompasses two different business configurations: the physical relocation of activities overseas through the establishment of overseas affiliates and offshore outsourcing. The first type of offshoring maintains the offshore activity within the boundaries of the firm while offshore outsourcing refers to the sourcing of intermediate inputs from overseas suppliers. Both types of offshoring are common. In what follows, we use the term "offshoring" to refer to the type of activity that maintains the offshore activity within the boundaries of the firm and the term "offshore outsourcing" to refer the sourcing of intermediate inputs from foreign suppliers.

Most of the evidence concerning the impact of offshoring on developing country labour markets is centred on estimating the impact of developed countries' FDI on developing country labour markets. This work misses an important part of the story: trade in intermediate inputs or offshore outsourcing. Offshore outsourcing has become increasingly important for both developing and developed countries. The impact of offshore outsourcing on employment and wages has been especially difficult to get a handle on for a number of reasons. Most important is the fact that many statistical agencies do not differentiate between trade in final goods and trade in intermediate inputs. For example, the US Bureau of Economic Analysis only collects data on imports by US-based MNCs, making no distinction between final goods imports and imported intermediate inputs.

Some studies have managed to get around these data limitations. For example, Goldberg et al. (2010) find that trade reform might have benefitted Indian firms by providing them access to a less expensive array of imported intermediate inputs. Their goal is to link the increased access to imported intermediate goods to dynamic gains from trade. This is innovative and important work but the implications for employment are unclear. Using cross-country data, Estevadeordal and Taylor (2008) find that liberalization of tariffs on capital and intermediate goods has a positive impact on economy-wide growth. "Liberalizers" have a 1 per cent higher annual growth rate. Again though, the implications for employment are ambiguous.

Understanding the employment effects of offshoring for developing countries is particularly important since unemployment in many of these countries tends to be very high. Indeed, the promise of job creation is one of the reasons developing countries set up investment offices and provide tax breaks to multinational corporations. Yet, we still know very little about the numbers and types of jobs created. The assumption is typically that jobs will be created and that this is a good thing, but this is not always the case. Take, for example, Chinese investors in Africa. Chinese construction projects in Africa are primarily carried out by state-owned enterprises that often employ imported Chinese workers. The reasons for this are discussed in greater detail in the next section. For now, it is sufficient to note that offshoring by "developing" countries is occurring at a rapid pace and we have very little hard evidence regarding its effect on recipient countries' labour markets.

One of the few papers that does ask about the effects of production offshoring from developed to developing countries in the receiving developing country is Feenstra and Hanson (1997). They consider the effects of relocating manufacturing activities from the United States to Mexico on the demand for labour in Mexico. For nine industries located across multiple regions in Mexico, they find that the demand for skilled labour is positively correlated with the change in the number of foreign affiliate assembly plants, and that FDI increases the wage share of skilled labour relative to unskilled labour. While this might seem counter-intuitive, the reason for this is that tasks performed by unskilled labour in the United States are performed by relatively skilled labour in Mexico. In a separate piece (Bergin, Feenstra and Hanson, 2009), find that offshoring by the United States increases wage inequality in the United States. They do not consider wage inequality in Mexico but the implications are clear. To the extent that offshoring increases the demand for skilled labour in Mexico, it would also increase inequality in Mexico. Feenstra indeed confirms this in a recent lecture on globalization and labour (Feenstra, 2007).

From this we can conclude that, overall, the effects of production offshoring on labour market outcomes in developing countries are likely to be mixed, and we still know too little about this issue. In some cases, there seem to be slightly encouraging effects, with production offshoring to developing countries helping to create new jobs of similar or even better quality than those offered by local companies. In other cases, the effects do not seem to be as positive for local workers. Significantly more research is needed to understand this type of trade and its impact on labour market outcomes in developing countries. Furthermore, there is a growing trend in South-South production offshoring, and the availability of data and studies of this kind of trade are scarce.

The available literature on the impact of production offshoring on employment in developed countries can offer some guidance on the probable effects in labour markets on the home country. This issue has been extensively studied and the results have often been contradictory. In one of the most recent papers, Harrison and McMillan (2009) find that the insights derived from trade theory go a long way towards explaining this apparently contradictory evidence on the relationship between offshoring and domestic manufacturing employment. For US parent firms primarily involved in horizontal activities, affiliate activity abroad substitutes for domestic employment. For vertically-integrated parent firms, however, the results suggest that home and foreign employment are complementary. Foreign wage reductions are associated with an increase in domestic employment. The results differ across high- and low-income affiliate locations, in part because factor-price differences relative to the United States are much more important in low-income regions. In low-income affiliate locations, a 10 percentage point reduction in wages is associated with a 2.7 percentage point reduction in the US parent company's employment for horizontal parents and a 3.1 percentage point increase in the parent company's employment for vertical firms.

Sethupathy (2010) also investigates the wage and employment effects of off-shoring. Using a theoretical framework that combines heterogeneous firms with wage bargaining, Sethupathy predicts that offshoring firms increase their productivity and profitability at the expense of firms that do not offshore. For firms that offshore, the productivity effect boosts wages while wages at the firms that do not offshore fall. The predicted effect for employment for firms that offshore is ambiguous, while the predicted effect for employment at firms that do not offshore is unambiguously negative. Using two events in Mexico as exogenous shocks to the marginal cost of offshoring to Mexico, Sethupathy (2010) tests the implications of his model using firm-level data on US multinationals. His empirical results support the predictions regarding wages. However, the author finds no evidence that job losses are greater at firms that offshore than at firms that do not offshore.

Both of these studies share important limitations. First, by their very nature, they are partial equilibrium studies that focus only on the traded goods sector. But as Grossman and Rossi-Hansberg (2008) stress, the spillovers associated with off-shoring require a general equilibrium framework in order to properly account for effects outside the traded goods sector. And second, since there are no details available on worker characteristics in the BEA data, it is difficult to know what to make of the results on wages. Harrison and McMillan (2009) do not use the BEA wage data for this reason. Ebenstein et al. (2009) get around both of these problems by matching data on offshoring from the BEA with data on wages and worker characteristics from the Current Population Surveys (CPSs). This has two advantages. First, in all of the wage regressions they are able to control for worker characteristics. And second, since the CPS encompasses workers from all sectors of the economy, they are able to ascertain whether trade and offshoring have been important drivers of the reallocation of labour across sectors. As discussed in great detail in section 2.3.1 of this chapter, they find that the effects of offshoring on wages and employment are small and that offshore outsourcing proxied for with import penetration does have significant effects on wages at the occupational level.

Over the past decade, trade economists have begun to study the implications of trade in services for employment and wages. Much of the work for developed countries has focused on defining a set of occupational characteristics that make occupations more or less offshorable. Jensen and Kletzer (2005) find that the total share of employment potentially affected by service trade is likely to be closer to 40 per cent. However, the empirical work that focuses on this issue generally finds that services trade has had a minimal impact on labour market outcomes in developed countries. This is partly due to the fact that previous studies have not used the most current data.

The work on the impact of services trade on labour markets in developing countries has been primarily anecdotal and focused on the cultural aspects of services trade. The publication by Messenger and Ghosheh (2010) is an exception to that rule. The authors examine and provide a historical context for the development of the business process outsourcing (BPO) industry, based on case study analysis of working conditions in four countries where this industry is large or growing – Argentina, Brazil, India and the Philippines. A mixed picture emerges from their analysis. On the positive side, and unlike previous assumptions, remote work jobs – such as jobs in BPO activities – are of a reasonably good quality by local standards. For example, wages of Indian workers are nearly double the average wages in other sectors of the Indian economy. In the Philippines, BPO employees earn 53 per cent more than workers of the same age in other industries. On the other hand, night work is common to serve customers in distant time zones in "real time" and work is generally stressful. BPO employees face heavy workloads backed by performance targets combined with tight rules and procedures, all this enforced via electronic monitoring. This type of high-strain work organization is well-known to produce high levels of job-related stress, according to the authors.

## 2.4 CAN GOVERNMENTS INFLUENCE THE RELATIONSHIP BETWEEN TRADE AND EMPLOYMENT?

Curiously, the most recent volume of the *Handbook of Development Economics* includes a chapter on trade, foreign investment and industrial policy for developing countries that completely side-steps the issue of unemployment.[20] The authors conclude that there is no strong case for tariffs, subsidies or tax breaks to protect industry in developing countries. Yet, as we noted in the introduction, unemployment is extremely high in many developing countries. This unemployment and underemployment is costly and the inefficiencies associated with the forms of industrial policy the authors focus on (tariffs and subsidies) must be weighed against the costs of potentially higher unemployment. This point is clearly made by McMillan, Rodrik and Welch (2003) who study the case of the Mozambique cashew sector. The efficiency gains of removing the export ban on raw cashew were almost completely offset by the costs of unemployment.

---

[20] See Harrison and Rodriguez-Clare (2010).

Nevertheless, Harrison and Rodríguez-Clare (2010) do envision a role for what they call "soft" industrial policy designed to shift attention from interventions that distort prices to interventions that deal directly with coordination failures. They go on to say that given the wide number of coordination failures, an exhaustive list of the appropriate industrial policies is impossible to provide. They do though suggest the following as possibilities: (i) policies to increase the supply of skilled workers; (ii) policies to encourage technology adoption; (iii) policies to improve regulation and infrastructure; (iv) public investment in infrastructure projects when there are strong investment complementarities; (v) policies to attract FDI that brings in "foreign" technologies; (vi) scholarships for study abroad in areas deemed important for growth; (vii) grants and prizes for innovation; and (viii) technical assistance. While some of this sounds good on paper, the key underlying assumption is that somehow these policies will stimulate growth and that *growth will lead to employment*. As we have argued above, and as Harrison and Rodríguez-Clare (2010) point out in section 4.2 of their paper, the link between trade and growth is not something that can be taken for granted. Even more tenuous is the link between growth and employment.

In what follows, we will argue that there is considerable scope for government policy to enhance the job-creation potential of trade and foreign direct investment in developing countries. To make this case, we focus on two recent, high profile, episodes of increased trade and investment in developing countries. First, we turn to the increased acquisition of land by foreign investors in developing countries across the globe and ask whether governments can use these investments to help create jobs. Then, we turn to the case of Chinese investment in Africa and ask: to what extent has this led to job creation and what can African governments do to enhance job creation in Africa by Chinese investors?

### 2.4.1 Land grab? The race for the world's farmland[21]

Nowhere is the scope for industrial policy more important than in the arena of foreign investment in agriculture. According to the World Bank (2007), agriculture provided jobs for 1.3 billion smallholders and landless workers in 2007. This number corresponds closely to the number of people living below the dollar a day poverty line. The process of modernization of the agricultural sector is likely to reduce the number of jobs in agriculture. Of course this does not mean that the process should be reversed; however, host country governments need to formulate strategies that incorporate the well-being of smallholders. Traditional trade policies such as tariffs and subsidies may be part of this strategy.

A case in point is Olam Nigeria. Olam Nigeria, a foreign affiliate of a Singapore-based multinational had been importing rice into Nigeria for years. Nigeria has the right conditions for rice cultivation but local production never satisfied local demand. Reasons for this had to do with low productivity due to inferior inputs and high

---

[21] The title of this section is borrowed from the publication "Land Grab? The Race for the World's Farmland", which was published in 2009 by the Woodrow Wilson International Center for Scholars.

transportation costs. As a result, Nigeria imported around 60 per cent of its total rice consumption. In 2005, the Government imposed high tariffs on imported rice. As a result, Olam Nigeria leased a mill from the Government and began processing locally produced rice. By 2007, the company had invested US$5 million in upgrading the mill and had doubled its capacity. To solve the problem of an insufficient supply of high-quality rice, the affiliate started an outgrowers programme for rice cultivation in Nigeria. Olam Nigeria provided credit to farmers, who used it to purchase inputs. eight thousand farmers participated in the programme during its first two years, and the number was expected to grow to 20,000 by 2009 (UNCTAD, 2009).

Figure 2.7 shows that 48 new land deals were signed between 2006 and 2009. It also shows that 27 of these deals took place in sub-Saharan Africa and that, of these 27, only five originated in China. One of the most pressing questions for policy-makers is how to harness these deals so as to maximize the welfare and employment gains to the host countries. It is too soon to tell what the effects will be but one thing is clear: the governments of the recipient countries are in the driver's seat. It is up to them to determine what, if any, impact on employment these investments will have.

According to Kugelman (2009), the magnitude of the effects could be huge. He notes that 15 to 20 million hectares of farmland in the developing world have been under negotiation over the past few years. According to *The Economist* (2009), this represents one-fifth of all the farmland in the European Union. Kugelman puts this in perspective when he writes:

> "One of the largest and most notorious deals is one that ultimately collapsed: an arrangement that would have given the South Korean firm Daewoo a 99-year lease to grow corn and other crops on 1.3 million hectares of farmland in Madagascar – half of that country's total arable land. However, according to a German press account, similar mega-deals have either been finalized or are in the works. Sudan has leased 1.5 million hectares of 'prime farmland' to the Gulf states, Egypt and South Korea for 99 years; Egypt 'plans to grow grain' on 840,000 hectares in Uganda; and the president of the Democratic Republic of Congo 'has offered to lease' an incredible 10 million hectares to South Africa. To get a sense of the enormity of such deals, consider that most small farmers own two- or three-hectare plots."

Considering the costs and benefits of these deals, a recent report by the Woodrow Wilson International Center for Scholars (2009) makes a number of important and sensible recommendations for host country governments. Most relevant to the issue at hand is their recommendation that governments uphold the right to food as a human right. To this end, they write, "host countries should impose tariffs or other protective measures to ensure local industries are not subjected to foreign investment that could jeopardize domestic food security or right-to-food measures."

Figure 2.7: Overseas land investment for agricultural production (2006-May 2009)

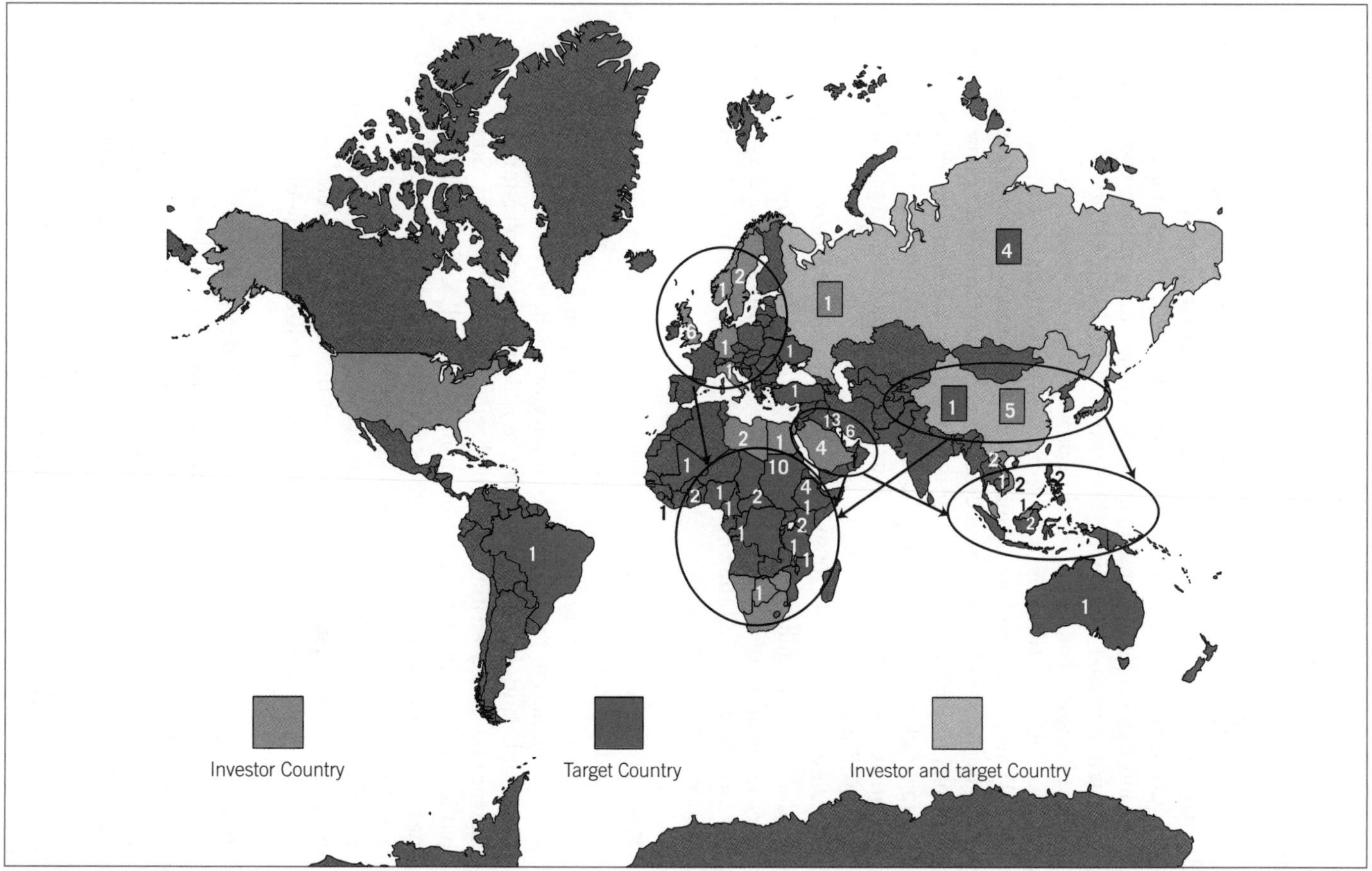

Investor Country    Target Country    Investor and target Country

Source: UNCTAD (2009).

Notes: This map covers only confirmed deals that have been signed, some of which have been implemented. However, not all signed deals have been implemented, and all signed deals that were rescinded by one or both parties before the end of May 2009 are excluded. Prospective deals reported in the press, but which have not progressed to the stage of agreement, are excluded. The total number of deals was 48, shown by both source and destination countries.

## 2.4.2 FDI inflows and development: The case of Africa

Unemployment and underemployment are a serious problem in most African countries, and not only in the poorest. For example, in Botswana, the so-called superstar of Africa, poverty, unemployment and inequality remain extremely high. Recent work by McCaig and McMillan (forthcoming) indicates that in 2002–03 (the latest year for which the Household Income and Expenditure Survey is available), the headcount poverty rate was 30.2 per cent, the Gini coefficient was 64.7 – making it the third most unequal society in the world – the overall unemployment rate was 24 per cent and the youth unemployment rate was closer to 50 per cent.[22] These facts should make any economist convinced that good governance and institutions are the key to economic success take pause. Botswana has experienced rapid economic growth and is well known for its efficient and practically corruption-free bureaucracy. But this growth has been largely based on the diamond industry which employs only around 7,000 people or 2.3 per cent of the labour force. The Government of Botswana is well aware of these problems and has implemented numerous schemes dedicated to creating employment in an effort to alleviate poverty and reduce inequality. Botswana has an official Institute for Development Policy Analysis (BIDPA) which is generally oriented towards employment creation and diversification of the economy. Yet, to date, industrialization has been elusive. The reasons for this are unclear and warrant further investigation. For now, the point is that even in the so-called superstar of Africa, efforts to industrialize and generate employment have not met with much success.

Like Botswana, Nigeria has a serious unemployment problem. The World Bank (2009) notes the following:

> "Public debate in Nigeria on the country's progress has been dominated by two seemingly opposed themes. The first is the strong growth performance of the non-oil economy since the return to democracy in 1999, and especially since 2003, which ushered in a period during which the Federal Government of Nigeria undertook debt restructuring and fiscal, financial, infrastructure, and institutional reforms. Strong growth during this period has been manifested in sharp increases in agricultural production, wholesale and retail trade, and construction, and in the emergence of new industries, particularly in the financial, telecommunications, and entertainment sectors. The second, opposing theme is that Nigeria's much improved economic performance seems to have done little to reduce unemployment, especially among the young. The consensus in society is that youth unemployment is on the rise, with an associated negative impact on public order and an increase in militancy."

---

[22] McCaig and McMillan's calculations based on Botswana's 2002–03 Household Income and Expenditure Survey.

53

On the likelihood of creating jobs in manufacturing, the report contradicts itself. First, quoting Paul Collier, the authors write that countries like Nigeria cannot compete with China and that perhaps upgrading the skills of the labour force to make Nigeria attractive for outsourcing is the way to go. However, the impressive annexes of the report provide detailed lists of manufacturing investors in several free trade zones throughout Nigeria. These projects include the manufacturing and/or assembly of all sorts of consumer products.

Where does trade policy play a role in all of this? Hundreds of newspaper articles claim that cheap imports from China are responsible for the decline in industrial employment in Africa. However, as Brautigam (2010) points out, China has been engaged in sub-Saharan Africa for decades. Brautigam writes that it is quite likely that imports from China have displaced some African workers. And given the nature of exports from Africa, it is unlikely that the increase in exports made up for the jobs lost. However, she is also optimistic about China's ability to stimulate entrepreneurial activity and create jobs in Africa. This is because China's industrial policy – China's *zou chu qu* or "go global" policy, launched in 1999 – has provided enormous incentives for private firms from China to invest in Africa. This is a clear break from the past when it was primarily state-owned Chinese enterprises investing in Africa. Brautigam also provides several anecdotes of successful Chinese-African manufacturing joint ventures.

A second reason to be optimistic about China's role in Africa is that Chinese firms are likely to be better equipped than their western counterparts to deal with the working conditions in Africa (Buckley et al., 2010). For example, Chinese firms are adept at operating successfully in environments characterized by uncertainty, opaque regulatory conditions and weak market-enhancing institutions. Buckley also asserts that developing country firms may be better able than industrialized countries to adapt their technologies, products and processes to local market conditions because they entered the product markets more recently than their western counterparts and therefore have more recent experience with labour-intensive low-cost manufacturing.

A third reason to be optimistic about China's investment in Africa is that China's strategy in Africa reveals a willingness to diversify and work in many different countries, all with their own sets of priorities and investment rules. This is important because Africa is home to an enormous amount of untapped potential in a variety of areas. For example, Africa's agro-ecological potential is huge compared to its current output. More than one-quarter of the world's arable land lies in the continent, but it only generates 10 per cent of global agricultural output. And in most African countries, upward of 70 per cent of the population relies on agriculture for a living.

It is up to African governments to decide how they can best harness the enthusiasm of the Chinese investors for job creation. There is in our view no reason to rule out tariffs and subsidies as tools for directing investment into labour-intensive activities.

## 2.5 POLICY IMPLICATIONS AND DIRECTIONS FOR FUTURE RESEARCH

Recent advances in economic theory have highlighted three issues that have potentially important implications for policy-makers in developing countries. The three most important implications are: (1) the extent of the gains in allocative efficiency associated with trade liberalization depends critically on the institutional setting; (2) exposure to international trade can have an impact on aggregate employment and therefore the rate of unemployment; and (3) exposure to international trade can increase wage inequality in both rich and poor countries.

Our examination of aggregate data provided at the beginning of this chapter reveals interesting trends that do not, however, explicitly confirm the theoretical predictions highlighted in the previous paragraph. We find that: (1) developing countries have significantly reduced industrial tariffs over the past decade; (2) two-thirds of industrial employment is now located in developing countries and that China drives this trend; and (3) at least in the aggregate, trade liberalization is not correlated with changes in real wages or employment.

On the other hand, the overview of country-level studies that represent the bulk of the discussion in this chapter provides a more nuanced picture that often supports theoretical predictions. In particular, our review of the most recent empirical literature on trade and employment reveals that in Brazil, South Africa and the United States, trade liberalization has been associated with employment losses in the industrial sector according to general equilibrium studies. In addition, recent empirical work on trade in tasks and employment suggest that trade in tasks results in a reallocation of workers from manufacturing to services and puts downward pressure on wages in home countries measured at the occupational level. Host countries, however, appear to benefit. If the host country is a developing country, wages in multinational enterprises are usually higher than those in domestic firms.

Those recent findings suggest that previous micro-studies that focus only on labour market outcomes within the traded goods sector are likely to miss an important part of the story.[23] Employment contractions (expansions) in the traded goods sector imply either employment expansions (contractions) in the non-traded goods, or changes in unemployment, or both. These movements of labour across sectors are likely to be associated with wage changes that have been missed by studies that focus solely on the manufacturing sector. In fact, given what we know about the impact of trade reform on efficiency gains, wages for workers who remain in manufacturing after trade liberalization are likely to rise. However, focusing only on these workers can easily lead to the wrong conclusion about the effects of trade reform on wages and inequality.

---

[23] Others have made this point, noting that in many cases the issue is data constraints (see, for example, Lee, 2005).

Another finding that is supported by recent empirical literature is that the extent to which trade liberalization has had an impact on employment varies enormously across countries. The case of Mozambique, for instance, illustrates the importance of taking into account initial conditions when thinking about the impact of trade liberalization on labour market outcomes. Trade liberalization also appears to have ambiguous impacts on the quality of jobs in terms of wages and employment opportunities: while it can raise the wages of workers who remain employed in the traded goods sector or of those finding a new job, it can at the same time expose workers to more job insecurity.

Last but not least, we argue in this chapter that the shift in manufacturing employment from developed to developing countries has probably weakened the bargaining power of workers in developed countries. Indeed, the empirical evidence discussed in this chapter supports the hypothesis that the nature of the bargaining relationship between labour and capital has changed as a result of exposure to international trade.

These findings have potentially important policy implications. In particular, they give no reason for complacency about the relationship between trade and jobs in developing countries. Many of the workers in the poorest developing countries continue to squeeze a living from land that has limited potential for productivity improvements.[24] Private schemes – such as Babajob – that address labour market frictions in developing countries can contribute to providing employment opportunities for the poor. But such schemes are no replacement for government policies that aim at creating alternative means of employment.

We conclude this section by saying that, while some of the recent literature on the effects of trade and jobs has found mixed effects, where there are job gains in some sectors but important losses in others, the most recent and detailed empirical studies seem to be challenging many of the traditional ideas in the trade literature. Very recent theoretical advances in the field have shed light on previously unaccounted effects of trade liberalization that, along with more ambitious empirical tests of these models using individual-level and firm-level data as well as sectoral-level liberalization variables, are clearing the way for a better understanding of the effects of trade liberalization on labour market outcomes. Moreover, applied studies like those by Menesez-Filho and Muendler (2007) and Ebenstein et al. (2009) have found important negative effects of trade liberalization on labour market outcomes both in developed and developing countries.

While we cannot give a final verdict on the impact of trade liberalization on employment (and we will probably not be able to do so, at least in the near future) these recent studies do raise important doubts over the previously held view that trade liberalization would yield employment benefits even in the long run. Moreover, there is the need to better understand experiences in other countries and the structural environments that would allow to minimize or contain the potentially negative effects of trade liberalizations on employment. It would seem, from what is suggested

---

[24] Yu, You and Fan (2010).

by the work of Rodrik (2006) and Menesez-Filho and Muendler (2007), that industrial policies, patterns of liberalization (for example, differences between liberalization in intermediate and final goods) as well as characteristics of the labour market (for example, how easy it is to reallocate workers) could have significant roles in determining whether workers in a country would be better off, which sectors would be affected and what policies could be pursued to smooth the transition.

# REFERENCES

Agenor, P-R.; Aizenman, J. 1996. "Trade liberalization and unemployment", in *Journal of International Trade and Economic Development*, Vol. 5, No. 3, pp. 265-286.

Artuç, E.; McLaren, J. 2010. "A structural empirical approach to trade shocks and labor adjustment: An application to Turkey", in G. Porto; B.M. Hoekman (eds): *Trade Adjustment Costs in Developing Countries: Impacts, Determinants and Policy Responses* (World Bank and CEPR).

Balassa, B. 1965. "Tariff Protection in Industrial Countries: An Evaluation", in *The Journal of Political Economy*, Vol. 73, No. 6, pp. 573-594, Dec.

Bergin, P.; Feenstra, R.C.; Hanson, G. 2009. "Offshoring and volatility: Evidence from Mexico's Maquiladora industry", in *The American Economic Review*, Vol. 99, No. 4, pp. 1664-1671.

Bernard, A.B.; Bradford Jensen, J.; Schott, P.K. 2006. "Survival of the best fit: Exposure to low-wage countries and the (uneven) growth of US manufacturing plants", in *Journal of International Economics*, Vol. 68, pp. 219-237.

Bertrand, M. 2004. "From the invisible handshake to the invisible hand? How import competition changes the employment relationship", in *Journal of Labor Economics*, Vol. 22, No. 4, pp. 723-765, Oct.

Blanchflower, D.G.; Oswald, A.J.; Sanfey, P. 1996. "Wages, profits, and rent-sharing", in *The Quarterly Journal of Economics*, Vol. 111, No. 1, pp. 227-251, Feb.

Brainard, L.S.; Riker, D.A. 1997a. "Are U.S. multinationals exporting U.S. jobs?", *NBER Working Paper* No. 5958.

Brainard, L.S.; Riker, D.A. 1997b. "U.S. multinationals and competition from low wage countries", *NBER Working Paper* No. 5959.

Brautigam, D. 2010. *The Dragon's Gift: The real story of China in Africa* (Oxford University Press).

Buckley, P.J.; Clegg L.J.; Cross, A.R.; Liu, X.; Voss, H.; Zheng, P. 2010. "The determinants of Chinese outward foreign investment", in P.J. Buckley (ed.): *In foreign direct investment, China in the world economy*, p. 240 (Palgrave McMillan).

Collier, P. 1993. "Higgledy-piggledy liberalization", in *The World Economy*, Vol. 16, No. 4, pp. 503-511.

Davidson, C.; Matusz, S.J. 2009. "Modeling, measuring, and compensating the adjustment costs associated with trade reforms", in *Adjustment costs and adjustment impacts of trade policy* (CEPR and World Bank), June.

Earle, J.S.; Telegdy, A. 2007. "Ownership and wages: Estimating public-private and foreign-domestic differentials using LEED from Hungary, 1986-2003", *NBER Working Paper* No. 12997, Mar.

Ebenstein, A; Harrison, A.; McMillan, M.; and Phillips, S. 2009. "Estimating the impact of trade and offshoring on American workers using the current population surveys", *NBER Working Paper* No. 15107.

Edmonds, E.V.; Pavcnik, N. 2005a. "Child labor in the global economy", in *Journal of Economic Perspectives*, Vol. 19, No. 1, pp. 199-220.

Edmonds, E.V.; Pavcnik, N. 2005b. "The effect of trade liberalization on child labor", in *Journal of International Economics*, Vol. 65, No. 2, pp. 401-419, Mar.

Edmonds, E.V.; Pavcnik, N.; Topalova, P. 2008. "Child labor and schooling in a globalizing world: Some evidence from urban India", mimeo (Dartmouth College), Sep.

Egger, H.; Kreickemeier, U. 2009. "Firm Heterogeneity and the Labor Market Effects of Trade Liberalization", in International Economic Review, Vol. 50, No. 1, pp. 187-216, Feb.

Estevadeordal, A.; Taylor, A.M. 2008. "Is the Washington consensus dead? Growth, openness, and the great liberalization, 1970s–2000s", *NBER Working Paper* No. 14264.

Feenstra, R.C.; Hanson, G.H. 1997. "Foreign direct investment and relative wages: Evidence from Mexico's Maquiladoras", in *Journal of International Economics*, Vol. 42, No. 3-4, pp. 371-394.

Feenstra, R.C. 2007. "Globalization and its impact on labour", *wiiw Working Paper* No. 44.

Goldberg, P.K.; Khandelwal, A.; Pavcnik, N.; Topalova, P. 2010. "Imported intermediate inputs and domestic product growth: Evidence from India", in *The Quarterly Journal of Economics*, Vol. 125, No. 4, pp. 1727-1767.

Goldberg, P.K.; Pavcnik, N. 2004. "Trade, inequality, and poverty: What do we know? Evidence from recent trade liberalization episodes in developing countries", in *Brookings Trade Forum 2004*, pp. 223-269.

Goldberg, P.K.; Pavcnik, N. 2007. "Distributional effects of globalization in developing countries", in *Journal of Economic Literature*, Vol. 45, No. 1, pp. 39-82, Mar.

Greenaway, D. 1993. "Liberalizing foreign trade through rose-tinted glasses", in *Economic Journal*, Vol. 103, pp. 208-223.

Grossman, G.M.; Rossi-Hansberg, E. 2008. "Trading tasks: A simple theory of offshoring", in *American Economic Review*, Vol. 98, No. 5, pp. 1978-1997, Dec.

Harrison, A.E.; McMillan, M.S. 2004. "The impact of overseas investment by US multinationals on wages and employment", Conference Paper presented at the 2005 ASSA Conference, see:

http://www.aeaweb.org/assa/2005/0108_1430_0402.pdf.

Harrison, A.E.; McMillan, M.S. 2009. "Offshoring jobs? Multinationals and U.S. manufacturing employment", *NBER Working Paper* No. 12372 (also in *Review of Economics and Statistics*, forthcoming).

Harrison, A.E.; Rodríguez-Clare, A. 2010. "Trade, foreign investment, and industrial policy for developing countries", in D. Rodrik; M. Rosenzweig (eds): *Handbook of Development Economics*, Vol. 5, pp. 4039-4214.

Harrison, A.E.; Scorse, J. 2010. "Multinationals and anti-sweatshop activism", in *American Economic Review*, Vol. 100, No. 1, pp. 247-273.

Helpman, E.; Itskhoki, O. 2009. *Labor market rigidities, trade and unemployment* (Harvard University).

Helpman, E.; Itskhoki, O.; Redding, S. 2009. "Inequality and unemployment in a global economy", *CEP Discussion Paper Series* No. 940.

Hoekman, B.; Winters, L.A. 2005. "Trade and employment: Stylized facts and research findings", *Working Paper* No. 102, pp. 33 (The Egyptian Center for Economic Studies), May.

Jensen, J.B.; Kletzer, L.G. 2005. "Tradable services: Understanding the scope and impact of services outsourcing", in S.M. Collins; L. Brainard (eds): *Brookings trade forum 2005: Offshoring white-collar work*, pp. 75-133 (Brookings Institution Press).

Kanbur, R. 2001. "Economic policy, distribution and poverty: The nature of disagreements", in *World Development*, Vol. 29, No. 6, pp. 1083-1094, June.

Kletzer, L.G. 2001. *Job loss from imports: Measuring the costs* (Institute for International Economics).

Krishna, A. 2007. "For reducing poverty faster: Target reasons before people", in *World Development*, Vol. 35, No. 11, pp. 1947-1960, Nov.

Krueger, A.O. 1983. *Trade and employment in developing countries, Volume 3: Synthesis and conclusions* (University of Chicago Press).

Krugman, P.R. 2008. "Trade and wages, reconsidered", *Brookings Papers on Economic Activity*, No. 1, pp. 103-154.

Kugelman, M. 2009. Introduction in M. Kugelman; S.L. Levenstein (eds): *Land grab? The race for the world's farmland*, p. 123 (Woodrow Wilson International Center for Scholars).

Kugelman, M.; Levenstein, S.L. 2009. *Land grab? The race for the world's farmland* (Woodrow Wilson International Center for Scholars).

Lee, E. 2005. "Trade liberalization and employment", *DESA Working Paper* No. 5.

Martins, P.; Esteves, L.A. 2007. "Is there rent sharing in developing countries? Matched-panel evidence from Brazil", *Working Papers* No. 0060 (Universidade Federal do Paraná, Department of Economics).

Mataloni, R.J. Jr. 1999. "U.S. multinational companies: Operations in 1997", in *Survey of current business*, July.

McCaig, B.; McMillan, M. Forthcoming, mimeo (International Food Policy Research Institute).

McMillan, M.; Rodrik, D.; Welch K.H. 2003. "When economic reform goes wrong: Cashews in Mozambique", in *Brookings Trade Forum*, pp. 97-165.

Melitz, M.J. 2003. "The impact of trade on intra-industry reallocations and aggregate industry productivity", in *Econometrica*, Vol. 71, No. 6, pp. 1695-1725, Nov.

Menezes Filho, N.A.; Muendler, M.A. 2007. "Labor reallocation in response to trade reform", *CESifo Working Paper* No. 1936.

Messenger, J.C.; Ghosheh, N. 2010. *Offshoring and working conditions in remote work* (Palgrave Macmillan).

Poterba, J.M. 1997. *Recent developments in corporate profitability: Patterns and explanations*, mimeo, Mar.

Robertson, R.; Brown, D.; Le Borgne Pierre, G. ; Sanchez-Puerta, M.L. 2009. *Globalization, wages, and the quality of jobs: Five country studies* (World Bank).

Rodrik, D. 1997. *Has globalization gone too far?* (Institute for International Economics).

Rodrik, D. 2006. "Understanding South Africa's economic puzzles", *CID Working Paper* No. 130 (Harvard University).

Rodrik, D. 2007. "Industrial development: Some stylized facts and policy directions", in D. O'Connor; M. Kjollerstrom (eds): *Industrial development for the 21st century: Sustainable development perspectives* (UNDESA).

Sethupathy, G. 2010. *Offshoring, wages, and employment: Theory and evidence*, mimeo (Johns Hopkins University).

*The Economist*. 2009. "Outsourcing's third wave", 21 May, see:

http://www.economist.com/displaystory.cfm?story_id=13692889.

UNCTAD. 2009. *World Investment Report 2009: Transnational corporations, agricultural production and development.*

World Bank. 1995. *World Development Report 1995:Workers in an integrating world.*

World Bank. 2007. *World Development Report 2008: Agriculture for development.*

World Bank. 2009. "Nigeria – Employment and growth study", *Public Sector Study Report* No. 51564.

Yu, B.; You, L. Fan, S. 2010. "Toward a typology of food security in developing countries", *IFPRI Discussion Papers* 945 (International Food Policy Research Institute).

# ASSESSING THE IMPACT OF TRADE ON EMPLOYMENT: METHODS OF ANALYSIS

# 3

*By Bill Gibson*

## 3.1    INTRODUCTION

Since Adam Smith, economists have laboured under the assumption that special-ization and trade is the cause of the wealth of nations. For developing countries, this has traditionally meant specialization in relatively labour-intensive branches of production and trade with more developed economies with abundant capital. Early ILO studies concluded that liberalization could facilitate labour absorption in the least developed countries (LDCs) and that, potentially, significant gains could follow (Lydall, 1975). Still, there is considerable scepticism whether trade remains the engine of growth and employment, in terms of both quantity and quality.

It is the purpose of this chapter to investigate the main methodologies that have been used to address the link between trade, growth and employment. Estimates of the employment impact of trade can provide useful information for policy design. How and for which purpose information based on estimates can be used will, to a large extent, depend on the methodology that has been used to generate the estimates. This chapter provides an overview of the different methodologies that exist, their respective advantages and disadvantages when it comes to implementing them and their strengths and weaknesses with respect to policy guidance.

Methodologies to evaluate the impact of trade on employment may be broadly classified as quantitative or qualitative. Quantitative methods include both econo-metrics and simulations. Qualitative methods involve case studies or consist of "thick description" of specific events, narratives, cultural histories, ethnographies or other portraits of the effects of job creation and destruction as a result of globalization. The bulk of this chapter is devoted to quantitative assessments, but qualitative methods are also discussed.

The discussion in this chapter illustrates that, despite the overwhelming his-torical evidence that trade and specialization are generally major contributors to the wealth of nations, it is not known with precision whether a marginal change in imports will increase or decrease employment opportunities. Indeed, most studies that investigate the employment impact of shifts in the volume and composition of trade show that the overall impact on employment is small. Baldwin (1994, p. 17), for instance, notes that the net employment effects of changes in exports and imports have not been significant in OECD countries, and this is the mainstream view. To a certain extent, these findings can be explained by the fact that models of trade produced by economists are not designed to take into account the aggregate employment effects of trade, despite public concern that "trade destroys jobs" (Davidson and Matusz, 2004). Standard models assume full employment and, in such models, a shift in the pattern of production in response to trade opportunities causes only a temporary decline in aggregate employment as workers relocate from declining to expanding branches of production. These temporary changes in employment are not a main focus of this chapter, as they are discussed at length in Chapter 6 in this volume.

One could even ask the question of whether a focus on employment effects is warranted at all. In standard economic analysis, a gain or loss of employment is only one part of overall welfare. A reduction in the total amount of employment can be compensated in part by a rise in leisure and opportunities for home production. It also affords individuals an opportunity to accumulate human capital by returning to school or acquiring specialized training. Still, few economists would doubt that trade may lead to large adverse changes in overall well-being, if it is the case that a significant number of quality jobs are destroyed.

Instead of focusing on the short-term effects of trade on employment, this chapter discusses methods to evaluate the long-term effects. Those long-term effects will to a large extent be determined by the interplay of three variables: trade, productivity and employment. Significant attention is therefore given in this chapter to the relationship between those three variables, both at the economy-wide level and at the cross-sectoral level within economies. The chapter also features a discussion of how the interaction between trade and productivity affects the quality of employment, notably in terms of wages and the wage premium between high- and low-skilled labour.

The chapter starts with a section that highlights the challenges faced by those who attempt to assess the employment effects of trade. The section contains a discussion of the need to understand the trade, productivity and employment (both in terms of quantity and quality) relationship. Challenges related to data requirements and model choice are also discussed in that section. Sections 3.3 and 3.4 provide detailed discussions of models available for conducting quantitative assessments of the employment effects of trade. Section 3.3 focuses on simulation methods and discusses different methods in order of increasing level of sophistication. Section 3.4 focuses on econometric approaches. Section 3.5 provides a short introduction into qualitative methods, and section 3.6 concludes with a number of key points that emerge from the preceding sections as to the proper way to model the relationship between trade and employment.

## 3.2 ASSESSING THE EMPLOYMENT EFFECTS OF TRADE: MAIN CHALLENGES

### 3.2.1 Trade, productivity and employment

Since Edwards and Edwards (1996), it seems clear that increased openness will initially cause a rise in unemployment in the affected sectors. Both the depth and duration of unemployment are correlated with the degree of import penetration. Matusz and Tarr (1999) survey more than 50 studies and conclude that trade adjustment is rapid with a short duration of transitory unemployment, quick recovery to net zero impact of liberalization, and rapid expansion thereafter. Temporary unemployment during the adjustment phase following trade reform represents an important policy concern that is discussed in detail in Chapter 6 of this volume.

This chapter, instead, focuses on the long-term effects of trade on employment. To evaluate those, it is important to understand how trade reform affects productivity, as the productivity increase triggered by trade reform will ultimately be a crucial determinant of labour market outcomes. Indeed, total employment $L$ is equal to aggregate demand $X$ multiplied by employment per unit of output $l$, as reflected in the following equation:

$$L = lX \qquad (3\text{-}1)$$

Taking growth rates of this equation

$$\hat{L} = \hat{l} + \hat{X} \qquad (3\text{-}2)$$

so that the rate of growth of employment is equal to the rate of growth of the labour coefficient plus the rate of growth of output. Productivity growth causes the labour coefficient to fall.[1]

From this simple demand-driven model, a fundamental truth about trade and employment is revealed. So long as productivity is increasing, aggregate demand must expand by $-\hat{l}$ in order for employment to remain stable. Or, to say the same thing differently, from equation (3-2) we would expect there to be a negative relationship between productivity growth and employment growth. There seems to be widespread empirical support for this account. Dew-Becker and Gordon (2005), for example, find strongly robust negative correlation between growth in labour productivity and growth in employment per capita across Europe. This places the burden of employment growth on the $\hat{X}$ variable, the growth in gross domestic product (GDP). If trade causes growth, it follows that employment can rise. There is one important caveat to this conclusion, however. Equation (3-2) relates the aggregate labour coefficient to employment growth. It is evidently possible to have all sectoral labour coefficients fall with productivity growth, yet the aggregate labour coefficient

---

[1] Underlying these aggregate changes might well be change in sectoral composition, technology, wages and many other institutional and economic factors. One might also wish to subtract the rate of growth of the population, as well, in order to focus on employment growth per capita.

rises, as the sectoral mix comes to favour more labour-intensive sectors. This could come about due to specialization in labour-using industries as the result of trade. This is an obvious point, but one that should be kept in mind throughout the discussion to follow. Still to a first order approximation, growth in demand per capita appears to be the main determinant of employment growth.

Supply side models with full employment might be applicable for developed countries but are much less convincing when applied to developing economies. Still, there are important links between the two: even in models without full employment, if trade can be shown to increase the rate of growth of output, then *ipso facto*, trade would increase the rate of growth of employment. The question of whether trade is good for employment then can evidently be decomposed into whether trade is good for growth and how growth and productivity change are related. Davidson and Matusz (2010) point out, though, that the trade-growth relationship may be affected if the labour market is characterized by imperfections. In their book on trade with equilibrium unemployment, they argue that multiple equilibria is more the rule rather than the exception in such cases. This implies that, with the same initial conditions, economies can follow a "low-trade" or "high-trade" growth path.[2]

The question of how growth and productivity changes are related has received a good deal of attention in theoretical discussions of the last century. For Keynes, in the *General Theory*, the decision to invest was shrouded in mystery. In the simplest account, investment is driven by profitability, which rises with productivity and capacity utilization. The relationship is complicated by the fact that current profitability might not be a good indicator of future profitability, and certainly it is the latter that drives investment. Moreover, investment does not occur in isolation: there are problems of coordination between sectors. Keynes' investors had to think both about what the future was to bring as well as what their colleagues thought about what the future was to bring. This was all too complicated for theory to handle so, for Keynes, investment was determined by a mixture of the objective measures of productivity and capacity utilization with a subjective component he called "animal spirits" (Keynes, 1936).

Other important theorists, such as Solow (1956), followed suit, taking the propensity to accumulate as essentially given and technical change as exogenous. *New growth theories* have attempted to endogenize technological change depending upon the path the economy takes, the availability of human capital, positive externalities or spillovers and deliberate investment in technical progress (Romer, 1986; Romer, 1990). These models, well worth exploring in their own right, are essentially elaborations of the problem identified by Keynes. In every case, productivity matters and is directly related to investment and growth.

---

[2] A fundamental finding is also that factor endowments no longer determine the pattern of trade-induced specialization, which can instead be driven by differential turnover rates across domestic sectors.

The connection to trade in this new way of thinking about investment and technical change is immediate. Consider a producer in a developing country who is limited by the extent of the domestic market. The producer is afraid to expand production and employment, fearing the price might fall and with it profitability. Similarly, she cannot easily expand output because the price of her *inputs* will go up, unless the local suppliers of those inputs also decide to invest at the same time. A classic "coordination" failure creates multiple equilibria: one in which output and employment are low and another when coordinated expansion leads to higher levels of both. In the first equilibrium, production is plagued by economies of scale in reverse, costs are high and profits and employment are low. The alternative equilibrium is the product of a virtuous cycle of increasing returns to scale, higher productivity, lower input prices and much higher employment, an accelerated accumulation of capital all woven together in a process of cumulative causation.[3]

## 3.2.2 Taking into account wage effects

When sectors expand in response to trading opportunities, this is precisely the moment at which technological change can occur. As a general rule, labour productivity is higher in export industries. Clerides et al. (1998) and many others find similar results.[4] The reason is evident: new investment brings with it state-of-the-art technology, often supplied by foreign investors and designed and developed to cope with the relative labour scarcity there. Indeed, the combination of high technology and extremely low wages is often irresistible, but the new capital employs far fewer people than in the past. The labour market effects of trade combined with technological change can take any combination of the following two forms: pressure on wages in the occupations or sectors most affected by the technological progress and/or employment losses in those occupations or sectors. Because of this combined effect on the quantity and quality of employment, a discussion of the employment effects of trade that only focuses on the quantity of employment would be incomplete.

Indeed, traditional trade models predict that the labour market effects of trade reform mainly take the form of changes in relative factor prices. Standard Heckscher-Ohlin-Samuelson (HOS) theory, for instance, suggests that firms in countries with excess supplies of labour will find it profitable to increase production of goods for

---

[3] What could shift the economy from the low- to high-level equilibrium? One answer is free international trade. Note that in a perfectly competitive economy none of the considerations of the last paragraph pertain. Each producer is so small that it is impossible to have an impact on the market as a whole. In developing countries, the scale of production is frequently large relative to the size of the internal market and so the assumption of a perfectly competitive economy scarcely applies. Free international trade, however, can restore the competition lost to the mismatch of technology to market size in developing economies. With trade, it is impossible to sustain a coordination failure.

[4] Abraham and Brock (2003) find that trade has induced changes in technology in the EU.

which cheap labour produces a cost advantage relative to competitors. As the trade-favoured sector expands, the contracting sector must then release the factors of production in proportions suited to its rival. If countries specialize in goods intensive in their most abundant factor, then the return to that factor should rise with trade. Since the inception of this theory, economists have held that poor countries should specialize in labour-intensive goods so long as capital is in short supply relative to labour. The expansion in demand for the labour-intensive good will then drive up the price of labour. HOS is a theory with fully employed factors of production, however, and so even though overall employment cannot rise, the quality of jobs in poor countries improves with the trade, in so far as quality is measured by the wage rate.

The HOS framework thus suggests that developing countries should specialize in labour-intensive goods, given their excess supply of labour. Here the aggregation across skill categories required for analytical models obscures the basic fact that labour is heterogeneous with respect to skill and experience. There is no reason to expect that an increase in demand for exports in a developing country would not cause some disruption in those labour markets, similar to what is experienced as a result of intra-industry trade in developed markets. While the broad range of developing country exports might well be more intensive in unskilled labour, it is impossible to ignore that in practice labour appears quite heterogeneous to firms in developing countries. In South Africa, for example, textile manufacturers frequently complain of a "labour shortage" despite the fact that there is 40 per cent unemployment. This will have to be explained by increasing the resolution in the labour market until differences as perceived by the firms themselves can be identified. Once the detailed nature of the market is analysed, it is far less surprising that a bubble in export demand might generate significant wage inequality, even in developing countries and contrary to what standard HOS models predict.

There is, indeed, evidence that relative wages, of skilled compared to unskilled workers, have tended to increase in numerous developed and developing countries in the aftermath of trade liberalization. Outsourcing provides one mechanism by which such wage inequality can legitimately arise.[5] To the extent that a ladder of comparative advantage exists, countries will simultaneously take advantage of opportunities to expand employment in a given skill category, while typically contracting employment in less-skilled branches. Part of the phenomenon is that as unskilled branches of production migrate from developed to developing countries, the demand for skilled labour rises in both. This increases skill-based wage inequality on both sides of the border. As the international division of labour progressively develops,

---

[5] Current account liberalization also forces lower middle-income countries to experience competition from even lower-income countries. Tariff reduction thus concentrates job opportunities on one rung of the ladder of comparative advantage. Those with the appropriate skills benefit from the increase in demand; those without suffer until their skills can be upgraded or they move into the local service economy, the non-traded sector.

large wage inequalities could naturally be expected to emerge and persist.[6] Only when the adjustment process is fully played out, will the wage gap close.[7]

The wage inequality that results from trade liberalization is not necessarily undesirable.[8] High wages signal the need for the formation of human capital specific to the demand for labour for the expanding sectors, and vice versa for those that are contracting. Any policy initiative that seeks to reduce inequality of this kind may well be counterproductive to the extent that it impedes the formation of specific human capital. Indeed, Wood (1997) notes that the skilled labour premium declined in the Republic of Korea, Singapore and Chinese Taipei as the virtuous cycle of rising exports, improved access to education followed by an increase in supply of skilled labour, took hold. Lopez-Calva and Lustig's recent work on Mexico shows that wage differentials in Latin America have eroded over time as markets adjust, much to the surprise of most observers (Lopez-Calva and Lustig, 2010).

Policy-makers nevertheless often decry the wage inequality that arises from "efficiency wages" paid to the workers lucky enough to find jobs in the export sector that in part reflect the comparatively vast quantities of capital with which they work. Some of the economic literature has taken up the task of explaining wage inequality as it presents an economic as well as sociological problem. Rodrik (1997) is an early attempt to promote globalization by way of calling for stepped-up public sector intervention to resolve wage and, more broadly, factor price inequality that seems to be emerging. More than a decade ago, Rodrik pointed out that the trend toward increased openness would increase competition. In highly competitive markets, there is little or no ability of producers to pass on idiosyncratic cost increases. Consequently, the demand for labour in competitive industries could be expected to become more elastic under a globalized trading system. Rodrik points out that larger, more aggressive public sector intervention may be required in order to prevent a backlash by those who have been hurt by globalization, free-trade and current-ac-

---

[6] One response to rising competitive pressure is an increase in informality. Gibson and Kelley (1994) define the informal sector in a general equilibrium context as those who are forced to operate production processes that fail to return the average rate of profit when paying the going wage rate. These processes are defective in the sense that formal sector capitalists will not operate them. They nonetheless exist and can be utilized by those who have no other options. This conceptualization of informality is useful in analysing the impact of tariff reductions. Formal sector firms rendered unprofitable by tariff reduction fail and disappear, while informal firms simply adjust to the new competitive reality by accepting a lower rate of return, possibly negative, when evaluated at the market wage rate. Informality rises with import penetration.

[7] Feenstra and Hanson (1997), for example, find that US firms outsourced mostly labour-intensive jobs, which raises equality both at home and in the host country.

[8] Trade liberalization can also contribute to reducing wage inequalities. One way that wage *equality* can be brought about by trade policy is by reducing rents that accrue to firms and their workers in protected industries. As long-standing tariff protection is eliminated, unemployment in local labour markets rises, reducing the gap between the wages of experienced workers with significant learning-by-doing skills and those that had had little formal-sector experience. The wage inequality that had previously existed in this case would be reduced or eliminated by pro-trade policies. This "levelling from below" is rarely an attractive process to observe in reality, but can in principle be defended on the grounds of standard economic theory.

count openness. How much of a problem this is in practice is still a matter of dispute. Indeed, since Samuelson-Stolper (as well as the factor-price equalization theorem), there has been an unresolved tension between trade theorists, policy-makers and even some members of the economics profession.[9]

Nothing about globalization prevents a developing country from adopting the labour standards and associated transfers to shape their societies in ways they see fit. Stepped-up public sector intervention to resolve wage inequality is wholly consistent with mainstream economic theory, so long as: (1) the citizens of the country authorize the expenditure in the form of voting for the required tax increases; and (2) transfers are made in lump sums and do not disturb the prices or wages prevailing in the market. To the extent that planning was an attempt to circumvent these conditions, it would not be sustainable in the long run.

The extent to which government intervention is desired may depend on the nature of trade and also on the extent of the positive supply response following trade reform. It is, for instance, often pointed out that within-sector trade tends to winnow less productive, uncompetitive firms from the branch of production, allowing the fitter firms to enjoy a Darwinian prerogative.[10] Workers need not be reskilled to suit the expanding subsector, since they were recently discharged from the similar firms. Excess supply, local to the branch in question, will reduce wage demands, which will help to maintain competitiveness of the survivors. Since the losers are probably less competitive precisely because they are more labour intensive, an expanded role of the public sector may still be called for if sectoral employment falls. The scope and potential damage to macroeconomic variables, such as the public sector borrowing requirement (PSBR) to GDP ratio and subsequent exchange rate overvaluation, is less if the emerging sector is successful. Indeed, if exports rise rapidly, the budgetary implications will be positive. Wage inequality will certainly emerge, but it will be a marker of the success, not the failure, of the policy.

It also needs to be pointed out that poverty may decrease in developing countries even in the context of increasing wage inequality. Indeed, many economists would agree that the poor benefit from trade reforms because they rely on local industries for most of the goods they consume, industries that escape the cost-reducing effects of competition (Hertel and Winters, 2006). Real income of the poor increases with the rate of growth of their share plus the rate of growth of real GDP. If trade then accelerates GDP growth but causes the share of the poor to fall in the same proportion then the poor are no worse off as a result of trade liberalization, despite

---

[9] Samuelson himself has recently argued that trade may well damage the interests of US workers (Samuelson, 2004).

[10] In a closed economy, the rising concentration ratios might well raise market-power flags. Trade, however, brings the best of both worlds in that firms enjoy increasing returns to scale yet, at the same time, foreign competition ensures that the benefits of scale economies are passed on to consumers.

the deterioration in the distribution of income. In this context, an important elasticity is that of the income of the least well off with respect to the real wage. If this is greater than one, then higher wages will benefit the least well off. If it is less than one, higher wages work against their interests. Trade that brings lower wages will then work to their benefit. The key to understanding how the lowest strata fare when there is trade liberalization lies in evaluating this elasticity. If higher wages lead to slower growth of GDP because of a loss in competitiveness, and the share of the poorest segments remains constant, then they are clearly worse off. If lower wages causes a rise in the share of the poor, because the elasticity of substitution of labour for capital is greater than one, and low wages improve competitiveness, then the poor are absolutely better off with low wages. In this case, the average wage can fall without having any individual suffer a decline in his or her own wage.

While trade may well be important on a case-by-case basis for developing countries to escape the bonds of their own weak internal markets, the same does not appear to hold true for developed countries. Developed countries have a much bigger impact on LDCs than the other way around. Well-known papers have repeatedly made this point, Freeman and Katz (1991), Revenga (1992) and others broadly agree that skill-biased technical change explains much more of the skilled wage differential than does trade. Moreover, trade and technical change may be highly collinear in that many studies confirm that trade induces technical change.[11]

If policy-makers nevertheless chose to address inequality through, for instance, transfers, such policies should, as mentioned above, not upset prevailing wages in that they carry signals, often the only signals available, to guide the behaviour of individuals in the economy. Wage differentials that result from trade-induced investment and technical change provide a strong incentive for the unskilled to improve their education and training, while at the same time demonstrating that semi-skilled employment is within reach and significantly more remunerative.[12] High wages would then signal the formation of human capital specific to the demand for labour for the expanding sectors and vice versa for those that are contracting. Any policy initiative that seeks to reduce inequality of this kind may well be counterproductive to the extent that it impedes the formation of specific human capital. Public sector intervention, instead, that makes skill upgrading affordable to families can be considered highly desirable.

Another welcome effect from wage reductions is that they could have salutary effect on exports, propelling the economy down an export-led growth path (Gibson,

---

[11] Trade and foreign direct investment (FDI) are widely recognized as the drivers of innovation. Abraham and Brock (2003) find that trade has induced changes in technology in the EU. Greenaway et al. (1999) indicate that open sectors in the UK tend to experience faster rates of technological change, and the same effect has been found for the US by Bernard and Jensen (1995).

[12] Feenstra and Hanson (1997) find this effect is strong along the Mexico-US border *maquiladora* zone in foreign affiliate assembly plants.

2005).[13] Indeed, why countries seem to believe that it is optimal to protect their low-skilled workers has been noted as a major "puzzle" by Hoekman and Winters (2005). Doing so effectively forces them to produce the "wrong" goods and, furthermore, effectively "protects" them from productivity-enhancing investment.

### 3.2.3 Which methodology?

In the context of the modern globalized economy, top-down planning in the traditional sense may be a lost art (Gibson, 2008a). Davidson and Matusz's (2010) abovementioned work on trade with equilibrium unemployment, however, describes a more bottom-up approach. Models should be constructed with clear attention to the incentives and constraints a microeconomic agent faces. Policy can then be designed around these incentives and constraints rather than reacting to the macro-level properties that the interaction of the agents creates.

One of the major challenges economists face when building relevant models, and subsequently trying to assess the employment impact of trade, is to control for the impact of other variables on employment and to establish that observed changes in trade flows or policy have actually caused changes in employment. Indeed, much of standard macroeconomic empirical work of the post-war period, for example, has been subjected to the debilitating criticism that *all* macroeconomic variables tend to be correlated over time and thus imputed causality of established studies is in fact only a correlation.

The gold standard for distinguishing causality from correlation is the so-called randomized controlled trial. In this procedure, subjects are randomly allocated to either a "treatment" or "control" group. The key is that they are *randomly assigned* and the resulting samples are statistically equivalent. This does not imply that samples are exactly the same, only that the reasons they differ are purely random. The "treatment" sample is then exposed to the shock that is the subject of analysis. For the purpose of this chapter, the shock would be a change in trade policy. If the protocol is observed, no sophisticated statistical processing is then required to assess the employment effect of a change in trade policy. One would only need to calculate the employment level in the treatment cohort and compare it with that of the control group. It is not straightforward to artificially construct randomized controlled trials. But social scientists sometimes benefit from so-called "natural experiments", ones

---

[13] Imperfectly competitive product markets might well enhance the adjustment process and produce as a by-product even more wage inequality. Harrison and Hanson (1999) and Currie and Harrison (1997) note that firms may well reduce their profit margins to establish themselves in the global market. Firms may also hoard labour if forecast growth is strong and they are investing in more productive capital equipment. Artificial wage differentials are another matter. If the public sector promotes wage differentials that would not be validated by the private market, serious distortions may result. Paraguay's policy of subsidizing tertiary education and then finding it necessary to provide public-sector employment for graduates is a classic and unfortunate example. Wage differentials that arise in this way cannot be defended as a normal market-signalling mechanism, indeed, quite the reverse.

they did not arrange, but came about through serendipity. An example would be a natural event such as an earthquake that damages one school district but leaves a neighbouring one intact, or the introduction of some policy in one jurisdiction but not another. Unfortunately, opportunities to apply natural experiments are relatively rare.

Standard econometric models are used when randomized trials are not possible, too expensive or ethically questionable. To mimic the randomized trial methods, econometric models "control" for systematic differences in the treatment and control group characteristics that are *not* in fact randomly distributed between the two. Such "observational" studies work at a disadvantage: to properly impute causality, the controls must remove any and all variation in the two subsamples that might be correlated with either the treatment or the outcome. The discussion in box 3-1 reveals that this can rarely be fully achieved. Econometric approaches have, nevertheless, become the traditional workhorse of quantitative analysis although randomized controlled trials have been effectively and impressively conducted by Duflo and Banerjee and their group at the Poverty Action Lab at the Massachusetts Institute of Technology (Duflo et al., 2007).

---

**Box 3-1: Separating causality from correlation in econometric models.**

Econometric techniques that fit a regression line to a set of points by minimizing the sum of squares of the error term can only uncover correlation. To elevate correlation to causality requires a second movement, often subtle, delicate and frequently misunderstood. The two problems that stand in the way are "omitted variable bias" and "reverse causality", a problem revealed in the correlation between the regression's independent variable and its error term.

Without delving into the technical details, omitted variable bias can be conceived as the imputing to one coefficient in a multiple regression the impact of some unknown variable acting through the estimated coefficient. In addition to this "hidden actor" problem, reverse causality robs many regressions of their ability to establish causal links by ignoring the correlation between the independent variable and the error term. If the latter is systematically elevated with large values of the independent variable, chances are there is a reason for this.

All econometric models are designed to test an underlying theory, and most theories in economics, think supply and demand, involve simultaneous equations. All such models have bidirectional causality, running from the independent variable to the dependent variable and in reverse. This is evidently a fundamental problem that must be addressed using sophisticated methods, such as instrumental variables, as discussed in some examples below.

---

The vast literature on the effect of trade on employment is increasingly dominated by methods that have little to do with econometric estimation. These are computable partial equilibrium (CPE) or computable general equilibrium (CGE) models that are built on extensive databases and employ a simulation methodology. These methods attempt to mimic a randomized controlled experiment by building their own subjects (e.g. consumers, firms) in what has been called "generative social science" (Epstein, 2006). Essentially, the argument is that if the researcher can build a computerized society that has the same large-scale properties as the actual, legitimate experiments can be run "en silica", that is on computers. Here, realism is of the essence: if the model conforms to some erstwhile theory, itself the product of an oversimplified view of a social process, the simulation is of less value that one that more accurately replicates the measured properties in the real economy.

Simulation methods are widely used in virtually every branch of scientific inquiry. They escape the fundamental problems of econometrics of omitted variable bias and reverse causality by providing a more complete account of the object of analysis. On the other hand, the models have been criticized as "works of fiction" by philosophers of science. Finally, as seen in detail below, different models yield different results and it is therefore incumbent on policy-makers to make their own judgment about the relative realism of the models at their disposal.

### 3.2.4 Overcoming implementation obstacles

As noted by Gibson (2008b), data in developing countries can be reliable, noisy and/or unreliable according to whether there are errors in the data collection process and whether these errors tend to cancel out.[14] Errors also result from changing definitions as well as the standard index number or aggregation problem. Populations tend to be more heterogeneous in developing countries and income is often badly distributed, leading to problems with aggregating rich and poor. Most fundamentally, aggregation problems are more likely to occur in developing countries because the social structure is rapidly changing.

Governments and non-governmental organizations (NGOs) often lack budgets to do an adequate job of collecting, cross-checking and validating data. The existence of a large informal or traditional sector also causes significant problems, especially in agriculture, which can make up more than half the economy. Auto-consumption and barter are perennial problems, of course, and investment in the informal sector is particularly difficult to track, often appearing in the national accounts as consumption (Taylor, 1979, p. 23). Employment data, especially when productive sectors are changing rapidly in response to trading opportunities, can be unreliable and tend to cover urban areas only. With technocrats in short supply, data gathering may be hampered by poorly trained or untrained field workers, especially for qualitative methods. Cost-minimizing sample design will lead to over-sampling of urban households (Deaton, 1995, p. 1790).

Gibson (2008b) lists specific sampling problems including: stratification and cluster bias; groups of individuals with similar unobservable characteristics, such as ability or entrepreneurship; weather; tastes; or prices. There is also selectivity bias,

---

[14] See the special issue of the *Journal of Development Economics* on data problems in developing countries. An overview is provided in Srinivasan (1994). There is no econometric test for unreliable data.

non-random reasons why some individuals enter a given sample. Uncertainty and inefficiency in tax laws may cause inaccurate reporting. There may also be principal-agent problems, in which respondents misrepresent their objective conditions when it is in their interest to do so.

Some data problems are specific to the models discussed in this chapter. Raw social accounting matrix (SAM) data, for example, is collected and processed by different agencies or ministries with different missions, budgets, effectiveness and capabilities. As noted in Gibson (2008b), most developing countries base their GDP estimates on the production rather than demand side. If the estimates are based on "flow of product" concepts, the underlying information will vary from sector to sector and reflect tax avoidance strategies.

Balance of payments data, necessary for trade analysis, may not agree with national accounts for exports and imports because of rapidly changing and distorted exchange rates, currency controls and import licensing. The ministry of interior or labour may handle household surveys with help from the World Bank, ILO or NGOs. Household surveys are often inconsistent with data for consumption in national accounts (Gruben and McLeod, 2002).

The two generally accepted methods of dealing with data problems in developing countries are cross-check and correlation. Correlation is a more elaborate process and integrates econometric methods into the process of consistent data generation, as for example is undertaken in the study cited above by Gruben and McLeod. Purchasing power parity (PPP) methods, which correct for the effect of asset demand on exchange rates, can be used for cross-country comparisons. Sequences of SAMs can be used to cross-check investment, depreciation rates and capital accumulation. Financial data from balance sheets from firms and central banks can also be used, although procedures are in their infancy. Data from agencies regulating financial practices, labour standards and environmental compliance may also be employed.

It must be borne in mind that models based on unreliable data are themselves unreliable, despite any other attractive properties they may possess. Unreliable data are data measured with error, but if the error is not random and does not cancel out, bias will result. Since data can be and often are produced by individuals who lack knowledge of proper sampling procedures, or indeed with political or self-interested motives, no corrective procedures are available.

## 3.3   ASSESSING THE EMPLOYMENT IMPACT OF TRADE: SIMULATION METHODS

Simulation methods of different levels of sophistication exist to evaluate the employment impact of trade. More sophisticated methods typically give a more complete picture of the employment effects of a change in trade policy or flows. Yet they also tend to be more difficult to use because they are more complex and tend to have ambitious data requirements. In the following, simulation methods are discussed in order of increasing level of sophistication.

## 3.3.1 *Factor content and partial equilibrium methods*

### 3.3.1.1 Looking at one market in isolation

The simplest trade model in economics is perhaps that of a single market in isolation. In such a model, the existence of other goods markets is ignored. How production factors, such as capital or labour, transit from one sector to the other is also not examined in detail. Instead, the outcome of the equilibration process in factor markets is taken as a given parameter, and the analysis focuses entirely on the market for the good in question. This partial equilibrium approach holds constant the effects of the changing price and quantity in the goods market of interest on factor markets and other goods. One of the ways in which the use of partial equilibrium models is justified is to say that competition in the factor markets equalizes factor returns. Any one market can only have a vanishing effect on this economy-wide equilibrium.

The advantage of using partial equilibrium model approaches is that it is significantly more straightforward than the use of a more complex and more accurate general equilibrium model. Indeed, partial equilibrium models represent probably one of the simplest models available for the analysis of the impact of trade on employment.

Trade models that look at one sector in isolation have often been used to quantify job losses due to import penetration. This is done by computing the "factor content" of displaced domestic production, i.e. the amount of capital and labour employed in production. When imports displace domestic production, the capital in the domestic sector is either retired or shifted to another sector. Partial equilibrium models do not account for this, but instead ask how much labour the domestic capital stock had employed in the import-competing sector. Displaced domestic production is then assumed to lead to displacement of workers and capital in the respective proportions. Not surprisingly, wiping out a labour-intensive sector will turn out to be worse for employment than wiping out its capital-intensive counterpart. Albeit the use of partial equilibrium models to evaluate employment impacts in import-

Table 3.1: Estimates of jobs lost when tariffs and quotas are removed

| Sector | Jobs lost | Costs to consumers[1] | | Jobs lost | Costs to consumers[1] |
|---|---|---|---|---|---|
| Ball bearings | 146 | 435,356 | Luggage | 226 | 933,628 |
| Benzoid chemicals | 216 | ≥ 1 mn | Machine tools | 1556 | 348,329 |
| Costume jewellery | 1,067 | 965,532 | Polyethylene resins | 298 | 590,604 |
| Dairy products | 2,378 | 497,897 | Rubber footwear | 1,701 | 122,281 |
| Frozen orange juice | 609 | 461,412 | Softwood lumber | 605 | 758,678 |
| Glassware | 1,477 | 180,095 | Women's footwear | 3,702 | 101,567 |

Source: Hufbauer and Elliott (1994).

Note 1: Per job.

competing sectors tends to lead to biased estimates, the use of partial equilibrium analysis has the great advantage of quickly and easily identifying the individuals who are likely to lose their jobs. The approach can thus be useful to provide guidance on the design of trade adjustment assistance, job retraining and other forms of transfers from the public sector.

One way to see what competition would do to employment is to ask the "dual" question of how tariffs protect jobs in a given sector. It follows that if tariffs were removed, the loss of jobs would be equivalent to those protected by the import tax. Removing a tariff is thus like a "natural experiment" and may provide the best partial equilibrium estimate of the employment-displacing effect of imports. Table 3.1 shows an estimate of the number of jobs saved by protection (tariffs and quotas) in the United States (US) in 1990.

### 3.3.1.2 Competitive and non-competitive imports

The distinction between competitive and non-competitive imports, while not theoretically self-evident, makes a big difference in determining the effect of liberalization of any particular product market. Indeed, in order to estimate how much domestic production is replaced by imports, it is important to have an understanding of whether and to which extent imports compete with domestic production. In this context, "competitive" imports are imports that compete directly with domestic production and therefore directly subtract from GDP in the aggregate demand equation. "Non-competitive" imports, while imports just the same, do not compete and are not a direct substitute for any domestically produced good. In the US, only some agricultural goods, cobalt and other rare minerals are considered non-competitive, but in developing countries some 50-75 per cent of imports are not produced, nor have any close local substitutes.

The impact of trade on employment, for non-competitive imports, has the opposite sign of that of competitive imports. As raw materials, intermediate goods, fuel or other specialized inputs, a reduction in non-competitive imports will always reduce GDP and employment. This is not just a generalization: any good or service that is an input into domestic production with no viable substitute will reduce the ability of the economy to generate employment if removed.

It follows that any partial equilibrium analysis of imports and their job-destroying capacity must take careful account of the critical component in production plans into which the import enters either directly or indirectly. Moreover, before policy-makers take steps to reduce imports of *any* good for the purposes of raising the employment response, it is incumbent on the analyst to examine the precise nature of the import with respect to its feasible and likely substitutes.[15]

First generation partial equilibrium models tended to assume perfect substitution between domestically produced goods and foreign imports in *consumption*. Those

---

[15] There is nothing in partial equilibrium analysis that says that policy-makers cannot determine the answer to this question, but much of economy theory holds that this information is all but impossible for policy-makers to collect and use effectively.

---

### Box 3-2: Employment effects of trade: A partial equilibrium example.

Imperfect substitution can be modelled by taking into account the elasticity of supply, demand and an estimated elasticity of substitution. Standard modelling techniques estimate an "Armington function" that essentially says that the demand for the domestic good $D$ to the import $D^*$ is given by

$$D = \frac{1-s}{s}\left(\frac{p}{p^*}\right)^{-\sigma} D^* \qquad (i)$$

where $s$ is the share of imports in domestic consumption, $p$ and $p^*$ are the domestic and foreign prices, respectively, and $\sigma$ is the Armington elasticity.[16]

Consider the following example: in light manufactured goods, the share of imports is given. Policy-makers are considering opening the market to imports but wish to know what the impact on local production and employment might be. It is known that demand for light manufactured goods, domestic or imported, is

$$C = p_c^{-\varepsilon} \qquad (ii)$$

while, for domestic production, it is

$$D = p^\mu \qquad (iii)$$

given that the consumer price is given by

$$p_c = (p^* D^* + pD)/(D+D^*) \qquad (iv)$$

Consumers respond to the price difference, increasing their demand by the Armington in equation (ii) above. How much employment will one lose in this industry as import prices fall?

This computable partial equilibrium model can be solved in Excel as a function of the foreign price, $p^*$ (Sadoulet and de Janvry, 1995). The results are given in figure 3-1. Given its simplicity, the model is a "quick and dirty" method that can be of some use to policy-makers in assessing possible employment loss. Its main advantage is that it recognizes the interplay of demand and supply elasticities, which might well be estimated from a variety of other sources, in the determination of the employment response.[17]

The result shows that the elasticity of transmission of import price is less than 1, and depends on the Armington elasticity $\sigma$ as shown in Figure 3-1.

---

models therefore generated "worst-case scenarios" for two reasons: first, they focused on import-competing sectors and ignored the possibly positive employment effects on other sectors and industries; second, by assuming perfect substitution, even a small price advantage enjoyed by the import will, in theory, reduce the domestic industry to rubble.

---

[15] There is nothing in partial equilibrium analysis that says that policy-makers cannot determine the answer to this question, but much of economy theory holds that this information is all but impossible for policy-makers to collect and use effectively.

[16] A particularly simple way of estimating this elasticity empirically is to take natural logs of both sides with the result that one has a linear equation in the coefficient $\sigma$.

[17] It is *extremely* simple in that the employment elasticity with respect to output is one.

Yet foreign products are not always able to satisfy consumers' preferences in precisely the same way that domestic production does. The point is that it is not really the same good for all consumers and so some are willing to pay the premium to "buy local" to keep domestic production viable. The imported and the locally produced goods are considered imperfect substitutes in this case, and two different prices will co-exist for the "same" good. The employment impact of tariff reductions will then crucially depend on the level of the so-called elasticity of substitution between imported and locally produced goods. This elasticity is called the "Armington elasticity" and is an important element of most trade-related simulation exercises. Box 3-2 provides details using the Armington elasticity to estimate the effect of cheaper imports on domestic employment.

The greater the consumer attachment to domestic goods vis-à-vis their foreign rivals, the smaller the $\sigma$ and the less job loss will occur.[18] Figure 3.1 reflects simulation results of the employment response to changes in foreign prices. The horizontal axis depicts foreign prices relative to domestic prices. If foreign goods are cheaper than domestically produced goods, the relative price on the horizontal axis is smaller than one. The vertical axis shows employment losses generated by reductions in foreign prices. The three curves depicted in the chart reflect employment losses corresponding to different levels of import substitution. The higher the level of substitution, i.e. the larger the Armington elasticity $\sigma$, the larger the employment losses resulting from import competition.

Many comparative static exercises could be undertaken with this simple model: the jobs response also depends on the initial share of imports and the supply elasticity, $\mu$, both of which can be changed. For $\sigma > \varepsilon$, job loss increases with the initial share of imports and decreases with the supply elasticity. Note the elephant in the room here: while there is job loss, the consumer price always *decreases*, leaving consumers better off than if trade barriers had not been lowered. This is the classic trade-off, captured in table 3.1 above, and now in this desktop CPE model.

Although partial equilibrium approaches have most frequently been used to assess the employment effects of increased imports, they can also be used to evaluate the employment effects of increased export opportunities. Not surprisingly, a focus on exporting sectors would tend to give an overly-optimistic picture of the employment effects of trade. As in the case of imports, the question of substitution between trade and domestically produced goods also arises in the case of exports. As noted in Sadoulet and de Janvry (1995), a bilateral choice model can be set up to extend to producers as well as consumers, as illustrated above. Exports in a world with competitive exchange rates may be very attractive for producers, but foreign markets also bear risks, many of which are absent in domestic markets. Quality control issues, forward markets for export earnings and other incentives may entice domestic producers to "sell local" when models with perfect substitution would suggest otherwise.

---

[18] Note that according to standard theory there is nothing inefficient whatsoever about this attachment.

Figure 3.1: Employment response as function of import price for various Armington elasticities (initial share of imports $= 0.1$, $\mu = 1$, $\varepsilon = 1.2$)

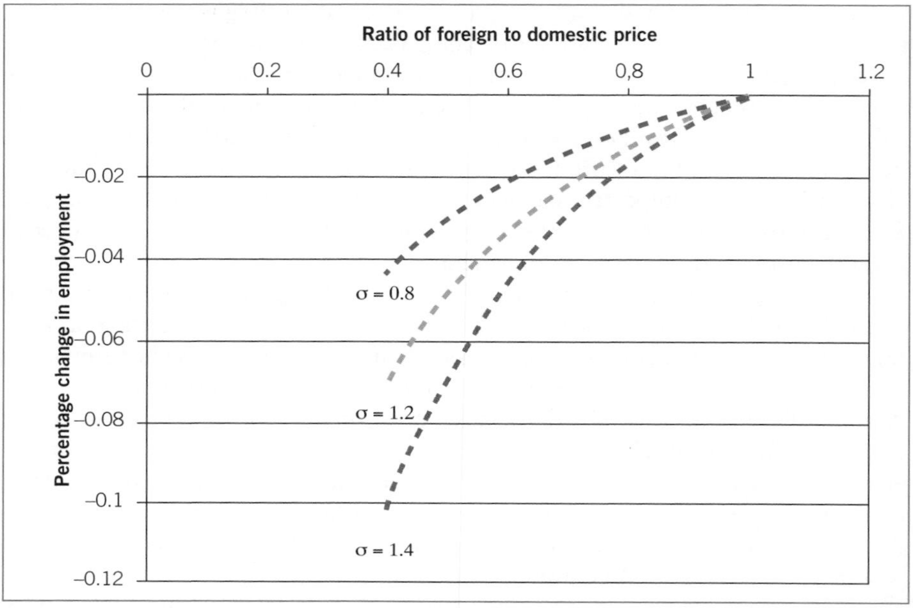

Source: Author's calculations.

It follows that reducing export taxes may not produce the expected job gains for the same reason that consumer preferences mitigated job losses in the demand-side analysis. Again the magnitude of the Armington elasticity will be crucial to the size of this effect, and must be carefully estimated.

### 3.3.1.3 Assessing the CPE method

An audit of costs and benefits of the CPE methods discussed in this section would conclude that the method could be implemented with minimal data and data-processing requirements, and relatively simple theoretical set-ups for local market structures. No teams or special clean rooms are needed, and all that is required is for policy-makers to think carefully about the applicability of framework to their economies.

The CPE method quickly and cheaply quantifies the effect of import competition, but its drawbacks as to the reliability of findings are significant. It certainly does not represent the end of the analysis of the effects of trade on employment. Why, for example, are computed job losses assumed not to affect the demand side of the model? Moreover, the lower price might not simply benefit consumers in this market but also *producers* in other markets. As those producers gain from cost savings, they might well expand, mitigating the job loss in the affected industry.

Finally, if there are many potential producers (and their consumers) who might benefit, the task of adding them all up becomes daunting.[19]

Note, however, that more lofty objectives in modelling see rapid escalation of data requirements as will become evident in the following sections. Policy-makers and experts will constantly face the trade-off between simplicity of the method and reliability of findings. Even stepping up from an assumption of perfect substitutability between imports and local products to a world of imperfect substitutability, as discussed above, requires substantially higher investment in the estimating of response elasticities. This is never easy or straightforward, and some policy-makers could be excused for substituting "sensitivity analysis", in which informal estimates of key parameters, such as response elasticities, are made and then are investigated for result robustness by simply varying the values within reasonable ranges. This is field dressing the model, but is clearly preferable in terms of reliability of outputs than taking fixed coefficients and calculating employment losses under the assumption of perfect substitutability.

### 3.3.2 Two-sector factor substitution models

#### 3.3.2.1 Allowing for more than one market

When the economy opens to international trade, producers begin to respond to the demand from the world as a whole. In general, this will lead to changing the autarkic proportions of production. In the most extreme case, producers specialize in one good to the exclusion of the other, but in real-world economies complete specialization is rare. If production were undertaken with the fixed proportions discussed above, the movement from autarky to trade would be catastrophic for at least some individuals. If producers specialize in the labour-intensive good, for example, the rate of return to owners of capital will literally collapse, since the capital-intensive sector will have more capital to transfer to the labour-intensive sector than it can possibly use. The excess supply of capital will drive its price to zero, at least in theory.

Factor substitution models are based on the proposition that this unfortunate sequence of events never takes place. They tend to be based on the HOS theoretical framework that usually assumes two goods and two factors of production. As the labour-intensive sector expands, the price of capital falls and producers find it profitable to employ more capital per unit of labour. Factor proportions are adjusting here and it is a striking fact that the capital-intensity of *both* sectors will rise in the process. Note further that the demand for labour has increased. While the expanding firm sees too much capital arriving on the capital market, the contracting sector never used much labour in the first place. If the expanding sector is going to meet world demand, it will want to hire more labour than is available in the market. In

---

[19] For this reason, economists developed early on in the last century a comprehensive methodology to cut through the "fictitious rounds" of seemingly infinite interactions between sectors. See sections 3.3.3 and 3.3.4 on input-output and CGE models, respectively.

response, the expanding sector substitutes capital for labour and, in the process, the marginal *productivity of labour* increases. Workers have more capital to work with and thus firms can pay higher wages. Again, note that this occurs in both sectors. Rising world demand has increased wages at the expense of profits, but the latter do not fall to zero because of factor substitution.

### 3.3.2.2 Elasticities of substitution matter yet again

It follows logically then, that the effect of trade on employment is crucially dependent on the possibilities of substitution. The elasticity of substitution is thus an important number to nail down empirically and must be done for each sector separately. The Cobb-Douglas production function, the workhorse of economic analysis for more than a century, is arguably of only limited use here. The elasticity of substitution is defined rather complexly as the percentage change in the capital-labour ratio with respect to the percentage change in the ratio of the cost of labour to the cost of capital. For the Cobb-Douglas case, it can be shown analytically that the elasticity is always equal to one for the constant returns to scale case.[20]

---

**Box 3-3: Why elasticities of substitution matter**

The elasticity of technical substitution is an important number to accurately estimate in simulations assessing the employment effects of trade. To see this, consider the following example. As trade starts to boom, the import-competing sector begins to contract, disgorging workers onto the labour market. In the expanding sector, labour demand increases, but there is a problem. Because of the low elasticity of substitution in the expanding sector, the capital per worker does not increase much, and therefore neither does the marginal productivity. Thus, real wages cannot rise and the incentives for labour to move, search out these newly emerging opportunities and obtain the skills necessary for the new job are all dampened. It is quite likely that skills will need some upgrading, since the expansion of the export sector will have attracted foreign capital with more advanced technology and higher demands on its workers. Retooling, as the sector expands, raises its elasticity of substitution and with it the marginal productivity of labour. Not as much labour is required, but those who do find jobs are well remunerated, at least comparatively. Slaughter (2001), for example, notes that changes in the elasticity of labour demand over time arise more from technological progress rather than trade itself.

---

After the Cobb-Douglas, the most popular production functions are constant elasticity of substitution (CES) production functions and translog, which closely approximates well-defined cost functions. These mathematical structures have elasticities of substitution that are different from one and can be estimated econometrically. All can be modified to use more than two factors so that, for example, the analysis

---

[20] For a Cobb-Douglas function of the form $Q = AK^{\alpha}L^{\beta}$, the elasticity of substitution is $1/(\alpha + \beta)$, where $Q$ is output, $A$ is scaling parameter and $\alpha$ and $\beta$ are the elasticities of $Q$ with respect to capital and labour $L$.

can include both skilled and unskilled labour or, indeed, as many labour categories as one wishes.[21]

If fixed coefficients is an excessively pessimistic foundation on which to analyse the effect of trade on employment, perhaps the Cobb-Douglas is at the other extreme. While fixed coefficient analyses implicitly assume an elasticity of substitution equal to zero, Cobb-Douglas production functions assume that factors can easily substitute one another. Ideally, one would want to pin down the "true" elasticity of substitution by collecting a sufficient quantity of relevant data and estimate either of the more sophisticated production functions mentioned above. An alternative to this relatively costly and time-consuming procedure would be to assume that the "truth" lies somewhere in the middle. This would correspond to running the simulation once under the assumption of fixed coefficients and once under the assumption of a Cobb-Douglas function. The generated employment effects would then arguably provide upper- and lower-bound estimates for the employment effects of trade.

A second point is time: like winter snows, the frozen elasticity of substitution in the fixed coefficients case will tend to melt away with time. Thus, a reasonable strategy might be to use the fixed coefficient model for small changes around the initial equilibrium, reserving the more sophisticated approaches for longer time frames and larger departures from the base data.[22] It has also been argued that the fixed coefficient case could provide estimates for economies characterized by low labour mobility.[23]

There is some evidence that for longer-term estimates in economies with sufficient labour mobility, Cobb-Douglas functions may actually represent good proxies for the actual elasticity of substitution. An early study of trade and employment in development was undertaken by Krueger and her associates for the NBER and published in a three-volume work (Krueger, 1983). Behrman (1983) in one chapter estimates a CES production for 70 countries for the period 1967-73. The total number of observations is increased by using data on 26 sectors per country, with a total $\eta$ = 1,723. The author finds, for this data set, that the Cobb-Douglas does indeed apply since the estimated CES elasticities of substitution are close to one. Behrman concludes that trade analysis based on fixed coefficients will be off the mark, as firms do actively substitute capital for labour as supplies of the latter dry up.

---

[21] For the CES function of the form $Q = A[\alpha K^{-\rho} + (1 - \alpha) L^{-\rho}]^{-1/\rho}$, where $Q$ is output, $A$ is scaling parameter, the elasticity of substitution is $\sigma = 1/(1 + \rho)$ and $\alpha$ is the share of the return to capital in output. As $\rho$ goes to zero, the CES approaches the Cobb-Douglas. The translog function takes the form: $\ln Q = \ln \gamma_0 + \alpha_1 \ln K + \alpha_2 \ln L + \beta_1 (\ln K)^2 + \beta_2 (\ln L)^2 + \gamma_1 (\ln K)(\ln L)$, where the elasticity of substitution is $\sigma = -[(A + B)/Q](A + B - 2\alpha_2 A/B - 2\beta_2 B/A - 2\gamma_1)^{-1}$ where $A = \beta_1 + 2\beta_2 \ln L + \gamma_1 \ln K$ and $B = \alpha_1 + 2\alpha_2 \ln K + \gamma_1 \ln L$.

[22] A subtle, but highly relevant, implication of the unitary elasticity of the Cobb-Douglas production function is the property that the total remuneration to a factor of production is constant with respect to changes in factor proportions. Thus, if the wage rate falls by $\varepsilon$ per cent, then employment increases by $\varepsilon$ per cent, and the wage bill remains fixed

[23] The issue of labour mobility is extensively discussed by Davidson and Matusz (2004; 2010). Labour mobility significantly affects the adjustment process following trade reform, as discussed in detail in Chapter 6 of this volume.

### 3.3.2.3 Assessing the two-sector substitution model

The strength of the two-sector factor substitution models approach is its simplicity and clarity in regard to basic principles of economics.[24] Factor share models are relatively cheap and easy to implement: Cobb-Douglas equations can be easily estimated and factor shares deduced. Since the wage bill is constant, two-sector substitution models based on Cobb-Douglas production functions can predict whether there will be a large quantity of new jobs with low wages or the reverse, so long as workers are paid their marginal product. In non-competitive environments, studded with minimum wages and other labour-market distortions, the marginal product of labour may be scarcely relevant. It is still possible, however, to say that if demand shifts from a sector with a low share of labour to one with a high share of labour, workers in some form or other will probably benefit.

A weakness of the HOS-inspired labour share approach is that it does not often take into account inter-industry relationships as do the input-output models discussed below. A second weakness of this approach is that the whole of traditional trade theory in the mould of HOS seems to be at variance with what is observed in the current trading arena (Hertel and Keeney, 2005). A serious objection to the HOS view of the world is that sectoral reallocation along the lines predicted does not typically take place. Instead, a sector expands to meet an increase in export demand. In exchange, the home country receives an import from the same sector of the trading partner's economy. No factors are reallocated. Both sectors must either experience a rise in labour productivity or increased employment. Aggregate employment will then rise if there was slack in the labour market initially and wages will increase otherwise. Referring to the effects of the formation of the European Economic Community (EEC) and the US-Canadian auto agreement, Hertel and Keeney (2005) observe:

> "Little resource reallocation took place; instead, trade seems to have permitted an increased productivity of existing resources, which left everyone better off."

### 3.3.3 Input-output framework

### 3.3.3.1 Taking into account indirect employment effects

The next step is to introduce multi-market equilibria by way of an input-output framework, a halfway house to the full general equilibrium specification.[25] These

---

[24] The HOS model does not allow for the possibility of intra-industry trade, i.e. the type of trade that typically takes place between industrialized countries. Although the bulk of trade still occurs between industrialized countries, trade between sectors with different capital labour ratios and radically different wages is still important and arguably increasingly so because of the increasing role of developing countries in global trade. The HOS model thus remains a valid instrument for trade analysis.

[25] These models have their roots in the model first described by the young Harvard graduate student W. Leontief just after the turn of the century.

---

**Box 3-4: Input-output models: Some technical details**

Input-output models are used to analyse the impact of a change in final demand, including *net exports* on the levels of production. The models assume fixed coefficients for labour, capital and intermediate inputs. Let $A = \{\alpha_{ij}\}$ be the *coefficient matrix* such that each $\alpha_{ij}$ describes the use of input $i$ for the production of one unit of output $j$ and $X = \{x_j\}$ be a column vector of gross outputs, including intermediate goods. So-called dual variables can also be defined and interpreted as prices, denoted here by row vector $P = \{p_i\}$. The equation dual to the material balance is then

$$P = PA + V_A$$

where $V_A$ is a row vector of value added, and may be disaggregated into wages, profits, imports, taxes and rents as needed.[26] *Final demand* is denoted by $F = \{f_j\}$, a column vector of outputs, and may be disaggregated into consumption, government spending, exports and imports as needed. The essential equation of input-output analysis, known as the *material balance*, is then

$$X = AX + F$$

One of the most basic measures of the effect of trade on employment comes from estimating *direct labour coefficients*, or the inverse of labour productivity. Census data provides measures of value added and employment by sector and thus an index of the number of workers employed by a unit of value added can be constructed.[27]

---

frameworks take into account backward linkages between trading sectors and the rest of the economy and therefore make it possible to assess the indirect employment impacts of trade reform or changes in trade flows. Economy-wide models of this type are usually based on either aggregate data from national income and product accounts or more disaggregated input-output tables. Regional models may link regional input-output matrices, analogous to the way international trade models link countries. The informal sector can also be treated in the same way, operating alongside the formal economy and trading with it.

Lydall's (1975) classic study for the ILO assumed that an increase in imports by a developed country of one of 12 different final processing ISIC industries, produced by a developing country, would replace an equal *value* (US$1 million at factor cost) of production in the developed economy. The question addressed was then: what is the effect of this replacement in the importing and exporting countries, respectively? The Lydall study takes into account not only the direct impact of the trade on producing sector employment but also the indirect employment effects by way of input-output analysis. These are the so-called "backward linkage" effects. These indirect effects naturally include the impact on the balance of other tradable goods.[28]

---

[26] Factors of production, labour, $L$, and capital, $K$, are treated separately, usually with fixed coefficients under the assumption that factor prices remain unchanged.

[27] The "unit" has to be in common currency and this presents problems of its own. Previous studies have used the official or prevailing exchange rate to convert value added to a common currency, usually US$.

[28] A recent study on the employment effects of changes in trade flows during the Great Recession (Kucera et al., 2010) finds that indirect employment effects may be about equal in size to the direct employment effects of a trade shock.

The input-output approach is still widely used. Revenga (1992), for example, looked at 38 US manufacturing industries for 1977-87 and found a fall in price of 1 per cent caused only a small loss in employment, between 0.24 and 0.39 per cent. She found almost no impact on nominal wages, and concluded that labour mobility prevented a significant decline in wages due to import penetration, despite job loss. This implies that the direct and indirect factor content of industries that contract is approximately the same as that of expanding industries, at least for the US data.

Box 3.5 illustrates using a hypothetical example of how trade-induced employment changes can be calculated on the basis of the input-output approach.

---

### Box 3-5: Using input-output methods to compute trade-induced changes in employment: a hypothetical example

The effect of trade on employment can be studied with the help of an input-output matrix, which shows the quantity of intermediate goods and services (both imported and domestically produced) required for the production of one unit of output. This is known as the Leontief matrix and is denoted by $A$:

|             | Agriculture | Industry | Services |
|-------------|-------------|----------|----------|
| Agriculture | 0.1         | 0.1      | 0.15     |
| Industry    | 0.2         | 0.25     | 0.12     |
| Services    | 0.1         | 0.2      | 0.24     |

Source : Author's calculations.

If $X$ is a column vector of gross outputs of the three sectors shown, then total intermediate demand is given by the vector product $AX$. Labour demand per unit of output ($L$) is written as a row vector and, for this example, is

|               | Agriculture | Industry | Services |
|---------------|-------------|----------|----------|
| Labour demand | 0.4         | 0.2      | 0.3      |

Source : Author's calculations.

Final demand is made up of three column vectors, domestic demand, $Y_d$, exports, $E$, and imports, $M$

|             | $Y_d$ | Exports | Imports |
|-------------|-------|---------|---------|
| Agriculture | 40    | 30      | 10      |
| Industry    | 45    | 5       | 15      |
| Services    | 60    | 10      | 20      |

Source : Author's calculations.

---

**Box 3-5: Using input-output methods to compute trade-induced changes in employment: a hypothetical example** *(Continued)*

Note that when all prices are equal to one, trade is balanced in this example. Gross output ($X$) would then be equal to

$$X = AX + Y_d + E - M,$$

which can be solved

$$X = (I-A)^{-1} (Y_d + E - M )$$

Here, I is the identity matrix, with ones on the diagonal and zero elsewhere. Computing $X$ can be done easily by way of Excel's array functions.[29]

|  | $X$ |
| --- | --- |
| Agriculture | 93.3 |
| Industry | 87.7 |
| Services | 101.1 |

Source : Author's calculations.

Total employment is then $LX = 85.2$.

On the basis of this exercise, a 1 per cent increase in imports in all sectors will lead to an employment level of 84.94, a decline of 0.26, since total output contracts. A 1 percent increase in exports, instead, will increase employment by 0.27 as output expands. Since trade was initially in balance, a 1 per cent change in both exports and imports has no effect on the total gross value of production but does change its structure.

The Leontief multiplier analysis emphasizes the need to count intermediate production, both direct and indirect, in order to assess employment effects. It assumes that wages are fixed and that the economy adjusts to changes in final demand, both in aggregate and structure, through proportional adjustments in employment levels *for each sector*. In this structuralist approach (see box 3-7), exports from sectors that are more labour intensive, directly *and* indirectly, cause employment to rise faster.

The methodology can be easily extended to assess the impact of productivity increases, which simply take the form of lower labour coefficients. If, however, lower employment leads to lower wages, and if profit-maximizing firms respond by hiring more labour, the linearity of the Leontief model is inappropriate and a more complex model is required.

---

An approach similar to that summarized in box 3-5 has been applied in the OECD (Baldwin, 1994) to assess employment changes following changes in trade flows for eight industrialized countries. Table 3.2 reports the findings of the exercise. Canada, as is seen, experienced a 2.38 per cent increase in employment from 1971

---

[29] One can use the command: "=MMULT(MINVERSE(I-A),Yd+E-M)", to compute $X$ with $I$, $A$, $Yd$, $E$ and $M$ all defined as ranges.

to 1986. This was due to a 3.56 per cent change in gross output, itself the product of a rise in domestic demand of 3.48 per cent and a rise in exports of 1.85 per cent. This was offset by a rise in imports of 1.58 per cent, a reduction in intermediate use of 0.19 per cent, as well as a change in productivity of 1.19 per cent. The latter enters with a negative sign since productivity reduces employment.

The table shows that import penetration slows employment growth most in the Netherlands, followed by Canada. The data for the US is broadly consistent with Revenga (1992). Table 3.3 combines the information of columns 4 and 5 of table 3.2. There it is seen that Japanese employment benefits from trade the most, with a change in employment growth of 0.71 per cent for the indicated period. Only the US and the UK seem have lost to trade, and this by small margins.

The exercise is consistent with the partial equilibrium models discussed above in that competition from abroad causes domestic prices and thus employment to fall. The same is true in input-output multi-sectoral environment. What is added is the *interactions* of the sectors and with it the possibility that jobs lost in one sector

Table 3.2: Decomposing the causes of employment growth

| | Employment growth | Change in gross output | Domestic final demand | Export growth | Import growth | Intermediate growth | Labour productivity |
|---|---|---|---|---|---|---|---|
| Canada[1] | 2.38 | 3.56 | 3.48 | 1.85 | −1.58 | -0.19 | −1.19 |
| Denmark[2] | 0.71 | 2.36 | 1.68 | 1.69 | −1.03 | 0.02 | −1.64 |
| France[3] | 0.03 | 2.3 | 2.15 | 0.95 | −0.71 | −0.09 | −2.27 |
| Germany[4] | 0.34 | 1.51 | 1.28 | 1.1 | −0.79 | −0.08 | −1.16 |
| Japan[5] | 0.66 | 4.2 | 4.38 | 1.13 | −0.42 | −0.81 | −3.52 |
| Netherlands[6] | 0 | 3.2 | 2.62 | 1.96 | −1.78 | 0.4 | −3.21 |
| UK[7] | −0.2 | 2.41 | 2.45 | 0.84 | −1.13 | 0.25 | −2.61 |
| US[3] | 1.96 | 2.8 | 2.82 | 0.35 | −0.46 | 0.09 | −0.84 |

Source: Baldwin (1994). Notes: 1. 1971–86. 2. 1972–88. 3. 1972–85. 4. 1978–86. 5. 1970–85. 6. 1972–86. 7. 1968–84.

Table 3.3: Net change in employment due to growth imports and exports

| | Canada | Denmark | France | Germany | Japan | Netherlands | UK | US |
|---|---|---|---|---|---|---|---|---|
| Imports | −1.58 | −1.03 | -0.32 | −0.79 | −0.42 | −1.78 | −1.13 | −0.46 |
| Exports | 1.85 | 1.69 | 1.02 | 1.31 | 1.13 | 1.96 | 0.84 | 0.35 |
| Imports and exports | 0.27 | 0.66 | 0.64 | 0.31 | 0.71 | 0.18 | −0.29 | −0.11 |

Source: Baldwin (1994).

through import penetration could be made up for, at least in part if not wholly, by jobs gained in a range of other sectors. Baldwin notes that when applied to manufacturing alone, the results are not as favourable in the above example. Canada, France, the UK and the US all suffer a net decline in manufacturing employment growth. The main point of this analysis, however, seems to echo the conventional wisdom: trade in the long run has mostly a small but positive impact on national employment growth.

### 3.3.3.2 Assessing input-output methods

As a result of the assumed linear production technology, input-output models are relatively inexpensive and easy to formulate and run. They can be made dynamic if investment, $I$, is first disaggregated from final demand, $F$, and then used to determine the time path of the capital stock.[30] Still, input-output models lack an internally consistent demand system and thus an endogenous balance of savings and investment. Productivity-enhancing trade flows may well kick up this investment in fully specified general equilibrium models, but for now that link is ignored. It follows that one would expect a reduced impact of trade on employment when using an input-output approach compared to partial equilibrium, but less than CGE models.

The disadvantages of input-output analysis mostly derive from the implicit assumption that factor content remains fixed over a long period of time and is therefore impervious to changes in policy, tastes or indeed any other behavioural variables. Moreover, the analysis takes the level of productivity as exogenously given, when a number of studies have shown that productivity growth rises with trade, both imports and exports.

As in partial equilibrium models, input-output does not track individuals to find out what they do when they are displaced from their jobs. In the short run the answer might be "nothing". This answer is not, however, plausible when one takes a longer historical view. In developing countries, the concentration of income due to trade or any other force opens up new areas of consumer goods that might not have been demanded in the past, or were seen as out of reach. In developing countries, transition from an agrarian-based economy to one based on manufacturing and ultimately services had to have begun with individuals "losing their jobs" in agriculture. Nobody wants to be the one to make the first move but, as Chamley (2004) notes in his work on rational herds, even penguins will push an unfortunate colleague into icy, orca-infested waters to test whether it is safe for the rest of the flock.

---

[30] This is done by way of the stock-flow equation $K_t = K_{t-1}(1-\delta) + I$, where $\delta$ is the depreciation rate. Consistent forecasts of intermediate demand, foreign exchange requirements and associated employment, for example, could then be made, contingent on a forecast for investment. The framework just presented is the *open Leontief model*, but a closed version is available in which all elements of final demand and value added are made dependent on gross output $X$. It was left to von Neumann to show that a maximum rate of sustainable growth is well defined by the model.

---

**Box 3-6: Linear programming: Another approach to assess
the employment effects of trade**

Linear programming models are an extension of input-output models that essentially
allow for multiple processes to produce the same good. Policy-makers lucky enough to
have detailed data on options that do not yet exist can add the technological coefficients
to the input-output matrix and ask a program such as LINDO (or even Excel if the
problem is small enough) for the "best" combination of sectors to maximize some
objective function.

Dorfman et al. (1958), the classic reference in the field, would use GDP as the welfare
function to be optimized. But it may occur to an enterprising policy-maker that she could
ask the program to maximize employment. She will be sorely disappointed, however,
since the program will almost certainly produce a nonsensical solution. It is obvious why:
employment was maximized when 100 per cent of the labour force was occupied in
agriculture or, for that matter, in hunter-gatherer activities.

Still, linear programming analysis can be highly useful for practical trade analysis in the
hands of skilled analysts and a relatively skilled data processing team. They must be
crafted for highly specific problems with well-defined constraints. The real value of the
approach comes not in solving the primal problem, the allocation of labour for example,
but in the duality theorem: the dual variable associated with a constraint that fails to
bind in the primal is always zero.

Consider an example in which a lengthy list of occupational categories is included in
the employment database. Calculate the primal solution that maximizes some agreed-
upon objective function. The dual variable is known as the shadow value because it
measures the change in the objective function, if some small additional amount of the
binding resource could be found. If it turns out that the shadow value of the $i$th skill
category is zero, then there is no reason to design policy to increase its supply, at least
in the short run. This idea of complementary slackness, the relationship between the
primal constraint and the value of the associated dual variable, is one of the most
profound in economics. It explains why factors get the returns they do, their shadow
values, in an economy that obeys the laws of perfect competition. To the extent that the
economy differs from the competitive ideal, some additional constraints would have to
be built in.

Linear programming has an illustrious history since it was first used by the US Army in
its operations research. Its glory has faded somewhat as vastly more sophisticated programs such as the General Algebraic Modelling System (GAMS) have become available.
This programming language, used extensively in CGE modelling, handles linear programming as a special case and as a result has relegated the method to use in problems of
such extreme dimensions that the non-linear counterpart fails.

---

## 3.3.4 Social accounting matrices and computable general equilibrium (CGE) models

### 3.3.4.1 An introduction into CGE modelling

As intimated above, CGE models are computer-based simulations capable of constructing counterfactual scenarios that have been found to be very useful in policy
discussions.[31] A counterfactual is the state of the world in which current policies are
not in force but some others are. The plausibility of the counterfactual depends on:

---

[31] See Ginsburgh and Keyzer (1997), Dervis et al. (1982) and Taylor (1990) for some general examples
of this literature. Of special interest on closure is Dewatripont and Michel (1987).

(1) the adjustment mechanisms built into the model; and (2) the data on which the counterfactual is based. CGE models can be static, designed for one period, and used for comparative static exercises, or they can be full-fledged dynamic models, similar to time series econometric models.[32]

---

**Box 3-7: Assumptions about the functioning of markets in different types of CGE models**

One adjustment mechanism used in economic models is that of perfectly competitive markets. CGE models based on perfect information, and perfect foresight in the dynamic versions, however, are usually unconvincing to policy-makers. *Structural CGE models*, on the other hand, are often more realistic, building in country-specific rigidities, such as foreign exchange constraints, parallel-market premia, informal sector and labour market rigidities, among others.

Structural models are often highly linearized with labour demand functions that are based on fixed labour coefficients, that is, labour demand functions that do not depend on the real wage. This is considered theoretically unrealistic, but is not necessarily a bad approximation for small changes. Certainly, models with fixed wages overestimate the damage done to employment by imports. If wages are flexible, then not all the adjustment to trade reform will take place through quantities (employment) and this is why economists usually back measures to increase labour-market deregulation.

---

Both structuralist and standard CGE models are typically calibrated to so-called social accounting matrices (SAMs) that extend I-O tables with a savings-investment balance and, as such, are simply dressed up input-output frameworks. It follows that they can be used in the same way, inverses calculated and direct and indirect variables computed, but in fact they are much more useful as simply databases to which CGE models are calibrated. Table 3-4 shows a simplified

Table 3.4: SAM for Chile, 1992

|  | **Agric** | **Non-Ag** | **HH** | **Invest** | **Govt** | **Expts** | **Total** |
|---|---|---|---|---|---|---|---|
| Agriculture | 2016 | 2174 | 1924 | −215 | 0 | 2373 | 8272 |
| Non-agriculture | 1718 | 9024 | 9645 | 2160 | 1454 | 2242 | 26243 |
| Households | 3318 | 8618 | | | 1162 | 125 | 13224 |
| labour skilled | 980 | 3045 | | | 908 | 43 | 4976 |
| labour unskilled | 314 | 861 | | | 254 | 83 | 1511 |
| Capital | 2024 | 4713 | | | | 0 | 6737 |
| Savings | | | 1101 | | 1236 | 2054 | 4391 |
| Government | 656 | 2626 | 277 | | | 425 | 3984 |
| Tariffs | 78 | 392 | | | | | 470 |
| Imports | 562 | 3801 | 276 | 2447 | 132 | | 7219 |
| Total | 8272 | 26243 | 13224 | 4391 | 3984 | 7219 | |

Note: Millions of 1992 local currency units (LCU).

---

[32] See Gibson and van Seventer (2000) and Gibson (2003) for some methodological details.

social accounting matrix adapted from the 1992 SAM for Chile. The full-sized SAM from which the table was taken has five household categories and a more complex system of domestic and foreign transfers than that shown here.

A SAM is not, formally speaking, a model inasmuch as it has no behavioural equations. It is rather a snapshot of economic activity on a given date, in this case 1992. A wide variety of models can be calibrated to the same SAM.[33] Desktop CGE models can be easily calibrated to SAMs of this size and then solved in Excel with limited need for advanced computer skills. More sophisticated software and stronger computer skills are necessary to calibrate CGEs to larger datasets. Decaluwe and his associates have, for instance, shown that CGE models can be merged with household survey data to provide a rich mosaic for policy analysis (Decaluwe and Martens, 1988). Households need not be aggregated at all and models with large numbers of household units, sometimes numbering into the thousands, can be handled in the CGE programming framework. Thus, the impact of trade policy can be finely dis-aggregated. Issues concerning both the size and functional distribution of income can be investigated and the impact on employment assessed. Since CGE models are typically multi-sectoral, one can easily examine the impact on workers of a certain skill category in a given sector of the economy.

CGE models need to make assumptions regarding the behaviour of consumers, firms and the government. The current account balance is also taken into account. One typically uses a linear expenditure system (LES) for the consumption function although other demand systems can also be used (Sadoulet and de Janvry, 1995). The addition of the LES closes the essential circular flow of income and it is left to the model builder to supply equations for other components of aggregate demand. Investment, for example, might be taken as a function of capacity utilization, the profit rate, or even the interest rate if a monetary side of the model were added. Government is usually taken as an exogenous policy variable on which to run comparative static exercises. For the purposes of this chapter, the net export function is key: net exports should rise with the real exchange rate, $ep^*/p$, where $e$ is the nominal exchange rate, $p^*$ is the foreign price and $p$ is the domestic price level, usually the GDP deflator or some other aggregate. Net exports should also fall with the level of income, according to some marginal propensity to import. Most models adhere to a version of the Marshall-Lerner condition, which ensures that a devaluation will not increase the *value* of imports in local currency so much that they more than offset the export response. The price level for each sector can either be determined by a flexible price that balances supply and demand at full capacity utilization or a markup on unit costs, including intermediate, wage and import costs. Indirect or value-added taxes are also added in.

---

[33] The simplest is perhaps a structuralist model in which aggregate demand determines the level of capacity utilization in a given period, with investment increasing capital stock in the next. The key to this kind of model is the distinction between investment by origin, that which contributes to aggregate demand, and investment by destination that causes an increase in productivity and capacity utilization for the next period.

Figure 3.2: Market structure in the sample CGE model

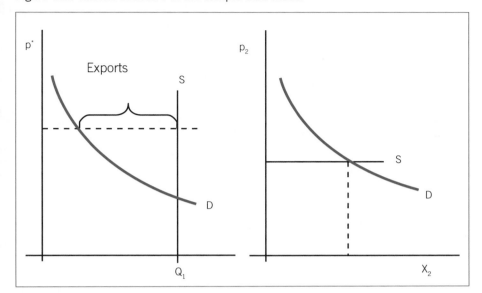

### 3.3.4.2 CGE simulations: A simple example

The sample model has the configuration in shown in figure 3.2 with export clearing in the agricultural sector, including mining and fix-price in the non-agricultural sectors. In this model, the nominal exchange rate continuously adjusts to keep the foreign and domestic prices of the first sector equal.[34]

Figure 3.3 provides an indication of the degree to which the model can be made to fit actual data. The figure depicts the actual evolution of GDP in Chile during the period 1992–2008. It also illustrates the predicted GDP evolution as simulated with the CGE model in our example. The crudeness of the model is evident in that the model undershoots and then overshoots the actual GDP path for the Chilean economy. The model nevertheless fits the actual data pretty well.

Having thus double-checked that the base model provides an adequate reflection of the actual economy, the model can now be used to estimate how small changes in trade policy might affect employment outcomes. One simple experiment that can be run in this kind of model is opening the economy to trade by reducing tariffs. The effect will not be large since tariffs are already extremely low in Chile, around 10 per cent of government revenue, as can be seen from the SAM in table 3.4.

---

[34] The spreadsheet for replication purposes is available at http://www.uvm.edu/~wgibson/. Further information is available in appendix 3.B of this chapter.

Figure 3.3: The base run of the small CGE for Chile

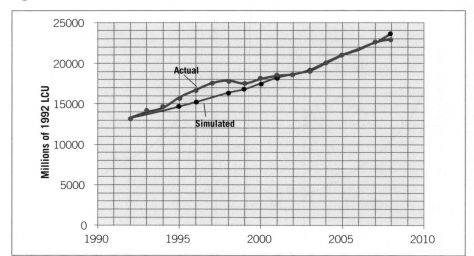

The results are shown in figure 3.4. Lowering tariffs only raises employment marginally, by about 2.3 per cent at the end of the simulated period. Real wages are the same in both simulations.

As is evident from the diagram, the impact of the tariff reduction is not large. The gain in employment amounts to a little more than 2.3 per cent at its maximum and that only after 25 simulated periods. The principal benefit of CGE models of this simple sort lies not in their predictive power, but rather in their elucidating the interactions of often complex mechanisms. In this case, the employment gain is due to the expansionary effect of lower tariffs, which after all, are just taxes. Thus, a tariff cut is likely to be expansionary simply because it amounts to an increase in net injections from the public sector.

This experiment is designed to do nothing more than illustrate how the CGE models can be used. Many alternative assumptions about how the model is configured are possible. Hammouda and Osakwe (2006), for example, note that CGE models are often designed to prevent revenues from falling, although the realism of this assumption is subject to question.

Perhaps the most important aspect of CGE modelling of the impact of trade on employment is due to accounting for the effect of productivity growth on investment. Models that examine the partial equilibrium impact of trade are useful but ultimately biased against trade openness because they can only "see" the negative impact. Not only is trade beneficial to consumers by lowering prices of goods directly and indirectly, it also stimulates productivity growth. This raises either wages, profits or both. If the productivity growth is captured by labour, demand will rise and increments in output will follow as capacity utilization rises. If profits increase, then investment is likely to rise as well. In both cases, the demand for labour will increase.

Figure 3.4: The impact of tariff reduction on employment

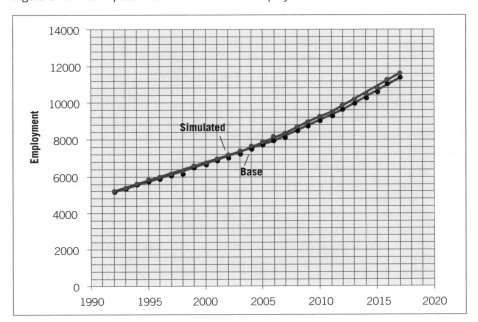

### Box 3-8: Trade and employment: The role of productivity

Gibson (2009) shows in a simple model that the relationship between trade and employment is essentially a relationship between productivity that reduces the demand for labour, *ceteris paribus*, and growth, which increases the demand for labour. The relationship between productivity and investment is a difficult one to measure with any precision, but one can be fairly sure that a rise in productivity will spur a rise in investment, output and *ultimately* the demand for labour.

Productivity gains are certainly lethal to employment in demand-driven models with fixed investment. The reason is obvious from the structure of demand that depends largely on consumption. Since consumption depends, for the most part, on labour incomes, a reduction in employment quickly drives down aggregate demand. When there is quantity clearing only, the effect can be quite strong, as shown in figure 3.5. There, employment in the Chile CGE for the base run is compared to a simulation with twice the base level productivity gain, from 0.5 per cent per year to 1 per cent. No other change is made. In particular, it is seen that the level of employment increases much less rapidly as a result of this small loss. There is much less inflation, of course, but the real wage for both skilled and unskilled labour remains fixed. Interestingly enough, real GDP in this simple model does not change. The country is producing exactly the same quantity of output but with less labour. Where does it go? There might well be re-distributional consequences, of course, but in reality, some of the output will filter down through the informal sector to the rest of the economy. Total labour hours will likely be the same or higher. This distribution of productive activity will be highly skewed, of course.

### 3.3.4.3 Labour market assumptions in CGE models

CGE models combine the logic of various partial equilibrium models into one, and so the process of profit maximization that is used to derive the demand for labour appears in both. Some combination of prices (in this case the wage rate) and quantities (employment) bring about an equilibrium. Structuralist CGE models, such as the prototype discussed in the example of Chile, typically assume fixed real wages and take investment as the independent variable of the system (Gibson, 2009; Polaski, 2006).[35] If the economy is demand driven, a rise in exports will increase employment, despite the rise in imports.[36] Structuralist models generate much higher employment multipliers than do standard CGE models, primarily because of the assumption of excess supplies of labour.

Kurzweil (2002) notes that the standard approach to modelling the labour market in a CGE model is based on the distinction between factors and goods. In the simplest framework, labour is a homogeneous factor of production and is used as an input into a production function that takes a Leontief (fixed coefficients), Cobb-Douglas, CES or translog form as discussed above. In static models, the supply of labour is usually taken as a given parameter but, in dynamic models, assumptions about the labour force participation rate can be combined with population forecasts to determine the supply endogenously.

Figure 3.5: Increasing the productivity growth rate by 0.5 per cent

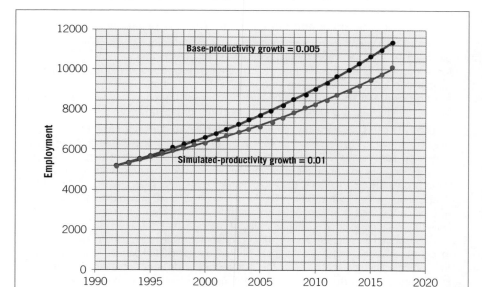

---

[35] Investment is often determined by "animal spirits" or some other exogenously specified variable.
[36] This shifts the focus to what determines investment and this is, of course, a notoriously difficult question as noted above.

The model may admit a wide range of labour types, degrees of mobility, forms of segmentation, costs and randomness of search depending on the assumptions deemed appropriate by the author.[37] Models with large numbers of labour categories are not uncommon and significant wage differences are often assumed, because of the assumption that skilled labour can compete with unskilled labour but not vice versa. This may be somewhat unrealistic, but skill categories are nonetheless useful ways of demarcating contours of labour mobility within a given sector.

Efficiency wage theory has also occasionally been integrated into applied models (Shapiro and Stiglitz, 1984). In LDCs, many firms pay workers higher than a market-clearing wage. Efficiency wage models explain this stylized fact by noting the principal-agent problem facing employers as workers may elect to work with less intensity than specified in the employment contract. One solution is monitoring, but this is expensive. Instead, workers are paid more to elicit higher productivity. This raises the cost of job loss to the worker and reduces shirking and turnover, attracts the best workers in the labour market and improves morale and productivity of workers happy to have a "really good" job.

In LDCs, efficiency wages may also have a biological component as caloric intake actually improves energy and effort and at the same time reduces absenteeism due to illness. While providing a theoretically cogent argument for high unemployment rates in developing countries, efficiency wage theory has not shown particular empirical strength. Since the optimal incentive wage is taken as a function of the unemployment rate, a rate that is very high when informal workers are considered unemployed, the efficiency wage premium is probably very small in LDCs.

Many structural CGE models do use a form of the Beverage curve, or wage curve, that relates search time to vacancies of employers (Gibson and van Seventer, 2000; Guichard and Laffargue, 2000). The curve serves to define the path of nominal wages in labour-market adjustment. When the rate of unemployment is higher than usual, nominal wage growth slows, and vice versa. In most CGE models, the agents (workers, firms and government) only control nominal variables, while general equilibrium essentially converts these nominal values into real, setting the stage for a reaction to the outcome in the next period. Reasonable paths for nominal variables are then required, which implies something like a Beverage curve for each segment of the labour market. Nothing prevents spillover here, such that unemployment in the skilled labour market reduces the rate of nominal wage growth for unskilled workers. It is also easy to build in a minimum wage option and then turn it on and off to see what the effects on employment and other variables, such as poverty, might be.

One innovative modelling technique in dynamic models is to use "complementary slackness", a term borrowed from the linear programming framework, as discussed above. Here, the labour constraint is written where

---

[37] Given the degree of aggregation at which most CGE models operate, it is not necessary to assume that any firm can substitute labour for capital, yet, for the sector as whole, it appears that substitution has taken place due to the changing patterns of aggregation.

$$(w / \overline{w})(\overline{L} - L) = 0 \qquad (3\text{-}5)$$

w is the nominal wage and $L$ is employment. Bars indicate a floor for the wage and full employment for labour. Thus, if there is slack in the labour market such that $\overline{L} - L > 0$, then the complementary condition holds as an equality, $w - \overline{w} = 0$, and vice versa. This approach can be used to model the boundary between full and less than full employment scenarios.

Another innovative example is to introduce labour unions in the labour market specification. Workers and firms can explicitly bargain over wages or employment levels, with the union setting the wage and firms making the employment decision. Unions may also decide to maximize employment subject to a minimum acceptable wage. A simple approach is to set up a monopoly model to endogenously define wage differentials to reflect union power as in Thierfelder and Shiells (1997).

Structuralist models are useful for the analysis of labour market deregulation and its effects on wages, employment and incomes of the economy as whole. The fine structure of these models is unhappily beyond the scope of this chapter, but note in passing there is a fundamental property of CGE models that can be at seen as both a strength and weakness. Supporters of living wage, fair trade, better factories and decent work initiatives can use CGE models to quantify the costs of these programmes in terms of the well-being of those left out of such programmes. Partial equilibrium models ignore the plight of rejected workers, but economy-wide models should not and often do not. Whether they fill the informal sector, return to school to acquire human capital, or enjoy their leisure time, these agents should be accounted for in the CGE. This may raise the cost of reformist policies to an unacceptable level, or the reverse, enable the political classes to make informed decisions about the cost of closing down "sweat shops" and the like.

The above illustrates that labour markets can be modelled in a variety of ways. One of the main attractions of CGE models is that they can incorporate a wide variety of adjustment mechanisms in markets, ranging from the extremes of pure price or quantity-clearing markets to rationing, monopoly pricing, administered or foreign border prices. In any given model, a number of these adjustment mechanisms can happily coexist, although subsequent interpretations of results can become somewhat opaque. It is, therefore, important to carefully chose labour market assumptions in accordance with the reality in the economy that is represented in the model.

Making the right choice is particularly important in dynamic models. The impact on employment of trade depends on the assumptions made and, since the effects are cumulative in dynamic models, there is a risk of creating a cumulative implausibility. The choice of CGE model also matters. The original CGE models were all one-period set-ups for which comparative static changes (derivatives) could be computed. Many standard CGE models remain static owing to the great technical difficulty of inserting (many simultaneous) intertemporal optimization models into a common framework. Once these formidable challenges have been met, however, they may still fail the test of plausibility, simply because their assumptions seem so unreal. Structuralist models deal with this problem by assuming simple stock-flow relationships, often linear, and then calibrating the model to actual data as shown in the simple CGE for Chile above.

### 3.3.4.4 Evidence based on SAM-CGE models

The largest impact of trade reform on employment seems to be from the effect that liberalization has on investment. Earlier CGE studies found that the gains from NAFTA-generated trade in Canada, Mexico and the US were small, less than 3 per cent of GDP over a decade. But standard CGE models do not typically address the inducement to invest in a dynamic context. The typical model has a neoclassical closure in which wages adjust to excess supply in the labour market and savings drive investment. With flexible product prices and elastic supply curves, an increase in the demand for exports can have a very small effect on wages and employment.

The Global Trade Analysis Project (GTAP) model is one of the most innovative CGE frameworks to appear in recent years (Hertel, 1997). The model's realism is enhanced by non-homothetic constant difference of elasticity (CDE) household preferences. It also incorporates international trade and transport margins as well as a banking sector that links system-wide savings and investment. Trade is modelled using bilateral trade matrices based on Armington elasticities. Factors include skilled and unskilled labour, capital, land and natural resources.

Kurzweil (2002) examines three specifications of the labour market in the GTAP model using the GTAP 5 database. The first is a "plain vanilla" trade liberalization experiment in which agricultural trade barriers are removed in the European Union (EU) by 50 per cent for African products. The second has the same tariff cut but low-wage workers in the EU are protected by a fixed real wage for unskilled labour in both low- and middle-income countries as well as in the EU. The third reduces the mobility of labour relative to the base GTAP assumption of perfect in-country labour mobility. Finally, a portmanteau simulation combines all the effects, liberalization, fixed real wage and labour mobility into one.

Kurzweil finds that the cut of the European tariffs on agricultural commodities raises welfare for the African regions. There is a slight decline in EU welfare. The different labour market extensions modify these results in various ways. Not surprisingly, the effect of labour immobility diminishes the impact of trade reform while the fixed real wage produces a large increase in welfare.

Note that this is the conjugate of the effect discussed above: when quantities adjust in the labour market rather than prices, that is wages, the employment effects are much more obvious. With the fixed real wage eliminated, employment gains in the formal sector are not as great as wages rise.

Kurzweil (2002) notes that "it becomes obvious that the characteristics of a country's labour market have a significant influence on the outcome of a trade liberalization scenario", but it would seem that the labour market structure is not what she is really getting at here. The difference in her simulations is how the model is closed, that is, with Keynesian demand-driven labour markets or with a more standard neoclassical flexible wage that eliminates excess demand or supply of labour. This point is fundamental to all CGE modelling: the nature of the closure is essential to

Table 3.5: Overall welfare gains from removal of all trade barriers in various
　　　　　CGE models

| Study | GTAP data | Sectors/ regions | Static/ dynamic | Returns to scale | Competition: perfect (PC) or monopolistic (MC) | Welfare gains ($US bn) |
|---|---|---|---|---|---|---|
| OECD[1] | 5 | 10/10 | Static | CRS | PC | 173.60 |
| Cline[2] | 5 | 22/25 | Static | CRS | PC | 227.80 |
| Anderson et al.[3] | 4 | 4/19 | Static | CRS | PC | 263.50 |
| Anderson et al.[4] | 6 | 25/27 | Dynamic | CRS | PC | 264.80 |
| Francois et al.[5] | 5 | 17/16 | Dynamic | Ag: CRS | Ag: PC | 367.30 |
| | | | | Mfg: IRS | Mfg: MC | |
| Brown et al.[6] | 4 | 18/20 | Dynamic | Ag: CRS | Ag: PC | 2154.50 |
| | | | | Mfg: IRS | Mfg: MC | |

Source: Piermartini and Teh (2005).

Notes: 1. OECD (2003); 2. Cline (2004); 3. Anderson et al. (2001); 4. Anderson et al. (2005);
5. Francois et al. (2003); 6. Brown et al. (2003).

the size and even direction of the results. There are fundamental differences between economies with surplus labour and those without (cyclical fluctuations notwithstanding) and it is this difference rather than the specific details of the labour market that must be pinned down before a model is ready for use in policy discussions.

Table 3.5 shows a summary of model structures and results for a number of models surveyed recently. As an example of how results from CGE models may vary with the database, structure of the models and the exact simulations undertaken, consider the information in table 3.5. The results of the studies in the table are presented as the total overall welfare gains from the removal of trade barriers, in the right-most column. From the table, the estimated gains range from a low of US$173.6 billion to a high of US$2,154.5 billion, with four of the six studies in a narrower range from US$227.8 billion to US$367.3 billion. The size of the gains increases as the models move from static to dynamic. Note also the assumptions about competition are altered in some studies to allow for imperfect competition, in the form of monopolistic competition. The effect is restricted to the manufacturing sector alone.

The table shows that structure makes a difference and this certainly irks some observers. Ackerman and Gallagher (2002) note that "the results of these models are typically reported as if they were hard, objective facts, providing unambiguous numerical measures of the value of liberalization". This could be a complaint made only by those with the most fleeting association with economic models of any kind and their use in modern political discourse. While it is possible to imagine that model results are sometimes presented in this way, there is certainly no shortage of scepticism in the eyes of the viewing public about virtually all models in virtually all disciplines. The picture illustrated in this table is that of a vigorous competition between modellers who believe that different aspects of an economy are of greatest importance. It is then up to the policy-maker, not the analyst, to choose the model deemed most appropriate to the policy question at hand.

Winchester (2008a) reviews 11 CGE studies of trade and wage inequality, including Cline (2004). Despite a wide variation in factors, sectors and regions, as well as trade scenarios considered, the models speak with one voice: the effect of trade liberalization on the relative skilled/unskilled wage is generally 5 per cent and often much less. The one outlier is Winchester (2008b), whose models claims a 27 per cent decrease for New Zealand in the skill premium. This is the product of an unusual experiment in which New Zealand returns to its agricultural roots, its true comparative advantage, and in the process requires much more unskilled labour. Ten of the 11 studies assume perfect competition and most have used an Armington function to distribute demand between imports and domestically produced goods. The changes are often quite large in these models: Theirfelder and Robinson (2002), for example, cut the price of imports by half, and Cortes and Jean (1999) double the size of emerging economies. Both get only a 1 per cent change in the skill premium.

In a particularly clear example of how large-scale structure can make an enormous difference in the way an economy responds to import penetration, Sadoulet and de Janvry (1992) use a CGE to study two archetypal low-income economies. In African countries, they note, cereal imports are non-competitive whereas in rice-producing Asian countries they are competitive with domestic production. The competitive/non-competitive import distinction was identified above as crucial to the impact of trade liberalization on employment. The authors use the same model (same closure and numéraire) with balanced fiscal intervention. Private and public investment has a long-run effect on total factor productivity. The models consider a 20 per cent increase in the price of cereals and animal products. In the African case, the price elasticity of the demand for cereals is, on net, less than one, leading to an increase in the import bill. Demand for local production falls and with it employment. To restore macroeconomic balance, a real devaluation is introduced, which reallocates labour to the agro-export sector. The devaluation steers resources to larger farmers who are the most capable of producing agro-exports. As a result, the distribution of income deteriorates, but a signal is sent to smaller farmers that producing food crops for domestic production is now a less viable option.

The Asian scenario is entirely different in that the rising cereal price benefits all farmers. There, cereal imports fall and macro-balance is achieved by way of a revaluation of the exchange rate. Since both countries depend on export taxes as the means to finance public-sector investment, the long-run effects are also the opposite. The Asian countries lose output and employment as budgets shrink, while the African countries, with rising trade taxes, have the resources to dedicate to public investment. The employment outlook is thus more positive for Africa relative to Asia in this simulation.

### 3.3.4.5 Assessing the CGE approach

One of the main weaknesses of the CGE approach is that the level of aggregation is very high and so it is not possible to identify where, when and for whom job loss will become a problem. Ackerman and Gallagher (2002) make three additional points when criticizing the use of CGE models to predict the gains from trade: First, in light of the fact that the projected benefits of liberalization of merchandise trade are small, especially for developing countries, and given the limited scope for future re-duction, trade liberalization is unlikely to help reduce poverty significantly. Second, the assumptions and structures of first-generation CGE models are undergoing serious modification and divergent results are undermining the minimal consensus there had been. Third, employment effects of liberalization, while of fundamental concern to policy-makers, are "excluded by design" from most CGE models. Models based on more realistic assumptions about how markets actually function would produce an auditing of winners and losers from trade that would differ from the standard results. In short, the authors make the case that trade liberalization is essentially over and that any future benefits will be on a margin that is seriously diminished.[38]

Table 3.6: Benefits of complete liberalization: GTAP versus LINKAGE

| Liberalizing sector | High income GTAP | LINKAGE | Developing World GTAP | LINKAGE | GTAP | LINKAGE |
|---|---|---|---|---|---|---|
| Total Amounts[1] | | | | | | |
| Agriculture | 42 | 128 | 12 | 54 | 56 | 182 |
| Textiles | 1 | 16 | 9 | 22 | 10 | 38 |
| Other | 17 | 57 | 1 | 10 | 19 | 67 |
| Total | 60 | 201 | 22 | 86 | 84 | 287 |
| Per capita[2] | | | | | | |
| Agriculture | 40 | 126 | 3 | 11 | 9 | 30 |
| Textiles | 1 | 16 | 2 | 4 | 2 | 6 |
| Other | 16 | 56 | 0 | 2 | 3 | 11 |
| Total | 57 | 199 | 5 | 17 | 14 | 47 |
| Percentage of GDP[3] | | | | | | |
| Agriculture | 0.16 | 0.38 | 0.24 | 0.50 | 0.18 | 0.44 |
| Textiles | 0.01 | 0.05 | 0.18 | 0.20 | 0.03 | 0.09 |
| Other | 0.07 | 0.17 | 0.03 | 0.09 | 0.06 | 0.16 |
| Total | 0.23 | 0.60 | 0.44 | 0.80 | 0.27 | 0.70 |

Source: Ackerman and Gallagher (2002).

Notes: 1. US$ billions. 2. US$ per person. 3. For LINKAGE, estimate for year 2015.

---

[38] Greenspan notes that the limits to the growth of benefits of globalization were already beginning to be felt in his administration as Chairman of the Federal Reserve (Greenspan, 2007).

World Bank economists have estimated global gains as much as US$520 billion with two-thirds of it going to developing countries. In the context of a US$50 trillion world economy, this is just over 1 per cent, observable, but not game-changing. Similarly, some 140 million people have escaped poverty due to trade liberalization according to World Bank economists. This effect is relatively larger; there are around 1 billion people in poverty worldwide, depending on how poverty is defined. Nothing in these numbers changes the general view that trade has only a peripheral impact on employment.

The discussion offered by Ackerman and Gallagher (2002) also highlights the role of data in the debate, weighing in against previous tales about how underlying SAMs to which CGE models had been calibrated were inadvertently switched, but with no perceptible effect on the outcomes of the simulations! The larger effect of liberalization observed in the GTAP 5 database seems to have diminished indeed. The GTAP 6 database describes the year 2001 and incorporates trade agreements reached through 2005, including China's entry into the WTO, the expansion of the European Union in 2004, and the end of the Multi-Fibre Agreement (Anderson et al., 2005; van der Mensbrugghe, 2007). The more up-to-date data incorporate the gains from previous tariff reductions, of course, but at the same time permit smaller gains from future reductions.[39]

On a more theoretical level, Hammouda and Osakwe (2006) note three sources of weakness in CGE models: the theoretical framework or structure; database availability and accuracy; and the distinction between model parameters and endogenous variables. The authors join Taylor and von Arnim (2006) in identifying the Armington function and its estimated elasticities, as a central vulnerability. In this view, policy recommendations seem to hinge on a parameter that cannot be estimated with great accuracy.[40]All CGE model critics note that strategic considerations, power relations, regional hegemony and other local rigidities are entirely left out of the model specification. To the extent that these models are guided by the spirit of the Walrasian general equilibrium system, they miss some of the features central to the development process, such as restricted or entirely absent credit markets, uncertainty around property ownership and title, asymmetric information problems and general coordination issues. Adjustment costs, too, are often left out of the models. Many of these criticisms can be addressed using agent-based methods, but that work remains in its infancy (Epstein, 2006).

---

[39] It is important to see, however, that tariff changes can happen in both directions, so the model is still useful in predicting what would happen, hysteresis aside, were some backtracking to occur. The tone of the critics notwithstanding, it is difficult to see the relevance of the critique of their CGE methodology as anything more than the recognition that diminishing returns to trade liberalization are setting in. The World Bank's LINKAGE model predicted, for example, a gain for developing countries of US$539 billion in 2003 but by 2005 the impact had fallen to US$86 billion. Hertel and Keeney (2005) use the GTAP model to estimate the benefits available from removal of all remaining barriers to merchandise trade, some US$84 billion, mostly from the liberalization of agriculture.

[40] The desktop CGE elaborated above can certainly be used to test this hypothesis. Raise the import price and lower the level of import growth: the model then mimics the presence of an Armington, without the computational complexity.

By far the most controversial assumption built into many CGE models is that of full employment. On the one hand, developing economies do have full employment: virtually everyone in an LDC is doing something all the time, especially in countries that provide no social safety net (Gibson and Kelley, 1994). Gibson (2005) uses a CGE model to incorporate the informal sector and this model effectively assumes full employment, just not all in the formal sector. The idea–implicit in full employment models–that wages would drop to the point that all those willing to work would find jobs in the formal sector is clearly a different kind of assumption and it is the one to which most critics most strenuously object.

The database critique does seem to have some validity. When CGE models are based on the MAcMAP or GTAP database, including vintage and MIRAGE models, many countries are left out.[41] Only 11 of the 48 in Sub-Saharan Africa are included in the GTAP 6 database (Hammouda and Osakwe, 2006).[42] The lacunae might or might not be pertinent to a specific policy issue but, at a minimum, should remind policy-makers that having a small pilot or desktop CGE for use in evaluating "black box" models linked to unrepresentative databases might be an investment well worth making. Models, for instance, that assume a common crop structure across an otherwise highly heterogeneous agricultural sector cannot hope to predict the effect of trade liberalization on employment in countries specialized in a limited number of agricultural products. This does not mean that CGE models are always wrong or of no use, but rather that they must be suited to both local rigidities and calibrated to relevant time scales.

### 3.3.5  Comparing different simulation methods

These and other criticisms frame the question of which is the more appropriate model, partial or general equilibrium. ATPC (2005) notes that computable partial equilibrium approaches, such as the World Integrated Trade Solution (WITS/SMART), are flexible enough to assess country- or sector-specific employment losses or gains associated with trade liberalization. The data for these models are certainly less synthetic than for SAMs and CGE models and thus present a higher resolution image of the sector in question. Moreover, CGE models are singularly unwilling to identify firms whose workers are in immediate need of trade

---

[41] The MIRAGE model has some interesting features: FDI flows are explicitly described, vertical product differentiation is introduced, by distinguishing two quality ranges, according to the country of origin of the product and trade barriers. These are described by the MAcMaps database, which also provides ad-valorem tariffs, ad-valorem equivalents of specific tariffs, tariff quotas, prohibitions and anti-dumping duties at the bilateral level for 137 countries with 220 partners. Preferential agreements are taken into account in a quasi-exhaustive way (Bchir et al., 2002).

[42] The Michigan model, on the other hand, is based on its own database and was used to analyse the employment effect of the Tokyo Round of Multi-lateral Trade Liberalization in 29 sector models of 18 industrialized and 16 developing countries (Deardorff and Stern, 1986.). This model was extended to include imperfect competition and some aspects of "new trade theory" for the analysis of the US-Canada free trade agreement (Brown et al., 2005).

adjustment assistance. Indeed, CGE models are all but blind to any but the largest contributors to GDP. The general rule of thumb is that sectors smaller than "1 per cent of GDP" do not matter and show up only as rounding error. The 1 per cent rule is hardly an adequate foundation on which to make policy except at the most aggregate level. In this important sense, partial and CGE models do not directly compete with but rather complement each other in any comprehensive policy analysis.

The large-scale optics of CGE models are made worse by the tendency of some modellers to regard their code as a commercial secret. There are two levels on which modellers can infringe. The first, mentioned by Hammouda and Osakwe (2006), is the obscurity with which model equations are described. Sensitivity testing of key assumptions is lacking too frequently, although in much of the professional literature it has become practically a requirement to post data and models on one's web page for replication purposes. In the case of some of the large CGE models, this certainly can present a practical problem.

Critics also complain that authors seem to be devoted to discussing the specific equations of their work without giving an overview of how the equations interact so that model results can be compared across various modelling approaches. For this reason, meta-studies are rare and not always of high value. The authors of the commercially available MIRAGE model, for a particularly egregious example, do not even supply a listing of their code, creating a box that is truly black.

As suggested above, data requirements of CGE are very different from those that feed econometric models. In addition to a base SAM, standard CGE models require elasticities of substitution between labour and capital, the income and price elasticities of household consumption demand, the elasticity of substitution for the Armington and an elasticity of transformation. These four key sets of elasticities cannot be estimated directly from the SAM and must, therefore, be derived from econometric or other sources (Sadoulet and de Janvry, 1995).[43]

## 3.4 ASSESSING THE EMPLOYMENT IMPACTS OF TRADE: ECONOMETRIC METHODS

Just articulating the nature of the problem that econometrics is designed to tackle unveils the difficulty in testing the hypothesis that trade liberalization causes employment to rise. The first problem that has plagued all econometric research is the nature of the subject. In principle, the subject should be an individual agent, rather than a country. Were all countries of the same size, it would be possible to renormalize

---

[43] "Other sources" include "guesstimation", i.e. educated guesses, but as Sadoulet and de Janvry (1995, p. 354) point out, "luckily, experience has shown that the empirical results obtained from simulations with CGEs are quite insensitive to specific values of all these elasticities ...". They go on to identify the Armington as one of the crucial parameters for which the proper "order of magnitude" must be obtained.

to the country unit without affecting the results. In the imagined randomized trial, most subjects will be from the large countries, randomly assigned to one group or the other.[44]

In the following, the discussion is structured around three types of regressions that have typically been conducted when analysing the relationship between trade and employment. The first subsection discusses an exercise in which sectoral information is explored to analyse how import penetration has affected sectoral employment within one single country. In the second subsection, the relationship between trade and the wage premium is discussed, a relationship that has been the object of a large body of econometric work. Last, but not least, a cross-country analysis is presented.

---

### Box 3-9: Econometrics: A reminder of the basics

To evaluate the econometric work done on the issue of trade and employment, it is best to keep in mind several basic ideas about what the method entails:

- First, all econometric models are (or should be) designed to mimic a randomized controlled trial. Hence, pick a group of country subjects, randomly assign them to two groups. Let one trade and the other not and then measure the employment response after a determinate length of time.

- Second, when working with observational data, the default interpretation of the results should be that the observations are correlated and that no causal relationship can be imputed. This "guilty until proven innocent" approach is the recommended way to avoiding type I errors, failing to reject a false hypothesis. This is because the overwhelming majority of theories in economics involve simultaneous causality.[45]

- Third, econometric tests can never "prove" anything. All that is possible is to fail to reject a theory that seems correct.

- Fourth, econometric methods cannot distinguish between theories since any given set of observations is likely to fail to contradict some theory. Data do generate theories, and working backward from data to theory ensures that the data will fail to contradict the theory and so will be of no intellectual value.

- Fifth, econometric models can test a theory "all up" in the sense of the overall direction of causality between independent and dependent variables, or it can test a component of a theory that is necessarily true if the theory as a whole is to work.

---

[44] Sometimes this can be done, or approximately so. Consider the coastal cities of China that are heavily involved in world trade. The rural counterpart is not, so in some sense there is a natural experiment. On closer inspection, the example fails, however, since the assumption that coastal and rural Chinese are statistically identical is obviously problematic. When subjects can self-sort into one of the two groups, control or treatment, the results are subject to "selection bias" and are generally not valid. See Kennedy (1998) for a non-technical discussion of selection bias.

[45] Paraphrasing Kennedy (1998), for any given set of variables some researcher is hoping that there will be a discernible relation between one and the others, while some other is hoping that there will not be (because of multi-collinearity).

### 3.4.1 Trade and sectoral employment

Consider first a naive regression, say the impact of imports on the industrial employment of some developing country. Could it be said that the imports "caused" the decline in employment, either quality or quantity of jobs, in that sector? Intuitively, the answer is yes. Even this simple relationship, however, is quite difficult to corroborate with empirical data.

A simple example is provided by Galiani and Sanguinetti (2003). The authors note that Argentina underwent a substantial liberalization beginning in 1990 that transformed the industrial sector. The tariff reductions resulted from multi-lateral negotiations at the General Agreement on Trade and Tariffs (GATT). Tariff barriers were reduced to an average level of 10 per cent and all import licences were eliminated. This was an impressive across-the-board liberalization, reducing protection from an average level of 45 per cent in 1988 to around 12 per cent in 1991.

During the next decade, total trade almost quadrupled, increasing its share in GDP from some 10 per cent to 18 per cent, with import penetration in manufacturing rising from 5.7 per cent in 1990 to 19 per cent in 1999. This was, then, a classic case of trade liberalization and it did lead to a reduction of employment in manufacturing. Here the "treatment" is the import penetration, which varies from sector to sector. The control group consists of the sectors with low or zero import penetration.

Do these sectors differ systematically? If so, then strictly speaking, any empirical results are meaningless since it will be uncertain whether the imports caused the decline in employment or it was some other unaccounted for factor. Surely the special circumstances of each of the industrial sectors must matter, how much capital they employ, the degree to which labour can be substituted for capital and what local labour rigidities might impinge on employment decisions. Even if there is no information about these and other factors, might it still be possible to apply the control group method?

The answer is broadly yes. The critical assumption is that the unobserved factors remain constant over the time frame for which the regression is run. If so, then it is possible to split the data set up into subsets, cancelling out the systematic difference between the two. Figure 3.6 shows how this is done. Let there be two sectors in the data set for some arbitrary country. Running a regression amounts to fitting a straight line through the data points as is done in the left-hand side of the panel. The regression slope there is positive as shown in the figure. In the right-hand panel, the data set is split into two, one for the first and one for the second sector. Now regressions are run for the two data sets separately and the difference in intercepts amounts to the "fixed effect" or sector-specific determinants of employment. Now the slopes have reversed their signs, as seen in the figure, so that an increase in import penetration shows a declining level of employment. Does the left-hand-side diagram contradict the theory that increased imports reduce employment? No, it does not, since the experimental design does not hold everything else but the treatment constant. On the other hand, the diagram on the right fails to contradict the hypothesis that higher imports lead to lower employment.

Figure 3.6: Fixed effects regressions

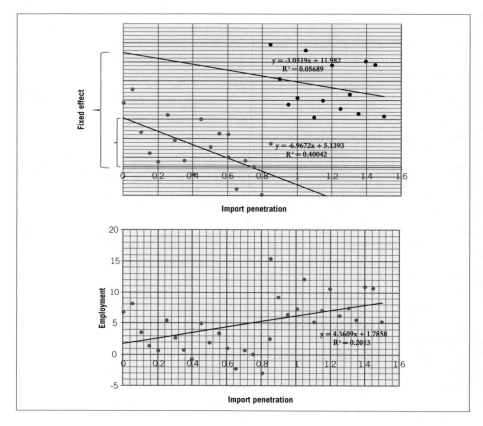

The coefficients on import penetration may nonetheless be incorrect if the unobserved factors held constant by way of splitting the data set are not, in fact, constant over time. If not, then there is omitted variable bias. What if, for example, employment were falling in all sectors over time as resources were reallocated from industry to services, a trend that seems to take place in most economies as they mature? The tendency for industrial employment to fall on its own would then "pile on" to the effect of trade liberalization, increasing the apparent effect of the latter. The improper attribution of time effects onto the import coefficient causes bias in the latter that will disappear even in large sample sizes. It is a fundamental defect of the experimental design.

Appendix table 3.A-1 shows data for Argentinean employment for 22 industrial sectors for the years 1994, 1996 and 1998. There are also data for imports as a percentage of valued added in those sectors for selected years from 1993 to 1998. Running a simple regression of employment on import penetration (IP) yields the

106

regression in the first column of table 3.7. While the sign is what might be expected, the coefficient is not significantly different from zero.[46] Regression 2 does not split the regression but nonetheless has a significant coefficient on import penetration lagged with a negative and *positive* and significant coefficient on lagged imports. The last two regressions sharpen the estimate a bit, effectively checking for the possibility of fixed sectoral effects (regression 3) and fixed time effects (regression 4). The general similarity of results suggests that these effects are not large in this sample. The quite negative effects of the year dummies show that *all* sectors are experiencing a decline in employment. Thus, the regression that seems most accurate is the last with fixed effects in both sector and time. It has the smallest coefficient for the import penetration variable.

Table 3.7: Dependent variable: Employment

| | Regression | | | |
|---|---|---|---|---|
| | 1 | 2 | 3 | 4 |
| IP | −0.022 | −0.242*** | −0.271*** | −0.163** |
| | (0.013) | (0.030) | (0.052) | (0.050) |
| IPL | | 0.227*** | 0.179* | 0.238*** |
| | | (0.024) | (0.067) | (0.058) |
| 1994 | | | | . |
| | | | | . |
| 1996 | | | | −9.594*** |
| | | | | (1.298) |
| 1998 | | | | −9.110*** |
| | | | | (1.776) |
| Constant | 86.306*** | 89.114*** | 92.829*** | 90.895*** |
| | (2.606) | (1.381) | (2.571) | (0.826) |
| $R^2$-adjusted | −0.009 | 0.081 | 0.253 | 0.68 |
| $R^2$ | 0.040 | 0.109 | 0.276 | 0.702 |
| Observations | 22 | 66 | 66 | 66 |
| F-stat | 2.562 | 49.166 | 14.007 | 20.771 |

Source: Galiani and Sanguinetti (2003).

Standard errors in parentheses. *** $p < 0.01$, ** $p < 0.05$, * $p < 0.1$.

Notes: 1.The dependent variable is the employment (1990 = 100).

2. The variable IP is the import penetration as a percentage of value added.

3. The variable IPL is the import penetration lagged one year.

---

[46] Running the regressions one at a time shows that, indeed, the coefficient on IP varies from positive to negative but is never significant.

What is remarkable about these regressions is that they seem to support the idea that imports destroy jobs in the current period, but build them back up in the second year.[47] Why might this be so? One answer is what the general equilibrium theories suggest above. Competitive imports do indeed reduce employment in the sectors with which they compete, but then the lower import prices also *raise* the profitability of import-using sectors. If and when these sectors expand in response to higher profitability, the demand for labour would then increase.

### 3.4.2  Trade and the wages of skilled and unskilled workers

Galiani and Sanguinetti (2003) show the effect of trade liberalization on the wages of skilled and unskilled workers. Import penetration will affect unskilled labour more if it is relatively immobile. Skilled workers may or may not have sector-specific skills, but to the extent that their skills are applicable in the expanding sectors, they will suffer less from import penetration.

Prior to liberalization, unskilled and semi-skilled workers kept pace with skilled workers in that the skill premium was relatively constant. After 1990, the premium began to accelerate. The premium is certainly correlated with the rise in imports as just discussed, but did liberalization *cause* the wage gap to rise?

All manufacturing wages were rising during the 1990s, skilled, semi-skilled and unskilled. Wages will rise with age and experience, so the researchers used information on these variables to control for the impact on wages. They then ask the question: holding the skill, experience and age of a worker constant, would an increase in import penetration raise the *slope* of the regression line more for semi-skilled and skilled workers relative to their unskilled counterparts? To analyse this question, the authors use an interaction term

$$w = \beta_0 + \sum_{j=1} \beta_j C_j + \beta_w C_s I \qquad (3\text{-}6)$$

where $\beta_0$ is a constant and $\sum_{j=1} \beta_j C_j$ the sum of the control variables multiplied times their coefficients $\beta_j$. The last term factors in the level of import penetration with the variable $I$. Note that it is multiplied times $C_s$, which is the variable to control for skills or education. The key to understanding this approach is to note that $C_s$ is *already included in the sum of controls*. So the effect of skills is not counted twice, once by itself and then multiplied by the import penetration variable. The change in wage with respect to skill is just the slope coefficient on the skilled variable but now it consists of *two* parts, a base slope and then, potentially, an addition for the fact that the worker is working in an industry with high import penetration. This extra boost on the *slope* coefficient is only "potential" because it might not be significantly different from zero. If so, then there is no difference in the skill premia

---

[47] This may be an interesting theory, but it is not tested by the data in table 3.8, simply because the idea emerged from the data. To check this theory further, some additional regressions would have to be run.

for workers in penetrated industries versus those in others. Return to figure 3.6 and consider that the interaction of the skilled premium with import penetration must there change the *slope* of each of the separate regressions in the right-hand panel.

Galiani and Sanguinetti (2003) find that the interaction terms are indeed significant but not large enough to explain the more than about 16 per cent of the skilled labour premium. This is certainly an interesting result and this methodology could easily be applied in a number of different countries. One important point to mention, however, is that since import penetration does not explain much of the rising skilled-labour premia, something else must. When the unknown effects are fully accounted for then perhaps it will be seen that import penetration suffers from omitted variable bias. Further research would be needed to answer this question definitively.

It should not come as a surprise that trade liberalization leads to an increase in the skilled-labour wage rate relative to the unskilled wage rate. As old sectors contract and new sectors expand, workers with greater mobility, non-specific creative abilities and generally higher levels of education will be in short supply, and even more so than in times of more balanced growth. The wage premium therefore reflects the reality that change requires adaptive talent, and the signal sent to those without that adequate human capital is that all the incentives are pointed in the direction of taking greater advantage of the educational system. Indeed, if skill bias in wage growth did not appear, one could be appropriately sceptical that any change was actually taking place in the economy.

### 3.4.3 Trade, productivity and employment

The previous section conveyed a story of rising demand for labour, but with a lag, as liberalization proceeds. Wage inequality sends a powerful signal that new opportunities for significantly better living standards are present if one takes the proper steps to prepare. This is an optimistic scenario and a reality that not all countries have experienced. The transition to openness might begin with significant import penetration, job loss, but then lack the investment necessary to open new branches of production with an export orientation.

Might it be possible to determine empirically the slope of the implied relationship between employment and productivity? The problems with a project of this nature are legion, however, in that one must deal with simultaneity (the correlation between the independent variable and the error term) as well as the usual problems of data reliability and comparability. Above all, there is the problem of lack of data on productivity and employment. Both have to be manufactured from existing data sources before any attempt at estimation can be made.

A second major estimation problem comes in the weighting of the data. Is it really possible to take one observation of a country the size of China and India along with states a micro-fraction of their size and deduce anything of scientific value? Finally, there is the problem faced by most time-series studies that spurious correlation must be removed by way of co-integration or other techniques. Despite these difficulties, it might be worthwhile to consult some data for an opinion as to the slope of the long-term relationship between trade, productivity and employment.

If trade is intended to promote higher levels of employment, it must do so through the mechanisms discussed above, notably, either that the economy must grow in a balanced fashion with no change in factor prices or, if growth is unbalanced, any subsequent rise in the aggregate labour coefficient should not offset the growth in output. So far, the empirical literature has not spoken with a consistent voice on the relationship between trade policy and employment. As noted, there are severe problems of endogeneity, with employment policy as a determinant of trade policy as much as the other way around.

Indeed, even *openness* itself is difficult to measure. Sachs and Warner's influential index of openness included a range of variables that would seem to be important (Sachs and Warner, 1997). It is a binary variable with a value of zero for a closed economy and one for an open economy. To qualify as closed, the economy must satisfy *only one* of the five following criteria: (1) average tariff rates exceed 40 per cent; (2) non-tariff barriers on more than 40 per cent of imports; (3) an explicitly socialist economic system; (4) a state monopoly on its major export; (5) a black-market premium on the exchange rate that exceeds 20 per cent during either the 1970s or 1980s.

A closed economy is thus defined somewhat subjectively, but this is more than a typical portmanteau regression variable in that economies can qualify as closed in a variety of ways, and introducing them separately may not yield stable *t*-scores due to their high levels of multicollinearity. The Sachs-Warner dummy has a high and robust coefficient when inserted into growth regressions and was subjected to exhaustive sensitivity analysis, including more than 58 potential determinants of growth.

Rodriguez and Rodrik (1999) point out that the variable actually measures *macroeconomic mismanagement*, especially around the real exchange rate, a key measure of competitiveness. This is, of course, broadly consistent with the major message of this chapter: employment, and derivatively, the quality of employment depends not on trade but rather on how well trade is managed. Rodriguez and Rodrik (1999) conclude that the Sachs and Warner indicator serves as a proxy for a wide range of policy and institutional differences and thus it yields an *upwardly biased* estimate of the effects of trade restrictions alone. Edwards (2002), correcting in various ways for heteroskedasticity, substitutes another linear combination, more heavily weighted toward even more subjective conceptions of openness, including an index compiled by the Heritage Foundation. Rodriguez and Rodrik are critical, noting numerous instances of judgment bias in sample selection and lack of counterparty robustness (robust in own but not other studies). They conclude that the relationship between trade and growth enjoys sketchy support at best and, while the econometric literature fails to soundly *reject* the null, it provides a weak foundation for policy advice (Rodrik, 1997).

As noted, a second major problem is simultaneity: in regressions of output per worker and employment, greater productivity can cause higher employment as easily as higher employment causes higher productivity. Recent attempts to solve this problem have instrumented employment by changes in labour taxes since the latter should be unaffected by changes in productivity. Several authors have found a strong *negative* relationship between productivity and employment, Beaudry and Collard (2002), among others.[48]

A casual conversation with the data does not lead to the same conclusion. Since reliable data for world employment are not readily available, a work-around is necessary. One approach is to replace employment with the labour force, a variable widely reported, under the assumption that there is no trend in unemployment rates over time. This proxy certainly reduces the variability of the dependent variable and leads to inflated *t*-statistics as reported below. Whether the resulting upward bias in reported *t*-ratios is sufficient to create a false impression of significance is a judgement left to the reader.

To counteract spurious correlation, the regressions below use time fixed effects as discussed above. Country fixed effects partially compensate for the endogeneity, since what would be a large error associated with a large value of the independent variable $\rho$ is absorbed into the dummy variable or constant term. The results of the regression are presented in table 3.8.

Table 3.8: Dependent variable: Employment

| | Regression | | | |
|---|---|---|---|---|
| | 1 | 2 | 3 | 4 |
| ln ipc | 0.307*** | 0.009 | 0.307*** | 0.285*** |
| | (0.013) | (0.008) | (0.013) | (0.018) |
| Trade | | | | 0.001*** |
| | | | | (0.000) |
| cons | 11.707*** | 14.641*** | 11.707*** | 11.779*** |
| | (0.130) | (0.088) | (0.130) | (0.176) |
| Observations | 4.568 | 4.568 | 4.568 | 3.536 |
| R² | 0.127 | 0.000 | 0.127 | 0.123 |
| R²-adjusted | 0.127 | 0.000 | 0.127 | 0.123 |

Source: Author's calculations based on World Bank (2009).

Standard errors in parentheses. *** p < 0.01, ** p < 0.05, * p < 0.1.

Notes: 1. The dependent variable is the log of the labour force.

2. The variable ln ipc is the log of income per capita.

3. The variable trade is the sum of exports and imports divided by GDP.

---

[48] This work would suggest that protection is the right way to save jobs since protection reduces productivity and therefore increases employment.

In table 3.8, regression 1 includes only *country* fixed effects while regression 2 has only *time* fixed effects. Regression 3 is estimated using two-way fixed effects, that is there as a dummy variable for every year and every country.[49] In both regressions 1 and 3, the coefficient on the measure of productivity (in log form in the equations) is positive and significant. Note that the time-only fixed effects model (regression 2) does not show a significant coefficient on the productivity variable.

The significance and positive sign of the coefficient on the productivity variable continue to hold for regression 4, which uses two-way fixed effects and includes the variable trade to measure openness in the economy (the ratio of the sum of imports and exports to GDP). Including trade in the model reduces slightly the coefficient on the productivity variable but it remains significant at the 1 per cent level. The coefficient on the trade variable itself is also positive and significant.

These simple regressions can only be suggestive, but they lend support to the notion that there is a positive relationship of labour productivity and trade with employment.

---

**Box 3-10: Structuralist and standard CGE models: Not that different after all?**

It was argued above that the full employment assumption underlying much of the research in CGE models seems inappropriate for countries with significant open unemployment and large informal sectors. Most of the standard CGE models assume that savings drives investment and that wages cannot remain in disequilibrium forever, and will eventually have to fall to the point that the labour market will clear. Structuralist models, as was seen above, are based on the reverse relationship, that investment drives savings and, moreover, that the long run is simply a sequence of short-run equilibria.

The difference in views of how the world works may not be as momentous as it first appears. Structuralist models assume that the independent variable of the system, investment, is driven over time by capacity utilization and profitability. Therefore, if trade brings technological change, which in turn causes productivity to rise faster than real wages, profits will have to rise. If it is institutionally possible for investment to increase, then indeed the structuralist model will come to resemble the standard model more closely. In other words, if productivity rises with trade liberalization, and investment rises with productivity, the employment must rise eventually.

The simple regression findings presented in the main text lend support to the notion that there is a positive relationship of labour productivity and trade with employment. This implies that the gulf between the standard and structuralist CGE models might not be as large as it seems.

---

## 3.5 ASSESSING THE EMPLOYMENT IMPACTS OF TRADE: QUALITATIVE METHODS

Qualitative methods in the social sciences start from the premise that the critical factor in understanding the world is *context*. This general point expresses concern about several specific features of quantitative analysis that, taken together, are seen as stripping away the necessary context (Chabal and Daloz, 2006). The first of these foundations of qualitative methods is the view that non-quantitative dimensions of experience and behaviour are ignored in quantitative techniques discussed in section

---

[49] Fixed effects models are voracious consumers of degrees of freedom, but the World Bank's development indicators database has (incomplete) data for a large number of countries back to the 1960s.

3.3 and 3.4 above. In discussions of trade, for example, deeply entrenched and powerful but difficult to measure factors such as gender and other social norms may limit the mobility of labour, retarding the employment response to trade liberalization. Similarly, critics of quantitative methods argue that randomized controlled experiments, as discussed above, are *not* possible. All the factors comprising the history of the agents acting in formal models cannot be captured as explanatory variables: quantitative studies can only give a partial and static snapshot in time.[50] Lacking the contextual detail leaves us with what critics of quantitative methods call "universalist and culture-free approaches to social phenomena" (Hantrais, 1995, p. 1), Therefore, quantitative methods are inherently "thin", only skimming the surface of social reality, whereas "thick" description admits a complex set of phenomena, themselves complexly superimposed and interrelated (Ryle, 1971).

What adds *thickness* to the alleged thinness of quantitative methods varies. The first of the two main positions holds that the most important context is the social nature of science itself as it is embedded in specific historical and cultural contexts. To do social science, this view believes, one must understand the "rhetoric of scientific authority" (Weinberg, 2002, p. 12).[51] A second main strand looks not only at the cultural imperatives of the researcher but also at the detailed histories of the studied population, with an eye toward identifying the multiple realities as seen by various members of the population and assigning meaning to the differences. The point then is to explore and interpret social phenomena for their meaning rather than to search for a covering law to confirm by way of standard hypothesis testing (Geertz, 2000).

Specific qualitative methods derived from these principles include participant observation, direct observation, unstructured interviewing and case studies. The last two are the most relevant for economic analysis and define clearly the difference between qualitative and quantitative methods. Unstructured interviewing is explicitly not based on survey instruments or protocols to be administered uniformly across the sample subjects, for example. Rather, open-ended questions, which can go in any direction the interviewees desire, form the basis of the qualitative study. Its results are not data that can be quantified or made comparable across respondents, but rather field notes that include enough detail, thick description, to account for what the researcher considers the most salient information (Trochim, 2006). Case studies in the same way are *sui generis*, with each case a reality in itself.

A good example of this methodology applied to the impact of trade on employment is a study of the lives of female factory workers in an export processing city in China (Chang, 2008). From interviews with workers, visits to their home villages and information from the author's family history, a complex portrait of the various strands of influence on the lives of factory workers is painted. Ancestral norms and expectations limit first the mobility of the women and then, once they break free of the village and migrate to urban employment, their decisions about acceptable

---

[50] The well-known "Hawthorne effect" eliminates the possibility of randomized controlled trials in context since the context is, by definition, made artificial by the presence of the study.
[51] See also McCloskey (1988).

forms of employment. At the same time, the new norms of the urban environment affect their experience by influencing how they spend their wages, the extent to which they invest in upgrading their skills and whether they maintain their ties to the village, including decisions about remittances. These decisions, in turn, seriously affect the evolution of their home communities in complex and contradictory ways that no formal model could predict.

Case studies of firms also look at the complexity of firm-level responses to trade liberalization. A good example of comparative case studies is D'Costa (2004), which examines the institutional features of automobile firms in India to assess the reasons some succeed and others fail to remain competitive. Consistent with thick description methods, the study incorporates but does not either quantify or attempt to rank formally the importance of a wide variety of institutional influences. These include factors external to the firm, such as cooperation between suppliers and buyers, the location of suppliers, partnership arrangements in the industry and government trade and industrial polices. Internal factors also play important roles, including the degree of worker participation and protection of worker rights, the form of innovation and the scale of operation. The point is that presence or absence of the *set* of institutions and their interaction, as a whole, is implicated in successful response to competition from imports. No one factor or subset is sufficient to capture the complex reality of the requirements for competitiveness. Moreover, what leads one firm to introduce an innovation such as worker participation is directly linked to the cultural history of the area in which the firm operates. Some firms are more tradition-bound than others by virtue of their location and heritage. In the original areas of India's industrial development, for example, firms are far more path dependent than in the call centres of Bangalore. While the narrative of qualitative analysis can capture these subtleties, they are often overlooked in formal models.

Both the strength and the weakness of qualitative methods lie in the degree to which cataloguing the richness and variety of individual experience is the goal of research. Unravelling the intertwined strands of experience to make any assessments of causal links is both difficult conceptually and subjective, based on the judgment of the participants and the researcher. By their nature, such studies cannot be replicated because the precise context cannot be reproduced, as noted above. It is left to the researcher to determine how thick the description must be to "account for the ever-changing context within which research occurs" (Trochim, 2006). An important weakness of qualitative methods is, therefore, that policy-makers are left with no firm ground on which to decide whether a particular case can be generalized as the basis for policy formulation.

## 3.6   CONCLUSIONS

As Jansen and Lee (2007, p. 20) observed, "due to a combination of methodological and data problems, it has been more difficult to provide robust empirical evidence for the relative impact of trade liberalization and other domestic policies on employment changes and economic growth". These authors conclude that the preponderance of studies do seem to show a consistent relationship between trade and growth in income per capita. An outward orientation does seem to be superior to an inward, self-sufficient course of growth. This seems to be the message of the models and literature reviewed in this chapter, but with some substantial caveats.

Given the complexity of the nature of the relationship between trade and employment, it is hardly a surprise to observe that the literature wanders somewhat aimlessly. One of the aims of this chapter has been to provide an overview of existing methods to evaluate the employment effects of trade. The methods discussed in this chapter and their respective characteristics are summarized in appendix table 3.A-2. Another aim of this chapter has been to narrow the field of possible methods to the point that they can converge to a common conclusion. While this chapter privileges no particular methods, several key points emerge as to the proper way to model the relationship between trade and employment:

(1)     An economy-wide model is necessary to study the complex interaction produced in a trading regime. Even the earliest ILO studies recognized this and it remains true today. Partial equilibrium accounts that conclude that the interests of some sectors have been damaged can lead to an anti-trade bias. This is simply because the partial equilibrium approach fails to see how seemingly unrelated sectors might benefit from the same trade policy that is so destructive to the sector in question.

(2)     Calibrated models, even if economy-wide, are not likely to produce good policy if there are inadequate micro-foundations. The reason a solid micro-foundation is necessary is that all policy must ultimately act on people, providing incentives that real-world agents can presumably understand and incorporate into their decisions. Policy directed at aggregate indicators is rarely successful; it must be directed to the people themselves. Many of the models surveyed in this chapter are properly micro-founded.

(3)     The data from econometric models should be used to test theories to the extent possible, but should not be used to build the theories. This will preclude the data from having any self-serving comment on the validity of the theory. What the data seem to show is that trade is important to virtually every country that has experienced large increases in employment. While openness is not sufficient to drive up employment, it does seem to be necessary for poor countries to break out of the cycle of poverty, low levels of human capital and large informal sectors.

(4)     It is important to note that people and not firms suffer adjustment costs. Standard economic theory suggests that policy should follow this logic, that is, direct assistance to individuals should be preferred to bailing out firms or sectors of the economy. This may be a difficult policy recommendation to follow in the real world, despite its pedigree among economists.

## APPPENDIX 3.A: TABLES

Appendix table 3.A-1:

Argentinean employment for 22 industrial sectors for the years 1994, 1996 and 1998.

| Sector | Employment | | | Imports as share of value added | | | | |
|--------|------|------|------|------|------|------|------|------|
| | 1994 | 1996 | 1998 | 1993 | 1994 | 1996 | 1997 | 1998 |
| Food | 100 | 91.1 | 88 | 2.9 | 2.4 | 3.0 | 3.4 | 3.7 |
| Tobacco | 89.9 | 72.5 | 67.2 | 0.1 | 0.1 | 0.1 | 0.2 | 0.2 |
| Textile | 90 | 83 | 81.2 | 13.6 | 11.5 | 15.1 | 16.9 | 18.7 |
| Apparel | 92.1 | 77.9 | 78.9 | 11.9 | 7.7 | 9.9 | 11.0 | 12.1 |
| Leather | 97 | 85.2 | 85.2 | 7.7 | 6.7 | 9.1 | 10.3 | 11.5 |
| Wood | 98.8 | 86.9 | 92.9 | 11.8 | 12.5 | 16.7 | 18.7 | 20.8 |
| Paper | 100.5 | 93.6 | 83.3 | 20.9 | 20.7 | 27.0 | 30.2 | 33.3 |
| Printing | 100.3 | 94.1 | 91.2 | 4.4 | 5.2 | 7.4 | 8.5 | 9.6 |
| Petroleum | 73.3 | 69.1 | 66.8 | 2.9 | 3.2 | 4.1 | 4.5 | 4.9 |
| Chemical | 97.4 | 94.6 | 93.4 | 25.3 | 29.9 | 36.4 | 39.6 | 42.8 |
| Rubber | 96 | 97.9 | 102.5 | 18.1 | 17.9 | 24.0 | 27.1 | 30.1 |
| Mineral | 95 | 84 | 83.9 | 7.3 | 7.3 | 9.2 | 10.2 | 11.2 |
| Basic metal | 96.3 | 93 | 93 | 15 | 15.4 | 19.6 | 21.6 | 23.7 |
| Metal products | 97 | 86.4 | 98.8 | 11.5 | 14.3 | 19.7 | 22.4 | 25.1 |
| Machinery | 95.9 | 89.2 | 90 | 60.5 | 55.5 | 72.6 | 81.1 | 89.7 |
| Computer | 97 | 92 | 76.3 | 308.5 | 259.1 | 324.9 | 357.8 | 390.7 |
| Engines elect | 94.9 | 82.2 | 84.6 | 44.2 | 43.4 | 56.9 | 63.7 | 70.5 |
| Audio | 89.1 | 64.8 | 66.2 | 83.7 | 71.8 | 89.8 | 98.8 | 107.7 |
| Instruments | 94.6 | 89 | 85.3 | 100.4 | 100.6 | 129.9 | 144.5 | 159.2 |
| Motor veh. | 103.5 | 85.8 | 91 | 28 | 27.4 | 36.8 | 41.6 | 46.3 |
| Transport | 87 | 73 | 83.3 | 99.4 | 97.8 | 140.5 | 161.8 | 183.2 |
| Furniture | 93.9 | 80.4 | 87 | 29 | 25.7 | 32.6 | 36.1 | 39.5 |

Source: Galiani and Sanguinetti (2003).

# APPPENDIX 3.A: TABLES

Appendix table 3.A-2: Methods matrix

| Model | Factor-content substitution | Partial equilibrium | Input-output LP | General equilibrium | Structural CGEs | Agent based | Econometric models | Social assessment | Qualitative approach |
|---|---|---|---|---|---|---|---|---|---|
| Description | Distinguishes L-K intensive processes | Single market equilibrium | Multi-market Supply-side | Multi-market Supply-Demand | Multi-market with structural constraints | Multi-market with structural constraints | Ex-post testing of existing theory | Survey methods with qualitative assessment | Case study anecdotal |
| Strengths | Consistency with first principles | Can be adapted to country-specific constraints | Compute direct plus indirect labour equirements | Full integration of demand side data | Realistic: calibrated to time series | Heterogenous agents bounded rationality | Inferential hypothesis testing possible | Additional detail captured | Highly detailed |
| Weaknesses | Ignores stylized facts | Good for small sectors only | Linear; good for small changes only; aggregated can only see sectors >1% of GDP | Comparative static exercises Dynamic results often unrealistic. For sectors >1% of GDP | Rigid | Emergent properties difficult to discern | Ambiguous causality due to OVB and simultaneity | Difficult to generalize | Highly difficult to generalize |
| Internal validity | High | High | Medium | High | Medium | Very high | Variable | Variable | Variable |
| External validity | Low | High | Medium | Low-medium | Medium-high | Low-medium | Variable | Medium-high | Low |
| Data requirement | Low | Low | Medium | Very high | Very high | High | Medium-high | Very high | Medium-high |
| | Low | Medium | Medium | High | High | High | Medium | High | High |

# APPPENDIX 3.A: TABLES

Appendix table 3.A-2: Methods matrix *(Continued)*

| Model | Factor-content substitution | Partial equilibrium | Input-output LP | General equilibrium | Structural CGEs | Agent based | Econometric models | Social assessment | Qualitative approach |
|---|---|---|---|---|---|---|---|---|---|
| Complexity | Staff requirement: 1 person | Staff requirement: 1-2 persons | Small team for gathering date; requirements low | Specialized professional staff needed; requires SAM, data-processing requirements hig | Specialized professional staff needed; requires SAM, data-processing requirements hig | Professional programmers required; multiple data sources | Small staff needed; requires professional analyst | Large staff of interviewers required; data-processing requirement higt | Small staff interviewers or individual |
| Programming | Excel, MatLab, Mathematica | Excel, MatLab Mathematica | Excel, Java, C or LINDO | GAMS, GTAP, Proprietary (MIRAGE) | GAMS, GTAP, DADS | Excel, Java, C or NetLogo | Stata, SPSS SAS | Excel | None |
| Policy relevance | Medium | Medium | High | Medium | Medium-high | Medium | High | Low-medium | |
| Labour market | Low | High | Medium/High | High | Rigid labour markets; fixed wages | Very high | High | High | |
| Main conclusions | HOS, Stolper-Samuelson | Biased against trade; overstates employment loss | Trade less damaging to employment | Trade effects small | Trade effects larger | Trade effects variable | Trade effects variable | Trade effects variable | |

## APPPENDIX 3.B

Model specification used for simple CGE simulation

The equations of the model used for the simulations in section 3.4.2 are first the consumption function (an LES) with $Y_j$ as household income for the $j$th income category

$$C_{ij} = C_{ij}(Y_{dj})$$

where $Y_{dj}$ is disposable income. The material balance is

$$X_i = \sum_{j=1} A_{ij} + C_{ij} + I_i + G_i + E_i$$

where government expenditure, $G_i$, and net exports, $E_i$, are taken from the base SAM and grow at an exogenous rate in the non-agricultural sector. For the agricultural sector, exports are determined as a residual from this same equation with

$$X_1 = Q(K_1 L_1)$$

where the production function is Cobb-Douglas. Investment, $I_i$, by destination is given by

$$I_i / K_i = I + \alpha_\mu u_2 + \alpha_r r$$

where $u_2 = X / Q_2$ and $r$ is the rate of profit. Household income is given by the value added in production plus domestic and foreign transfers.

# REFERENCES

Abraham, F.; Brock, E. 2003. "Sectoral employment effects of trade and productivity in Europe", in *Applied Economics*, Vol. 35, No. 2, pp. 223-235, Jan.

Ackerman, F.; Gallagher, K.P. 2002. "The shrinking gains from global trade liberalization in computable general equilibrium models: A critical assessment", in *International Journal of Political Economy*, Vol. 37, No. 1, pp. 50-77, Apr.

Anderson, K.; Dimaranan, B.; Francois, J.; Hertel, T.; Hoeckman, B.; Martin, W. 2003. "The cost of rich (and poor) country protection to developing countries", in *Journal of African Economies*, Vol. 10, No. 3, pp. 227-257.

Anderson, K.; Martin, W.; van der Mensbrugghe, D. 2005. "Agricultural trade reform and the Doha development agenda", in *Market and welfare implications of the Doha reform scenarios* (World Bank).

ATPC. 2005. *The economic and welfare impacts of the EU-Africa economic partnership agreements*, Briefing 6 (African Trade Policy Centre, Economic Commission for Africa).

Baldwin, R.E. 1994. "The effect of trade and foreign direct investment on employment and relative wages", in *OECD Economic Studies*, Vol. 23, pp. 7-54.

Bchir, H.; Decreux, Y.; Guérin, J-L.; Jean, S. 2002. "MIRAGE, a computable general equilibrium model for trade policy analysis", *CEPII Working Paper* No. 2002-17.

Beaudry, P.; Collard, F. 2002. "Why has the employment-productivity tradeoff among industrialized countries been so strong", *NBER Technical Report* No. W8754.

Behrman, J.R. 1983. "Country and sectoral variations in manufacturing elasticities of substitution between capital and labor", in O.E. Krueger (ed.): *Trade and employment in developing countries, Vol. 2: Factor supply and substitution* (NBER).

Bernard, A.B.; Jensen, J.B. 1995. "Exporters, jobs, and wages in U.S. manufacturing: 1976-1987", in *Brookings Papers on Economic Activity*, Vol. 1995.

Brown, D.K.; Deardorff, A.V.; Stern, R.M. 1995. "Expanding NAFTA: Economic effects of accession of Chile and other major South American nations", in *The North American Journal of Economics and Finance*, Vol. 6, No. 2, pp. 149-170.

Brown, D.K.; Deardorff, A.V.; Stern, R.M. 2003. "Multilateral, regional and bilateral trade-policy options for the United States and Japan", in *The World Economy*, Vol. 26, No. 6, pp. 803-828, June.

Chabal, P.; Daloz, J-P. 2006. *Culture troubles: Politics and the interpretation of meaning* (University of Chicago Press).

Chamley, C.P. 2004. *Rational herds: Economic models of social learning* (Cambridge University Press).

Chang, L.T. 2008. *Factory girls: From village to city in a changing China* (Spiegel & Grau).

Clerides, S.K.; Lach, S.; Tybout, J.R. 1998. "Is 'learning by exporting' important? Micro-dynamic evidence from Colombia, Mexico and Morocco", in *Quarterly Journal of Economics*, Vol. 113, No. 3, pp. 903-960, Aug.

Cline, W. 2004. *Trade policy and global poverty* (Institute for International Economics).

Cortes, O.; Jean, S. 1999. "Does competition from emerging countries threaten unskilled labour in Europe? An applied computable general equilibrium approach", in P. Brenton; L. Pelkmann (eds): *Global Trade and European Workers* (Macmillan), pp. 96-122.

Currie, J.; Harrison, A.E. 1997. "Sharing the costs: The impact of trade reform on capital and labor in Morocco", in *Journal of Labor Economics*, Vol. 15, No. 3, pp. S44-S71, July.

Davidson, C.; Matusz, S.J. 2004. *International trade and labor markets: Theory, evidence, and policy implications* (Upjohn Institute for Employment Research).

Davidson, C.; Matusz, S.J. 2010. *International trade with equilibrium unemployment* (Princeton University Press).

D'Costa, A.P. 2004. "Flexible practices for mass production goals: Economic governance in the Indian automobile industry", in *Industrial and Corporate Change*, Vol. 13, No. 2, pp. 335-367, Apr.

Deardorff, A.V.; Stern, R.M. 1986. *The Michigan model of world production and trade: Theory and applications* (MIT Press).

Deaton, A. 1995. Data and econometric tools for development analysis", in H. Chenery; T.N. Srinivasan (eds): *Handbook of development economics (Vol. 3A)*, Ch. 33 (Elsevier).

Decaluwe, B.; Martens A. 1988. "CGE modeling and developing economies: A concise empirical survey of 73 applications to 26 countries", in *Journal of Policy Modeling*, Vol. 10, No. 4, pp. 529-568.

Dervis, K.; de Melo, J.D.; Robinson, S. 1982. *General equilibrium models for development planning* (Cambridge University Press).

Dew-Becker, I.L.; Gordon, R.J. 2005. Where did the productivity growth go? Inflation dynamics and the distribution of income", *NBER Working Paper* No. 11842.

Dewatripont, M.; Michel, G. 1987. "On closure rules: Homogeneity and dynamics in applied general equilibrium models", in *Journal of Development Economics*, Vol. 26, No. 1, pp. 65-76.

Dorfman, R.; Samuelson, P.A.; Solow, R.M. 1958. *Linear programming and economic analysis* (McGraw-Hill).

Duflo, E.; Glennerster, R.; Kremer, M. 2007. "Using randomization in development economics research: A toolkit", *CEPR Discussion Paper* No. 6059.

Edwards, S. 2002. "Openness, trade liberalization, and growth in developing countries", in International Library of Critical Writings in Economics, Vol. 140, No. 3, pp. 78-116.

Edwards, S.; Edwards, A.C. 1996. "Trade liberalization and unemployment: Policy issues and evidence from Chile", in *Cuadernos de Economia*, Vol. 33, No. 99, pp. 227-250.

Epstein, J.M. 2006. *Generative social science: Studies in agent-based computational model* (Princeton University Press).

Feenstra, R.C.; Hanson, G.H. 1997. "Foreign direct investment and relative wages: Evidence from Mexico's maquiladoras", in *Journal of International Economics*, Vol. 42, No. 3-4, pp. 371-393, May.

Francois, J.; van Meijl, H.; van Tongeren, F. 2003. "Trade liberalization and developing countries under the Doha round", *CEPR Discussion Paper* No. 4032.

Freeman, R.B.; Katz, L.F. 1991. "Industrial wage and employment determination in an open economy", in J.M. Abowd; R. Freeman (eds): *Immigration, trade and the labor market* (University of Chicago Press).

Galiani, S.; Sanguinetti, P. 2003. "The impact of trade liberalization on wage inequality: Evidence from Argentina", *Working Paper* No. 011 (Department of Economics, Universidad Torcuato Di Tella).

Geertz, C. 2000. *Thick description: The interpretation of cultures: Selected essays* (Basic Books).

Gibson, B. 2003. "An essay on late structuralism", in A. Dutt; J. Ros (eds): *Development economics and structuralist macroeconomics: Essays in honor of Lance Taylor*, Ch. 2, pp. 52-76 (Edward Elgar).

Gibson, B. 2005. "The transition to a globalized economy: Poverty, human capital and the informal sector in a structuralist CGE model", in *Journal of Development Economics*, Vol. 78, No. 1, pp. 60-94, Oct.

Gibson, B. 2008a. "Economic planning in developing economies", in A. Dutt; J. Ros (eds): *International Handbook of Development Economics (Vol. 2)*, Ch. 57, pp. 341-355 (Edward Elgar).

Gibson, B. 2008b. "Data Problems and Empirical Modeling in Developing Economies", in A. Dutt,; J. Ros (eds): *International Handbook of Development Economics*, pp. 83-96 (Edward Elgar).

Gibson, B. 2009. *Trade and employment* (University of Vermont). Available at: http://www.uvm.edu/~wgibson/ (accessed 9 June 2011).

Gibson, B.; Kelley, B. 1994. "A classical theory of the informal sector", in *The Manchester School*, Vol. 62, No. 1, pp. 81-96, Mar.

Gibson, B.; van Seventer, D.E. 2000. "A tale of two models: Comparing structuralist and neo-classical computable general equilibrium models for South Africa", in *International Review of Applied Economics*, Vol. 14, No. 2, pp. 149-171, May.

Ginsburgh, V.; Keyzer, M. 1997. *The structure of applied general equilibrium models* (MIT Press).

Greenaway, D., Hine, R.C.; Wright, P. 1999. "An empirical assessment of the impact of trade on employment in the United Kingdom", in *European Journal of Political Economy*, Vol. 15, No. 3, pp. 485-500, Sep.

Greenspan, A. 2007. *The age of turbulence* (Penguin Press).

Gruben, W.; McLeod, D. 2002. *Choosing among rival poverty rates*. Available at: http://dallasfed.org/research/claepapers/2003/lawp0301.pdf (accessed 9 June 2011).

Guichard, S.; Laffargue, J-P. 2000. "The wage curve: The lessons of an estimation over a panel of countries", *CEPII Working Paper* No. 2000-21.

Hammouda, H.B.; Osakwe, P.N. 2006. "Global trade models and economic policy analyses: Relevance, risks, and repercussions for Africa", *ATPC Work in Progress* No. 47.

Hantrais, L. 1995. "Comparative research methods", *Social Research Update* No. 13 (University of Surrey).

Harrison, A.E.; Hanson, G.H. 1999. "Who gains from trade reform? Some remaining puzzles", *NBER Working Paper* No. 6915.

Hertel, T.W. 1997. *Global trade analysis: Modeling and applications* (Cambridge University Press).

Hertel, T.W.; Keeney, R. 2005. "What's at stake? The relative importance of import barriers, export subsidies and domestic support", chapter in *Agricultural trade reform and the Doha development agenda* (World Bank).

Hertel, T.W.; Winters, L.A. 2006. *Poverty and the WTO: Impacts of the Doha development agenda* (Palgrave Macmillan and World Bank).

Hoekman, B.; Winters, L.A. 2005. *Trade and employment: Stylized facts and research findings* (World Bank).

Hufbauer, G.C.; Elliott, K.A.1994. *Measuring the costs of protection in the United States* (Peterson Institute for International Economics).

Jansen, M.; Lee, E. 2007. *Trade and employment: Challenges for policy research* (ILO).

Kennedy, P.E. 1998. *A guide to econometrics* (MIT Press).

Keynes, J.M. 1936. *The general theory of employment, interest and money* (Palgrave Macmillan).

Krueger, A.O. 1983. *Trade and employment in developing countries, Volume 3: Synthesis and conclusions* (University of Chicago Press).

Kucera, D.; Roncolato, L.; Von Uexkull, E. 2010. Trade contraction in the global crisis: Employment and inequality effects in India and South Africa, in *ILO Employment Sector Working Paper* No. 54

Kurzweil, M. 2002. "The need for a 'complete' labor market in CGE modeling", in *Landbauforschung Völkenrode*, Vol. 52, No. 2, pp. 107-119.

Lopez-Calva, L.F.; Lustig, N.C. 2010. *Declining inequality in Latin America: A decade of progress?* (Brookings Institution Press and UNDP).

Lydall, H.F. 1975. *Trade and employment: A study of the effects of trade expansion on employment in developing and developed countries* (ILO).

Matusz, S.J.; Tarr, D. 1999. "Adjusting to trade policy reform", *World Bank Policy Research Paper* No. 2142.

McCloskey, D.N. 1988. "Thick and thin: Methodologies in the history of economic thought", chapter in *The Popperian legacy in economics* (Cambridge University Press).

van der Mensbrugghe, D. 2007. *Modeling the impact of trade liberalization: A structuralist perspective?* (World Bank).

OECD. 2003. *The Doha development agenda: Welfare gains from further multilateral trade liberalization with respect to tariffs.*

Piermartini, R.; Teh, R. 2005. "Demystifying modelling methods for trade policy", *WTO Discussion Paper* No. 10.

Polaski, S. 2006. *Winners and losers: Impact of the Doha round on developing countries* (Carnegie Endowment for International Peace).

Revenga, A.L. 1992. "Exporting jobs? The impact of import competition on employment and wages in U.S. manufacturing", in *Quarterly Journal of Economics*, Vol. 107, No. 1, pp. 255-284, Feb.

Rodriguez, F.; Rodrik, D. 1999. "Trade policy and economic growth: A sceptic's guide to the cross-national evidence", *CEPR Discussion Paper* No. 2143.

Rodrik, D. 1997. *Has Globalization Gone too Far?* (Peterson Institute for International Economics).

Romer, P.M. 1986. "Increasing returns and long run growth", in *Journal of Political Economy*, Vol. 94, No. 5, pp. 1002-1037, Oct.

Romer, P.M. 1990. "Endogenous technological change", in *Journal of Political Economy*, Vol. 98, No. 5, pp. S71-S101, Oct.

Ryle, G. 1971. *The thinking of thoughts: What is 'le Penseur' thinking?* (Hutchinson).

Sachs, J.D.; Warner, A.M. 1997. "Fundamental sources of long-run growth", in *American Economic Review*, Vol. 87, No. 2, pp. 184-188, May.

Sadoulet, E.; de Janvry, A. 1992. "Agricultural trade liberalization and low income countries: A general equilibrium-multimarket approach", in *American Journal of Agricultural Economics*, Vol. 74, No. 2, pp. 268-280, May.

Sadoulet, E.; de Janvry, A. 1995. *Quantitative Development Policy* (Johns Hopkins University Press).

Samuelson, P.A. 2004. "Where Ricardo and Mill rebut and confirm arguments of mainstream economists supporting globalization", in *Journal of Economic Perspectives*, Vol. 18, No. 3, pp. 135-146.

Shapiro, C.; Stiglitz, J.E. 1984. "Equilibrium unemployment as a worker discipline device", in *American Economic Review*, Vol. 74, No. 3, pp. 433-444.

Slaughter, M.J. 2001. "International trade and labor-demand elasticities", in *Journal of International Economics*, Vol. 54, No. 1, pp. 27-56.

Solow, R.M. 1956. "A contribution to the theory of economic growth", in *The Quarterly Journal of Economics*, Vol. 70, No. 1, pp. 65-94, Feb.

Srinivasan, T.N. 1994. "Data base for development analysis: An overview", in *Journal of Development Economics*, Vol. 44, No. 1, pp. 3-27, June.

Taylor, L. 1979. "Macro models for developing countries", *Economic Handbook Series* (McGraw-Hill).

Taylor, L. 1990. *Socially relevant policy analysis: Structuralist computable general equilibrium models for the developing world* (MIT Press).

Taylor, L.; von Arnim, R. 2006. *Modelling the impact of trade liberalisation: A critique of computable general equilibrium models* (Oxfam International Research Report).

Thierfelder, K.; Shiells, C. 1997. "Trade and labor market behavior", chapter in J.F. Francois; K.A. Reinert (eds): *Applied methods for trade policy analysis: A handbook* (Cambridge University Press).

Trochim, W.M. 2006. *Qualitative research methods* (Web Center for Social Research Methods).

Weinberg, D. 2002. *Qualitative research methods* (Blackwell Publishers).

Winchester, N. 2008a. "Trade and rising wage inequality: What can we learn from a decade of computable equilibrium analysis?", chapter in *Globalisation and labour market adjustment* (Palgrave MacMillan).

Winchester, N. 2008b. "Searching for the smoking gun: Did trade hurt unskilled workers?", in *Economic Record*, Vol. 84, No. 256, pp. 141-156, June.

Wood, A. 1997. "Openness and wage inequality in developing countries: The Latin American challenge to East Asian conventional wisdom", in *World Bank Economic Review*, Vol. 11, No. 1, pp. 33-58, Jan.

World Bank. 2009. *World Development Indicators 2009* (Washington, DC).

# TRADE AND THE INFORMAL ECONOMY

# 4

*By Anushree Sinha[1]*

## 4.1   INTRODUCTION

It was generally understood during the 1960s and 1970s that, with economic growth, the informal economy would shrink. But despite strong global growth that coincided with a massive increase in international trade, many jobs in developing countries remain in the informal economy. The share of employment in the informal economy has been persistent in many developing countries over recent decades and even increased in some regions. On average, 60 per cent of employment in developing countries is in the informal sector. Research findings from the 1990s and 2000s indicate that globalization and trade reforms have shown a tendency to encourage precarious forms of work. In contrast to developed countries' experiences, the formal sector in developing countries has not been able to absorb informal workers and production processes as expected. In fact, many studies suggest that globalization and trade reforms lead to competition in the formal sector, which may result in a reduction in formal employment, at least in the short run. Today's global value chains combine various modes of production, such as traditional, semi-industrial and fully industrial production mechanisms. The downside of such a system is that processes can be outsourced into the informal sector and larger firms tend to capture a major part of capital, leaving little for informal enterprises, which generally continue to remain small scale and less productive. Moreover, workers in the informal economy are

[1] I am grateful for the comments received at the Expert meeting on Assessing and Addressing the Effects of Trade on Employment held at the ILO, Geneva, in December 2009; especially from Marco Fugazza and Henrik Huitfeldt. Thanks are also due to the anonymous reviewers who provided valuable comments on the chapter. I am also thankful to Susmita Dasgupta for her editorial support and input. Finally, I would like to acknowledge Sadhana Singh for providing technical support in writing this chapter.

generally not covered by social protection mechanisms and have a high incidence of poverty.

The informal economy, though, has provided employment opportunities for both the newly unemployed and certain informal workers who have little opportunity to enter the formal workforce without planned interventions. The high proportion of employment in the informal economy in developing countries was, by the late 1990s, recognized as being of enormous importance (Meagher and Yunusa, 1996; Ranis and Stewart, 1997; Sinha, 1999). Given the considerable influence exerted by the informal economy, it is important to study how it interacts with other economic variables. In fact, for more than two decades, scholars and policy-makers have paid increasing attention to the informal economy as they grapple with the challenges faced by many developing countries. Moreover, new understanding of the informal economy has surfaced. In earlier discussions, the informal economy was often viewed as an underground economy or illegal sector that was detrimental to healthy growth, and squeezed out resources from formal and legal activities. However, this perception began to change because of a series of studies, led by de Soto (1989). De Soto argued that policies and certain circumstances prevented people in the informal economy from improving their own lives through entrepreneurial endeavours. They could, if not constrained, make an important contribution to economic and social progress. De Soto's book on Peru's informal economy opened up discussions about informal economies around the world.

With global trade reaching 60 per cent of the world's gross domestic product (GDP), and trade liberalization continuing across the globe, it is important to review the impact of trade and trade liberalization on employment, wages and welfare in the informal economy. Studies conducted since the late 1990s have indicated that, contrary to classical trade theories, trade liberalization does not necessarily lead to rising welfare of unskilled labour. In fact, opening economies up to trade may instead lead to informalization of work, increased wage differentials across formal and informal manufacturing and market segmentation, rather than a greater degree of economic integration. Stallings and Peres (2000), Sinha and Adam (2000), Carr and Chen (2002), Harriss-White (2003), Sinha et al. (2003, 2007), and others have described the rapid expansion of informal economies, which contradicts assumptions of neoclassical economic theories of international trade.

This chapter surveys various theoretical and empirical studies to examine the link between trade and informality, and attempts to identify the specific contexts where they are positively or inversely related. In addition, the study provides guidance on how to develop a model to assess the impact of trade on informality. Examples of data sources from four countries are provided (Bangladesh, Benin, Guatemala and Indonesia). Such a model can help policy-makers and social partners develop a sound understanding of the impact of trade and labour market policies on the informal economy. When combined with background information on their linkages, such a model could constitute a global knowledge tool on trade and informality.

The rest of this chapter is organized as follows. Section 4.2 discusses the definition of the informal economy that has evolved over time. Section 4.3 briefly provides some stylized facts about the informal economy, and identifies the theoretical links between trade and informality. Qualitative and quantitative approaches to assess the impact of trade on informality are shown in section 4.4, where case studies, empirical studies and general equilibrium models are discussed. Policy recommendations are provided in section 4.5, and section 4.6 concludes.

## 4.2    THE CONCEPT OF THE INFORMAL ECONOMY

Different characterizations of informality have been used during recent decades – shifting the focus away from economic units toward workers – and increasingly heterogeneous phenomena have emerged.

Hugon (1990) is often an accepted starting point for the conceptualization of the informal economy. Hugon characterized the informal sector as a production process that uses a specific type of technology that is not capital intensive, produces different kinds of goods, and accesses different types of markets. The *Fifteenth International Conference of Labour Statisticians* (ILO, 1993) defined the informal sector as follows:

(1)    The informal sector may be broadly characterized as consisting of units engaged in the production of goods or services with the primary objective of generating employment and incomes to the persons concerned. These units typically operate at a low level of organization, with little or no division between labour and capital as factors of production and on a small scale. Labour relations – where they exist – are based mostly on casual employment, kinship or personal and social relations rather than contractual arrangements with formal guarantees.

(2)    Production units of the informal sector have the characteristic features of household enterprises. The fixed and other assets used do not belong to the production units as such but to their owners. The units as such cannot engage in transactions or enter into contracts with other units, nor incur liabilities, on their own behalf. The owners have to raise the necessary finance at their own risk and are personally liable, without limit, for any debts or obligations incurred in the production process. Expenditure for production is often indistinguishable from household expenditure. Similarly, capital goods such as buildings or vehicles may be used indistinguishably for business and household purposes.

(3)    Activities performed by production units of the informal sector are not necessarily performed with the deliberate intention of evading the payment of taxes or social security contributions, or infringing labour or other legislations or administrative provisions. Accordingly, the concept of informal sector activities should be distinguished from the concept of activities of the hidden or underground economy.

127

Table 4.1: The informal (sub)sector within the sector concept

| Corporations sector | Household sector | | | |
|---|---|---|---|---|
| | | **Informal sector** | | |
| Quasi-corporate household enterprises | Unincorporated enterprises owned by households, engaged in *farming* | Unincorporated enterprises owned by households, engaged in *non-farm* production with *fixed* location | Unincorporated enterprises owned by households, engaged in *non-farm* production with *non-fixed* location | Illegal activities |

Source: Advisory Expert Group on National Accounts, SNA/M2.04/12; New York, 8-16 December 2004.

Hussmanns (2004), in turn, defined employment in the informal sector as including all jobs in the informal sector enterprises or all persons who, during a given reference period, were employed in at least one informal sector enterprise, irrespective of their status in employment and whether it was their main job. Illegal activities, however, are not part of the informal sector definition.

The broader concept of an informal economy as a composite of production-unit and labour-process aspects of informality has been recognized and defined by the ILO Task Force (ILO, 2002a) and in Sinha (1999) and Sinha and Adam (2000), in contrast to earlier studies, which indentified only production units. The "informal economy" captures employment relations as well as enterprise relations. The concept of "informal employment" refers to the production unit and the characteristics of the job or worker.

---

**Box 4-1: The ILO framework of informality**

The 2002 ILO International Labour Conference Resolution concerning decent work and the informal economy provided a framework rather than a specific definition. The term "informal economy" refers to "all economic activities by workers and economic units that are – in law or in practice – not covered or insufficiently covered by formal arrangements. Their activities are not included in the law, which means that they are operating outside the formal reach of the law; or they are not covered in practice, which means that – although they are operating within the formal reach of the law, the law is not applied or not enforced; or the law discourages compliance because it is inappropriate, burdensome, or imposes excessive costs". (ILO, 2002b)

The term "informal employment", as used by the ILO Task Force (ILO, 2002a), defines employment that has no secure contracts, worker benefits or social protection. So the major components of such employment are: (a) self-employment in the informal economy; and (b) paid employment in informal occupations. The latter could also be in the formal sector. Thus, it includes casual and precarious work within the formal economy.

More precisely, at the Seventeenth International Conference of Labour Statisticians (ICLS), it was agreed that informal employment comprises the following types of jobs (ILO, 2003):

- Own-account workers who have their own informal sector enterprises and no employees (cell 3 in table 4.2).

- Employers with employees who have their own informal sector enterprises (cell 4) (the informal nature of their jobs follows directly from the characteristics of the enterprise).

- Contributing family workers, irrespective of whether they work in formal or informal sector enterprises (cells 1 and 5).

- Employees who have informal jobs, whether employed by formal sector enterprises, informal sector enterprises, or as paid domestic workers by households (cells 2, 6 and 10) (employment relationship is not subject to standard labour legislation, taxation, social protection or entitlement to certain employment benefits).

- Employees, who hire more than six to nine workers are generally considered formal (cell 7).

- Members of informal producers' cooperatives (cell 8) (not established as legal entities).

- Persons engaged in the own-account production of goods exclusively for own final use by their household (cell 9).

The three aspects of informal economy defined by the 15th ICLS (as noted above) are useful for analysing informality, both as traditionally defined (based on what might be called the "production unit view" (see table 4.1) that focused on the type of production unit (rows)) and according to the newer focus (defined according to the "social protection" or "legalistic" view by job status). Informal sector enterprises are defined as production units operated by single individuals or households that are not constituted as separate legal entities independent of their owners and in which capital accumulation and productivity are low. This includes "family units" (those operated by non-professional own-account workers with or without contributing family workers) and "micro-enterprises" (productive units with no more than five employees). Furthermore, taking the 17th ICLS on board, table 4.1 shows that total employment in the informal sector includes the self-employed,

Table 4.2: ILO conceptual framework: Informal employment

| Production unit by type | Job by status in employment | | | | | | | | |
|---|---|---|---|---|---|---|---|---|---|
| | Own-account workers | | Employers | | Contributing family workers | Employees | | Members of producers' cooperatives | |
| | Informal | Formal | Formal | Informal | Informal | Formal | Informal | Formal | Informal |
| Formal sector enterprises | | | | | 1 | 2 | | | |
| Informal sector enterprises[a] | 3 | | 4 | | 5 | 6 | 7 | 8 | |
| Households[b] | 9 | | | | | 10 | | | |

Source: Hussmanns, 2004.

Note: Cells shaded in dark blue refer to jobs that, by definition, do not exist in the type of production unit in question. Cells shaded in light blue refer to formal jobs. Unshaded cells represent the various types of informal jobs.

Informal employment: cells 1-6 and 8-10. Employment in the informal sector: cells 3-8.

Informal employment outside the informal sector: cells 1, 2, 9 and 10.

[a] As defined by the Fifteenth International Conference of Labour Statisticians 1993 (excluding households employing paid domestic workers).

[b] Households producing goods exclusively for their own final use and households employing paid domestic workers.

own-account workers, with or without family workers, micro-entrepreneurs and their employees. The more recent shift to a "legal" definition of informality recognizes that "informal employment" can be found both within and outside the small-firm sector. Consequently, informal employment now also includes informal contractual arrangements in firms that are otherwise formal (cells 1 and 2 in table 4.2). In this chapter, we follow the ILO concept of informality where both definitions, i.e. definition by activities (economic units/enterprises) and definition by employment categories are considered (15th and 17th ICLS).

It is important to get meaningful data on the informal economy for making effective economic policy decisions. This economy mainly develops due to tax evasion tactics carried out by enterprises and employers. The informal economy discussed so far is one where the concern is in understanding the status of workers, or small firms who are not in the position to pay any direct taxes whatsoever. However, they could be hired by informal enterprises or firms who are in a position to pay taxes, but are evading making such payment. Feinstein (1999) attempts to close the gap between research on tax evasion and the shadow economy. In a study to relate tax rates and the shadow economy, Schneider and Neck (1993) investigate why such tax evasion occurs by examining how a tax structure can affect the size of the shadow economy. The authors argue that a more complex income tax regime leads to higher rates of tax avoidance than a simpler one. On the other hand, other studies (for example, Johnson et al., 1998a, 1998b) argue that it is government regulations and the ineffective and discretionary application of taxation, rather than high tax rates per se, that lead to expansion of the shadow economy. Loayza (1996) states that when the statutory tax burden is larger than optimal, and when it is weakly enforced, there is an increase in the relative size of the informal economy. This restricts economic growth, since resources are diverted toward an unofficial and unaccounted economy. Loayza further shows empirically that, in Latin American countries, when the shadow economy increases by 1 percentage point of GDP – everything else remaining the same – the official GDP declines by 1.2 percentage points. Naturally, when the shadow (illegal) economy has such an adverse impact, the informal sector is considered a negative phenomenon. The effects of the shadow economy on economic growth remain a matter of concern. It is, however, important to distinguish between the informal economy (which is informal due to lack of resources) and the shadow economy, which is sometimes considered "informal" but where the driving factor is that of hiding resources from the authorities. Thus, various studies have shown that over-regulation and labour costs (such as the level of minimum wages) in the official labour market are driving forces for the shadow economy. However, most studies consider only one particular factor, the tax burden, as a cause of the shadow economy. The shadow economy has a strong adverse influence on the allocation of resources and causes loss of revenue for the State. What is even more important is the negative impact that the shadow economy has on official institutions, norms and rules of the State (Schneider and Enste, 2000).

## 4.3   THE INFORMAL ECONOMY AND THE RELATIONSHIP BETWEEN TRADE AND INFORMALITY

### 4.3.1  The informal economy

In developing countries, the informal economy plays an important role in income generation and employment creation, with the majority of the workforce – over 60 per cent – located in the informal economy. Figure 4.1 shows that, on average, the share of informal employment has remained high in Africa, Asia and Latin America, with Asia leading in informal worker share. Although detailed statistics about the informal economy remain fragmented in many countries, existing data reveal that informal employment is a persistent feature in developing countries.

Although figure 4.1 provides a compelling overview, it is also important to compare data from individual countries within the three regions. Figure 4.2 shows that Paraguay has a very large share of informal workers: 74 per cent compared to 32 per cent for Chile. Similarly, Africa has a wide variation between countries. In Asia, India shows the highest share in the region, at 93 per cent.

Figure 4.1: Informality around the world (relative to total employment, per cent)

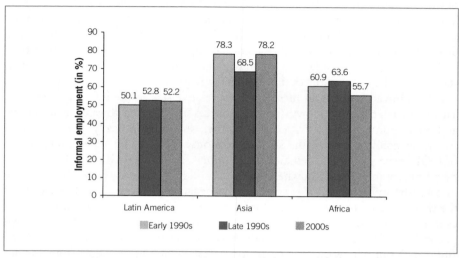

Note: Latin America: Argentina, Chile, Colombia, Costa Rica, Ecuador, Mexico, Panama, Uruguay and Venezuela; Asia: China, India, Indonesia, Pakistan, Sri Lanka and Thailand; Africa: Botswana, Cameroon, Egypt, Ethiopia, Ghana, Kenya, Malawi, South Africa, United Republic of Tanzania, Zambia and Zimbabwe. Source: IILS estimates based on the IILS Informality Database.

Figure 4.2: Within-region variation of informality rates (relative to total employment, percentage)

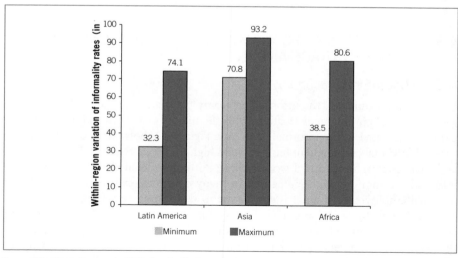

Source: IILS estimates based on the IILS Informality Database.

The informal economy has traditionally been viewed to be the last resort for workers who cannot find a job in the formal economy and who need to engage in small economic activities to earn a living. The informal economy is diverse, reaching from home-based producers, casual wage workers and own-account workers to informal employers. On average, workers in the informal economy earn less and have less job security compared to their counterparts in the formal economy. Both capital intensity and productivity are considerably lower than in the formal sector. Women tend to be more likely to be informal workers than men, and the probability of working in an informal job is highly correlated with the skill level of individuals (ILO and WIEGO, 2000). The less educated are more likely to be in the informal economy. This skill difference is likely to be of importance given the observed skill-biased nature of international trade (Bacchetta, Ernst and Bustamante, 2009).

## 4.3.2 Trade and the informal economy: Theory and concepts

The issues surrounding the informal economy and trade can be conceptualized either as trade influencing the degree of informality in the economy or as the degree of informality influencing the potential gains from trade. A significant number of studies have addressed these issues. Different theoretical models and concepts were developed to analyse the link between globalization and informality. The different concepts reflect the variety of views of the informal economy and its links to the formal economy. No universally accepted concept exists, but the three main views that can be identified are dualist, legalist and structuralist in nature:

- The dualistic view states that no direct link exists between the formal segment and the – inferior – informal segment of the labour market. Often, it is assumed that only the formal economy can engage in international trade.

- The legalistic view sees the informal sector as existing only because of rigid government regulations. Micro-entrepreneurs operate informally to avoid costs associated with registration.

- The structuralist view asserts that the informal economy serves as a refuge or a residual strategy for those who are excluded from the formal economy. The informal economy supplies cheap labour and inputs to larger formal firms. The two segments are connected and interdependent. Informality is therefore seen as a rational response to the obstacles faced in economic development.

Within the dualistic structure, there are models with differentiated wages, which emphasize constraints on the mobility between formal and informal labour markets based on, e.g. differences in skills or access to capital, etc. Through such conceptualization of dualistic models, one could show that the number of jobs available in the formal economy could be restricted, for example, due to lack of potential profitability and cost-cutting ventures.

### 4.3.2.1 The impact of trade on the informal sector

The three schools of thought are reflected in theoretical models, which describe how trade can influence the informal economy. The studies based on the dualistic model have broadly followed the Harris and Todaro (1970) dual economy model, in which the economy is divided into rural and urban sectors. Differences between the two sectors are marked by both wage differentials and income expectations. The two sectors are separated by space, access to information, market principles, bargaining power and structures of employment and capital intensities. Studies on the impact on the informal economy provide varied conclusions depending on the assumptions they have used. For instance, various studies have assumed that the informal economy produces: final goods, tradable goods or both tradable and non-tradable goods; they also acknowledge the existence of urban unemployment, the duality of the credit markets and capital immobility across the sectors (Gupta, 1993). The majority of these studies find that trade tends to increase employment in the informal economy. The impact on wages in the informal economy varies depending upon the assumptions of the models.

Marjit and Acharyya (2003) find that, when capital is mobile between the formal and the informal economy in a dualistic model, the opening up of trade raises wages in the informal economy, whereas, with immobile capital, trade depresses the wages in the informal economy. If the informal economy produces tradable goods and services, opening up of trade through a decline in tariffs raises both wages and employment in the informal economy. Marjit and Beladi (2005), and Chandra and Khan (1993), seem to corroborate this thesis, provided capital is mobile across informal and formal sectors. With declining tariffs, the formal sector faces competition, thus its return on capital decreases. As capital moves into the informal economy, the rental income of capital in this sector declines and capital intensity of production increases, raising the wages of formal workers.

Studies based on wage differentials – in which the wages in the formal and informal economy are clearly different due to differences in skills, availability of capital, credit and information and various barriers on spatial mobility – suggest that the opening up of trade may shift production to the informal economy, where wages remain stagnant or may even decline. Kar and Marjit (2001) find that opening up of the economy does not increase the welfare of workers in the informal economy, even in cases where activities in the informal economy increase with reduction in tariffs. Marjit and Maiti (2005) observe that the wages may decline even with an increase in employment in the informal economy if capital is immobile across sectors. However, if capital is mobile, wages improve significantly in the informal economy as activities and employment in this sector increase. Goldberg and Pavcnik (2003) note that with the opening up of trade there is a reallocation of production from the formal to the informal economy and the workers in the formal sector face the threat of lay-off. As a result, employment shrinks in the formal sector and new employment is created in the informal economy, but wages in the formal sector rise while those in the informal economy fall. Marjit and Maiti (2005) show that a limited degree of capital mobility between the formal and informal sectors increases employment in the informal sector, which leads to lower wages; however, a lack of capital mobility would constrain such informalization. The total wage bill of the informal economy, however, is predicted to increase after trade liberalization. Chaudhuri and Mukherjee (2002) insist that restructuring of employment and informalization of production and employment is bound to increase wages in the informal economy due to reallocation of capital into this sector.

Cimoli and Porcile (2009) argue from a structuralist stance that, with the opening up of trade in Latin America, production units in the formal sector started specializing in goods for export and that the production of non-export goods and services was relegated to the informal economy, leading to an expansion in the formal sector and inhibiting the growth of employment in the formal sector. Such a situation emerges when exporting firms try to claim a greater share of the existing demand pattern of the traded good rather than face an expanding market. Major fluctuation in trade leads to the less-responsive firms becoming less viable. Hence, it is necessary to build capabilities to address new and sophisticated exports markets. Cimoli and Porcile (2009) suggest that this happens because productivity gains in the formal sector do not translate into overall productivity gains across the economy due to overall demand constraints. Therefore, the ability of gains of the export sector to generate activity in the rest of the economy depends on the trajectory and robustness of economic growth. Thus, it is not trade per se that could be leading to informalization but rather the internal structure of the economy, the degrees of specialization and the levels of skills therein.

Although the majority of the theoretical models find that trade liberalization increases informal employment in developing countries (see also box 3.1 in Bacchetta, Ernst and Bustamante, 2009), and wide-ranging trade reforms carried out in developing countries – including Latin America in the 1990s – often coincide with higher informality, it may still be argued that the effects of trade on informality are not conclusively proven. On the one hand, cheaper imports, which could also result from

---

## Box 4-2: Traditional trade theories

Traditional trade theories distinguish between labour, capital-intensive goods and different levels of skills that correlate only partly with the formal or informal status of workers. Nevertheless, ex post empirical studies (discussed in section 4.4.2) have reviewed two major aspects arising from the Heckscher-Ohlin model. The Heckscher-Ohlin theorem states that a labour-abundant country will export the labour-intensive good, and the Stolper-Samuelson theorem predicts gains for the return to labour in labour-abundant countries with the opening up of trade. However, while there was often an increase in the labour-intensive informal sector with trade opening, incomes in the informal sector did not always rise as predicted by the Stolper-Samuelson theorem within the overall framework of the Heckscher-Ohlin model.

A caveat of applying the traditional trade theory to informality is that the informal economy appears to produce non-tradable goods rather than tradables as assumed in the Heckscher-Ohlin model.

appreciation of a trading partner's currency, may introduce pressure on domestic prices, drive local firms out of business, reduce their incentives to open new positions, or push them toward cheaper means of production in the informal economy. In the model proposed by Fiess et al. (2006), this could be seen as a negative productivity shock to the formal/traded sector, the adjustment to which would depend on the degrees of rigidity in the formal sector, but would in any case lead to a decline in formal sector employment. The increase in salaried informality could be manifested through two channels. The negative shift of the demand curve for formal labour would lead to lower employment and earnings in the formal sector. Part of the fall in earnings could occur through lower benefits, an effect that might be exacerbated if wages were relatively rigid. The same scenario would lead to hiring workers without benefits or subcontracting tasks to lower-paid external workers.

On the other hand, lower tariffs may also foster the import of technology and capital from abroad, thereby increasing the demand for complementary skilled labour that, in the long run, tends to lead to greater formality. Generally speaking, industries that are more exposed to trade tend to pay higher wages and be more formal (de Ferranti et al., 2001), given the human capital of their workers. In addition, the availability of higher-quality or lower-cost intermediate inputs in essence constitutes a positive productivity shock to the formal sector and leads to lower informality. Furthermore, Aleman-Castilla (2006) develops a dynamic industry model with firm heterogeneity in which import tariff elimination could reduce the incidence of informality by increasing the profitability for some firms to enter the formal sector, forcing the less productive informal firms to exit the industry, and inducing the most productive formal firms to engage in trade.

The above studies on the impact of trade on the informal economy suggest that capital mobility and formalization of credit, as well as upgrading of skills, are crucial for the informal economy to benefit from trade. Trade may lead to an expansion of the informal economy if it pushes firms to cut production costs and overheads.

### 4.3.2.2 The impact of the informal economy on trade

A large informal economy can in turn have an impact on a country's ability to benefit from international trade. Empirical evidence suggests, for example, that it is often the bigger and more productive companies that benefit from trade liberalization. A small formal sector with few large firms may thus limit the potential to benefit from international trade.

Conceptually, the impact of informality on trade may vary according to the three main views of informality. According to the dualistic view, only the formal economy can engage in international trade and hence the existence of large informal economies is detrimental to trade. The legalistic view treats the informal sector as one that exists only because of rigid government regulations that can hardly match up to the pace of developments in the real world. Hence, informality indicates the failure of the government to address trade and economic development and, to this extent, informalization can retard trade. According to the structuralist view, the informal economy is a rational response to the obstacles faced in economic development and hence informalization indicates the limitations of the economy in absorbing the gains from trade. However, the possibility of subcontracting and using cheaper informal labour may provide companies with a competitive advantage and, thus, may have a positive impact on exports. De Soto (1989) and others suggests that the informal sector is an engine of growth.

### Empirical analysis[2]

Empirical analysis of the impact of informality on the capacity to benefit from trade is rare. However, a related literature strand that has looked at informality, growth and inequality provides some insights. Most of the studies suggest that a large informal sector has an adverse effect on international trade. Short-term cost advantages may be possible, but this appears to be at the expense of longer-term dynamic gains.

Several studies attribute adverse effects to the small size of entities in the informal sector. La Porta and Shleifer (2008) observe that the informal economy, due to the small size of firms, is less likely to find good talent and hence economies with a predominance of such firms are not likely to specialize or become competitive enough to benefit from trade. Elbadawi and Loayza (2008) find that, in Arab countries, informality has negative marginal effects on small enterprise performance and conclude that informal establishments have difficulties penetrating regional or international markets. Smaller firms cater to local markets and larger firms are more likely to serve international markets. In the case of such neat divisions, the informal economy must become formal in order to be able to participate in global trade. Such a process of formalization may require easier access to credit, capital and skills. In another study, Inshengoma and Kappel (2006) observed that home-based production usually comes with marginalization of economic resources and economic agents by limiting their access to social services and also to capital. This phenomenon therefore tends to impact trade adversely, since such micro-firms are not able to function in a competitive trading framework.

Some studies find a positive effect on trade, often linked to subcontracting. Carr and Chen (2002) recognized the potential of the informal economy to help expand opportunities in trade in cases where firms are vertically linked with the formal sector – such as outsourcing and subcontracting. The informal economy, as observed by the authors, helps to minimize production costs and overheads. Under some conditions, positive effects are also found in studies reflecting the dualistic approach. Davis and Haltiwanger (1990, 1992), and Davis et al. (1996), observe that informality helps trade, provided job switches are possible from the informal to the formal sector with skill upgrading and new skills. Trade destroys jobs in both sectors and creates new ones according to new demands. This requires certain levels of education, opportunities for retraining, and so on.

---

[2] Although section 4.3 discusses theories and concepts, empirical results of the impact of informality on trade is discussed here since the literature on this topic is small.

However, cost advantages from informality may only provide short-term gains. Farrell (2004) observes that low-cost and small-sized firms grow less and hence cannot contribute to long-term productivity growth. Davis (2004) corroborates this observation and adds that, despite being low cost, the informal economy constitutes a drag on the economy due to its low productivity growth.

UN DESA (2005) finds that income inequality retards access to education and health, and eventually blocks access to capital, skills, infrastructure and markets and hence depresses trade. The main finding of this study is the linkage of informality with income inequality. Hall and Sobel (2008) argue that the owners of informal production units face enormous hurdles in the form of regulations, and that this increases the transaction costs for these businesses. Bigsten and Söderbom (2005) state that the existence of government regulations traps workers in the informal economy with poor wages. Low wages keep workers in poverty and prevent them from overcoming their low skills and asset bases. The informal economy appears to keep the poor as poor and does not help create real productivity gains, and hence retards development as well as trade.

A main area of concern raised by these studies is the finding that informality itself exists due to income inequalities. Rising informality therefore indicates rising inequality, which in turn implies that the distributive structures in the economy are retarding the process of specialization and growth, and hence trade. Thus, trade and social policies, including labour market policies, need to be coherent and sensitive to the impact of informality and inequality on the potential to benefit from trade.

Gravity models have not yet been used to assess the effects of informality on trade. Although there has been significant progress in gravity models to understand factors determining trade, the author of this chapter is not aware of any study incorporating the informal economy in any gravity model – for example, the gravity models dealing with trade issues in Wright (2004), Anderson and Wincoop (2001), and Matthieu and Mehl (2008), do not discuss the impact of trade on the informal economy.

## 4.4 APPROACHES TO ASSESS THE IMPACT OF TRADE ON THE INFORMAL ECONOMY

The theoretical models identify several mechanisms through which trade can impact the informal sector, and vice versa. In most modelling approaches, trade liberalization increases informal employment, but the extent is unclear. Moreover, the impact on wages in the informal economy is ambiguous and the impact of informality on the ability to benefit from trade is unclear. Therefore, since a large proportion of the population is involved in informality in developing countries, contributing a major share to GDP, there is a need to carefully assess the informal economy to help in formulating and implementing appropriate policies. Such policies need to address both productivity and employment rights, including social security.

For more than two decades, quantitative and qualitative studies have tried to assess the impact of trade liberalization on the informal sector and the presence of a large informal sector on export competitiveness. Three approaches have been used and are discussed below:

- Qualitative studies (case studies, partly using data).

- Quantitative ex post studies (econometric analysis).

- Quantitative ex ante studies (mainly computable general equilibrium (CGE) models).

In quantitative studies, published or specifically collected data are used to analyse the relationship between trade and informality for policy analysis. Quantitative studies can be exact in establishing relationships between variables in order to track the impact of tariff reduction, for example, while field studies can establish nuances that cannot be easily captured through data and models. Moreover, qualitative studies use cases from the field. Policy-makers are interested in studying the impact of particular policy measures, such as the impact of a change in income tax on welfare of people below poverty lines and other socio-economic categories of households. It is possible to study the impact of policies that are targeted and are not likely to have major indirect impact on other variables of an economy through focused case studies.

Econometric exercises have also used samples to establish relationships between informalization and other variables. Econometric studies allow determination of the significance of a relation between variables using established statistical methodologies. Most of the studies, with certain exceptions,[3] have used micro-level (i.e. firm- or industry-level) data in specific countries to draw their conclusions.

Economy-wide analysis is essential when the indirect impact of policy changes is potentially wide and other groups and other markets may be affected as a result of a policy change. CGE models take the entire macroeconomy into consideration. To provide a framework, in which the influence of policy changes or any exogenous change can be traced through different sectors and different socio-economic classes, it would be helpful to use a multi-sectoral model in which informal transactions and "agents" can explicitly be tracked. In such a model, the magnitude of the impact of different policies can be quantified to identify sectors that respond more strongly through production, to analyse the impact on the demand for informal factors, and eventually to identify income generation for the households belonging to the informal economy. Moreover, through their expenditure pattern, second-round effects on the economy can be identified. For instance, through simulations based on government investment expenditure or alternative trade policies, it is possible to explore the inter-relationships among the various economic factors considered. A particular expansion of sectoral exports may bring about repercussions that could be counter-intuitive. For example, if the objective is to raise informal incomes in the

---

[3] Sinha (1999), Sinha et al. (2003), Sinha and Adam (2006), and Sinha (2009).

short term, it might be more beneficial to encourage export in specific sectors, such as agriculture and allied activities, rather than in traditionally accepted sectors like manufacturing.

The impact of trade policy changes on the informal economy needs to be examined to better understand how such policies should be designed, modified if necessary, and implemented. Impact analysis can be carried out through many approaches. Qualitative and quantitative and, in this case, econometric and general equilibrium analysis approaches have different strengths and weaknesses and are suitable for different research questions (see Annex 4.A). In this section, the three approaches that were used are discussed.

### 4.4.1 Qualitative approach (micro-level studies)

Case studies and field surveys have been undertaken to collect and analyse information about the nature of the trade liberalizations, how policies are implemented and the resulting impact on different groups of people within the area surveyed. The studies attempt to build reasonable linkages between the reforms and the changes in the welfare of different groups of the labour force, such as informal and formal workers.

The field studies discussed here clearly indicate that the informal economy is structurally connected to the formal economy and does not have a distinct existence. Thus, this economy seems to defy the very premises of dual economy.

Several field studies have analysed the effects of policy changes in developing countries on poverty and inequality. Squire (1991) and Van der Hoeven (1996) conducted reviews of the linkage between adjustment and poverty during the 1980s. The findings of qualitative analysis of the relationship between reforms and poverty are presented in a short review by Killick (1995), and White (1997) provides a more recent review on this. Such work describes methodically the reforms undertaken in a selected country and the changes in a variety of welfare indicators among different households and socio-economic groups. Studies have also been reported in a series of Background Papers on "globalization with a human face" prepared for the Human Development Report 1999 (UNDP, 1999). Similarly Cornia (1999), Handa and King (1997), and McCulloch et al. (2000) provide similar analyses for different African countries.

Glick and Roubaud (2004) investigate the impact of the establishment of an export processing zone (EPZ) on earnings, employment and the gender composition of employment as well as gender-specific wage differentiation from 1995 to 2002 in Antananarivo, Madagascar.[4] The authors find that, in the aftermath of globalization, there is a decline in: (a) women's participation in the workforce; (b) the total number of self-employed and private informal workers; and (c) the number of firms in the informal economy. At the same time, there was a disproportionate rise of female

---

[4] In fact, the study uses time-series labour force survey data and is thus an econometric analysis, but the authors also describe the sector qualitatively and use descriptive data so that it is also a case study.

workers in the EPZ. The formal sector outside the EPZ remained largely unaffected. The wages in the EPZ, though lower than in the formal sector, were higher than in the informal sector. Again using a field study in 2005, Marjit and Maiti (2005) investigated in the state of West Bengal, India, how the Government's trade-opening policies affected the informal economy. The survey found that, with the growth of dedicated export sectors, the production units in the informal economy became tied to formal units through various types of agent. The informal economy existed and even expanded; but it expanded as a web of relationships with the formal units, rather than as independent units, and consequently exhibited trends such as adoption of technology and even growth.

In a case study conducted by Singh and Sapra (2007) in the industrial clusters of Tiruppur (southern India) and Delhi, garment factories that were linked to the global value chain were found to operate in clusters, and were considered informal since they hired casual, temporary and daily-wage labour. The lower castes formed the bulk of such informal labour in Tiruppur, but migrant workers formed most of the labour force in Delhi. Labour had no bargaining power and, over the years, the entire hiring and firing process seemed to have been taken over by the labour contractor. What was important was that even within the informal economy there seemed to be a division between "factory" and "home-based" work, in which the latter was a further subcontracted form of the former. There was also a hierarchical division of work, with the better-paid and skilled jobs going to males and the lower-paid jobs going to women, reflecting that informal work was at the lower end of the production value chain and women within the informal economy were at the bottom of this chain.

## 4.4.2 Empirical quantitative studies

Similar to some qualitative case studies, several empirical studies on the informal sector shed light on the structure of the informal economy and its link to the formal economy. Agenor and Aizenman (1994) employ an econometric model using data from both the formal and the informal economies to show that the efforts of workers to find formal employment depend on the wage differentials between the formal and the informal sectors. Bauch (1991) uses econometric models using firm-level data across the economy to examine the relationship between firm size, employment and minimum wages, and observes that the insistence on minimum wages creates the formal-informal duality. Fortin et al. (1997) use an econometric model including firm-level data to observe formal and informal firms in the same productive sector of the economy, and find that market segmentation takes place due to scale of the operation, the evasion of taxes and the wages paid to workers. Following liberalization, trading countries want to become more competitive, reducing the wages of workers and cutting down on overheads associated with the regulations of the formal sector. This desire to minimize the costs of labour, and other costs of compliance such as fees and taxes, informalizes both firms and employment.

Most of the empirical literature on trade and informality is focused on Latin America, including Argentina, Brazil and Mexico. From the data presented in the various OECD papers (e.g. OECD, 2009; see http://www.oecd.org/dataoecd/4/49/42863997.pdf), we observe the gradual informalization of the workforce across developing countries. With gradual integration into the global economy, countries either expand production bases for exports or improve competitiveness of home industries to withstand cheaper imports. In either case, a desire to reduce costs leads to informalization of production as well as employment. In Mexico, changes in the distribution of formal employment across age groups over the last decades, in which trade was liberalized remarkably, have been minimal, with some loss of formality (with absorption in both informal salaried and independent work) among prime-age males and perhaps older workers in the 1987–96 period. There were no substantial changes in the 1996–2004 period. In Brazil, however, the 1990–2002 period brought a decrease in formal employment of roughly 10 percentage points across the whole age spectrum, with a fall of 20-30 percentage points for young workers. In Argentina, a similar pattern has prevailed, with one exception. Although the similarly dramatic losses of formal jobs among young workers, in their early life cycle in the 20's, in Brazil the greatest losses level out at about 20. Moreover, there is a marked decrease in formalization among workers over 45 years of age that is roughly double that of the prime-age males. In light of this, concern in Argentina about the increased informalization of the workforce is high. Argentina, one of the richest countries in Latin America, once had a consistently high formal employment rate of almost 70 per cent, where 17-year-old workers had the same access to formal sector jobs as prime-age males. The situation now more closely resembles Mexico, especially in the preservation of formal sector employment, except that large firms in Mexico are relatively more formal than those in Argentina. At the very least, this represents different experiences with trade liberalization. But the summary picture is striking. Mexico's far-reaching trade liberalization, which began in 1987, coincides with small changes of informality and small changes of its allocation across age groups or firm sizes. Meanwhile, Brazil has experienced an increase in informality in terms of its labour force, although investments in informal and formal firms remain proportionately the same as in Argentina. The above section suggests that, although the allocation of capital remains more or less unaffected in proportion to expansion in economic activity through trade liberalization, employment tends to be tilted in favour of the informal sector rather than toward firms in the formal sector.

## Small impact of trade on the informal economy

Econometric studies have tried to determine whether there is a statistically significant link between trade and informal employment and wages in the informal economy. In Latin America, empirical evidence on the impact of openness to trade on levels of informality is mixed, but it generally suggests marginal effects. Goldberg and Pavcnik (2003) find a very modest impact from trade reforms in Colombia on informality, and none in Brazil. Bosch et al. (2006), revisiting the Brazilian case through the lens of job creation and destruction, find again a small but positive impact (whereby trade liberalization increased informality). In the absence of trade liberalization, formal employment may have been higher (Shimer, 2005). The evidence from Mexico also does not suggest a large impact. As noted by García-Verdú (2007), among others, given the dramatic unilateral liberalization beginning in 1987 and then continuing through the North American Free Trade Agreement (NAFTA), there is little trend in informality.

## Some studies find that trade liberalization increases informality ...

Goldberg and Pavcnik (2003) use data from Brazil and Colombia, countries that experienced large trade barrier reductions in the 1980s and 1990s, and examine the response of the informal sector to liberalization. The authors build a model in which firms optimize the share of formal and informal workers that are employed and relate changes in the likelihood of informal employment to tariff changes in each sector. Underlying the model is the observed premise that mobility across the formal and informal sectors within an industry is greater than mobility across industries. For Brazil, the authors do not find evidence of a relationship between trade policy and informality. For Colombia, they find weak evidence of such a relationship and show that trade liberalization leads to an increase of the informal economy. However, this link depends on the labour market structure, since the impact is only significant for the period prior to a reform that increased the flexibility of the Colombian labour market. Prior to that reform, the opening up of trade led to a reallocation of production from the formal to the informal economy, and the workers in the formal sector faced higher threats of lay-offs and retrenchments. Employment shrank in the formal sector and new employment was created in the informal economy. Wages in the formal sector rose while those in the informal economy fell. In other words, wage differentials seem to persist between the formal and the informal economies despite the restructuring, leading to an increase in informalization of employment, notwithstanding capital mobility.

Mondino and Montoya (2002), and World Bank (2007), show a very large increase in the share of informal salaried workers in Argentina in the early 1980s. Though the last round of trade liberalization began only in 1990, reforms in the late 1970s radically lowered tariffs and led to an appreciated exchange rate. Galiani and Sanguinetti (2003), and Porto and Galiani (2006), find that the decreased protection had some effect on both the absolute level of wages and the gap between skilled and unskilled labour. To the degree that downward pressure on unskilled wages came through the reduction of benefits, or subcontracting, it seems possible that trade liberalization had an impact. However, preliminary analysis replicating the Goldberg-Pavcnik exercise for Argentina suggests that the impact of trade reform per se had a magnitude similar to that in Brazil – i.e. very low direct impact – on employment although there was a downward pressure on wages (however, there may have been significant additional impacts from the various periods of sustained currency over-evaluation).

**... while, under some circumstances, trade liberalization can reduce informality**
When examining how trade liberalization affects informality in Mexico, Aleman-Castilla (2006), broadly following the Goldberg-Pavcnik (2003) methodology, finds that industries that were more exposed to trade saw higher increases in the rate of formality. The author argues that the impact on product prices was minor, while the reduction in import prices raised the productivity of the tradables sector and, hence, expanded the demand for formal labour overall. The results are based on data for the period 1988–2002 and the study focuses on trade liberalization under NAFTA. Aleman-Castilla models the decision process of firms facing the option of producing either in the formal or the informal sector. Secondly, the author incorporates a framework that explains how trade liberalization affects the performance of firms. And thirdly, these two points have been put together. The author uses a dynamic industry model with firm heterogeneity similar to that used by Melitz (2003) to describe the way in which trade liberalization could affect the rate of informality. The original model shows how exposure to trade induces only the more productive firms to export while simultaneously forcing the least productive firms to exit. Both the exit of the least productive firms and the additional export sales gained by the more productive firms reallocate market shares towards the more productive firms and contribute to an aggregate productivity increase. Profits are also reallocated towards more productive firms.

---

**Box 4-3: Individual characteristics of informal workers**

Apart from providing estimates of industry informality differentials, the first stage estimation of Aleman-Castilla (2006) is also useful to study the determinants of informal labour at the individual level. As expected from the human capital theory, the probability of being informal decreases with years of experience and schooling. It is also lower for married workers, but not for those cohabiting with a partner without being married. Males seem to be more likely to be informal than females. This result does not seem to support what Roberts (1989) finds for the labour market of Guadalajara, Mexico, but is consistent with Goldberg and Pavcnik's (2003) findings for Colombia. Within a household, the likelihood of informality is significantly lower for the first provider of income and significantly higher for the second provider, which supports the results of Roberts (1989) and Maloney (1999). The findings are reasonable considering that, as found by Roberts and argued by Maloney, the deductions made for social welfare in formal employment are perceived as a disadvantage by many workers. Since social welfare in Mexico normally covers not only the worker but his family as well, there is no benefit for the second provider of income to work in the formal sector and pay the welfare deductions to get his or her own social insurance.

---

The findings from Aleman-Castilla (2006) reveal interesting results regarding the geographic characteristics of informality. The probability of informality varies significantly across cities. The probability of informality appears to be positively correlated with the population of the city where the worker lives,[5] and also with the

---

[5] More precisely, the natural logarithm of the population.

proximity to the city (relative distance). Workers are more likely to be informal when they live closer to Mexico City than to the US-Mexico border. However, the estimated coefficients are statistically significant only for a few years of the sample. Furthermore, the estimates indicate that the likelihood of informality is significantly lower for workers living in a state with high exposure to globalization (for nine years of the sample) and higher for those living in a state with low exposure to it (for eight years of the sample). In most cases, these indicators were individually and jointly statistically significant, suggesting that geographic location is an important determinant of the likelihood of informality and that informality in Mexico is lower in states with a high exposure to trade.

Goldberg and Pavcnik (2003) state that part of the variation in informal employment that cannot be explained by worker characteristics can be explained by coefficients reflecting workers' industry affiliations. The authors call these coefficients industry informality differentials.

Goldberg and Pavcnik show that trade reforms affect tariff rates differentially in different sectors. They argue that sectors with traditionally high protection rates, such as textiles and apparel, experience sharper reduction in tariff. On the other hand, sectors with relatively low rates of protection experience smaller tariff cuts. Such differential tariff rates are examined by the authors across industries in order to identify the effects of tariff changes on informality. A high measure of year-to-year correlations of industry informality differentials in Brazil suggest that trade policy changes are unlikely to be associated with changes in informal employment. On the other hand, the lower correlation coefficients in informality differentials in Colombia suggest that trade policy could at least in principle affect the incidence of informal employment in this country.

From the second stage results, the estimates suggest a significant effect of trade liberalization on the probability of informal employment. Specifically, a 1 percentage point decline in the Mexican import tariff is associated with a 0.392 percentage point reduction in the likelihood of informality. The US import tariff does not seem to have a significant effect, which is a reasonable outcome considering its already low level in the pre-NAFTA period. The analysis also suggests that the benefits of trade liberalization have not spread over to the labour force in the non-tradable sectors, at least in a statistically significant sense.

Recent trends in Mexico also seem related to international exposure. The sharp increase in both self-employment and informal salaried work after 2000 has occurred concomitantly with the entry of China as a major competitor in some areas of Mexico's comparative advantage. Therefore, while Mexico saw an increase in the formal sector after NAFTA, the entry of another developing country such as China informalized the Mexican economy. Hanson and Robertson (2006) argue that, had China's growth in export capacity remained unchanged after 1995, Mexico's annual export growth rate of Chinese-substitutable goods would have been 1.5 percentage points higher in the late 1990s and 3.0 percentage points higher than the 1.9 per cent it experienced going into the new millennium. This does suggest that international competition is constraining the expansion of some formal export jobs. On the other

> **Box 4-4: Methodology suggestion to quantify trade liberalization to capture effects on non-tradables**
>
> Apart from using the standard import tariffs, the effect of trade liberalization on informality can also be estimated by using an input-output matrix (IOM) to calculate an import tariff that reflects the taxes payable on imported inputs more precisely. The input-output matrix shows the intersectoral transactions at current producer prices, which can be expressed as shares of the total output of each sector. Moreover, the input-output matrix also contains the share of imported inputs for each sector. Therefore, apart from summarizing the intersectoral dependence, the IOM tariff also reflects the relative importance of imports across sectors. Among other virtues, this tariff allows assignment of a real import tariff to the non-tradable sectors, because of their interactions with the tradable ones.

hand, Lederman et al. (2006), using estimations of the gravity model of trade, argue that there is little evidence that Mexican (and Central American) non-fuel overall exports were affected. It is also noteworthy that the sharp increase of informality seems to occur with the relaxation of restrictions on Chinese textiles and apparel imports in the United States. The overall reduction in exports due to the US recession may have had a straightforward impact through a reduction in productivity that, in the absence of wage rigidities, led to depreciation of the currency concomitant with a rise in relative sector size and relative employment in non-exporting firms. It is likely that with a slowdown in the US economy, the opportunities became relatively better in informal micro-enterprises. In Mexico, medium-sized and large firms are still becoming more formal over time. Therefore, the shifts in informality measured may be due to the increased relative attractiveness of working for micro-enterprises over the preceding five-year period, and not to greater subcontracting or within-large-firm informality due to trade opening in Mexico.

Overall, the econometric analysis provides supporting evidence for the hypothesis that the tariff elimination process undertaken by Mexico when joining NAFTA in 1994 has helped reduce the incidence of informality. Increasing competition from other developing countries in areas where Mexico has a comparative advantage could lead to increasing informality.

The studies discussed above analyse specific developing countries and provide interesting insights into the impact of trade on informality. However, due to the specific circumstances in each country, results cannot easily be generalized. Fiess and Fugazza (2008) tried to work through statistical macro-level and internationally comparable data to attempt to find relationships between trade and informality. But the results yield a mixed picture. While cross-sectional data suggest that opening up of trade reduces informality, panel data suggests that the reverse is true. Micro-level data seem to suggest that lower tariffs and lower restrictions reduce informality in countries. In a dynamic panel estimation set-up that accounts for endogeneity, the authors find that informal employment decreases with deeper trade liberalization, while informal output increases. The authors argue that their results may suggest that the productivity of the informal sector increases after trade liberalization. Due to the partly conflicting results, Fiess and Fugazza call for more research in this important area that involves trade and poverty.

Another strand of econometric literature focuses on turbulence in employment. This is related to the creation and destruction of jobs in certain sectors and the mobility between sectors, including between the formal and the informal sector due to fluctuation in trade. Blanchard (2005) analyses trend data from industrialized countries and shows that the gradual restructuring of such economies towards greater openness does not lead to more turbulence in employment. Turbulence emanates from restructuring within economies and, contrary to what trade theories suggest, leads to job reallocations within sectors rather than across sectors. Jansen and Turrini (2004) also observe that turbulence in employment does not mean net job loss. Comin and Philippon (2005) use firm-level data to construct sales volatility and find that higher volatility need not mean higher job creation or job loss. Ljunqvist and Sargent (1998, 2005) insist that turbulence increases skill specialization and wage differentials and that this may actually create rigidity in labour movement across sectors.

The findings suggest that the outcomes of trade liberalization depend more on the structure of the individual economy rather than in the intrinsic nature of trade liberalization. Neoclassical economics predict that open trade will generate gains from trade. However, various econometric studies reveal that this is not always the case. Econometric studies indicate that conditions specific to each country determine the outcome of trade more than the fact of open trade. In this sense, the CGE models are capable of capturing the structures intrinsic to each country and examining the impact of open trade therein.

### 4.4.3 Computable general equilibrium (CGE) models

Quantitative studies based on CGE models are useful in examining the impact of policy changes on production, employment, wages and other variables by sector, including informal units and informal workers. General equilibrium models are useful when a policy change that targets a specific sector has an effect on other sectors or has second-round effects, such as income effects. Since the informal economy is so large in many developing countries, it is important to assess the impact of trade policy changes on the economy using general equilibrium models.

Some studies have used CGE models in relation to the informal economy. Savard and Adjovi (1997), and Paquet and Savard (2009), study Benin's informal sectors in response to changes in Government policies. Gibson and Godoy (1993) study Bolivia through a 38-sector social accounting matrix (SAM) that helped them to assess the short-term impact on the earnings of workers in the informal sector. Gibson (2005) studies Bolivia through a CGE model and presents findings showing that a rise of the informal sector had reduced the output of the formal sector. Bautista et al. (1998) study Zimbabwe using a CGE model to quantitatively examine the income and equity effects of trade liberalization, fiscal and land policies. The exercise reveals that positive effects on income may not have a positive impact on equity. Kelley (1994) studies Peru through the CGE model and observes that the informal sector emerges because the formal sector cannot serve the highly segmented and differentiated market for goods and services. Sinha and Adam (2006) study India through a labour-segmented CGE model and find that casualization of work leads to loss of labour welfare and a reduction in the wages of informal workers. The study by Agenor et al. (2003) uses the integrated macroeconomic model for poverty analysis (IMMPA) to analyse rural and urban areas as the poor recover from the effects of earlier financial policies and the transmission of external shocks. Other CGE studies that analyse the impact of policy changes on the informal economy include Savard and Adjovi (1997), Sinha (1999), and Sinha and Adam (2000).

## CGE models

CGE models are theoretically founded upon neoclassical theories. Such models are generally short term with a comparative-static framework using mainly relative prices for commodities with excess capacity so that prices and quantities adjust to changes in demand and markets are cleared. However, dynamic CGE models can also be developed that have potentially longer time-period analysis, since many variables may have different trajectories over the longer term. In both static and dynamic models, consumers are utility maximizers while producers are profit maximizers. Circular flow of income between firms and the household is incorporated, as is the government, though the latter is not an optimizer. The standard feature of such models consists of an imperfect substitution between imports and domestic demand for goods, known as the Armington assumption. Firms are assumed to be perfectly competitive, produce a homogenous output with imperfect transformability between production for domestic and foreign markets at the sectoral level, determined by a constant elasticity of transformation function. The treatment of export and import in such models allows autonomy to the domestic prices to adjust to changes in the world prices of sectoral substitutes and assumes that the country under consideration cannot affect world prices. Such models are often used for developing countries to observe the impact of structural adjustment on economies. The CGE is a model in which micro-level decision-making parameters of firms can be related to the macro-level policies of countries.

In these models, factors of production, mostly labour and sometimes land and capital, are assumed to behave differently for different markets. Though full employment and perfect mobility of factors of production are possible in the long run, in the short run, capital is assumed to be fixed for each sector and immobile across sectors, thus possibly creating excess and unutilized capacities. Aggregate domestic demand in such models has four components, namely: consumption, intermediate demand, government and investment. The major macroeconomic parameters that are supposed to balance are savings and investments and government deficit and balance of trade. Markets for goods and services respond to the forces of the market, and market forces are affected by government policies and the external environment. The CGE and other general equilibrium models are usually Walrasian in nature with all markets in balance. Each sector produces a fully differentiated good so that there is no overlap. The goods are produced through various combinations of labour and capital with constant elasticity of substitution (CES). The domestic output of the sector is derived from a CES function of factor inputs and the intermediate good used in the sector. Chapter 3 of this book discusses further details of CGE models used in relation to trade policy analysis.

## Application of CGE models to the informal economy

The CGE models characterize informality through various markets. The assumptions underlying these characteristics depend on concepts regarding informality in goods markets and factor markets. Hence, it is important to conceptualize the differences of the output of the formal and informal sectors for modelling purposes and to build the specifications carefully. Even when formal and informal output is similar, it has been observed from field studies that product differentiation and imperfect substitutability between the two sectors often exist. Informal entrepreneurs generally do not cater to a large market, can have differences in the quality of goods and can occupy different outlets (e.g. streets as vendors, flea markets) as compared to the formal retailers. Another example involves exclusive goods, where limited market size precludes efficient formal sector production. These factors need to be built into a CGE structure. In order to capture these differences in the model, the outputs of the two sectors are treated as imperfect substitutes in many CGE models. Relative prices and the degree of substitution between the outputs of the respective sectors determine the composite good's make-up in each sector's output. Regarding the input factors, there could be two types of capital, one in the formal and the other in the informal economy. The CGE models incorporating the informal distinction also need to distinguish labour by informality. Various types of labour could be identified as either formal or informal.

## A CGE model for India

The CGE work by and Sinha and Adam (2006) for India includes four key aspects on informality. First, there is product differentiation between the informal and formal sectors as they are shown to produce very different products. Second, the formal and informal economies use different technologies. Third, the formal and informal factors of production are distinct, especially since the formal wage is rigid. Finally, the informal sector does not pay taxes on the factor incomes. The model identifies ten sectors. Agriculture and construction are wholly informal while government and capital goods sectors are wholly formal. The rest, namely manufacturing, services and agro-processing have both formal and informal units. Both the formal and the informal units export, and both use informal factors. Total capital is fixed by sectors. The model is set up in two versions, one in which full employment is assumed and the other in which wages are rigid in the formal sub-sectors while they are totally flexible in the informal economies, and workers from the formal sector can join the informal sector. The simulations quantify the employment effects of two types of trade reforms: a revenue-neutral 60 per cent tariff reduction across the board, and a corresponding reduction of quantitative restrictions where they exist. The main findings of this exercise are that trade reforms lead to an inter-sectoral balancing of production away from the formal economy and toward the informal economy as the formal economy must cut costs due to the increased competition that opening up of trade brings about. Under flexible labour markets, the informal economy workers benefit at the cost of entrepreneurs, while in rigid labour markets the urban self-employed tend to benefit more. It may be noted here that different approaches often lead to similar results.

### Description of a Benin model

A CGE model for Benin was developed by Paquet and Savard (2009) using 1999 macroeconomic data. In the model, the authors distinguish between formal and informal households (households that work in the informal economy), and also the re-exportation industry, by dividing into Benin's eight most important export sectors. The model has incorporated informality aspects in a stylized form where the informal sector undertakes trade with Nigeria. Paquet and Savard carry out simulations where import tariffs were reduced. The model findings demonstrate a great sensitivity of government revenue to the activity of the informal economy. The SAM helps in identifying the imports that went into the re-exporting sector because all imports are categorized as domestic consumption. The SAM is also useful in identifying product-by-product trade. There are two factors of production: labour and capital. The agents in the model are the Government, households, firms, the rest of the world and Nigeria (because Benin's economy relies on re-exportation to Nigeria). All households are separated into formal and informal types. Informal households are the ones that work in the informal economy of re-exports while the formal households are those that work in any other sector of the economy. We assume that the workers in the informal and the formal sectors are distinct and separate. The informal economy is more capital intensive, contrary to the general idea that low capital intensity is a

---

### Box 4-5: Building a global knowledge tool to analyse trade and the informal economy

There is a need for wider use of national-level data and government statistics to develop a database that could capture and assess the impact of open trade policies on the organization of production and employment, and hence on wages, wage differentials and worker welfare. The economy-wide models based on macro-level data as developed in India could be used to develop further the framework with which to incorporate the informal economy and trade into CGE models.

The CGE studies discussed in this chapter have used national-level data to analyse the issue of informality and have demonstrated that such analyses are possible. Studies by Sinha and Adam (2006), Sinha (2009), and Paquet and Savard (2009), show the possibility of using economy-wide models to study the impact of globalization on informal workers, employment and wages.

Annex 4.A provides additional details on how to design a CGE model that can be used to analyse the impact of trade on informality. These can be used to provide policy-makers with advice based on quantitative analysis to design policies aimed at improving the informal sector's efficiency as well as addressing equity concerns, such as poverty reduction. It can thus be part of a global knowledge tool on trade and employment.

property of informality, and hence 70 per cent of value-addition goes to capital and 30 per cent to labour. The total input is imported and the total output is sold to Nigeria. The exports to the rest of the world take place in the formal sectors, while the informal economy exists only as a re-exporter to Nigeria. Paquet and Savard (2009) carry out two simulations in their paper: (a) simulation with a 20 per-cent decrease in tariffs across the board; and (b) simulation with 10 per cent appreciation of the Nigerian naira compared to the CFAF currency. The findings show that the simulated changes strongly influence the wealth of informal households, but have marginal impact on the formal households. The authors state that informal households are worse off than formal households for the first simulation and just the opposite results are seen by conducting the second simulation.

## 4.5   POLICY RECOMMENDATIONS

Economic trends show that the informal economy is not likely to wither away soon without focused intervention. On the contrary, there is concern that the informal economy will be a permanent feature during the development process. Growth in informal employment is of great concern. Indeed, in some countries, all segments of the informal workforce, i.e. micro-entrepreneurs, the self-employed, as well as casual, piecemeal, temporary and part-time workers, appear to be growing. The informal workforce is generally not covered by any form of social protection and average wages tend to be very low. Another concern is that the opportunity of economies to benefit from trade and trade liberalization appears to be hampered by the existence of a large informal sector.

On the other hand, the informal economy makes substantial economic contributions, and it also has the ability to mould itself to the changing conditions. The informal economies in Asia, Africa and Latin America have demonstrated that the informal economy is counter-cyclical and helps absorb shocks of lay-offs and unemployment by absorbing labour. There is a need for governments to be aware of the contribution made by the informal economy, both in providing jobs and removing extreme poverty, and thus unemployment-related social evils. Unfortunately, governments generally have a tendency to look at the informal economy as one that evades taxes and therefore creates a fiscal burden, not one that provides jobs to fit available skill and human capital and increases the domestic demand for goods, which results in higher retail tax collection. Governments need to develop innovative and supportive policies that recognize the contributions of this important sector and its workforce, including their constraints and needs. Governments, as well as the economy, will benefit through the release of entrepreneurial effectiveness and the improved well-being of the workforce.

### A need for policy measures
It is important to examine the informal economy to be able to recommend policies that help improve the quality and productivity of such work and its workers. Policy-

making needs to take into account the impact of the global economic structure and the international trading system on the size and the conditions of the informal economy worldwide. Domestic policies, both trade and labour-market policies, as well as other measures such as economic reforms, impact the effects of trade on informality as well as the potential of economies to benefit from trade liberalization.

It stands to reason that informality is not only a matter of concern in terms of social equity, but also in terms of the improved economic efficiency of a country. There is a major concern that the persistent or rising informalization of work in the developing and even developed countries could adversely impact human capital and social progress. Thus, the main reasons for governments to intervene in the informal economy are based on the principles of developing a mechanism to utilize the potential productivity of the informal labour force, poverty reduction, and equity considerations.

Economic policies impact both the informal and the formal economy, but in different ways. Standard economic policies do not have the same effects on the informal economy, where responses are much more varied, as on the formal economy. Hence, it is important to develop policies that fully recognize the interrelationship between the informal and formal economy and other economic and social agents. The informal economy is very much affected by the objects of economic regulation as well as their impact (e.g. the price of capital, labour, inputs and outputs). Trade and industry policy also provides incentives to large formal businesses to increase their international competitiveness, from which small informal businesses in the same industry or sector may not benefit. Proactive policy on the informal economy would shift the structure of aggregate demand, the prices of inputs and outputs, and the set of incentives and subsidies in favour of informal enterprises. Appropriate economic policies on the informal economy should balance incentives, tax burdens and statutory benefits (e.g. unemployment insurance and pension funds) between large and small businesses, and between employers and informal workers.

Clearly, a reappraisal of the impact of existing economic policies and the need for supportive economic policies is needed, since these policies impact the process of redistribution between the formal and informal economies. Policy analysis needs to determine whether the informal economy shares in benefits that result from government expenditure and procurement policies. New methods for assessing government budgets – called social audits or people's budgets – can be used to assess the differential impacts of policies on the formal and informal economy. However, there is a clear need for improved statistics on the informal economy. Collection of budget data is difficult, since allocations affecting those who work in the informal economy may be the responsibility of many different government departments, such as labour, housing, small enterprise development and public health.

Policies towards the informal economy have the potential to create a new contract between the State, business, organized labour and other social actors (including organizations of informal workers and producers). Without addressing the employment needs, constraints and vulnerabilities of those who work in the informal economy, efforts to reduce poverty will not succeed. International labour conventions also mandate governments to intervene on behalf of all workers, including those who work in the informal economy.

## Policy measures on equity and efficiency grounds

Workers in the informal economy are more likely to be poor than those working in the formal economy. Since the informal economy is so closely linked with poverty, it is important to address the various needs and constraints of informal workers in order to alleviate poverty. A large segment of workers in developing countries are in the informal economy, and these workers are a vulnerable group who need certain interventions to improve their welfare. Equity and welfare rationales for government intervention in the informal economy stem from the vulnerability of those in the sector.

Progressive tax policies that would benefit informal workers include lowering taxes on goods and services whose consumption constitutes a high fraction of their spending, and lowering taxes in firms in which the poor are likely to be engaged (Guillermo et al., 2007). Given their poverty, workers in informal employment spend a higher percentage of their incomes on food than other workers, and they are particularly affected by flat value-added tax rates on basic foodstuffs. User fees for social services such as health care and education also affect poor workers disproportionately. Governments need to recognize that formal institutions, such as those dealing with training and credit, often stigmatize workers in the informal economy.

As a large share of the population is involved in the informal economy, policies that improve their welfare would be more conducive to equitable and sustainable growth. With the reduction of poverty and concomitant improvement in standards of health and education, workers in informal employment will become more efficient contributors to the national economy.

In addition, support to informal enterprises will lead to higher productivity of the informal sector and sustainable growth. As the informal economy is a major contributor to GDP and to economic development in general, governments should intervene to promote productivity and growth of informal enterprises.

## Policies adapted to the needs of different parts of the informal economy

While recommending policy interventions, at the very outset, it is important to distinguish between illegal activities producing illicit goods and services and informal activities that produce legal goods and services. Admittedly, some informal entrepreneurs deliberately conceal their activities from public authorities to avoid taxes or compliance with bureaucratic procedures. Moreover, in the case of informal wage workers, it is the employer – not the worker – who does not comply with labour legislation or pay payroll taxes (Arias et al., 2007). And many informal wage workers are employed by formal firms either directly or indirectly through subcontract arrangements.

It is important to distinguish between how policies and regulations affect informal enterprises as compared to how they affect informal employment relations. There is also an urgent need to develop policies and regulation for different categories of workers in this sector. For example, the two types of home-based workers, i.e. micro-entrepreneurs or own-account workers who work from their homes, need different kinds of policies than subcontract workers or industrial outworkers who work from their homes (called home workers).

There is a pressing requirement for governments to develop policies that recognize the informal economy's importance, and to regulate it where necessary so that there is progress and improved well-being for informal workers, which constitute a majority of the workforce in many nations. Therefore, governments should design policies that help increase productivity and promote better working conditions of those who work in the informal economy.

### Policies for informal enterprises

Possible policy interventions include providing certain micro-enterprise development programmes for own-account workers to increase their knowledge of, access to, and bargaining power in markets. Governments can support small-scale entrepreneurial activities through training, credit and marketing support. It has been shown above that capital mobility between the formal and the informal economy is essential for a positive impact of trade on incomes in the informal economy. Thus, policies facilitating informal firms' access to capital would have a positive impact on their productivity.

The policy package should be concerned with fiscal policies, trade policies, welfare policies, education, training and labour policies. While considering policy packages for sustained job creation, investment climate reforms need to be given top priority. Need for reforms can be identified by using investment climate surveys that include informal sector enterprises and own-account workers. Labour market regulations are also important but need to be considered within a broader institutional and policy framework. Improving labour market outcomes entails implementation of a set of comprehensive and complex policy reforms that remove a wide range of constraints to business operation. In the Russian Federation and Ukraine, for example, growth in private-sector employment has been achieved mainly thanks to a relatively low tax burden. However, the poor investment climate has impeded job creation. Specifically, heavy market regulations, high administrative barriers to firm formation and poor access to finance, have all slowed the pace of private-sector employment growth.

Apart from the potential to increase the productivity of informal enterprises, policies facilitating graduation to formal enterprises should be pursued. International evidence suggests that governments need to take two approaches to encourage firms to become formal (World Bank, 2005). First, recognizing that formalization will take time, governments can provide a supportive environment for the growth of productivity and improvement in working conditions in the informal sector. The key step here is to remove disincentives to growth. In India, for example, growth-restricting policies include reserving sectors for small-scale firms, regulations that raise transaction costs and costs when firms grow beyond a certain size, and other regulatory barriers discussed earlier. Another prominent example of a regulation that taxes firm growth in India is Clause VB of the Industrial Disputes Act, which severely restricts the rights of firms employing more than 100 workers to retrench labour. In general, many procedures can be simplified (Chen, 2006). Governments can directly and indirectly (e.g. through private-sector associations) provide business services and access to capital for informal sector firms to grow. Second, governments can gradually improve enforcement by raising incentives for firms to join the formal sector and impose penalties for non-compliance with formal-sector regulations. A range of tax and regulatory reforms that reduce concessions to informal sector firms, and lower taxes, social security contributions and regulatory burdens on formal sector firms, can be employed for this purpose. In implementing the second step to increase the penalties for non-compliance, however, governments should proceed with caution. Eliminating informality can lead to high costs in the short term in terms of firm closures and worker redundancies. Rather, the spirit should be to encourage growth and increase the incentives for firms to become formal, because this will enable them to gain access to services and benefits, and grow faster.

**Policies for informal workers**
Informal workers can be supported by governments through training and better labour rights. However, training and credit from formal sources tend to be administered by bureaucracies that are generally unfriendly to the poor, women and those with low literacy, who predominate in the informal economy. Economic policy needs to address the disadvantages and vulnerability of the informal economy that derives from its lack of access to formal training and credit institutions. Kenya and India each provide examples of governments enacting national economic policies to encourage the informal economy.

**Labour rights**
Although the majority of workers in developing countries are involved in informal work, these informal jobs are often not covered by labour laws or notable social protection. Thus, the informal economy is where most jobs – but few workers' rights – are to be found. Today, informal workers and labour advocates around the world are demanding workers' rights for all workers, including informal workers. Some of the impetus behind the demand for workers' rights for the informal workforce relates to concerns about globalization. Though all types of informal wage workers are, in principle, covered by almost all international labour conventions, such internationally recognized rights of informal workers are generally not addressed in the country-specific labour law and, more importantly, they are hardly enforced.

Home workers, who mainly do the work of factory workers but are stationed at home, also need labour rights. However, there is a need to first get information about such workers, and how to reach them, before policy intervention to govern and protect their employment relations can be implemented. There is a lack of data on home-based factory workers in most regular labour surveys, which makes it difficult to understand the concerns and constraints faced by such workers.

---

## Box 4-6: India: National Commission for Enterprise in the Unorganized Sector (NCEUS)

One of the major highlights of the Fourth Report of NCEUS (2007) was the official quantification of unorganized and informal workers, defined as those who do not have employment security, work security and social security. These workers are engaged not only in the unorganized sector but in the organized sector as well.

Examination of the regulatory framework for ensuring minimum conditions of work for unorganized wage workers shows that: (1) there is a lack of comprehensive and appropriate regulations in India; and (2) even where regulations exists, they are in-adequately and ineffectively implemented. The Commission reviewed and analysed the various perspectives on a comprehensive legislative framework for unorganized wage workers and made appropriate recommendations. The Commission established at a very high government practice level the need to make separate policies for informal workers and women workers.

Source: NCEUS, 2007.

---

## Box 4-7: International labour standards

Throughout the ILO, a system of international labour standards and labour Conventions was developed during the last century. Workers' rights include both core labour standards around which there is widespread international agreement and other basic rights. The core rights, encompassed in international Conventions, include freedom of association and the right to collective bargaining; elimination of all forms of forced or compulsory labour; elimination of discrimination in respect of employment and occupation; and the effective abolition of child labour. The longstanding commitment of the ILO to protecting the core rights of all workers irrespective of where they work was reinforced in 1998 when the International Labour Conference unanimously adopted a Declaration on Fundamental Principles and Rights at Work that applies to all those who work, regardless of their employment relationship. Most recently, the ILO has explicitly incorporated the informal economy in its policy framework called "Decent Work".

Most ILO standards apply to all workers or, if targeted at workers in the formal economy, have explicit provisions for extension to other categories of workers. One ILO Convention – the Home Work Convention, 1996 (No. 177) – focuses on a specific category of worker in the informal economy: home workers or industrial outworkers who work from their homes. And two ILO Conventions – one on rural workers, the other on indigenous and tribal peoples – focuses on groups who are often in the informal economy.

Source: ILO: *Decent work and the informal economy: Abstracts of working papers* (Geneva, 2002).

## Box 4-8: Example from India on labour rights

The National Commission for Enterprises in the Unorganized Sector (NCEUS) was created in 2004 to develop, implement and enforce national labour legislation in the unorganized sector (India's term for the informal economy). Earlier labour commissions in India neglected the informal or unorganized workforce.

The NCEUS mandate was to review:

- The status of unorganized/informal sector in India.
- The nature of enterprises.
- Their size, spread and scope, and magnitude of employment.
- Constraints faced by small enterprises with regard to freedom to carry out enterprise.
- Access to raw materials, finance, skills, entrepreneurship development, infrastructure, technology and markets.
- Measures to provide institutional support and linkages to facilitate easy access.
- Legal and policy environment to govern informal/unorganized sector for growth.
- Government of employment, exports and export promotion.
- Existing programmes relating to employment generation in informal/ unorganized sector and suggest improvements for redesign.
- Innovative legal and financing instruments to promote the growth of the informal sector.
- Existing arrangements for estimating employment and unemployment in the informal sector, and examine why the rate of growth in employment stagnated in the 1990s.
- Elements of an employment strategy focusing on the informal sector.
- Indian labour laws, consistent with labour rights, and with requirements of expanding growth of industry and services, particularly in the informal sector, to improve productivity and competitiveness.
- Social security system availability for labour in informal sector, and make recommendations for expanding their coverage.

The Study Group on Women Workers and Child Labour, one of five study groups set up under the Commission, recommended broadening the definition of workers to accommodate more categories of informal workers, promoting equal pay for men and women workers, extending maternity coverage to many informal workers, and mandating the provision of childcare facilities in small- and medium-sized enterprises. Some of the other recommendations of this study group include concrete and comprehensive ideas of how to extend national labour legislation to cover informal women workers.

The Government, through municipalities, has to facilitate career development so that informal traders can progress from the informal to the formal sector. Government officials must ensure that informal economy actors are well trained on policies and legislation that affect their operations. There is also a need for mentors to follow up on training sessions to see if there are any changes in the way training beneficiaries conduct business.

International labour standards need to be ratified and enforced by individual countries. In consultation with organizations of workers in the informal economy, national governments need to review how existing labour regulations can be extended to protect the rights of workers in the informal economy and whether additional labour regulation needs to be introduced to adequately protect the rights of the informal workforce. Some countries have adopted progressive labour regulation that addresses the insecurity and disadvantages of specific categories of informal or non-standard wage workers, including home workers (Canada), temporary workers (France) and sweatshop workers (California, US).

The Sector Education and Training Authority (SETA) is established to improve the skill levels of low-skilled workers. There are a number of people throughout the developing world who want and need to learn new skills. Many of the potential workers in such countries are still in schools or colleges and require special training through SETA. Even when certain workers are employed, they still need to improve their skills and learn new ones as well as to improve their productivity and get involved as formal/regular workers. In South Africa, for example, an estimated 4.3 million people are unemployed and many of them have little training and low skills. So it is clear that skills development, along with training and education, are vital elements for people in developing and middle-income countries to improve their own income and the GDP of their respective countries.

Given that a large number of people are still low skilled in many middle- and low-income countries, the majority of informal workers within these countries have little formal education. Hence, through SETA, there is a need for basic literacy and numeracy training as well as courses in areas such as managing a business, financial management, pertinent legislation and general life skills. Municipalities should work hand-in-hand with SETAs, other departments and organizations to implement training programmes aimed at building the capacity for informal-economy actors. Understanding regional differences is an important aspect in providing equal opportunities to all workers in a country. Therefore, regional governments within a country should conduct a comprehensive survey to establish training service providers who are currently working in the informal sector. Regional and local governments should play a role in facilitating and supporting skills development in these areas, for the benefit of all concerned.

## 4.6 CONCLUSIONS AND THE WAY FORWARD

Over 80 per cent of workers in low-income countries, 40 per cent of those in middle-income countries and 15 per cent of those in high-income countries are employed in the informal economy. While these shares are persistent, or in some regions even increasing, trade has increased dramatically during recent decades. Home-based work, piecemeal jobs, subcontracting and outsourcing have for decades been recognized as institutional means whereby employers can avoid the costs of compliance with labour regulations by shifting risks and various social obligations away from the parent company. However, the contemporary era has seen an unprecedented increase in casual labour employed in a range of rights-less contracts and appalling working conditions.

This chapter presents studies that attempt to conceptualize and formalize how trade and trade liberalization influences the informal economy, and how the informal economy impacts on the potential of a country to benefit from international trade. In this chapter, the term informal economy refers to "all economic activities by workers and economic units that are – in law or in practice – not covered or insufficiently covered by formal arrangements" and thus it includes self-employment in the informal economy and paid employment in informal occupations. Casualized and precarious work within the formal economy is therefore also included.

The informal economy has been addressed in this chapter in terms of three approaches, namely dualistic, legalistic and structuralist. Theoretical studies on the impact on the informal economy have emerged with varied conclusions depending on the assumptions they have used. Many studies find, however, that trade liberalization leads to an increase in the size of the informal economy. The impact on wages in the informal economy is less clear and depends on the specific assumptions in the model. One critical element is the mobility of capital. If capital can flow between the formal and the informal sectors, trade liberalization is likely to lead to higher wages in the informal sector. On the other hand, wages come under pressure if capital is not mobile.

Several econometric studies, mainly from Latin America, confirm a statistically significant link between trade and informality. Although the causality is not unambiguous, liberalization policies may have created incentives to cut costs by registered firms and to outsource into the informal economy. The identified impact of trade on informality is, however, small in most studies. For Brazil, studies failed to find a significant impact. In Colombia, trade increased employment in the informal sector, and in Mexico studies show that trade liberalization has led to formalization. Hence, one could conclude that the trade composition, supply capacity, details of the trade liberalization scenario and other specific circumstances, such as labour market conditions, determine the direction of the impact of trade on employment. Labour markets that facilitate adjustment processes, low administrative barriers, capital mobility and certain forms of regional trade integration are among those circumstances that may support formalization of the informal economy.

Empirical ex post studies have also reviewed standard trade theories and indicate that, contrary to traditional theses, trade liberalization does not necessarily lead to rising welfare of unskilled labour. In general, it has been shown that the impact of trade on the informal economy cannot be separated from the impact on employment as a whole. Development in the informal sector is linked to the overall impact that trade has on employment.

This chapter also presents ex ante approaches to observe the impact of trade on the informal economy. Ex ante studies have tried to anticipate the likely impact of trade on informal production, employment and wages. An advantage of these CGE models is that they cover the whole economy and are thus useful instruments if effects from trade policy changes spread into all sectors and if second-round effects (e.g. through income effects) exist. This chapter also describes several CGE methodologies that take household-level data and labour market segmentations into account. Models for India and Benin are discussed in some detail. Furthermore, this chapter provides guidance for developing a model on trade and informal employment that can be used for policy analysis to support policy-makers' and social partners' decisions regarding the informal sector.

Trade reforms in certain cases have improved linkages between formal and informal economies and have benefited informal workers (e.g. in dedicated export processing zones). Although the relatively low productivity of the informal economy remains a major concern, its dynamism and flexibility may have helped countries to adapt to a new reality whereby the informal economy makes a substantial contribution to both national GDP and employment. Moreover, the informal sector provides an important opportunity for those who cannot find jobs in the formal economy to engage in small-scale economic activities to earn a living. It is important that these contributions are acknowledged by policy-makers.

Nevertheless, for a large share of workers in developing countries involved in informal work, these informal jobs often generate a low level of income compared to formal sector jobs and do not provide coverage by labour laws nor notable social protection. In many countries, the majority of the workforce is in the informal sector and workers in the informal economy are more likely to be poor than those working in the formal economy. Thus, without addressing the employment needs, constraints and vulnerabilities of those who work in the informal economy, efforts to reduce poverty will not succeed. Therefore, governments need to intervene to support small-scale entrepreneurial activities and informal economy workers to improve the productivity of informal workers and the ability of the economy to absorb such trained workers. International labour conventions also mandate governments to intervene on behalf of all workers, including those who work in the informal economy.

Policies and regulations generally have a different effect on formal and informal parts of the economy and, within the latter, effects on informal enterprises and on informal employment relations are likely to differ. Policy analysis needs to determine the various effects and identify appropriate equity and efficiency policies. The policy package should be concerned with fiscal policies, trade policies, welfare policies, education, training and labour policies. Support to informal enterprises through training, credit and marketing support will lead to sustainable growth. As the informal economy is a major contributor to GDP and to economic development in general, governments should intervene to promote productivity and growth of informal enterprises. Furthermore, appropriate economic policies on the informal economy should balance incentives, tax burdens and statutory benefits (e.g. unemployment insurance and pension funds) between large and small businesses, and between employers and informal workers. Proactive policy on the informal economy could shift the structure of aggregate demand, the prices of inputs and outputs, and the set of incentives and subsidies in favour of informal enterprises. Governments need to improve the perception of workers in the informal economy by formal institutions, including those dealing with training and credit. The disadvantages and vulnerabilities of informal workers arising from limited access to formal training and credit institutions should be addressed. Graduation from the informal to the formal sector needs to be facilitated by, for example, low administrative barriers.

Some progress has been made. Both Kenya and India, for example, provide examples of governments enacting national economic policies to encourage the informal economy, though much still needs to be done in actual implementation of interventions in these countries. It is important that national governments consult workers' organizations in the informal economy, review existing labour legislation and extend it to protect the rights of workers in the informal economy. In addition, additional labour legislation needs to be introduced whenever necessary to adequately protect the rights of the informal workforce. Such policies will also enable countries as a whole to benefit from trade and globalization.

# REFERENCES

Agenor, P-R.; Aizenman, J. 1994. "Macroeconomic adjustment with segmented labor markets", *NBER Working Paper* No. 4769.

Agénor, P-R.; Izquierdo, A.; Fofack, H. 2003. "IMMPA: A quantitative macroeconomic framework for the analysis of poverty reduction strategies", *Policy Research Working Paper* No. 3092 (Washington, DC, World Bank).

Anderson, J.E.; van Wincoop, E. 2001. "Gravity with gravitas: A solution to the border puzzle", *NBER Working Paper* No. 8079.

Bacchetta, M.; Ernst, E.; Bustamante, J.P. 2009. *Globalization and informal jobs in developing countries* (ILO and WTO).

Bauch, P.A. 1991. "Linking reasons for parent choice and involvement for minority families in Catholic high schools", in *International Journal of Educational Research*, Vol. 15, No. 3-4, pp. 311-322.

Baulch, B.; Cherel-Robson, M.; McCulloch, N. 2000. "Poverty, inequality and growth in Zambia during the 1990s", *EconWPA Econometrics* No. 0004004.

Bautista, M.R.; Lofgren, H.; Thomas, M. 1998. "Does trade liberalisation enhance income growth and equity in Zimbabwe? The role of complementary policies", *TMD Discussion Paper* No. 32 (Trade and Macroeconomics Division, International Food Policy Research Institute).

Bigsten, A.; Söderbom, M. 2005. "What have we learned from a decade of manufacturing enterprise surveys in Africa?", *Policy Research Working Paper* No. 3798 (World Bank, Washington, DC).

Blanchard, O. 2005. "European unemployment: the evolution of facts and ideas", *NBER Working Paper* No. 11750.

Bosch, M.; Goñi, E.; Maloney, W.F. 2006. *The determination of rising informality in Brazil: Evidence from gross worker flows* (World Bank, Washington, DC).

Carr, M.; Chen, M.A. 2002. "Globalization and informal economy: How global trade and investment impact on the working poor", *Working Paper on the Informal Economy* (ILO).

Chandra, V.; Khan, M.A. 1993. "Foreign investment in the presence of an informal sector", in *Economica*, Vol. 60, No. 237, pp. 79-103, Feb.

Chaudhuri, S.; Mukherjee, U. 2002. "Removal of protectionism, foreign investment and welfare in a model of informal sector", in *Japan and the World Economy*, Vol. 14, No. 1, pp. 101-116, Jan.

Chen, M. 2006. *Formalization of informal enterprises: Which, what, how and why?*, presentation to World Bank, Mar.

Cimoli, M.; Porcile, G. 2009. "Sources of learning paths and technological capabilities: An introductory roadmap of development processes", in *Economics of Innovation and New Technology*, Vol. 18, No. 7, pp. 675-694.

Comin, D.; Philippon, T. 2005. "The rise in firm-level volatility: Causes and consequences", *NBER Working Paper* No. 11388.

Cornia, G.A. 1999. "Social funds in stabilization and adjustment programmes", *Research Paper* 48 (World Institute for Development Economics Research).

Davis, L.S. 2004. "Explaining the evidence on inequality and growth: Informality and redistribution", *DEGIT Conference Paper* No. c009_032 (Dynamics, Economic Growth and International Trade).

Davis, S.J.; Haltiwanger, J. 1990. "Gross job creation and destruction: Microeconomic evidence and macroeconomic implications", in O.J. Blanchard; S. Fischer (eds): *NBER macroeconomics annual 1990: Volume 5.*

Davis, S.J.; Haltiwanger, J. 1992. "Gross job creation, gross job destruction, and employment reallocation", in *Quarterly Journal of Economics*, Vol. 107, No. 3, pp. 819-863, Aug.

Davis, S.J.; Haltiwanger, J.; Schuh, S. 1996. *Job creation and destruction* (MIT Press).

Elbadawi, I.; Loayza, N. 2008. "Informality, employment and economic development in the Arab world", in *Journal of Development and Economic Policies*, Vol. 10, No. 2, Mar.

Farrell, D. 2004. "Boost growth by reducing the informal economy", in *The Asian Wall Street Journal*, 18 Oct.

Feinstein, J.S. 1999. "Approaches for estimating noncompliance: Examples from federal taxation in the United States", in *The Economic Journal*, Vol. 109, No. 456, pp. 360-369, June.

de Ferranti, D.; Lederman, D.; Malloney, W.; Perry, G. 2001. "From natural resources to the new economy: Trade and job quality" (World Bank).

Fiess, N.M.; Fugazza, M.; Maloney, W.F. 2006. "Informal labor markets and macroeconomic fluctuations", *Working Paper* No. 2006_17 (Department of Economics, University of Glasgow).

Fiess, N.M.; Fugazza, M. 2008. "Trade liberalization and informality: New stylized facts", *Policy Issues in International Trade and Commodities Study Series* No. 43 (UNCTAD).

Fortin, B.; Marceau, N.; Savard, L. 1997. "Taxation, wage controls and the informal sector", in *Journal of Public Economics*, Vol. 66, No. 2, pp. 293-312, Nov.

Galiani, S.; Sanguinetti, P. 2003. "The impact of trade liberalization on wage inequality: Evidence from Argentina", in *Journal of Development Economics*, Vol. 72, No. 2, pp. 497-513, Dec.

García-Verdú, R. 2007. *Measurement of the shadow economy or shadowy measurement?* (World Bank).

Gibson, B. 2005. "The transition to a globalized economy: Poverty, human capital and the informal sector in a structuralist CGE model", in *Journal of Development Economics*, Vol. 78, No. 1, pp. 60-94, Oct.

Gibson, B.; Godoy, R. 1993. "Alternatives to coca production in Bolivia: A computable general equilibrium approach", in *World Development*, Vol. 21, No. 6, pp. 1007-1021, June.

Glick, P.; Roubaud, F. 2004. "Export processing zone expansion in an African country: What are the labor market and gender impacts?", *DIAL Working Papers* No. DT/2004/15 (Développement, Institutions et Analyses de Long terme).

Goldberg, P.K.; Pavcnik, N. 2003. "The response of the informal sector to trade liberalization", in *Journal of Development Economics*, Vol. 66, No. 1, pp. 75-105, May.

Gupta, M.R. 1993. "Rural-urban migration, informal sector and development policies: A theoretical analysis", in *Journal of Development Economics*, Vol. 41, No. 1, pp. 137-151, June.

Hall, J.C.; Sobel, R.S. 2008. "Freedom, entrepreneurship, and economic growth", in A.V. Llosa (ed.): *Lessons from the poor* (The Independent Institute), pp. 247-268.

Handa, S.; King, D. 1997. "Structural adjustment policies, income distribution and poverty: A review of the Jamaican experience", in *World Development*, Vol. 25, No. 6, pp. 915-930, June.

Hanson, G.H.; Robertson, R. 2006. *China and the recent evolution of Mexico's manufacturing exports* (University of California).

Harris J.R.; Todaro, M.P. 1970. "Migration, unemployment & development: A two-sector analysis", in *The American Economic Review*, Vol. 60, No. 1, pp. 126-142, Mar.

Harriss-White, B. 2003. *India working: Essays on society and economy* (Cambridge University Press).

Hugon, P. 1990. "The informal sector revisited (in Africa)", in D. Turnham; B. Salomé; A. Schwarz (eds): *The informal sector revisited* (OECD).

Hussmanns, R. 2004. *Defining and measuring informal employment* (Bureau of Statistics, ILO).

ILO. 1993. Fifteenth International Conference of Labour Statisticians (ICLS), Resolution concerning the International Classification of Status in Employment (ICSE), in *Bulletin of Labour Statistics* (Geneva).

ILO. 2002a. *Decent work and the informal economy: Abstracts of working papers*, International Labour Office, Geneva, 2002.

ILO. 2002b. *Decent work and the informal economy*, Report VI, International Labour Conference, 90th Session, Geneva, 2002.

ILO. 2003. Seventeenth International Conference of Labour Statisticians (ICLS), *Report I: General Report* (Geneva).

ILO; WIEGO. 2000. *Social protection for women in the informal economy*.

Ishengoma, E.K.; Kappel, R. 2006. "Economic growth and poverty: Does formalisation of informal enterprises matter?", *GIGA Working Paper* No. 20 (German Institute of Global and Area Studies).

Jansen, M.; Turrini, A.A. 2004. "Job creation, job destruction, and the international division of labor", in *Review of International Economics*, Vol. 12, No. 3, pp. 476-494, Aug.

Johnson, S.; Kaufmann, D.; Zoido-Lobaton, P. 1998a. "Regulatory discretion and the unofficial economy", in *American Economic Review*, Vol. 88, No. 2, pp. 387-392, May.

Johnson, S.; Kaufmann, D.; Zoido-Lobaton, P. 1998b. "Corruption, public finances and the unofficial economy", *World Bank Discussion Paper*.

Kar, S.; Marjit, S. 2001. "Informal sector in general equilibrium: Welfare effects of trade policy reforms", *in International Review of Economics & Finance*, Vol. 10, No. 3, pp. 289-300, July.

Kelley, B. 1994. "The informal sector and the macroeconomy: A computable general equilibrium approach for Peru", in *World Development*, Vol. 22, No. 9, pp. 1393-1411, Sep.

Killick T. 1995. "Structural adjustment and poverty alleviation: An interpretative survey", in *Development and Change*, Vol. 26, pp. 305-331.

La Porta, R.; Shleifer, A. 2008. "The unofficial economy and economic development", *NBER Working Paper* No. 14520.

Lederman, D.; Olarreaga, M.; Soloaga, I. 2006. "The growth of China and India in world markets: Opportunity of threat for Latin America exporters?", background paper for regional study: *Latin America and the Caribbean respond to the growth of China and India* (World Bank).

Ljungqvist, L.; Sargent, T.J. 1998. "The European unemployment dilemma", *in Journal of Political Economy*, Vol. 106, No. 3, pp. 514-550, June.

Ljungqvist, L.; Sargent, T.J. 2005. "Jobs and unemployment in macroeconomic theory: A turbulence laboratory", *CEPR Discussion Paper* No. 5340.

Loayza, N.V. 1996. "The economics of the informal sector: A simple model and some empirical evidence from Latin America", in *Carnegie-Rochester Conference Series on Public Policy*, Vol. 45, No. 1, pp. 129-162, Dec.

Maloney, W.F. 1999. "Does informality imply segmentation in urban labor markets? Evidence from sectoral transitions in Mexico", in *World Bank Economic Review*, Vol. 13, No. 2, pp. 275-302, May.

Marjit, S.; Acharyya, R. 2003. *International trade, wage inequality and the developing economy – A general equilibrium approach* (Physica-Springer Verlag).

Marjit, S.; Beladi. H. 2005. *International trade and interregional disparity* (City University of Hong Kong), mimeo.

Marjit, S.; Maiti, D.S. 2005. "Globalization, reform and the informal sector", *Working Paper* No. RP2005/12 (World Institute for Development Economic Research).

Matthieu, B.; Mehl, A. 2008. "China's And India's roles in global trade and finance: Twin titans for the new millennium?", *Occasional Paper Series* No. 80 (European Central Bank).

Meagher, K.; Yunusa, M-B. 1996. *Passing the buck: Structural adjustment and the Nigerian urban informal sector* (United Nations Research Institute for Social Development).

Melitz, M.J. 2003. "The impact of trade on intra-industry reallocations and aggregate industry productivity", in *Econometrica*, Vol. 71, No. 6, pp. 1695-1725, Nov.

Mondino, G.; Montoya, G. 2002. "The effects of labor market regulations on employment decisions by firms: Empirical evidence for Argentina", in J. Heckman; C. Pages (eds): *Law and employment: Lessons from Latin America and the Caribbean* (University of Chicago Press).

NCEUS. 2007. *Report on conditions of work and promotion of livelihoods in the unorganised sector* (National Commission for Enterprises in the Unorganised Sector, Government of India).

Neck, R.; Schneider, F. 1993. "The development of the shadow economy under changing tax systems and structures", in *Finanzarchiv*, Vol. 50, No. 3, pp. 344-369.

OECD. 2009. "Is informal normal? Towards more and better jobs in developing countries", in J. Jutting; J. de Laiglesia (eds): *An OECD development centre perspective*.

Paquet, M.; Savard, L. 2009. "Impact of informal re-exports between Benin and Nigeria: A CGE analysis", *Working Paper* No. 09-14 (Departement d'Economique de la Faculte d'administration à l'Université de Sherbrooke).

Peattie, L. 1987. "An idea in good currency and how it grew: The informal sector", in *World Development*, Vol. 15, No. 7, pp. 851-860, July.

Perry, G.E.; Maloney, W.F.; Arias, O.S.; Fajnzylber, P.; Mason, A.D.; Saavendra-Chanduvi, J. 2007. *Informality: Exit and exclusion* (World Bank).

Porto, G.; Galiano, S. 2006. "Trends in tariff reforms and trends in wage inequality", *Policy Research Working Paper* 3905 (World Bank).

Ranis, G.; Stewart, F. 1997. "The urban informal sector within a global economy", in U. Kirdar (ed.): *Cities fit for people* (Unite Nations, New York).

Roberts, B.R. 1989. "Employment structure, life cycle, and life chances: Formal and informal sectors in Guadalajara", in L.A. Benton; M. Castells; A. Portes (eds): *The informal economy: Studies in advanced and less developed countries* (Johns Hopkins University Press).

Savard, L.; Adjovi, E. 1997. "Adjustment, liberalisation and welfare, in presence of health and education externalities: A CGE applied to Benin", *Cahier* No. 97-07 (Centre de Recherche en Économie et Finance Appliquées).

Schneider, F.; Enste, D.H. 2000. "Shadow economies: Size, causes and consequences", in *Journal of Economic Literature*, Vol. 38, pp. 77-114, Mar.

Schneider, F.; Enste, D.H. 2000. *Schattenwirtschaft und schwarzarbeit: Umfang, ursachen, wirkungen und wirtschaftspolitische empfehlungen* (Munich).

Shimer, R. 2005. *Reassessing the ins and outs of unemployment* (University of Chicago).

Singh, N.; Sapra, M.K. 2007. "Liberalization in trade and finance: India's garment sector", in B. Harriss-White; A. Sinha (eds*): Trade liberalization and India's informal economy* (Oxford University Press).

Sinha, A.; Adam C.S. 2000. *Trade policy reform and the informal sector in India*, paper presented at the Thirteenth International Conference on Input-Output Techniques at Macerata, Italy, Aug.

Sinha, A.; Adam C.S. 2006. "Reforms and informalization: What lies behind jobless growth in India", in B. Guha-Khasnobis; R. Kanbur (eds): *Informal labour markets and development* (Palgrave Macmillan).

Sinha, A.; Siddiqui, K.A.; Munjal, P. 2007. "A SAM framework of the Indian informal economy", in B. Harriss-White; A. Sinha (eds): *Trade liberalization and India's informal economy* (Oxford University Press, India).

Sinha, A.; Siddiqui, K.A.; Sangeeta, N. 2003. *The impact of alternative economic policies on the informal sector: A multisectoral study* (NCAER).

Sinha, A. 1999. "Trade liberalisation and informal households: A study using a CGE model for India", *Research Report* No. 26 (Queen Elizabeth House, University of Oxford).

Sinha, A. 2009. "Impact of global slowdown on employment and income in India: A CGE model analysis", prepared for a study on *The consequences of the global economic crisis* (NCAER and World Bank), mimeo.

de Soto, H. 1989. *The other path: The invisible revolution in the Third World* (Tauris).

Squire, L. 1991. "Poverty and adjustment in the 1980s: Introduction", in *World Bank Economic Review*, Vol. 5, No. 2, pp. 177-185, May.

Stallings, B.; Peres, W. 2000. *Growth, employment and equity: The impact of the economic reforms in Latin America and the Caribbean* (Economic Commission for Latin America and the Caribbean and Brookings Institution Press).

UNDP. 1999. *Human development report 1999*.

UN DESA. 2005. *The inequality predicament: Report on the world social situation 2005*.

Van der Hoeven, J. 1996. "Differential and mixed differential - difference equations from the effective viewpoint". Preprints.

White, H. 1997. *Poverty and adjustment in Sub-Saharan Africa: A review of the literature*, report prepared for the evaluation of SPA (Institute of Social Studies).

World Bank. 2005. "The informality trap, private sector development", *View Point Note* No. 301 (Washington, DC).

World Bank. 2007. *Argentina poverty assessment – Informal employment in Argentina: Towards understanding its causes and consequences*.

Wright, M.L.J. 2004. "New empirical results on default: A discussion of 'A gravity model of sovereign lending trade, default and credit'", *IMF Staff Papers*, Vol. 51.

## ANNEX 4.A: DEVELOPING A KNOWLEDGE TOOL ON TRADE AND INFORMALITY

This annex provides information for the development of a knowledge tool on trade and informality. Such a tool could serve to train relevant government ministry officials and researchers to support policy-makers in designing policies that address the challenges of trade and informality.

First, an outline for the background information is provided. This information is provided in this chapter and could be complemented by additional information from other parts of this book, especially the overviews of trade and employment (Chapter 2) and methodology (Chapter 3), but also the chapter on gender and trade and trade adjustment (Chapter 6).

Second, information about strengths and weaknesses of different analytical approaches is provided in a structured form.

Third, for the development of a CGE model, data requirements are discussed and four examples of possible data sources are provided.

### 4.A.1 Outline of background information for a knowledge tool

---

**Module 1: What is informal work: Concepts and status**
1.1      Overview
1.2      Aims of the module
1.3      Why measure informal work?
1.4      The status and trends in data collection on informal employment

**Module 2: Guide to policy options, responses and advocacy on informal work**
2.1      Overview
2.2      Aims of the module
2.3      Integration of informal work in national policies
2.4      What are the perspectives in analysing policy implications of informal work?
2.5      Informal work in labour-market and employment policies
2.6      Policy options and responses for informal work

**Module 3: Guide on methods for measuring informal work through case studies**
3.1      Overview
3.2      Aims of the module
3.3      Concepts and terminology
3.4      Building a system of interaction with respondents in the informal economy
3.5      Building focus-group discussion issues using good practices
3.6      Build field-study questionnaires using good practices

**Module 4: Guide to building analytical tools for integrating informal work in quantitative models**
4.1      Overview
4.2      Aims of the module
4.3      Best practices for quantitative techniques to study trade and informality
4.4      Guide to building SAMs
4.5      Guide to building CGEs

---

## 4.A.2 Strengths and weaknesses of possible analytical approaches

### Qualitative approach
*Strengths*
Qualitative approaches, through the use of various case studies and focus-group discussions of informal worker and enterprises, could provide a very detailed understanding of the focus of the trade reforms (see, for example, Singh and Sapra, 2007). Information on the exact implementation procedures and the changes experienced by the group in which the researchers are interested can be obtained.

### Some disadvantages
However, this approach cannot identify the exact linkage between, for example, trade or fiscal reforms and the welfare changes, as these cannot be tested. The results seen after a policy change could be due to other reasons or mixed outcomes, and no direct linkage can be traced without any quantitative connection. Moreover, in cases where there is no impact observed after a policy change, this could in fact be due to some countering factors, even though policy changes had a direct impact on the stated objective. Also, the conclusions drawn from qualitative analyses cannot be taken as general, and should be limited only to the specific group analysed. Such studies, in spite of being very valuable for in-depth understanding, have significant limitations. The inability of descriptive studies to provide a robust causality between impact and result is one of the reasons for the popularity of research based on quantitative approaches.

### Quantitative approaches
*Strengths*
Quantitative approaches, such as those based on CGE models, are numerical representations of economic theory and intuition. The models can be used to address a broad range of policy issues and can take into account "second-round" effects of policy changes (in circumstances where basic intuition can carry us only so far).

–   It is important to note that CGE models:

–   Can be used to decompose the effects of policy changes.

–   Can be used to track the distributional consequences of policy choices.

–   Can evaluate feasible policies or "policy packages" in a systematic fashion.

–   Can assist in policy formulation by permitting comparisons across the set of compatible policy combinations.

–   Are explicitly structural (they do not encounter the identification problems associated with econometric models).

–   Force modellers to be explicit about assumptions (which can be changed).

–   Offer considerable scope for altering aggregation (across sectors, institutions, households).

168

- Demand and enforce data consistency, thus identifying data gaps.

- Demand clarity in specification.

- Help prioritize areas of data collection.

## Some disadvantages

- CGE models are complex and require skilled maintenance.

- Quantitative CGE models are data-demanding: they do not tolerate inconsistencies in data.

- CGE models are not "forecasting" tools.

### 4.A.3   Information to develop an informal-economy related CGE model

In its simplest form, the application of CGE simulation techniques is identical to the procedures followed in disaggregating household categories in a standard SAM model. The steps outlined here relate to data requirements to build an informal economy in a SAM that drive the building of a CGE model for technical assistance projects.

## Social accounting matrix (base data set for developing CGE)

**Bangladesh**
Social accounting matrix, 1993–94; available at:
http://www.ifpri.cgiar.org/datasets/results/taxonomy:5169?page=2.
Social accounting matrix, 2005; available from Selim Raihan, University of Dhaka, Bangladesh, at: selim.raihan@gmail.com.

**Benin**
Social accounting matrix, 2006 (Benin's Finance Ministry, Cotonou).
Paquet and Savard (2009).

**Guatemala**
Alarcón, J. 2006. "Matriz de Contabilidad Social para Guatemala (2001)", final report, Institute of Social Studies (ISS) and Secretaría General del Consejo Nacional de Planificación Económica de Guatemala (SEGEPLAN), The Hague, Feb.

**Indonesia**
Social accounting matrix, 1995 (in billions of rupiah at purchasers' prices).
Source: Biro Pusat Statistik. 1998. *Sistem Neraca Sosial Ekonomi, 1995* (Jakarta), tables 3 and 6.
Dimensions: 109 accounts and employment of 16 categories of labour.
Imports: Imports c.i.f., duties and taxes are considered negative in the final demand columns of an input-output table.
Available at: http://storm.ca/~sdamus/io_data.htm.

169

## Input-output tables

### Bangladesh
Input-output table, 1962/63 (in 100,000 rupees at current purchasers' prices).
Source: Khan, A.R.; MacEwan, A. 1967. *Regional input-output tables for East and West Pakistan* (Pakistan Institute of Development Economics).
Dimensions: 35 sectors, industry by industry.
Imports: c.i.f. plus duty column in the final demand wing. Imports from West Pakistan are shown in a separate column.
Exports: In two columns for exports to West Pakistan and other exports.
Available at: http://storm.ca/~sdamus/io_data.htm.

### Benin
Not available in the public domain.

### Guatemala
Input-output table, 1971 (in quetzales, at producers' prices).
Source: Centro de Estudios Centroamericanos de Integración y Desarrollo. 1978. *Relaciones económicas intersectoriales: matrices de insumo-producto de Guatemala, año 1971.*
Dimensions: 45 sectors, industry by industry.
Imports: In one intermediate input row, including duties.
Available at: http://storm.ca/~sdamus/io_data.htm.

### Indonesia
Input-output table, 1995 (in millions of rupiah at producers' prices).
Source: Biro Pusat Statistik. 1998. *Table input-output Indonesia, 1995, Vol. I* (Jakarta), table 2.
Dimensions: 66 sectors, commodity by commodity.
Imports: Imports c.i.f., duties and taxes in negative F.D. columns.
Available at http://storm.ca/~sdamus/io_data.htm.

# GENDER ASPECTS OF TRADE

5

*Günseli Berik[1]*

## 5.1    INTRODUCTION

Expansion of trade has been one of the major forces of global integration of economies in the last quarter of the twentieth century. Trade liberalization policies that were implemented through multi-lateral, regional or bilateral trade agreements have been instrumental in this expansion of trade. Since the early 1980s, developing and industrial countries alike have reduced tariffs and have shifted away from quantitative restrictions to tariffs. In many developing countries, trade liberalization was implemented as part of structural adjustment programmes that aimed to bring macroeconomic stability and growth. Even when countries moved out of the debt crises that initially launched these market reforms, these sets of policies have often continued. The ongoing trade negotiations that focus on removal of various controls, protections and export subsidies continue to emphasize the benefits of trade liberalization in bringing prosperity to low-income countries and reducing inequalities between countries.

This study examines the literature relating to the effect of trade liberalization and subsequent trade expansion on employment and wages of women and gender inequalities. The main question is the extent to which trade policies have enhanced women's economic and social status and reduced within-country gender inequalities. The relationship between gender and trade has been examined in the scholarly literature since the early 1980s, which has shown the gender-differentiated effects of macroeconomic policies (Çağatay and Elson, 2000). The topic is receiving increasing attention in trade policy discussions as well, with calls for concrete policy measures to gender-mainstream trade policies. From a trade-policy perspective, the interest centres on the potential benefits of promoting gender equality for favourable trade outcomes and growth. In addition, there is desire for better anticipating the

---

[1] I thank, without implicating, Marion Jansen, Ralf Peters, David Kucera, Alessandra Lustrati and Naoko Otobe, and an anonymous reviewer, for useful comments on this paper.

gender-differentiated impacts of trade liberalization so as to respond to any adverse impacts and promote gender-equitable adjustments (Coche et al., 2006; Beviglia Zampetti and Tran-Nguyen, 2004).

Gender-aware research on trade has identified several channels by which trade policies and outcomes interact with gender relations.[2] One pathway is the change in the level and distribution of employment and wage levels in response to the change in the structure of production. The degree of economic volatility entailed by production for the world market could also affect the stability and security of employment. Another channel is the effect of trade liberalization on prices of tradable goods and services and, thus, livelihoods of households. Yet another pathway is the impact of tariff cuts on government revenues available for spending on social programmes and infrastructure. These effects in turn have implications for household-level resource and time allocation. Trade impacts differ by gender, however, since policies are implemented in the context of gendered social structures. Often, women are more adversely affected by trade policies, given that they have less skills and fewer resources compared to men, and thus have greater difficulty in both coping with the adjustments entailed and taking advantage of new employment or income opportunities generated by trade. Moreover, policy-making compounds these difficulties when the policy-makers presume gender-equitable impacts.

Gender inequalities also affect trade and industrialization strategies and long-run growth (Seguino, 2000; Klasen, 2002; Klasen and Lamanna, 2009). While policy-makers are keen on emphasizing research findings that indicate the long-run benefits of promoting gender equality in education, employment and access to assets for growth, it is also the case that major exporter countries have benefited from women's lower wages relative to men in achieving export success, at least in the short run (Seguino, 2000; Busse and Spielmann, 2006). Specifically, gender wage inequalities have provided advantages for many developing countries to gain a foothold in labour-intensive manufacturing exports. Some of these countries have used the proceeds of growth so achieved to finance investments in more diversified production structures and to promote improvements in women's well-being over the long run.

This chapter evaluates the state of the knowledge on this two-way relationship between gender and trade. As the chapter shows, the assessment is fraught with difficulties. Not only do gender inequalities precede trade reforms and provide the context for the trade impacts, but also it is difficult to disentangle trade impacts from changes in other macroeconomic policies. Moreover, data limitations and related research gaps constrain a comprehensive assessment of trade impacts that would trace effects from the labour markets (macro-) and institutional, public services (meso-) levels to the household (micro-) level, and especially in the domain of unpaid reproductive or subsistence work. Nonetheless, since trade liberalization has been so widely embraced, the economic experiences of otherwise diverse economies have been similar and common gendered patterns and trends in economic outcomes have emerged. A substantial body of research has focused on the quantity and quality of employment

---

[2] For a recent compilation of the gender-aware research on trade, see Çağatay et al. (2007).

and income-earning opportunities generated by trade reforms, particularly in the manufacturing and agricultural sectors. This evaluation shows a variety of gender impacts of trade reforms. On the whole, trade reforms have brought expansion of jobs for women in export sectors, with some likely positive feedback effects on women's status and autonomy in the household, but the working conditions in these jobs have often fallen short of complying with ILO Conventions. Agricultural trade liberalization has generally put women farmers at a disadvantage. With respect to policy, this chapter's argument is that in order to make trade reforms a force for reducing gender gaps and promoting gender-equitable improvements in livelihoods, gender-equity policies must be situated within a coherent framework of gender-sensitive trade and macroeconomic policies that aims to generate employment and income security.

## 5.2   ASSESSING GENDER IMPACTS OF TRADE

### 5.2.1   Gender inequalities precede trade reforms

Trade policies have different impacts on men and women in a given society because of the existence of gendered social structures. Each society has a gender system, socially constructed on the basis of biological differences between women and men. In most societies, women are primarily responsible for daily reproductive tasks in the household as the extension of their biological capacity to bear children and care for infants. That said, in pre-industrial societies, the gender division of labour was fairly flexible as it was organized around the household as the site of production, the primary focus of which was subsistence.

The gender division of labour that is characteristic of most contemporary societies has emerged with industrialization when the locus of production moved from the household to a dedicated space outside the household (the factory or the mine) and broke up the integrated nature of the household production process. This separation of home and workplace sharpened the division of labour as women became primary caregivers in the family and men became the "breadwinners". The gender division of labour was reinforced by gender ideologies of women's domesticity and men's authority in the household that are embedded in all institutions of society. In twentieth century agrarian societies, often shaped by colonial labour policies, women engaged in subsistence production along with caring tasks, while men migrated to mining or industrial areas to engage in wage work.

In late twentieth century agrarian and urban communities alike, this gender division of labour was commonly associated with women's weaker bargaining power in the household (figure 5.1, panel A). In the context of an expanding monetary economy, when confined to domestic and unpaid homestead pursuits, women's economic contribution to the household can be less visible and valued. Furthermore, women will likely have weaker perceptions of their self-interest (as distinct from family concerns), and a weaker fallback position (e.g. little income-earning ability) in the event of a family break-up (Sen, 1990). Weaker bargaining power in the household, in turn, contributes to and reinforces women's weaker access to household resources and is instrumental in inter-generationally transmitting inequalities between men and women. Women have no/little formal asset ownership, less education and training than men, and in many societies women also have less access to health care than men, which results in poorer health outcomes. These household-level inequalities are, in turn, associated with a particular set of economic outcomes for women in the monetary economy, which have weak feedback effects to alter the intra-household status of women (figure 5.1, panel B).

Development histories of several Asian and Latin American economies show that male workers constituted the first and main industrial workforce in the import-substituting industrialization drives of the twentieth century (Berik et al., 2008). In this phase, women workers accounted for a small share of the industrial labour force and were concentrated in a few labour-intensive industries, such as food and clothing, which were deemed gender-appropriate extensions of women's domestic work. Women, almost always young and unmarried, constituted a high share of workers in these industries. Married women were virtually absent from industrial wage work, consistent with gender norms and the actual division of labour in the household (figure 5.1, panel A).

Within industries, gender norms likewise shaped occupational (vertical) segregation, whereby women staffed less-skilled, non-supervisory assembly line positions, while men filled managerial positions or jobs that were deemed skilled. Associated with this industrial and occupational segregation by gender was a wage differential that signalled and reinforced women's dependence on men. Women's lower wages were shaped by not only their lower education levels and fewer years of work experience compared to men but also their low aspirations, lack of options and employer perceptions of women as short-term labour market participants. Thus, wage inequalities by gender were based on both the actual and perceived lower skill levels of women relative to men and societal views of appropriate pursuits for women and men. The societal norms that devalue women's labour and render them less deserving of wages paid to men were embedded in workplace practices (Elson, 1999).

These were the stylized features of the gendered context of the urban labour market when many developing economies embarked on trade liberalization and began orienting their domestic production toward exports in the last quarter of the twentieth century. In addition, in rural communities women were scarce in cash-crop production or entrepreneurial activities, except as unpaid family workers. These gender inequalities in employment and wages are salient in evaluating the impacts of trade policy changes on women and men. Different outcomes by gender (and more adverse outcomes for women) are expected since trade policy is implemented in the context of gendered social structures of the economy that are marked by inequalities – the household, legal systems, the labour market. Figure 5.1 presents a stylized representation of the gender inequalities characteristic of this stage of economic development, and the linkages between household-level inequalities and inequalities in the labour market and the monetary economy.

Figure 5.1: Description of gender inequality in the economy

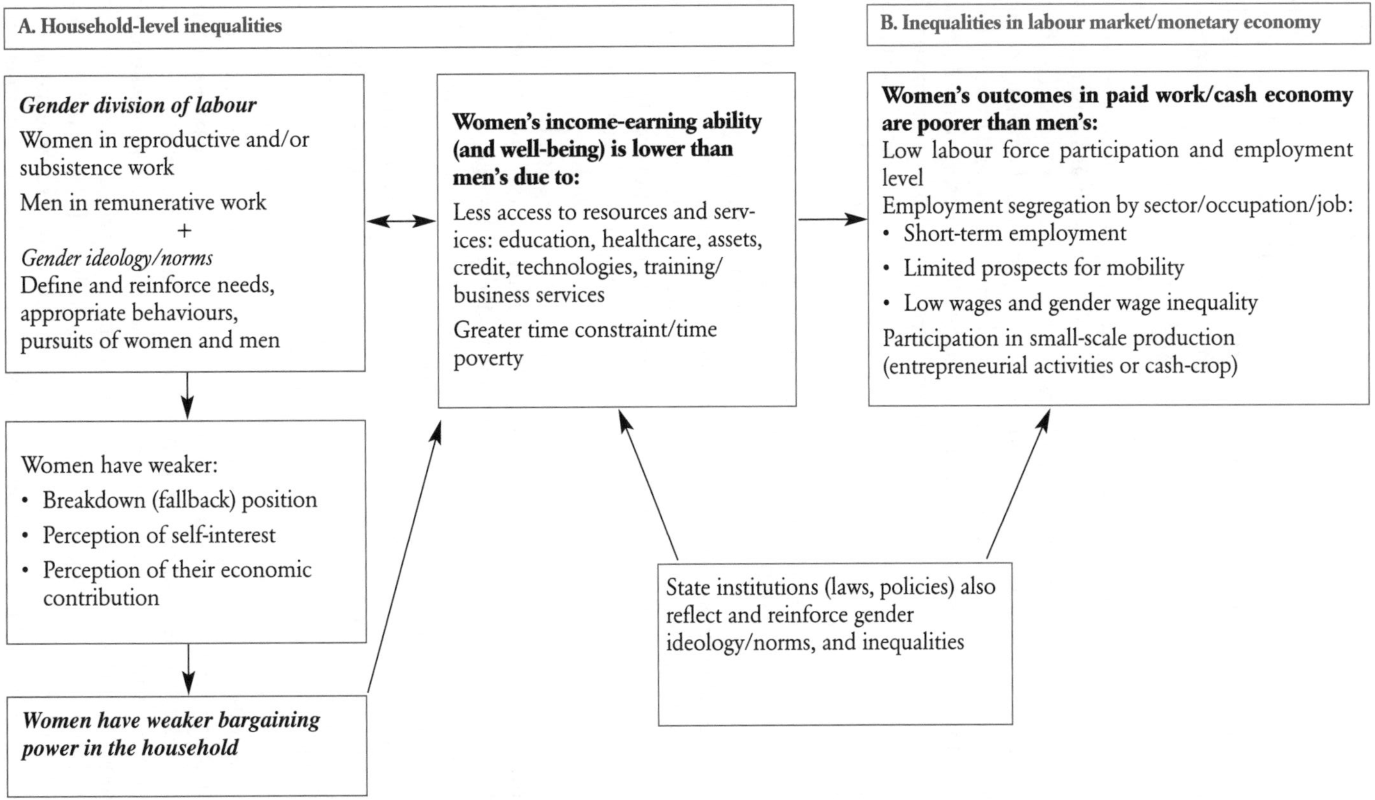

**A. Household-level inequalities**

**B. Inequalities in labour market/monetary economy**

**Women's outcomes in paid work/cash economy are poorer than men's:**
Low labour force participation and employment level
Employment segregation by sector/occupation/job:
- Short-term employment
- Limited prospects for mobility
- Low wages and gender wage inequality

Participation in small-scale production (entrepreneurial activities or cash-crop)

**Women's income-earning ability (and well-being) is lower than men's due to:**

Less access to resources and services: education, healthcare, assets, credit, technologies, training/business services

Greater time constraint/time poverty

State institutions (laws, policies) also reflect and reinforce gender ideology/norms, and inequalities

*Gender division of labour*
Women in reproductive and/or subsistence work

+

Men in remunerative work

*Gender ideology/norms*
Define and reinforce needs, appropriate behaviours, pursuits of women and men

Women have weaker:
- Breakdown (fallback) position
- Perception of self-interest
- Perception of their economic contribution

*Women have weaker bargaining power in the household*

Adapted from Beviglia Zampetti and Tran-Nguyen (2004), Ch.1, Figure 1; Sen (1990).

### 5.2.2 Methodological considerations: Identifying the gender impacts of trade

Trade policies affect individual well-being via three channels: (i) the price of goods consumed by the households; (ii) the household income, which includes labour income, income from sales of agricultural products, and government transfers; (iii) the generation and distribution of government revenues. Each of these pathways affects resource and time allocation and livelihoods at the household level.

In examining the trade-gender nexus, a variety of research methodologies has been used to infer changes in women's well-being, and gender inequalities and trade outcomes: cross-country, country or sector multiple regression analysis; computable general equilibrium (CGE) models; and descriptive statistical analyses. The first and main challenge in the assessment of trade impacts by gender is the paucity of gender-differentiated statistics. Most gender-differentiated employment and earnings data are for the manufacturing sector and for middle-income countries. As a result, much of the research on gender impacts of trade has focused on labour market impacts. Even for the manufacturing sector, however, data shortfalls at detailed sector, occupational and skill levels hinder assessment of the employment dislocation and churning in the labour market that are expected from a change in the trade regime.

Another data constraint is that survey data in developing countries tend to be more accurate in reflecting employment in formal establishments (and often those above a certain size). These statistics will not reflect the changes in the workforce that is employed in small establishments or at home, who are predominantly women. For example, the growth in female share of employment might be underestimated in the context of informalization, if former women workers in export factories move to home-based work or women enter the labour force as home-based workers. Both groups of women are likely to be hidden from statistical records.

Second, there are methodological difficulties in assessing gender impacts, such as sorting out the trade impacts from impacts of other macroeconomic policies or identifying the overall welfare impacts of trade that work through various channels. While not specific to gender-aware analysis, these difficulties render the analysis of gender impacts of trade invariably a partial one.

A major difficulty concerns differentiating trade impacts from the impacts of other macroeconomic reforms that accompany trade liberalization. Trade liberalization is adopted as part of the package of market reforms that often included: capital account liberalization; financial liberalization; deregulation of domestic economies; fiscal restraint; and the privatization of services, infrastructure and production that were previously provided by the public sector. One or more of these policies may work at cross purposes with trade reforms and undermine the anticipated benefits of trade expansion, at least in the short run. For example, while growth in exports of labour-intensive manufactures generates employment for women, the investment liberalization may make it difficult for workers to secure higher wages or better conditions in these jobs over time. Investors may respond to such worker demands by moving to other countries that offer lower labour costs. This failure to generate good jobs over time would not be due to trade liberalization per se, but to investment liberalization (and/or the diminished capacity of the government to pursue industrial policy to move up the industrial ladder and attract the investment that will bring more sophisticated technologies).

Furthermore, it is difficult to differentiate overall welfare impacts of trade liberalization, even from a single channel, such as price changes. While import liberalization is likely to reduce prices of tradable consumer goods available in the domestic market, it may also contribute to increases in prices of non-tradable goods, such as health services. Increase in (or introduction of) fees for such services may be necessary in order for governments to remedy the shortfall in tax revenues. Thus, the welfare gains associated with tariff reductions may be offset by the subsequent price effects. Low-income consumers, particularly women, are disproportionately affected by these impacts, yet it is difficult to determine the net consumption gains, even in overall terms.

Additionally, the standard variables used in assessing the gender impacts of trade – employment levels, employment segregation or gender wage gaps – may not pick up or can obscure the absolute improvements for women made possible by the growth generated by trade policies. Specifically, most statistical studies examine the change in earnings of women relative to men. While an increase in the relative earnings of women is important for achieving gender-equitable development, attention to absolute gains in earnings of both men and women is necessary for inferring changes in well-being. An historical perspective on Asian development shows that over the long run women have benefited from the changes brought by export successes of these economies (Chataignier and Kucera, 2005), even if these export successes cannot be attributed to internal or external liberalization:[3] labour force participation rates and educational attainment of women and men converged; real wages increased; and child labour declined. Women's and children's health and educational outcomes improved (table 6.1 of Berik, 2008; table 7.5 of Doraisami, 2008).[4] Thus, it is important to complement wage and employment analysis with broader gender well-being indicators in assessing gender impacts of trade policies and to include absolute as well as relative measures in evaluation.

Notwithstanding these data constraints and methodological caveats in assessing the gender impacts of trade, there is a sizeable empirical literature on gender and trade that allows some generalizations. Most of these studies are, in some cases implicitly, anchored in either neoclassical economic theory or heterodox economic approaches.

---

[3] It is now widely accepted that the export success and the consequent improvement of living standards in East Asian economies are the product of careful management of various macroeconomic policies, including trade policy and foreign direct investment flows, together with favourable initial conditions (for example, relatively low income inequality and pioneer status in implementing the export model).

[4] These absolute achievements in health are overshadowed by the emergence of high sex ratios at birth (that is the number of males per 100 females) in the Republic of Korea and Taiwan (China) in the mid-1980s. This key indicator of societal discrimination against women has emerged as the unforeseen side effect of a decline in fertility in the context of strong preference for sons rather than daughters.

177

## 5.3 THE GENDER IMPACTS OF TRADE ON EMPLOYMENT AND WAGES

### 5.3.1 Theoretical approaches

Within neoclassical (mainstream) economic theory, two arguments predict gender-equitable effects of trade liberalization and expansion in developing countries: the standard international trade theory (Hecksher-Ohlin-Stolper-Samuelson) and Gary Becker's theory of labour market discrimination. According to standard international trade theory, countries that specialize in production and trade based on their relatively abundant factor endowment will benefit from trade. Free trade in this case is expected to bring about increase in demand for the relatively abundant type of labour – relatively less-skilled labour in developing countries and relatively skilled labour in industrial economies. Sustained expansion of demand for the relatively abundant factor, in turn, is predicted to induce an increase in its relative return. To the extent that women workers predominate in less-skilled jobs in both developing and industrial economies, this theory predicts employment gains for women in export sectors of developing countries and employment losses for women in industrial countries. In developing countries, women workers are expected to see a rise in their wages relative to men in skilled jobs and a decline in the gender wage gap. Conversely, for industrial economies, disproportionate job losses for unskilled workers (women), and a widening wage gap between skilled (men) and unskilled (women) labour are expected.[5]

According to a recent interpretation of Becker's theory of labour market discrimination, a similar demand-induced dynamic toward greater gender equity is expected to ensue from increased competition generated by trade expansion (Becker, 1971; Black and Brainerd, 2004). Becker's theory predicts decline in labour market discrimination in response to increasing competition in product markets. These effects are more likely to be observed in concentrated industries since more competitive industries are already expected to have less or no discrimination against women workers. In this framework, women workers are assumed to be equally skilled/productive as male workers, hence the term "discrimination". The theory conceptualizes discrimination as a cost to the firm, which pays a wage differential that is higher than the marginal product of labour ("rent") to male workers. In the open economy context, the prediction is that import competition will discipline firms in concentrated industries and help reduce the gender wage differential via erosion of rents to male workers and an expansion in the relative demand for female labour.

---

[5] The restrictive assumptions of the theory – two-good, two-country world economy with no market imperfections, full employment – do not allow consideration of the interdependence between domestic sectors and the likely adjustments whereby the job losses for unskilled workers (women) in the manufacturing sector could be compensated by expanding opportunities in services.

By contrast, non-neoclassical (heterodox) approaches do not predict gender-equitable effects of trade expansion (Albelda et al., 2004). In this approach, wages and access to jobs are determined by the relative bargaining power of groups of workers, which are shaped by both worker skills and job characteristics. Heterodox labour market analyses do not explicitly address impacts of international trade but they conceive of the employment adjustments that ensue as a source of intensified competition among groups of workers to secure good jobs. In the case of import expansion, for example, job competition among workers in import-competing industries is likely to adversely affect wages of workers who are in a weaker position in terms of their skill levels, seniority or sector of employment. Thus, women workers may bear the brunt of job losses, have limited access to the newly created higher-paying jobs and may experience slower wage growth relative to men. When exports expand, on the other hand, women workers may experience job gains but not necessarily decline in wage discrimination, since discrimination is viewed as a routine feature of the economy. Specifically, labour market discrimination is both an adaptation to the prevailing gender norms in society, which shape occupational distribution and wage levels, and a conscious employer strategy to boost profits.

The predictions of the two neoclassical theories for developing countries are consistent: trade expansion sets off a process of closing of gender wage gaps that is associated with the increase in demand for women workers and the downward pressure on labour costs. The heterodox approach, premised as it is on the power differences between groups of workers and workers vis-à-vis employers, is less optimistic about the ability of women workers to gain ground in closing the gender wage gaps or otherwise improving working conditions, even if they gain access to new jobs.

### 5.3.2 Empirical evidence: Global feminization of employment

A major feature of the late twentieth century process of global integration has been the rapid incorporation of women in export sectors producing manufactured goods, agricultural products and services such as tourism and data processing (Mehra and Gammage, 1999).

This trend has been referred to as "global feminization of labour," where often a double meaning is invoked: the increase in women's share of employment and the spread of conditions of employment – part-time, temporary work with low pay and no or limited benefits – which traditionally characterized jobs held by women (Standing, 1989, 1999). The positive correlation between export orientation and female intensity of manufacturing employment has been confirmed by several studies and has become a stylized fact in the development economics literature (Özler, 2007; Seguino, 2000).

The structural adjustment programmes of the 1980s and 1990s, which heightened job and income insecurity among workers, also boosted employment growth in export sectors. Job losses of men in import-substituting industries subject to increasing import competition likely reinforced the feminization process as they pushed more women into the labour force. These results are consistent with empirical analysis of 16 medium- and low-income countries during the 1970–2003 period that shows that global feminization is the net outcome of the greater export response relative to the import response to trade openness (Heintz, 2006). Overall, the expansion of exports had a strong positive impact on women's employment, while import growth negatively affected men's employment.

Export processing zones (EPZs), also known as free trade zones (FTZs) or special economic zones (SEZs), have been integral to the export-led growth strategy and contributed to the export success of many industrializing countries since the late 1960s. Initially, EPZs recruited young, unmarried women workers, mostly from rural areas. Subsequently, they have increasingly drawn upon a more diverse workforce, consistent with the changing age-labour force participation profiles of women (Horton, 1996; Domínguez et al., 2010).

Far from losing their importance, EPZs have continued to proliferate along with trade liberalization. Many countries create and operate EPZs as areas where national labour laws are not fully enforced in addition to offering financial incentives for investors. The estimated numbers employed in EPZs have risen dramatically, tripling between 1997 and 2006 (Amengual and Milberg, 2008). China accounts for the majority of EPZ employment worldwide. EPZs produce a high proportion of exports, on the order of 80 per cent in several developing countries in 2006.

According to the latest ILO statistics, women workers constituted around 70 per cent of EPZ employment in 2005–06, ranging from a low of 10 per cent in Bahrain to 90 per cent in Jamaica and Nicaragua (Boyange, 2007). Women are prominent in EPZs, and export sectors in general, because they enable exporters to attain lower unit labour costs than is possible with male workers. This outcome is due to: the lower wage rates of women relative to men in comparable jobs; the high productivity levels of women; and the flexibility and lower risk women workers allow for exporters.

Each of these characteristics of women workers is sustained by societal gender norms. As Elson and Pearson (1984) emphasize in a classic contribution, abundant low-cost (female) labour is not a natural factor endowment of developing countries, but rather produced through concerted efforts of employers and governments in the context of gender norms.

First, women workers earn lower wages compared with men because of employment segregation. Employers often segregate women in unskilled positions because women are perceived as unskilled workers according to the gender schema of most societies. Further, the gender norms that designate men as the breadwinners and women as their dependents provide the rationale for hiring women into low-wage insecure jobs, considered befitting their role as secondary wage earners. Case studies also show that gender wage gaps are produced by the State and employers through gendered employment rules, lack of training for women, application of two-tier wages in EPZs, and suppression of union rights in export sectors (Seguino, 1997; Doraisami, 2008; Berik, 2008).

Second, export sectors attain high labour productivity with women workers due to the temporary nature of their employment. Short employment tenure is commonly the result of marriage or childbearing, which are often explicit grounds for termination. Limited tenure and high turnover allow factories to benefit from women workers' productivity at its peak and to maintain these as low-wage jobs. Women workers' docility, willingness to accept managerial discipline, and suitability for tedious, monotonous work are also likely to contribute to high productivity of women. While these qualities of women's labour are often played up as "natural" and "innate," they are the product of years of gender socialization and informal training in the home, prior to entry into employment in export factories (Elson and Pearson, 1984).

Institutional arrangements supported and enforced by governments and export factory employers also contribute to high productivity of export sector workers. Ngai (2007) shows that in China's export factories, where employment is temporary and conditional on urban residency permits, rural-urban migrant workers' compliance with shop-floor discipline and willingness to work overtime are high. These permits, along with short-term employment contracts, also allow factories to keep wage growth in check. In addition, by housing workers in dormitories adjacent to the factory, employers are able to draw upon labour rapidly (to meet shipping deadlines, for example) and to maintain extremely long hours of work.

In export factories both inside and outside EPZs, working long hours, including excessive overtime, is the norm. Especially in the apparel and footwear industries, where suppliers face tight shipping deadlines and seasonal peaks in demand and where export performance depends on increasing the export volume rather than the unit price, excessive overtime and continuous work schedules are widespread (Berik and Rodgers, 2010; Amengual and Milberg, 2008). Furthermore, excessive overtime is correlated with low wage levels, reinforcing the achievement of lower unit labour costs. For example, survey results and interviews with workers in Bangladesh indicate that, due to low wage rates, workers are eager to work overtime, since they could earn a higher overtime rate or even earn additional income at the same regular hourly rate (Bhattacharya, Moazzem and Rahman, 2008; Bhattacharya, Khatun, Moazzem, Rahman and Shahrin, 2008; Berik and Rodgers, 2010). For women workers in Bangladesh, whose base pay in 2006 was between 72 and 80 per cent of the earnings of male workers who perform identical work, the pressure is especially high to keep up with overtime and periodic continuous work schedules, sometimes up to 20 days.

Third, export sectors also achieve flexibility and lower risk with women workers who are employed in informal jobs or home-based work, characterized by job insecurity, unregulated contracts and openness to external labour market pressures (Balakrishnan, 2001). Women workers predominate in the lower rungs of global supply chains and provide the highly flexible workforce that absorbs the risks of shifting global orders, falling unit prices and falling lead times (Carr et al., 2000; Barrientos, 2007). Especially in countries where women are physically immobile due to gender norms, home-based work creates a vulnerable workforce that is unable to improve their terms of employment. These conditions also contribute to the attainment of lower unit labour costs with women workers.[6]

Underlying the global tendency for an increase in women's share of employment is a churning of the global labour market whereby women's job gains in some countries come at the expense of women workers in other countries. As predicted by standard trade theory, the increase in developing countries' labour-intensive exports produced by women workers has come at the expense of destruction of jobs held by women through import competition in high-income economies. OECD trade with developing countries provides a striking example. Kucera and Milberg (2007) found that the expansion of the OECD trade with developing countries over the 1978–95 period resulted in disproportionate job losses for women in OECD countries, who constituted the majority of workers in import-competing industries such as textiles, garments, footwear and leather goods. Such trade-related job losses have continued in the United States (US) in the late 1990s and early 2000s, with losses falling disproportionately on women workers (Callahan and Vijaya, 2009). These job losses have been compensated to some extent by the growth of service sector jobs, but whether the wage levels and the gender wage gaps in these growing sectors are more favourable is the subject of ongoing research.[7]

The intensified trade competition among developing countries following the end of the Agreement on Textiles and Clothing (ATC) on 31 December 2004 provides a more recent example of women workers competing for jobs in the same industries. The liberalization of trade in garments has brought a shift in exports, and thus in employment, from Central America and Africa toward Asia, especially toward China. The Dominican Republic, El Salvador, Honduras and Mexico experienced sharp declines in the export value and volume to the United States (Emerging Textiles, 2007). China and India increased their share of imports in the European Union and the United States while smaller economies – Fiji, the Maldives, Mongolia, Nepal – experienced absolute decline in their exports. In each of these cases, women's jobs and livelihoods were disproportionately adversely affected. Mauritius, which was highly dependent on the trade protections provided by the Multi-Fibre Agreement (MFA), and its successor the ATC, lost its export competitiveness with the end of the ATC, and experienced sharp declines in exports and employment, especially for women (Otobe, 2008). Other Asian countries have faced price competition that puts down-

---

[6] While home-based work predominantly draws on women's labour, men have been also increasingly employed as home-based workers under increased competitive pressures. For example, in the 1990s, firms in several of India's import-competing manufacturing sectors sought to lower costs by hiring workers in small-scale, home-based workshops where wages were lower (Rani and Unni, 2009).

[7] Kongar (2008) shows that the gender wage gap in the US services sector widened between 1990 and 2001, even as occupational segregation declined. In high-income developing countries, such as the Republic of Korea and Taiwan (China), there were differing trends over 1980–2002. While gender earnings gaps declined in services sectors where women's share of employment was rising, especially in Taiwan, after the Asian financial crisis (1997) the earnings gaps have widened in several services sectors in the Republic of Korea (Berik, 2008).

ward pressure on wages and other labour costs and hence working conditions (Adhikari and Yamamoto, 2006). While these shifts do not necessarily result in a zero-sum change in employment, they underscore the instability of trade-related jobs and suggest large-scale hardships of adjustment due to trade liberalization and preference erosion.

In sum, women in developing countries achieved employment gains during the era of trade reforms of the late twentieth century since they facilitate lower unit labour costs for employers than is the case with their male counterparts. However, the relative employment gains of women overall should not obscure the costs of adjustment generated elsewhere: job losses of both male workers in import-competing industries and the jobs lost for women workers elsewhere in export industries that experienced erosion of competitiveness.

### 5.3.3 Empirical evidence: Wage levels, wage growth and gender wage gaps

Wages are often used as the key indicator to track changes in job quality associated with international trade. If trade reforms have led to growth in women's employment opportunities relative to men, have these job options offered women higher wages relative to their alternatives and allowed wage growth so as to break the low-wage mould for women's jobs?

The wage levels and working conditions in EPZs/export-factories and their trajectories have been contentious issues. In a classic contribution Lim (1990) and recently Kabeer (2004) contested the argument of critics that export sector jobs represent poor options for women in developing countries. Lim argued that critics focused on the early stages of EPZs and relied on case studies that did not use a multivariate approach in examining working conditions. She argued that jobs in EPZs offered higher wages to women workers compared to their alternatives in the local economy, and challenged critics to use a local yardstick in assessing these jobs. Further, she predicted that over time working conditions in EPZs would improve as the EPZs matured and the demand for women's labour continued to grow.

Recent evidence on relative wage levels in EPZs is generally consistent with Lim's and Kabeer's argument. Wage levels and non-wage benefits are generally better than in non-EPZ factories and wages in alternative employment in the economy (Amengual and Milberg, 2008; Glick and Roubaud, 2006; Kabeer and Mahmud, 2004). Thus, EPZ jobs provide greater potential for alleviation of income poverty. Based on a 2001 survey of women workers in Bangladesh, Kabeer and Mahmud (2004) further argue that EPZ workers' earnings are well above the local poverty line. That said, EPZs in Mauritius, Mexico and Central America provide contrary evidence: real monthly earnings in large EPZ establishments in Mauritius have been below the average earnings in large non-EPZ establishments after 1991 (Otobe, 2008). In a study that aims to take stock of relative wages in *maquiladoras* (assembly factories that produce for export) after two decades of operation, Fussell (2000) finds that the EPZ workers constitute the lowest paid workers in the local labour market. Based on a review of studies for 2006–09 in Mexico and Central America, Domínguez et al. (2010) also argue that *maquiladora* workers often earn less than self-employed women, earn less than the industrial sector minimum wage or earn a salary that is insufficient to cover basic needs.

In making EPZ/non-EPZ wage comparisons, studies do not factor in the long hours and excessive overtime endemic to EPZ jobs. The use of monthly or annual earnings in making wage comparisons, without taking into account the working hours, is likely to overstate the relative advantage of EPZ jobs. EPZ factory workers have longer hours than their non-EPZ counterparts, which may even make the hourly EPZ pay lower than the hourly pay in alternative jobs. While a higher annual or monthly income may be more attractive for workers and will make a bigger dent in the income poverty rate, this income is attained at the expense of women workers' physical well-being as well as possibly being at lower hourly wages in comparison to alternatives.

Use of the local poverty line as the yardstick is equally problematic. Domestic poverty lines are often very low, and are not sufficient to support adequate livelihoods. Use of the minimum wage as the yardstick, as is common in policy discussions, is likewise inadequate when there is a clear erosion of the minimum wage over time. Such was the case in Bangladesh, for example, where the 2006 minimum wage adjustment for the garment sector left the real minimum wage for entry-level garment workers below its 1993 levels (Berik and Rodgers, 2010).

Lim's hypothesis about the long-term trajectory of EPZ working conditions has been examined by Fussell (2000). Based on data from a 1993 survey of women workers in Tijuana along the Mexico-United States border, Fussell shows that as global competition from Mexico's competitors intensified *maquiladora* employers not only reduced average real wages but also tapped into a workforce of older, married women with the lowest levels of schooling. These women lack better alternatives in the local labour market and are therefore a stable workforce for *maquiladora* employers. While the change in composition of *maquiladora* employment implies that younger women have improved their job options in the local labour market, possibly in the service sectors, Fussell shows that growth of *maquiladora* employment over the course of the 1980s and early 1990s has not brought about improvement in wages in this sector. Similarly, in Mauritius, between 1991 and 2004 the growth of EPZ earnings lagged behind non-EPZ earnings, resulting in a widening earnings gap, even though EPZ earnings more than doubled over this period (Otobe, 2008).

Studies that focus on non-EPZ export sectors find that average wage rates of both women and men in export sectors are lower than in non-export sectors. Inter-industry analysis of wages conducted for Mexico (2001–05) and Taiwan (1984–93) indicates that the export orientation of a sector exerts downward pressure on wages of women and men over and above the effect of a host of other industry characteristics such as skill composition, female share of industry employment and capital intensity (Brown-Grossman and Domínguez-Villalobos, 2010; Berik, 2000).

In sum, trade expansion has created better employment options for women in EPZ factories in most cases, but export sectors overall appear to provide lower-wage jobs relative to sectors that produce for the domestic economy. Country wage trajectories are also likely to be contingent on the dynamism of the sector: workers in EPZs facing intense competition from fast-growing countries (for example, Mauritius and Mexico vis-à-vis China) are likely to experience real wage erosion while wage growth is rapid in expanding export sectors/EPZs (for example, in China, where average wage growth has been more rapid than the global average (ILO, 2010)).

## 5.3.4 Empirical analyses of trade impacts on gender wage gaps

### 1) Does increased demand for female labour reduce gender wage gaps?

The standard international trade theory has not fared well in predicting wage gaps in developing country cases. Far from narrowing, wage gaps between skilled and unskilled labour (not differentiated by gender) have widened in many developing countries under the impact of trade, whether the latter is measured in terms of import expansion, protection rates, trade reform or export orientation. Occupational-level analysis for 1990–2000 also finds that wage inequality between high-skilled and low-skilled occupations widened due to the faster wage growth in high-skilled occupations (Corley et al., 2005).

Studies that examine trends in gender wage gaps without directly linking them to trade policy changes find some decline in gender wage gaps in manufacturing from the mid-1980s to the early 2000s (Tran-Nguyen and Beviglia Zampetti, 2004; Corley et al., 2005). However, as the researchers observe, even in the most successful East Asian economies the gender wage ratios varied between 59 and 65 per cent in the early 2000s. Almost all of the developing countries that narrowed gender wage inequalities between 1996 and 2003 had very high levels of gender wage inequality. Moreover, gender wage inequality increased in developing countries that had low levels of inequality.

A meta-study of a large number of industrial and developing country analyses shows that between the 1960s and 1990s gender wage gaps narrowed owing to the increasing education levels of women, but there is no evidence that the discriminatory portion of the gender wage gap – which focuses on wages of equally skilled women and men – narrowed (Weichselbaumer and Winter-Ebmer, 2005).[8] This evidence suggests that, while women are making progress in closing the earnings gaps, they are not reaping the full benefits of their rising education levels. In major exporter countries with strong demand for women's labour, the discriminatory gender wage gaps increased over the course of the 1990s and early 2000s. In Bangladesh, for example, the gender wage ratio in apparel manufacturing declined from 66 per cent in 1990

---

[8] Much of the research indicates that gender gaps are only partly due to productivity differentials, with about two-thirds of the gender gaps attributable to discrimination. See, for example, Horton (1996) and Psacharopoulos and Tzannatos (1992).

to 50 per cent in 1997 (Majumder-Paul and Begum, 2000). When differences in worker skills are controlled for, the female-male wage ratio that was fairly high in 1991–95 (95 per cent) declined (to between 72 and 80 per cent) by 2006 (Bhattacharya, Khatun, Moazzem, Rahman and Shahrin, 2008). In China, the discriminatory portion of the gender wage gap also widened in the 1990s (Maurer-Fazio et al., 1999). In 2008, 40 per cent of the gender wage gap among migrant workers in China was attributable to discriminatory treatment (ILO, 2010).

### 2) Does trade competition reduce gender wage gaps?

Studies that examine Becker's hypothesis, on the other hand, have generally not found support for the argument that trade competition undermines gender wage discrimination, i.e. the gender wage differencial among equally skilled workers.[9] Oostendorp's cross-country analysis of gender wage gaps at the detailed occupational level does not find evidence for the effect of trade (or foreign direct investment) in low- or lower-middle income countries during the 1983–99 period (Oostendorp, 2009).[10]

In one of the first studies to test the open-economy version of Becker's hypothesis, Black and Brainerd (2004) find that, in the US during the 1976–93 period, import expansion contributed to decline in wage discrimination in less competitive manufacturing industries. They attribute this favourable impact of trade to firms' cost-cutting measures, including cutting rents paid to male workers.[11] However, this study does not shed light on the direction and magnitude of changes in women's and men's earnings and changes in their employment levels that underlie the narrowing of gender wage gaps. A re-examination of the "importing equality" hypothesis shows that import competition in the US during this period reduced gender wage gaps via decline in the relative demand for less-skilled production workers in concentrated industries where women workers experienced heavier job losses (Kongar, 2007). It was the departure of low-skilled women workers, rather than the decline in wage discrimination against women workers, that increased average female wages and narrowed the gender wage gap.

Mexico provides mixed evidence depending on the export sector and the period under consideration. Trade liberalization over the 1987–99 period was associated with

---

[9] This empirical strategy has high data demands that impede its widespread application. Gender-differentiated data on individual worker characteristics – such as education, work experience – are necessary to isolate the wage differentials that arise from productivity differentials from those that cannot be explained ("the residuals"), which are usually attributed to discrimination.

[10] Oostendorp (2009) used the ILO October Inquiry data for 161 detailed occupations and 83 countries. He infers discrimination if average wages of men and women differ in the same narrowly-defined occupation where skills are relatively homogeneous.

[11] The dependent variable in this model is the residual wage gap – the portion of the wage gap that cannot be explained by observed productivity differences between women and men. The key independent variable is the interaction term between trade share of output and domestic industrial concentration by industry. Domestic concentration by industry and trade share by industry and year serve as control variables.

lower gender earnings discrimination in the non-EPZ manufacturing sector (Hazarika and Otero, 2004). Further, only those sectors of non-EPZ manufacturing that had achieved complete elimination of import tariffs by 1999 experienced decline in gender wage gaps. However, the gender wage gap trends in the EPZ (*maquiladora*) sector in the same study indicate that the *maquiladora* gender earnings gap, which was substantially smaller than in the rest of Mexico, widened after 1987 when Mexico liberalized its trade.

Other developing country research has produced evidence contrary to Becker's hypothesis. Based on panel data for Taiwan (China) and the Republic of Korea for the 1980–99 period, Berik et al. (2004) do not find support for a decline in wage discrimination with trade expansion. Specifically, in the case of Taiwan, increased import expansion was associated with a rise in wage discrimination. Furthermore, the study suggests that a Becker-type adjustment process is implausible: there is no evidence for the static implications of Becker's theory (on the contrary, wage gaps in competitive sectors were in fact wider than in concentrated sectors), and the widening wage gaps in fact accompanied decline in relative demand for women workers. In addition, the institutional context of the labour market at the time was characterized by discrimination against women and resistance to reducing discrimination. Thus, the authors interpret the adverse impact of import expansion on gender wage gaps as the outcome of disproportionate lay-offs by women workers in Taiwan's manufacturing industries. These lay-offs and associated wage gaps provide support for an underlying process that is consistent with non-neoclassical approaches that emphasize relative bargaining power of various groups in determining wage outcomes.

India's industrial and trade liberalization policies since 1991 were also associated with wider gender wage gaps in manufacturing industries (Menon and Rodgers, 2009). The policy reforms led individual firms in India to face greater competition both from abroad and from other domestic firms in the same industry. Menon and Rodgers attribute growing gender wage gaps to the relatively weak bargaining power of women workers who are less able to negotiate for favourable working conditions and higher pay.

Thus, this particular strand of research has not produced support for the argument that trade liberalization narrows discriminatory gender wage gaps. The widening gender wage gaps in the Asian country studies and Mexican *maquiladoras* present a challenge for both Becker's theory and the standard trade theory. As argued in debates on industrial economies, skill-biased technological change may be at work, whereby the demand for labour increasingly favours skilled workers and dominates the wage-equalizing effects of trade. It is also possible that the large supplies of surplus labour (domestic or migrant labour) and other features of globalization discussed below prevent a relative increase in the wages of relatively less-skilled (women) workers.

Other research methodologies that examine the effect of trade on unadjusted gender wage gaps indicate mixed results. For Mexico, an inter-industry wage analysis shows that, during the 2001–05 period in the non-EPZ manufacturing industry (subsequent to the period examined by Hazarika and Otero, 2004), openness of sector was associated with wider gender wage gaps (Brown-Grossman and Domínguez-

Villalobos, 2010). The period examined by this study was one during which the sector faced increasing competition from new players in global product markets, notably from China. Since the average skill level of workers in the sector also declined during this period, Brown-Grossman and Domínguez-Villalobos rule out skill-biased technological change as an explanation for the widening gender wage gap. By contrast, simulations within the CGE framework show that in economies where women are employed in the export sector (Bangladesh, Pakistan) trade reforms reduced the gender wage (or wage income) gaps (Fontana, 2007; Siddiqui, 2009).

### 3) Ongoing surplus labour generation in the global economy

The wage and gender wage gap trajectories in tradable sectors discussed above can be explained by the ongoing generation of low-skilled surplus labour in the global economy fuelled by a number of features of the current global integration. Trade liberalization is only one of these features.

First, the underemployed or unemployed labour is constantly generated domestically or recruited through international labour migration in many countries. The ongoing unravelling of the smallholder sector in Mexican agriculture under the impact of agricultural trade liberalization, for example, means that the surplus labour that is released from rural areas will keep the pressure on the wages of *maquiladora* workers (Perez et al., 2008). Several successful exporters – such as Malaysia, Mauritius and Taiwan – import labour from poorer countries for work in various sectors, including manufacturing, which slows down wage growth. Women workers in export factories not only are engaged in low-wage/low-value-added activities but also face intense competition from other workers around the world, notably from China after the latter's accession to the WTO and the liberalization of the textile and clothing trade. When export sectors lose dynamism due to trade preference erosion or loss of competitiveness, export sector workers join the ranks of underemployed labour and keep wage growth in check in the local economy.

A related set of pressures on wage growth emanates from the increased global mobility of foreign investors and corporate buyers in the context of decentralized organization of international production. In many products, international firms with market power subcontract production of lower value-added activities – sometimes the entire production process – to firms that operate in a highly competitive global market (Heintz, 2006). Investment liberalization since the 1980s has made it easier for firms to shift production from one country to another when faced with adverse cost pressures. As a result, much of the value produced in global production chains goes to brand name companies that have a high degree of flexibility in where they place orders, and women workers who predominate in the lower tiers of production have little means for improving their wage levels (Carr, Chen and Tate, 2000).

### 4) Weakening of labour rights

One consequence of the ongoing generation of surplus labour in the global economy and increased labour substitution possibilities globally has been the erosion of union rights. This trend has been documented in detail for the US, where companies in mobile industries secure concessions from their workers by making credible threats to move company operations outside the US (Bronfenbrenner, 2000). Workers fear that if they try to organize into unions, strike or otherwise struggle to improve working conditions, they will lose their jobs. Even if workers do not lose their jobs immediately, they are prevented from exercising their right to freedom of association and collective bargaining.

Developing country governments, on the other hand, have been reluctant to enforce labour laws in general and to support union rights in the EPZs or non-EPZ export factories in particular for fear of losing foreign direct investment. In countries that rely on exports of labour-intensive manufactures to generate much-needed foreign exchange, there is an obvious incentive not to undermine the competitiveness of the export sectors. Moreover, most developing country governments lack the resources to enforce their labour laws, particularly under the budget constraints brought by market reforms. As a result, in developing and developed countries alike, workers lose the key means for improving wages and working conditions.

Absence of effective union rights is especially of concern in reducing gender wage gaps. Doraisami (2008) attributes the persistent gender wage gap in Malaysia's manufacturing sector to the prohibition of union rights in foreign-owned, export-oriented enterprises. She argues that the absence of national-level unions, along with the lack of a legally established minimum wage, prevented women workers, who were concentrated in export industries, from improving their earnings. Even when new laws that grant union rights in EPZs are phased in, their implementation has fallen behind schedule or has been postponed (Berik and Rodgers, 2010).

The cross-country and panel analysis by Busse and Spielmann (2006) further underscores the appeal of the low-wage strategy. Taking as the point of departure the standard trade theory, this study provides robust evidence to support the positive association between comparative advantage in labour-intensive manufactured goods and gender wage inequality. Gender wage inequality has a consistent positive effect on trade outcomes, measured variously as the ratio of labour-intensive exports to total exports and the revealed comparative advantage in labour-intensive exports.[12]

### 5) Does moving up the industrial ladder reduce gender wage inequalities?
If gender wage inequality strengthens comparative advantage in labour-intensive man-ufactures, then a prerequisite for promoting gender-equitable development is for developing countries to move out of this particular export niche to diversify the pro-duction structure and produce higher-value-added products. Such a move would make possible payment of higher wages commensurate with productivity growth and closing of gender wage gaps. The Republic of Korea and Taiwan (China), which are the most

---

[12] Busse and Spielmann's study of the effects of gender wage inequality on trade competitiveness includes 29 countries in the cross-section analysis for 2000, and 40 countries in the panel analysis for the period 1975-2000.

successful practitioners of export-led growth, have made this transition based on the stimulus to trade, investment and growth provided by gender earnings inequalities (Seguino, 2000; Blecker and Seguino, 2002). In the Republic of Korea, the State directed the foreign exchange to build capacity in strategic industries such as automobiles, semiconductors, steel and shipbuilding and moved the country up the industrial ladder (Seguino, 1997, 2000).[13] The question is whether these transitions have sustained the strong demand for women's labour and helped reduce gender wage gaps.

In East Asia, as countries moved up the industrial ladder to more skill-intensive manufacturing, there has been a defeminization of the manufacturing workforce. The growing sectors have been male-dominated ones where women have not been able to make inroads. Between 1980 and 2004, women's share of manufacturing employment declined from 50 per cent to 41.4 per cent in Taiwan (China) and 39 per cent to 35 per cent in the Republic of Korea (Berik, 2008). These shares further declined to 37 per cent in Taiwan (China) and 32 per cent in the Republic of Korea by 2008 (ILO, 2011). Thus, an increase in women's share of manufacturing jobs appears to be specific to a particular export niche among developing countries and hence subject to reversal once economies move out of that niche.

The pattern holds more generally as well. A recent cross-country study shows that during the 1985–2006 period in middle-income countries the growth of the female share of employment was inversely related to the growth rate of both capital intensity and value added per worker in manufacturing (Milberg and Tejani, 2010). South-East Asian manufacturing growth, which was characterized by higher productivity growth and capital intensity than manufacturing in Latin America, was associated with defeminization of employment.

The processes underlying this trend are illustrated by evidence from Taiwan (Berik, 2000). During the mid-1980s and early 1990s, domestic industries in Taiwan underwent technological upgrading and investors relocated the labour-intensive industries to South-East Asia and China. Women workers experienced a larger share of the job losses, which led to decline of both women's share of wage workers and the average gender wage ratio in manufacturing. Industry-level panel analysis shows that the rising skill composition of this sector contributed to wage gains for men but adversely affected women's wages in both absolute and relative terms. This result suggests that, as the occupational mix of industry changed towards greater reliance on technical skills, a new occupational segregation pattern emerged that placed women in lower paying jobs. Over a decade hence, in 2008, women's earnings reached 70 per cent of men's earnings, up from a low of 62 per cent in 1992 (Berik, 2008; ILO, 2011). In

---

[13] Gender inequalities in the household also supported this change in export structure. In Taiwan, young women workers in export industries in the 1970s helped finance the education of their brothers whose schooling was prioritized in accordance with gender norms (Greenhalgh, 1985). The intra-household gender inequality in the allocation of household resources, in turn, expanded the supply of educated workers who were then able to take up the more skilled jobs that became available as the country moved up the industrial ladder in the 1980s and 1990s.

the Republic of Korea's manufacturing sector, they stood at only 58 per cent in 2007 (ILO, 2011).

The obvious candidate for explaining women workers' inability to move into higher-paying, more-skilled jobs, and the slow narrowing of gender wage gaps with upgrading in manufacturing industries, is women's limited skills compared to men (Doraisami, 2008; Berik, 2000). Even if the skills-mismatch explanation has become increasingly untenable in light of women's educational gains in recent years (Milberg and Tejani, 2010), a shortfall in educational qualifications still is likely to be valid. Measures such as years of schooling or gross enrolment ratios may not be good measures of the required skill levels in particular industries and occupations. As Rodgers, Zveglich and Wherry (2006) show in the case of vocational training in Taiwan, women are not as well placed as men to qualify for the high-paying jobs offered by industries that are upgrading. To the extent that workforce development policy does not set separate targets for women and men, most women specialize in clerical occupations and most men major in technical ones. Sex segregation in specialization in vocational schools thus widens the gender disadvantage in access to new employment and is reflected in wage premium differentials of women and men.

In addition, skills are filtered through the prism of gender norms, as pointed out earlier. Gendered notions of women's and men's work and the underlying abilities of women and men shape employer perceptions of women's and men's abilities, their hiring practices and the patterns of employment segregation. Thus, employer discrimination in hiring and placement may also be preventing women from gaining access to jobs that are deemed to require skilled labour. In the context of industrial upgrading, women may not be able to shake off their association with unskilled work and have difficulty moving into skilled positions in manufacturing. And with the relative growth of the service economy, women may be perceived as more suitable to staff lower-paying occupations that are consistent with gender norms (such as caring jobs). Thus, the policy challenge is to ensure job gains for women in the growing sectors by making sure that women have the requisite skills to take these jobs and to support this outcome through the enforcement of antidiscrimination policies and upholding of collective bargaining rights.

All in all, in absolute terms, women in developing countries have benefited from employment opportunities created in export sectors. Women now earn incomes that are higher than their income from alternative jobs (or the case of no jobs). Trends in wages and gender wage gaps, on the other hand, suggest that trade liberalization, together with the decentralization of global production and investment liberalization, contributes to the generation of large labour supplies in the global economy. These processes have placed women workers in tradable sectors in a vulnerable position as firms compete in the global market and have more freedom to relocate. As a result, working conditions in export jobs fall short of complying with ILO Conventions, and much has to be done on the policy front to ensure that employment gains remain and increase and women are able to gain access to new, higher-paying jobs when the economy moves up the technology ladder.

## 5.4 TRADE LIBERALIZATION IN AGRICULTURE: WOMEN FARMERS AND AGRICULTURAL WORKERS

While manufacturing for export has received the most attention in the literature, agricultural trade liberalization has also affected women's livelihoods as farmers, unpaid family workers and agricultural wage workers. Women farmers predominate in subsistence agriculture and in smaller scale cash-crop production compared to men due to constraints of access to land, credit and inputs. These constraints on the expansion of women's farm incomes have been documented prior to agricultural trade liberalization, which has exacerbated these difficulties (Beviglia Zampetti and Tran-Nguyen, 2004).

Agricultural trade liberalization affects farmers via both agricultural exports and agricultural imports. In general, trade liberalization tends to favour the production of cash crops over food crops and to encourage farmers to diversify crops and engage in off-farm activities to generate cash incomes (Beviglia Zampetti and Tran-Nguyen, 2004). However, small farmers have difficulty competing with large farms in producing crops for the world market. Moreover, growth of export agriculture has brought about competition for water and prime land and pushed small farmers to less fertile land. This shift in production structure has increased the workloads of small farmers, especially of women, and undermined their livelihoods. Many have abandoned food production or farming altogether and migrated out of rural areas. As a result, the commercialization trend has been associated with decline in viability of small-scale farming and the concentration of land ownership in many parts of the world (Perez, Schlesinger and Wise, 2008).

The expansion of non-traditional agricultural exports (NTAEs), promoted as a strategy to counter the decline in world prices in the main export crops of developing countries, has created jobs for rural women (and men). NTAEs are undertaken in large factory farms that are part of the global network of production controlled by a small number of North American and European supermarkets. Women are prominent in the production of many of these crops, such as asparagus, bananas, eucalyptus and cut flowers in the Philippines; cut flowers in Tanzania; grapes in Chile; maize, beans and flowers in Uganda (Beviglia Zampetti and Tran-Nguyen, 2004; Barrientos et al., 1999; Blackden et al., 2007).

While NTAE production has provided jobs for rural women, some of whom are displaced from the land they used to farm, the working conditions are poor. Not only are the workers only seasonally employed but also they work in environments of high pesticide use that pose serious health risks. Gender-segregated employment similar to the one in export manufacturing is prevalent: women constitute a high proportion of the low-skilled, low-paid temporary workers and men staff the supervisory or more-skilled positions. Where women horticulturalists supply the export crop (such as shea butter), their income constitutes a tiny fraction of the overall value generated from the sale of the product to the consumers (Carr et al., 2000). Further, the scope for future expansion of NTAEs is limited (Beviglia Zampetti Tran-Nguyen, 2004).

Agricultural import liberalization, on the other hand, has compounded women farmers' difficulties in taking advantage of export markets as food imports displace domestic production. Koopman's (2009) examination of the modernization of agriculture in the Senegal River Valley since the 1970s is a striking story of how a series of development interventions led by international agencies undermined food security in a region of sustainable self-reliant agriculture.[14] From the 1980s onward, small farmers in the region have faced not only higher input prices due to removal of state supports for agriculture but also falling farm prices due to import liberalization, a squeeze that is also demonstrated for other African economies and Latin America (Van Staveren, 2007; Perez et al., 2008). Koopman's 2003 village case study shows that the farm income generated by women on small garden plots is vital for livelihoods of impoverished rural households. Yet women's insecure land rights together with competition from subsidized European food imports, which reach even the most remote stretches of the Senegal River Valley, constrain women farmers' attempts to grow vegetables for the market and household subsistence. While the European Union (EU) allows duty-free and quota-free imports from LDCs and countries covered by the Economic Partnership Agreements (EPAs) and these countries benefit from exporting to the EU – tomatoes in the case of Senegal, for example – when cheap tomato imports flood the market, women farmers cannot compete (Van Staveren 2007). Koopman (2009) is concerned that the consolidation of liberalized trade through the EPAs sought by the European Union will threaten the livelihoods of the majority of Africa's farming families. She predicts that, unless import liberalization is tackled, women farmers will not be able to compete with imported food in local markets, even when they hold land titles.

The overall benefits of agricultural trade liberalization largely depend on whether countries are net buyers or net sellers of food.[15] However, even in many net-exporting countries, a majority of the rural people are net buyers of food, and hence are viewed as potential beneficiaries of the decline in domestic food prices resulting from tariff reductions. On the basis of this metric and an analysis for 15 developing countries, Hertel et al. (2009) argue in favour of further reductions of tariffs on staple food products in developing countries (over and above those negotiated in the Doha Round) as an effective poverty-reduction strategy. However, this argument assumes smooth transition of all farmers into producing export crops or otherwise generating the cash income necessary to purchase food. And the focus on net gains of food imports at the national level overlooks the hardships faced by many groups. If the women farmers highlighted by Koopman's study are unable to switch to cultivating crops that offer a stable income source to purchase food, they will likely be further impoverished. Small net sellers of food that produce only for the local markets and do not export due to their small size would lose from a reduction of trade barriers

---

[14] Creation of a capital-intensive farming system, supported by dams and irrigation schemes, resulted in an unsustainable debt burden that led the country to implement market reforms.

[15] The impact of trade liberalization on government revenues and its capacity to deliver services to farmers is an additional consideration.

in their own counties since this would lead to lower domestic prices and thus less income.

In sum, agricultural trade liberalization has put small farmers in peril. Not only are export markets beyond reach for most small – especially women – farmers but also these farmers are unable to produce for the domestic market when food imports displace domestic production. These developments have undermined self-reliance and social safety nets in rural areas and contributed to hardship and dislocation of poorer rural inhabitants. Such impacts are likely to be far-reaching in countries where agriculture predominates production and export activity.

## 5.5 INTRA-HOUSEHOLD EFFECTS OF TRADE LIBERALIZATION: TIME AND RESOURCE ALLOCATION

Changes in employment opportunities and earnings, prices and tariffs ushered by trade liberalization are expected to affect time- and resource-allocation in the household. While the effects of trade policy on intra-household dynamics are more difficult to assess compared to its effects on employment and wages, there is some evidence on impacts on women's unpaid workloads, the nature and level of consumption, and women's decision-making power.

### 5.5.1 Time allocation

In assessing individual-level impacts of trade, gender-aware analysis has to take into consideration the integrated set of paid and unpaid activities undertaken by individuals. Women are responsible for a wide range of unpaid reproductive tasks to ensure the well-being of family members. In rural areas and poorer households, these tasks are more extensive and include tending to small gardens for food crops, and management of the energy and water needs of the household, as well as cooking, cleaning and caring for children, the elderly and the ill.

A direct channel whereby trade reforms affect unpaid work is through the household-level response to women's additional work hours in export sectors. When added to women's care work in the household, paid work will lengthen their working day, unless paid work is accompanied by a redistribution of household tasks among family members. When young women engage in export sector work, their housework responsibilities are assumed by older women or siblings. However, as noted earlier, a rising proportion of the workforce in export manufacturing is comprised of married women with children, whose overall workloads intensify. Excessive overtime and continuous work schedules, typical of export sector employment, create severe time poverty for married women (Berik and Rodgers, 2010). Mothers' participation in NTAE production results in a shift of household tasks to daughters to the detriment of the daughters' schooling (Fontana, 2008). Only rarely is there a gender redistribution of housework as men pick up some of the housework tasks usually performed by women.

Studies using a gendered CGE framework tend to confirm these findings. Fontana (2007) constructs gendered social accounting matrices for Bangladesh for 1994 and for Zambia for 1995 and shows that tariff reductions in both countries increased time spent in export production and reduced both leisure hours and the unpaid work performed. For Pakistan, Siddiqui (2009) shows that among poor households trade reforms contributed to higher gender gaps in domestic labour.

Another channel whereby trade affects the amount of unpaid work performed is through the impact of tariff cuts on government revenues. Tariff revenues are the major source of public sector revenue for low-income country governments. In theory, trade expansion following trade liberalization should expand the tax base (Ebrill, Stotsky and Gropp, 2001). However, as Khattry and Rao (2002) show for a sample of 80 countries over the 1970–98 period, reduction of tariffs has contributed to lost tax revenues. Baunsgaard and Keen (2005) investigate whether or not countries have been able to recover revenues from other sources, for example, through a domestic tax reform as recommended by Ebrill et al. (2001). In a study of 111 countries for the 1975–2000 period, Baunsgaard and Keen show that, except for the high-income group, countries have not been able to recover lost trade tax revenues. Low-income countries, in particular, face severe public revenue shortfalls. Exploring the fiscal squeeze, Khattry (2003) found a variety of responses to the decline of revenues across country income groups. Low-income countries, for example, relied on external funding and took on more debt to maintain spending levels, raising interest debt. A general pattern in response to lost revenue from trade taxes between 1970 and 1998 was reduced spending on physical infrastructure.

When governments attempt to make up for the shortfall in tariff revenues by cutting public expenditures and/or raising sales and other indirect taxes, these burdens are likely to fall most heavily on the low-income consumer groups, among which women are over-represented (Williams, 2007). Gender-aware research, mostly on the earlier episodes of structural adjustment, has highlighted the greater adverse effects of cuts in public spending on women compared to men (Çağatay and Elson, 2000). For example, to make up for declines in subsidies on food or public transportation, women have had to increase their labour market hours, often in informal jobs, and spend more time in household production. As a result, women's overall work burden has risen (Gladwin, 1991; Benería and Feldman, 1992; Elson, 1995). Similarly, women's unpaid labour burden has increased due to reductions in health-care expenditures. Faced with increased user fees in public hospitals, low-income women have taken on the care of ill family members at home. These additional burdens limit women's ability to spend time in remunerative activities and increase time poverty. In some cases, daughters have been taken out of school to help with the increased overall work burden of mothers (Elson, 1995). Shortfalls in spending on physical infrastructure are also likely to increase women's unpaid labour burden. As roads deteriorate, or energy and clean water supplies become increasingly scarce, securing these supplies can take up a large portion of each day. Thus, an increase in trade-related employment, especially in the context of the fiscal squeeze experienced in many developing countries, is expected to increase women workers' overall work burden and intensify time poverty of women.

### 5.5.2 Resource allocation

Cross-cultural evidence shows that women's consumption patterns benefit children's well-being more than does men's expenditures (Hoddinott and Haddad, 1995). As a result, job creation for women has a greater pay-off, not only in delivering immediate improvements in family well-being but also making the future labour force more productive, setting in motion a virtuous cycle of interactions between gender equality and growth (Klasen, 2002; Klasen and Lamanna, 2009). The key mediating variable in consumption spending, however, is the extent to which women control the income generated, since earning an income does not guarantee income control. Case studies of commercialization of agriculture, for example, suggest that rural women tend to lose income control, while women wage workers in export manufacturing tend to increase their control of income (Fontana, 2008). In addition to making possible consumption spending that improves children's well-being, engaging in paid work also has the potential to increase women's decision-making and self-esteem, and enhance the value of daughters.

The intra-household process that makes possible these positive outcomes is highlighted in figure 5.1. Expansion of employment opportunities for women in export sectors alters gender division of labour and can be expected to strengthen women's fallback position, awareness of their self-interest and economic contribution, and hence their bargaining power in the household (feedback from panel B to panel A). Access to income is likely to provide women the possibility of negotiating a fairer distribution of family resources, which in turn can improve their own and their children's well-being and break up the cycle of inter-generational transmission of gender inequalities. Women's employment may also alter parental perceptions of girls, leading parents to view them as potential income earners and valuable members of the family (Sen, 1990). Researchers hold three distinct positions on the strength of these feedback effects from the labour market to the household.

Some argue that having a job that pays more than the available alternatives is a major step in enhancing women's decision-making power in the household (Kabeer, 2004). An example is increased decision-making by women over marriage and fertility decisions, as identified by export sector workers in Bangladesh (Fontana, 2008).

Second, research shows that the profile of export sector workers is relevant for assessing possibilities for paid work and enhancing women's self-esteem and autonomy. Young, unmarried women, in particular, report an increase in their self-esteem and ability to make a wider range of life choices. An early 1980s' study of workers in Mexicali found that women, especially those with a higher education level, view themselves as choice-making individuals with some degree of control over their lives (Fiala and Tiano, 1991). For older, married women, however, export sector work is argued to be no more than a means of economic survival that results in intensification of women's overall workload (Domínguez et al. 2010).

A third view is that the type of jobs held by women matter in shaping women's fallback position in the household. The emphasis in much of the literature is on creating jobs for women outside the household, away from the nexus of kinship relations (Sen, 1990), but even that may not be sufficient. As Fiala and Tiano (1991) show, for example, the extent of women's empowerment is directly related to their employment in less patriarchal factory settings. Low-skill, low-wage jobs generated by labour-intensive export industries, especially in their home-based extensions, however, are likely to have a limited effect on women's chances for economic security, their well-being and decision-making power in the household (Koggel, 2003; Domínguez et al., 2010). Thus, the effects of engaging in paid work on women's status and autonomy are not uniform and invariably positive. The policy challenge is to generate jobs under decent conditions with adequate wages, which offer greater prospects for personal autonomy and economic security.

## 5.6   CONCLUSIONS AND POLICY IMPLICATIONS

### 5.6.1  Main findings

This study has provided a gender analysis of trade and trade liberalization in developing countries, mainly focusing on gender inequalities in wages and employment in the manufacturing sector. The research reviewed has relied on existing theoretical frameworks and pursued a plurality of methodologies, including cross-country or country-level econometric analyses, descriptive statistical analyses and CGE models.

Figure 5.2 provides a schematic description of the gender impacts of the late twentieth century trade liberalization and expansion that highlights the dimensions of gender inequality examined in this chapter. Trade expansion has brought an increase in employment for women workers in labour-intensive export-oriented industries since the late 1970s. These jobs often provide better employment options than alternatives in the local economy, and have contributed to women's economic autonomy and status in the household, though they have also increased the overall workload of married women. The conditions of work in these industries have been poor, often marked by persistent low wages, gender wage inequalities, extremely long hours, hazardous conditions and job instability. Despite gains in education, women also appear not able to reap the full returns as evidenced by persistent or growing discriminatory wage gaps that are associated with trade expansion in some developing countries. A likely explanation for these wage trends is that trade liberalization, accompanied by other market reforms and global processes, undermines women workers' bargaining position vis-à-vis employers. Decentralization of global production, increased corporate buyer and investor mobility, together with trade liberalization, contribute to the generation of surplus labour in the global economy, which may adversely affect wage growth for workers who are concentrated in export sectors and prevent closing of gender wage gaps. These same processes also undermine the capacity and willingness of governments to enforce labour laws and support workers' struggles to improve working conditions.

Figure 5.2: Gender effects of trade liberalization and expansion in late twentieth century globalization

| Trade impacts | Gender-differentiated impacts | |
|---|---|---|

**Trade impacts**

Change in structure of labour demand:
Shift from non-tradables to tradables.

Shift from subsistence to cash-crop production.

Reduction in tariffs:
• Increase in import competition
• Decline in tax revenues

Growth impacts of trade:
Via magnitude of foreign exchange earnings and policies for industrial upgrading.
→ Potential to move the economy out of low-wage, low productivity activities
→ Potential to increase tax revenues and spending on public services, infrastructure.
(The case of East Asian economies)

**Gender-differentiated impacts**

*Manufacturing/Urban labour markets:*
• Increase in women's labour force participation rates.
• Increase in women's employment opportunities.
• Increase in (mostly male) unemployment in import-competing sectors.
• Employment segregation in export sectors: women concentrated in labour-intensive, low-value added sectors, low-skill occupations.
• Slow closing of gender wage gaps; persistent/increase in wage discrimination.

*Agriculture:*
• Rural women (and small farmers, in general) are poorly-positioned to take advantage of new cash-crop opportunities; some move out of farming/rural areas.
• Food imports undermine domestic markets for small (women) farmers.
• Expansion of women's employment opportunities in non-traditional agricultural export (NTAE) crops in large farms; but employment segregation and poor working conditions.

• Potential to create highly-paying jobs.
• Gender composition of these jobs is contingent on complementary policies (e.g. antidiscrimination, training).
• Potential to promote absolute gains in well-being and gender equality in education/training, and thus future growth. (The case of East Asian economies, except for defeminization and slow closing of gender wage gaps in tradable sectors).

*Intra-household effects:*
Time allocation:
• Work for pay/profit increases overall work burden of women (and daughters).
• Increase in women's unpaid work burden in low-income countries due to fiscal squeeze and cuts in social services and infrastructure generated by reduction of tariffs.

Resource allocation:
• Work for pay/profit has potential to increase women's bargaining power and initiate a process of changing intra-household distribution of resources in favor of women and girls

*Intra-household effects:*
Time allocation:
Potential to alleviate women's unpaid work time constraints.

Resource allocation:
Potential to reduce gender inequalities in the household.

Agricultural trade liberalization and expansion has created hardships for subsistence and small farmers, especially for women. Women farmers' inability to compete with large farms in export markets and with food imports in domestic markets has reduced the viability of these farms and undermined rural livelihoods. While non-traditional agricultural exports have created jobs and incomes for rural women in many countries, these jobs replicate the unstable and insecure employment patterns observed in export manufacturing.

Finally, decline in tariff revenues has constrained public spending on social services and infrastructure in low-income developing countries. This fiscal squeeze has greater adverse effects on women, who intensify their unpaid labour to make up for the reduced availability of public services and infrastructure as well as increasing their hours in paid work.

Trade liberalization also has growth effects. Most developing countries are highly dependent on exports of a few key sectors where women workers predominate to alleviate the foreign exchange constraint and sustain growth. A small number of countries have used trade surpluses to implement industrial policy to diversify their production structure. Moving to higher-value-added production is desirable not only for improving wages and working conditions and generating higher incomes, but also for countering the risks associated with the export niche of labour-intensive (income-elastic) goods. However, in East and South-East Asian countries that were able to move up the technology ladder and diversify exports, women's employment opportunities relative to men have declined in export sectors and gender wage gaps have narrowed only slowly. This outcome may be partly due to limited job-specific skills of women in the new sectors. These skill deficits may interact with gender norms and stereotypes about women's weaker commitment to the workforce and less need for income to shape employer hiring and placement decisions. These stereotypes, in turn, continue to be reinforced by the persistent gender division of labour in the household, which assigns women the primary responsibility for caring tasks.

## 5.6.2 Policy recommendations: Promoting gender-equitable job creation and economic security

Based on these main findings, figure 5.3 identifies a set of policies to achieve a more gender-equitable distribution of the benefits of expanded trade and to provide income, employment and livelihood security for women workers and small farmers. The policy challenge is to improve the quality of jobs for women and to make the job gains for women in the first round of globalization sustainable as countries seek to diversify and upgrade production.

The following specific goals and policies can contribute to achieving gender-equitable job creation and economic security: (1) increase and improve women's employment options through investments in education and easing of unpaid workloads by providing childcare and infrastructure investments; (2) improve the quality of jobs that are generated through stronger enforcement of labour regulations, infrastructure investment and organizational adjustments in the workplace; (3) support

Figure 5.3: Gender equity policies

| Post-trade reform problem | Policy |
| --- | --- |
| Employment segregation in export sectors/lower skill occupations and rise in informal jobs that have:<br><br>• Low wages<br>  ⇒ High poverty risk<br>  ⇒ Weak feedback to intrahousehold gender inequalities<br><br>• Slow wage growth<br>  ⇒ Persistence of income poverty<br>  ⇒ Low productivity production structures<br>  ⇒ Negative feedback effects on supply of educated labour<br><br>• Persistent gender wage gaps<br>  ⇒ Persistence of intrahousehold gender inequalities<br><br>• Other working condition problems<br>  ⇒ Negative well-being effects<br><br>Decline in viability of small farming (women farmers) and inability of small/medium enterprises to compete leads to:<br>• Decline in small farms, small enterprises<br>• Decline in food security<br>• Unravelling of the countryside<br>• Accelerated outmigration. | In the context of policy space for macroeconomic policies and pro-poor international development stance:<br><br>• Education and training for women.<br>• Childcare for low-income women/parents and infrastructure investments to ease women's unpaid work.<br>• Promotion of decent work via:<br>  o Social clauses in bilateral trade agreements.<br>  o ILO's tripartite process (with emphasis on union rights, regulation and enforcement).<br>  o Better Work programmes.<br>  o Pedagogical approach to reduce non-labour costs and spread best practices.<br>  o Investments to reduce non-labour costs of export factories.<br>• Reduce gender gaps in assets, credit, technologies and business services.<br>  o Support small farmers and small/medium entrepreneurs;<br>  o Develop niche export products<br>  o Support cooperative development.<br>• Gender-sensitive trade policies.<br>  o Assess gender impacts of trade agreements (and make adjustments).<br>  o Integrate gender equity goal in trade agreements.<br>  o Revisit pace and extent of trade liberalization. |

rural livelihoods and incomes of women farmers and small producers through reduction of gender gaps in assets and inputs and encouragement of producer
cooperatives; (4) provide stable and secure economic activity options for all, and prevent abrupt adjustments and hardships for more vulnerable groups through adoption
of a pro-poor stance in trade negotiations and gender-sensitive trade policies.

Achieving these goals requires a broad set of policy tools that go beyond com-
pensatory schemes to address gender inequalities in education, time- and
resource-allocation. Gender-equity policies must be situated within a coherent macroeconomic (including trade) framework, an effective regulatory framework, and a
coherent set of initiatives at the international level. Different policies must work in
a complementary and virtuous manner to pursue gender equity. In particular, it is
important to avoid one set of policies from undermining the gender-equitable effects
of other policies. Thus, if trade liberalization in interaction with investment liberalization and restrictive fiscal policy creates adverse gender effects, then these policies
must be revisited to make adjustments so as to generate more equitable, pro-poor
development.

Several studies have emphasized the imperative for developing country governments to have the policy space to manage macroeconomic policy and the international
support to pursue a development strategy that harnesses the benefits of trade and
foreign direct investment to their advantage (Heintz, 2006; Grown and Seguino,
2007). Through productivity-enhancing investments and judicious management of
foreign direct investment, these economies can then move toward a more diverse
production structure. In addition, others have raised concerns about the sustainability
of relying on an export strategy of low wages and gender wage gaps and have urged
policies to move away from excessive reliance on exports (Beviglia Zampetti and Tran-
Nguyen, 2004; Berik and Rodgers, 2010; ILO, 2010). The concerns with this strategy
centre on the decline in terms of trade when a large number of developing countries
are concentrated in producing the same set of products for the world market and the
vulnerability to export market fluctuations (Beviglia Zampetti and Tran-Nguyen, 2004).
In addition, persistence of low-skilled and low-value-added export activities in countries
with low levels of educational attainment is likely to have detrimental effects on
economic growth and well-being of workers (Wood and Ridao-Cano, 1999). Given
the nature of the labour demand, women, in particular, may have little incentive to
seek higher levels of education (Vijaya, 2003).

The pursuit of industrial policy by developing country governments can move
the economy out of low-wage, low-productivity activities into higher-value-added activities that can create high-paying jobs with decent working conditions. While this
transition creates the possibility of gender-equitable access to the new jobs created,
it does not guarantee this outcome. A complementary set of policies is necessary to
pursue this goal.

First, countries have to continue emphasizing girls' education and must close
gender gaps in not only the quantity of education but also its quality. Education
policy has to promote girls' enrolments and ensure that they complete the school
cycle successfully. One promising policy that targets very low-income households is

the conditional cash transfer approach that is being implemented in several countries. The policy aims to provide economic incentives for families to encourage long-term attendance and school completion by girls (Latapí and de la Rocha, 2009). These schemes are proving effective in increasing school attendance by girls, improving health outcomes of children and reducing income poverty, and could be replicated in other developing countries. The challenge is for such schemes to also promote skill development by encouraging girls to study subjects that do not replicate the gender-segregated patterns of low-wage employment.

More generally, gender inequalities in the type of schooling received need to be addressed through curriculum reforms so that schools develop skills in a gender-equitable manner, especially technical skills that are needed to enable access to the new jobs in technology- and skill-intensive sectors. As Rodgers et al. (2006) emphasize, governments need to be proactive in creating incentives for girls to go into fields that prepare them for high-paying jobs and open up access to new training opportunities through stronger enforcement of equal opportunity legislation.

In addition, in each sector of the economy, there is scope for promoting skills for women entrepreneurs that, along with technical and financial support, can help them gain entry and be successful in the more competitive and export sectors of the economy (Coche et al., 2006). For wage workers, the policy objective is to improve women's skill sets so that they are able to qualify for jobs in sectors that are upgrading and expanding. Retraining workers who are likely to be disproportionately affected by shifts in trade composition of a country to provide for a smoother and gender-equitable transition to the newly emerging job opportunities is an option, though it is difficult to identify affected workers.

Second, another set of policies will have to address women's unpaid care workload that constrains their employment options and underlies stereotypes about women's weaker labour force commitment. Provision of quality, affordable and convenient childcare is an initiative that could be pursued to support secure and stable employment for low-income women, promote women's well-being and increase workplace productivity. As Hein and Cassirer (2010) show, public policies and services concerning childcare are rarely adequate, especially in developing countries, but public support is needed to meet the childcare needs of low-income workers.[16] In addition, some types of infrastructure investments are more likely to benefit women as a group than men, given women's time poverty, as well as improving economic efficiency

---

[16] However, where governments legally require employers to provide on-site childcare in establishments that employ above a certain number of female employees, such as in Brazil, China and India, this requirement has functioned as a disincentive for hiring women. On the other hand, since most workplace initiatives provide childcare for higher-level workers in large firms, and in financial or business services, there is an unmet demand for childcare by low-wage workers. There are only a few examples of workplace initiatives that could be viewed as best practice cases in developing countries. Case studies of Chile, Kenya and Thailand provide examples of childcare provision for rural agricultural workers in a gender equitable manner through public-private partnerships and tax incentives for employers (Hein and Cassirer, 2010).

overall. Improving access to clean water and clean energy sources for cooking, for example, would reduce women's unpaid care burden, enable their labour force participation and help promote women's health.[17]

Third, women workers in export sectors have to be supported through policies that facilitate the creation of decent jobs. In sectors where international competition has intensified in recent years, such as garments, as highlighted by this study, women workers face high risks of not only downward pressure on wages and working conditions but also employment insecurity due to export volatility. While the currently available jobs in export sectors are often better than the available alternatives (which in some cases are non-existent), policy should aim to set in motion a process of creation of decent jobs that are consistent with ILO Conventions and that achieve an adequate local living wage.

The main obstacle in improving working conditions is weak enforcement of legislation, given that most countries have ratified the core ILO Conventions, including those pertaining to equal pay and non-discrimination at work, and have national laws that are consistent with these Conventions. Many developing country governments lack the resources or the will to uphold their labour laws to fight gender discrimination and give workers greater bargaining power. Far from protecting workers, governments seek to establish EPZs as islands where they do not fully implement national labour laws. Short of an international standard that prevents countries from implementing a two-tier application of their national labour laws (for example, in the form of an ILO Convention), there is little incentive for individual countries to do away with the EPZ exceptions in their own territory. In such a political-economic context, a useful strategy for nudging countries toward enforcement of labour laws is to set in motion international mechanisms to actively support developing country workers' right to organize and collectively bargain so that workers themselves are able to push for improvement in working conditions. In addition, explicit international support for a broader set of ILO Conventions could leverage union rights.

Currently, there are three options at the international level for promoting decent working conditions in tradable sectors. The EU and US can promote union rights in developing country trading partners through social clauses in regional or bilateral trade agreements, but this tool has weak enforcement mechanisms that need to be strengthened. Second, the ILO's tripartite process, which has been energized by the Decent Work initiative after 1999, constitutes a pressure point at the national level that can be strengthened by building capacity for enforcement of national legislation. The third option is the corporate social responsibility (codes of conduct) approach, which holds the least promise despite being the most high-profile approach since the late 1990s. This approach not only has limited and uneven reach but also does not emphasize union rights or making improvements beyond a narrow set of corporate-defined goals.

---

[17] Reducing reliance on solid fuels for cooking and heating will help decrease high levels of indoor air pollution and premature deaths of mostly women and children.

A recent variant on the codes of conduct approach is the *Better Work* programme, which is a joint initiative of the ILO and the International Finance Corporation (IFC) of the World Bank. The programme, currently being implemented in several developing countries, is based on the idea that compliance with labour standards is good for business. *Better Work* was originally implemented as the *Better Factories Cambodia* programme, which grew out of the trade agreement negotiated between the Cambodian and US Governments in 1999. This agreement was the first to explicitly assign a monitoring role to the ILO, as Cambodia agreed to allow the ILO to inspect its factories to ascertain progress toward decent working conditions, upon verification of which the United States would increase Cambodia's export quota of garments.

In the post-ATC era, when use of quotas is no longer a trade policy tool, the programme relies on the incentive for supplier factories to reach buyers interested in sourcing from suppliers with better working conditions. There is evidence that companies that source from developing countries attach a premium to labour standards monitoring via the ILO.[18] As a result, since 2007, the *Better Work* programme has been extended through the partnership of the IFC and the ILO. A number of countries – Haiti, Lesotho, Jordan, Nicaragua and Viet Nam – have voluntarily entered the programme and most have required all garment factories to participate in the programme as a condition for export.

Evidence based on factory inspection reports indicates that under the *Better Factories* programme, Cambodia has achieved improvements in working conditions while at the same time increasing garment exports and employment (Polaski, 2009; Berik and Rodgers, 2010). Chief among the achievements is the correct payment of wages (minimum wage or overtime wages) in the garment sector, which is a major step forward, given widespread reports of non-payment or incorrect payment of wages in garment factories globally.

However, Cambodia's programme does not monitor wage growth in supplier factories but only their compliance with the minimum wage law. A crucial complement for the programme to achieve sustained improvements in standards of living in local terms could, therefore, consist in encouraging periodic and adequate adjustments in the minimum wage and upholding of union rights so that wage growth can proceed commensurate with productivity gains. These policy goals, in turn, reinforce the need for a factory-level programme such as *Better Work* to be well integrated with national-level implementation of labour laws and for the ILO's tripartite process to work at the national level. Moreover, there may be scope for adjustments in the *Better Work* approach itself. For example, the identities of buyers and of factories that source them could be disclosed and factory adherence to laws regarding union rights could be more closely monitored. Finally, to be effective in increasing wage levels and raising

---

[18] According to a 2004 World Bank survey, Cambodia's key overseas buyers rated highly the credibility of ILO monitoring and expressed their preference to source from Cambodia over Bangladesh, China, Thailand and Viet Nam due to the working conditions of the Cambodia's Better Factories programme (Foreign Investment Advisory Service, 2004).

the global floor in wage rates and non-wage working conditions, however, *Better Work* has to be simultaneously implemented in the poorest garment-exporter countries.

While wage growth is often viewed as a threat to jobs in export sectors, Harrison and Scorse (2010) show that substantial wage growth in Indonesia (achieved via the anti-sweatshop campaigns in the 1990s) did not undermine employment growth in unskilled work in export sectors. Moreover, improvements in wages and non-wage working conditions are consistent with the development strategy of moving up the industrial ladder. Wage gains can be growth enhancing and instrumental in moving the manufacturing sector toward a higher productivity path based on upgrading and diversification of export production. In addition, in heavily export-reliant economies, wage growth can help strengthen domestic consumption demand as a more reliable source of demand and promote sustainable economic growth (ILO, 2010). Accordingly, effective wage policies that not only hold up the lower end of the wage distribution (through minimum wage policy) but also improve the link between wage growth and productivity growth (through effective collective bargaining rights) are necessary.

In addition, the efforts to improve working conditions in developing countries must include domestic policies that strengthen non-labour aspects of export competitiveness. Non-labour costs and supply bottlenecks often impede competitiveness and create non-negotiable costs, resulting in downward pressure on labour costs. Investments could address persistent bottlenecks in quality of port, road and air transport infrastructure, and quality of electricity supply, thus reducing non-labour costs.

A related approach seeks to remove the production bottlenecks in export firms that give rise to many of the working condition problems (Amengual, 2010). According to this *pedagogical approach*, global non-governmental organization (NGO) and local government monitors help firms improve their compliance with national labour laws by working with firms to solve the production process bottlenecks and helping to spread the best practices in addressing these problems. Thus, for example, through workplace reorganization, non-labour costs could be saved and the need for overtime work could be minimized.

Fourth, domestic and international resources should be directed to reducing gender gaps in assets, inputs and access to marketing expertise. In order to strengthen rural livelihoods of small (women) farmers, domestic policies should support the production of goods that have the potential to occupy niche markets, such as organic agricultural products or textile handicrafts. The development of cooperatives would also help counter the disadvantages faced by small producers and horticulturalists in markets dominated by large farms and corporate buyers. Additionally, development assistance (for example, Aid for Trade) could be extended to support women farmers' capacity to produce for domestic and international markets.

In order to generate jobs and avoid saturation of local product markets, the support for women producers should go beyond micro-entrepreneurs. Trade financing or technology upgrades for exports by women-owned small- or medium-sized firms would help reduce gender inequalities in the small business sector as well as contributing to growth through employment generation in these firms. Legal reforms to support small-business development and creation of networks of women business owners would also reduce the barriers to women's business success.

Fifth, trade policies must become gender sensitive. With respect to trade agreements, this means that the likely gender impacts of trade agreements must be assessed prior to their ratification, and policy must be formulated and implemented to avoid increasing gender inequalities or to mitigate existing gender inequalities. Van Staveren (2007) proposes a set of gender and trade indicators to gauge the responsiveness of gender outcomes to various trade variables in order to mainstream gender equality goals in trade agreements.[19] These indicators could be used to provide a baseline prior to the negotiation of a trade agreement, to assess gender impacts during the negotiations, and to make trade policy changes or adopt complementary policies as the agreement is being implemented. In addition, commitment to gender equity must be integrated in texts of trade agreements and various other documents pertaining to their implementation so as to maintain awareness of gender-equity goals and ensure progress towards their achievement.

In general, if trade negotiations are development-centred, as envisioned by the Millennium Development Goal (MDG) 8 (Develop a global partnership for development), they would provide the necessary conditions for gender-equitable development. To this end, trade negotiations must revisit the terms – the pace and extent – of agricultural trade liberalization in developing countries and build in protective measures in order to mitigate adverse impacts. The changes in rural production structures spearheaded by agricultural trade liberalization have serious well-being consequences over the long run. They create major social dislocations in rural areas of developing countries and can have wide-ranging implications for the EU and North American economies through the illegal international migration they fuel. In addition, it may be necessary to avoid rapid trade liberalization in order not to destroy a greater number of jobs in import-competing industries than the ones being generated by exports (Heintz, 2006).

In sum, gender equity in a globally integrated context can be promoted within the framework of a macroeconomic policy environment that aims to generate employment and income security. Gender-equity policies, situated in this broader framework, would seek to address the bargaining power deficits of women workers and farmers and ensure the creation of decent jobs and income security. Investments in education, social services and infrastructure required by these gender-equity policies will promote both gender-equitable employment and economic growth. Reforms at the international level have to create the enabling framework for domestic policies as well as ensuring that trade liberalization proceeds in a manner that promotes secure livelihoods.

---

[19] Constructing 11 elasticities, Van Staveren focuses on the effect of trade on gender equalities in income, employment, wages and unpaid domestic work, and uses this framework to evaluate gender impacts of the 2000 European Union trade agreement with Mercosur countries.

# REFERENCES

Adhikari, R.; Yamamoto, Y. 2006. "Sewing thoughts: How to realise human development gains in the post-quota world", Tracking Report, Asia-Pacific Trade and Investment Initiative (UNDP Regional Centre in Colombo).

Albelda, R.; Drago, R.; Schulman, S. 2004. *Unlevel playing fields: Understanding wage inequality and discrimination* (Economic Affairs Bureau, second edition).

Amengual, M. 2010. "Complementary labor regulation: The uncoordinated combination of state and private regulators in the Dominican Republic", in *World Development*, Vol. 38, No. 3, pp. 405-414, Mar.

Amengual, M.; Milberg, W. 2008. *Economic development and working conditions in export processing zones: A survey of trends* (ILO).

Balakrishnan, R. 2001. *The hidden assembly line: Gender dynamics in subcontracted work in a global economy* (Kumarian Press).

Barrientos, S. 2007. "Gender, codes of conduct, and labor standards in global production systems", in N. Çağatay; I. van Staveren; D. Elson; C. Grown (eds): *Feminist economics of trade* (Routledge), pp. 239-256.

Barrientos, S. et al. 1999. *Women and agribusiness: Working miracles in the Chilean fruit export sector* (Palgrave MacMillan).

Baunsgaard, T.; Keen, M. 2005. "Tax revenue and (or?) trade liberalization", *IMF Working Paper* No. WP05/112.

Becker, G.S. 1971. *The economics of discrimination* (University of Chicago Press, second edition).

Benería, L.; Feldman, S. 1992. *Unequal burden: Economic crises, persistent poverty, and women's work* (Westview Press).

Berik, G. 2000. "Mature export-led growth and gender wage inequality in Taiwan", in *Feminist Economics*, Vol. 6, No. 3, pp. 1-26, Nov.

Berik, G. 2008. "Growth with gender inequity: Another look at East Asian development", in G. Berik; Y. Rodgers; A. Zammit (eds): *Social justice and gender equality: Rethinking development strategies and macroeconomic policies* (Routledge).

Berik, G.; Rodgers, Y. 2010. "Options for enforcing labour standards: Lessons from Bangladesh and Cambodia", in *Journal of International Development*, Vol. 22, No. 1, pp. 56-85.

Berik, G.; Rodgers, Y.; Zammit, A. 2008. *Social justice and gender equality: Rethinking development strategies and macroeconomic policies* (Routledge).

Berik, G.; Rodgers, Y.; Zveglich, J. 2004. "International trade and gender wage discrimination: Evidence from East Asia", in *Review of Development Economics*, Vol. 8, No. 2, pp. 237-254, May.

Beviglia Zampetti, A.; Tran-Nguyen, A-H. 2004. *Trade and gender: Opportunities and challenges for developing countries* (United Nations).

Bhattacharya, D.; Moazzem, G.M.; Rahman, M. 2008. *Bangladesh's apparel sector in post-MFA period: A benchmarking study on the ongoing restructuring process* (Dhaka, Centre for Policy Dialogue).

Bhattacharya, D.; Khatun, F.; Moazzem, K.G.; Rahman, M.; Shahrin, A. 2008. *Gender and trade liberalization in Bangladesh: The case of the ready-made garments* (Dhaka, Centre for Policy Dialogue).

Black, S.E.; Brainerd, E. 2004. "Importing equality? The impact of globalization on gender discrimination", in *Industrial and Labor Relations Review*, Vol. 57, No. 4, pp. 540-559, Jul.

Blackden, M. et al. 2007. "Gender and growth in Sub-Saharan Africa: Issues and evidence", in G. Mavrotas; A. Shorrocks (eds): *Advancing development: Core themes in global economics* (Palgrave Macmillan).

Blecker, R.A.; Seguino, S. 2002. "Macroeconomic effects of reducing gender wage inequality in an export-oriented, semi-industrialized economy", in *Review of Development Economics*, Vol. 6, No. 1, pp. 103-119, Feb.

Boyange, J-P.S. 2007. "ILO database on export processing zones (Revised)", *Working Paper* No. 251 (Sectoral Activities Programme, ILO).

Bronfenbrenner, K. 2000. *Uneasy terrain: The impact of capital mobility on workers, wages, and union organizing* (U.S. Trade Deficit Review Commission).

Brown-Grossman, F.; Domínguez-Villalobos, L. 2010. "Trade liberalization and gender wage inequality in Mexico", in *Feminist Economics*, Vol. 16, No. 4, pp. 53-79.

Busse, M.; Spielmann, C. 2006. "Gender inequality and trade", in *Review of International Economics*, Vol. 14, No. 3, pp. 362-372, Aug.

Çağatay, N.; Elson, D. 2000. "The social content of macroeconomic policies", in *World Development*, Vol. 28, No. 7, pp. 1347-1364, July.

Çağatay, N.; van Staveren, I.; Elson, D.; Grown, C. 2007. *Feminist economics of trade* (Routledge).

Callahan, D.; Vijaya, R.M. 2009. *Hidden casualties: Trade, employment loss and women workers* (Demos, A network for ideas and action). Available at: http://demos.org/publication.cfm? currentpublicationID=9FF1DD5A-3FF4-6C82-561B3FBA17F043E3 (accessed 8 June 2011).

Carr, M.; Chen, M.A.; Tate, J. 2000. "Globalization and home-based workers" in *Feminist Economics*, Vol. 6, No. 3, pp. 123-142, Nov.

Chataignier, A.; Kucera, D. 2005. "Labour developments in dynamic Asia: What do the data show?", *Working Paper* No. 61 (Policy Integration Department, ILO).

Coche, I.; Kotschwar, B.; Salazar-Xirinachs, J.M. 2006. *Gender issues in trade policy-making*, OAS Trade Series (Organization of American States). Available at: http://www.sice.oas.org/genderand-trade/genderissuesintp_e.asp (accessed 7 June 2010).

Corley, M.; Perardel, Y.; Popova, K. 2005. "Wage inequality by gender and occupation: A cross-country analysis", *Employment Strategy Paper* No. 2005/20 (ILO).

Domínguez, E. et al. 2010. "Women workers in the maquiladoras and the debate on global labor standards", in *Feminist Economics*, Vol. 16, No. 4, pp. 185-209.

Doraisami, A. 2008. "The gender implications of macroeconomic policy and performance in Malaysia", in G. Berik; Y. Rodgers; A. Zammit (eds): *Social justice and gender equality: Rethinking development strategies and macroeconomic policies* (Routledge).

Ebrill, L.; Stotsky, J.; Gropp, R. 2001. "Revenue implications of trade liberalization", in D. Peretz; R. Faruqi; E.J. Kisango (eds): *Small states in the global economy* (Commonwealth Secretariat).

Elson, D. 1995. "Male bias in macroeconomics: The case of structural adjustment", in D. Elson (ed.): *Male bias in the development process* (Manchester University Press, second edition).

Elson, D. 1999. "Labor markets as gendered institutions: Equality, efficiency and empowerment issues", in *World Development*, Vol. 27, No. 3, pp. 611-627, Mar.

Elson, D.; Pearson, R. 1984. "The subordination of women and the internationalization of factory production", in R. McCullagh; C. Wolkowitz; K. Young (eds): *Of marriage and the market: Women's subordination internationally and its lessons* (Routledge & Kegan Paul).

Emerging Textiles. 2007. *US apparel imports in 2006 (statistical report)*. Available at: http://www.emergingtextiles.com (accessed 7 June 2011).

Fiala, R.; Tiano, S. 1991. "The world views of export processing workers in Northern Mexico: A study of women, consciousness, and the new international division of labor", in *Studies in Comparative International Development*, Vol. 26, No. 3, pp. 3-27, Dec.

Fontana, M. 2007. "Modelling the effects of trade on women, at work and at home: A comparative perspective", in N. Çağatay et al. (eds): *The feminist economics of trade* (Routledge), pp. 117-140.

Fontana, M. 2008. "The gender effects of trade liberalization in developing countries: A review of the literature", presented at the UNCTAD India International Seminar *Moving Towards Gender Sensitization of Trade Policy*, 25-27 February.

Foreign Investment Advisory Service. 2004. *Cambodia: Corporate social responsibility and the apparel sector buyer survey results* (World Bank and International Finance Corporation).

Fussell, E. 2000. "Making labor flexible: The recomposition of Tijuana's maquiladora female labor force", in *Feminist Economics*, Vol. 6, No. 3, pp. 59-79, Nov.

Gladwin, C.H. 1991. *Structural adjustment and African women farmers* (University of Florida Press).

Glick, P.; Roubaud, F. 2006. "Export processing zone expansion in Madagascar: What are the labour market and gender impacts?", in *Journal of African Economies*, Vol. 15, No. 4, pp. 722-756.

Greenhalgh, S. 1985. "Sexual stratification: The other side of 'growth with equity' in East Asia", in *Population and Development Review*, Vol. 11, No. 2, pp. 265-314, June.

Grown, C.; Seguino, S. 2006. "Gender equity and globalization: Macroeconomic policy for developing countries", in *Journal of International Development*, Vol. 18, No. 8, pp. 1081-1104.

Harrison, A.; Scorse, J. 2010. "Multinationals and anti-sweatshop activism", in *American Economic Review*, Vol. 100, No. 1, pp. 247-273.

Hazarika, G.; Otero, R. 2004. "Foreign trade and the gender earnings differential in urban Mexico", in *Journal of Economic Integration*, Vol. 19, No. 2, pp. 353-373, June.

Hein, C.; Cassirer, N. 2010. *Workplace solutions for childcare* (ILO).

Heintz, J. 2006. "Globalization, economic policy and employment: Poverty and gender implications", *Employment Strategy Paper* No. 2006/3 (ILO).

Hertel, T. et al. 2009. "Why isn't the Doha development agenda more poverty friendly?", in *Review of Development Economics*, Vol. 13, No. 4, pp. 543-559.

Hoddinott, J.; Haddad, L. 1995. "Does female income share influence household expenditure patterns: Evidence from Côte d'Ivoire?", in *Oxford Bulletin of Economics and Statistics*, Vol. 57, No. 1, pp. 77-96, Feb.

Horton, S. 1996. *Women and industrialization in Asia* (Routledge).

ILO. 2010. *Global wage report 2010/11: Wage policies in times of crisis* (Geneva).

ILO. 2011. *LABORSTA Labour Statistics Database*. Available at: www.laborsta.ilo.org (accessed 14 July 2011).

Kabeer, N. 2004. "Globalization, labor standards, and women's rights: Dilemmas of collective (in)action in an interdependent world", in *Feminist Economics*, Vol. 10, No. 1, pp. 3-35, Mar.

Kabeer, N.; Mahmud, S. 2004. "Globalization, gender and poverty: Bangladeshi women workers in export and local markets", in *Journal of International Development*, Vol. 16, No. 1, pp. 93-109.

Khattry, B. 2003. "Trade liberalization and the fiscal squeeze: Implications for public investment", in *Development and Change*, Vol. 34, No. 3, pp. 401-424, June.

Khattry, B.; Rao, J.M. 2002. "Fiscal faux pas? An analysis of the revenue implications of trade liberalization", in *World Development*, Vol. 30, No. 8, pp. 1431-1444, Aug.

Klasen, S. 2002. "Low schooling for girls, slower growth for all? Cross-country evidence on the effect of gender inequality in education on economic development", in *The World Bank Economic Review*, Vol. 16, No. 3, pp. 345-373, Dec.

Klasen, S.; Lamanna, F. 2009. "The impact of gender inequality in education and employment on economic growth: New evidence for a panel of countries", in *Feminist Economics*, Vol. 15, No. 3, pp. 91-132.

Koggel, C. 2003. "Globalization and women's paid work: Expanding freedom?", in *Feminist Economics*, Vol. 9, No. 2-3, pp. 163-184, Jan.

Kongar, E. 2007. "Importing equality or exporting jobs? Competition and gender wage and employment differentials in U.S. manufacturing", in N. Çağatay et al. (eds): *The feminist economics of trade* (Routledge), pp. 215-236.

Kongar, E. 2008. "Is deindustrialization good for women? Evidence from the United States", in *Feminist Economics*, Vol. 14, No. 1, pp. 73-92.

Koopman, J. 2009. "Globalization, gender, and poverty in the Senegal River Valley", in *Feminist Economics*, Vol. 15, No. 3, pp. 253-285.

Kucera, D.; Milberg, W. 2007. "Gender segregation and gender bias in manufacturing trade expansion: Revisiting the 'wood asymmetry'", in N. Çağatay et al. (eds): *The feminist economics of trade* (Routledge), pp. 185-216.

Latapí, A.E.; de la Rocha, M.G. 2009. "Girls, mothers, and poverty reduction in Mexico: Evaluating progresa – Oportunidades", in S. Razavi (ed.): *The gendered impacts of liberalization: Towards embedded liberalism?* (Routledge).

Lim, L. 1990. "Women's work in export factories: The politics of a cause", in I. Tinker (ed.): *Persistent inequalities: Women and world development* (Oxford University Press).

Maurer-Fazio, M.; Rawski, T.G.; Zhang, W. 1999. "Inequality in the rewards for holding up half the sky: Gender wage gaps in China's urban labour market, 1988–1994", *The China Journal*, Vol. 41, pp. 55-88, Jan.

Mehra, R.; Gammage, S. 1999. "Trends, countertrends, and gaps in women's employment", in *World Development*, Vol. 27, No. 3, pp. 533-550, Mar.

Menon, N.; Rodgers, Y. 2009. "International trade and the gender wage gap: New evidence from India's manufacturing sector", in *World Development*, Vol. 37, No. 5, pp. 965-981, May.

Milberg, W.; Tejani, S. 2010. "Global defeminization? Industrial upgrading, occupational segmentation and manufacturing employment in middle-income countries", *SCEPA Working Paper* No. 2010-1 (New School for Social Research).

Ngai, P. 2007. "Gendering the dormitory labor system: Production, reproduction, and migrant labor in south China", in *Feminist Economics*, Vol. 13, No. 3-4, pp. 239-258.

Oostendorp, R. 2009. "Globalization and the gender wage gap", in *World Bank Economic Review*, Vol. 23, No. 1, pp. 141-161.

Otobe, N. 2008. "The impact of globalization and macroeconomic change on employment in Mauritius: What next in the post-MFA era?", *Employment Working Paper* No. 9 (Employment Policy Department, ILO).

Özler, S. 2007. "Export led industrialization and gender differences in job creation and destruction: Micro evidence from the Turkish manufacturing sector", in N. Çağatay et al. (eds): *The feminist economics of trade* (Routledge), pp. 164-184.

Paul-Majumder, P.; Begum, A. 2000. "The gender imbalances in the export oriented garment industry in Bangladesh", *Working Paper* No. 12 (Development Research Group, World Bank).

Perez, M.; Schlesinger, S.; Wise, T.A. 2008. *The promise and the perils of agricultural trade liberalization: Lessons from Latin America* (Washington Office on Latin America and The Global Development and Environment Institute, Tufts University).

Polaski, S. 2009. "Harnessing global forces to create decent work in Cambodia", *Research Series* No. 119 (ILO).

Psacharopoulos, G.; Tzannatos, Z. 1992. *Case studies on women's employment and pay in Latin America* (World Bank).

Rani, U.; Unni, J. 2009. "Do economic reforms influence home-based work? Evidence from India", in *Feminist Economics*, Vol. 15, No. 3, pp. 191-225.

Rodgers, Y.; Zveglich, J.; Wherry, L. 2006. "Gender differences in vocational school training and earnings premiums in Taiwan", in *Feminist Economics*, Vol. 12, No. 4, pp. 527-560, Oct.

Seguino, S. 1997. "Gender wage inequality and export-led growth in South Korea", in *Journal of Development Studies*, Vol. 34, No. 2, pp. 102-132.

Seguino, S. 2000. "Accounting for gender in Asian economic growth", in *Feminist Economics*, Vol. 6, No. 3, pp. 22-58, Nov.

Sen, A. 1990. "Gender and cooperative conflicts", in I. Tinker (ed.): *Persistent inequalities: Women and world development* (Oxford University Press).

Siddiqui, R. 2009. "Modeling gender effects of Pakistan's trade liberalization", in *Feminist Economics*, Vol. 15, No. 3, pp. 287-321.

Standing, G. 1989. "Global feminization through flexible labor", in *World Development*, Vol. 17, No. 7, pp. 1077-1095, July.

Standing, G. 1999. "Global feminization through flexible labor: A theme revisited", in *World Development*, Vol. 27, No. 3, pp. 583-602, Mar.

Van Staveren, I. 2007. "Gender indicators for monitoring trade agreements", in N. Çağatay et al. (eds): *The feminist economics of trade* (Routledge), pp. 257-276.

Vijaya, R. 2003. "Trade, skills and persistence of gender gap: A theoretical framework for policy discussion", *International Gender and Trade Network Working Paper* (Washington, DC). Available at: http://www.iiav.nl/epublications/2003/Trade_skills.pdf (accessed 14 July 2011).

Weichselbaumer, D.; Winter-Ebmer, R. 2005. "A meta-analysis of the international gender wage gap", in *Journal of Economic Surveys*, Vol. 19, No. 3, pp. 479-511, July.

Williams, M. 2007. "Gender issues in the multilateral trading system", in N. Çağatay et al. (eds): *The feminist economics of trade* (Routledge), pp. 277-291.

Wood, A.; Ridao-Cano, C. 1999. "Skill, trade, and international inequality", in *Oxford Economic Papers*, Vol. 51, No. 1, pp. 89-119.

# TRADE ADJUSTMENT COSTS AND ASSISTANCE: THE LABOUR MARKET DYNAMICS

# 6

*By Joseph Francois, Marion Jansen and Ralf Peters*

## 6.1 INTRODUCTION

To benefit from trade and trade liberalization, economies have to reallocate factors of production within and between sectors. This structural change is the source of gains from trade but brings with it costs of adjustment. Evidence has, for instance, confirmed that some groups of workers tend to face temporary unemployment and lower income when their jobs are lost as a result of international competition

Adjustment to trade reform or to changes in trade flows have always tended to be rather high on policy-makers' agendas. In the United States, for instance, the Trade Adjustment Assistant programme (US-TAA) was established as early as 1974. The programme aims at assisting workers and enterprises that are negatively affected by trade reforms or changes in trade flows. The European Union (EU) introduced a similar programme, the European Globalization Adjustment Fund, in 2006. Also at the multilateral level, trade negotiators have felt compelled to deal with the issue of adjustment. The World Trade Organization's (WTO's) Agreement on Safeguards and Countervailing Measures, for instance, contains explicit references to the adjustment process following changes in trade flows. The adjustment process following trade reform has also been the subject of studies published by relevant international institutions[1] and is being discussed in the context of Aid for Trade.[2]

Compared with the attention that adjustment challenges have received in the political debate, the academic literature on the subject is rather meagre, notwithstanding a certain revival of interest in the subject in recent years. This lack of academic interest in the topic may be due to the fact that in early empirical work, adjustment costs were estimated to be negligible when compared to the long-run gains for the

---

[1] See, for instance, OECD (2005a), UNCTAD (Laird and de Córdoba, 2006), and the references to Brahmbhatt (1997) and Bacchetta and Jansen (2003) in Chapter 9 of Davidson and Matusz (2010).
[2] See, for instance, ILO, OECD, World Bank and WTO (2010).

economy as a whole. It can also partly be explained by the difficulty in obtaining data necessary to estimate adjustment effects and by the complexities adjustment considerations introduce into standard trade models.

Because of this relative lack of analytical and empirical work on the phenomenon of adjustment to trade, policy-makers often look in vain for clear answers on crucial policy questions, such as the duration of the adjustment process following trade reform, the likelihood and extent of unemployment surges following trade shocks or reforms and the best policies to facilitate relevant adjustment processes. Finding answers to these questions is of political importance for a variety of reasons:

- Policy-makers need to be able to evaluate the political and economic (for example, budgetary) consequences of possible temporary drops in gross domestic product (GDP) or surges in unemployment.

- Evidence suggests that the distribution of adjustment costs is skewed and that adjustment costs can, as a consequence, be very substantial for certain individuals. Policy-makers may wish to consider assisting individuals suffering from particular hardship during adjustment processes.

- Costly adjustment processes reduce the net gains from trade reform. This is particularly worrisome if poorly executed adjustment processes impede economies from reaching the optimal equilibrium.

- Those suffering during the adjustment process following trade reform may oppose trade reform. Guidance on how to pre-empt such opposition would be beneficial for policy-makers and in the long-run for the economy as a whole.

This chapter tries to address these and other relevant questions by providing a summary of the existing economic literature on the subject of adjustment to trade liberalization. After a presentation of the definition of adjustment costs used in this chapter, the measurement of adjustment costs is discussed in detail in section 6.3. In particular, indices measuring intra-sectoral employment churning are developed. In that section, different methodologies to measure adjustment costs, both ex-ante and ex-post, are presented and a summary of existing empirical evidence and simulation exercises is provided. Most of the empirical evidence focuses on industrialized countries, as evidence on developing countries is particularly scarce. In section 6.4, arguments in favour of adjustment assistance are presented, based on a discussion of the relevant theoretical economic literature. A discussion of different policy options to address adjustment challenges and of existing evidence on the effectiveness of different policy options follows. Section 6.5 concludes.

## 6.2   DEFINING ADJUSTMENT COSTS

The measurement of the effects of trade liberalization on welfare generally involves comparison of welfare levels before and after liberalization, i.e. after all factors of production have found their new long-run occupations. However, such calculations need to be adjusted for possible losses during the transition to the new long-run situation, in particular if this transition takes a long time. That is, proper welfare calculus needs to allow for social *adjustment costs*.

One standard metric of the adjustment costs an economy faces is the value of output that is foregone in the transition to new long-run production patterns because of the time taken to reallocate factors from their pre- to their post-liberalization occupations. In figure 6.1, the long-run equilibrium path is represented by $Y_T$. If trade liberalization takes place at time=0, output would jump from $Y_0$ to $Y_T$ in the absence of adjustment costs. In the presence of adjustment costs, instead, output will follow a path as the curved line Y(t), i.e. output may drop below the original output level $Y_0$, remain below it until $t_{Y0}$, and ultimately exceed $Y_0$ to slowly approach $Y_T$.

Adjustment costs would, therefore, correspond to the properly discounted difference between $Y_T$ and the curve Y(t) in figure 6.1.[3] In this chapter, we refer to this value as gross adjustment costs. Gross gains correspond to the discounted value of $Y_T$ minus $Y_0$. As a consequence, net gains from trade reform equal the discounted value of Y(t) minus $Y_0$.

In the left-hand part of figure 6.1, it is assumed that output drops temporarily below the output level $Y_0$ that preceded trade reform. In many of the papers discussed in this chapter, adjustment costs are considered to be only those costs that bring output below its pre-reform level. In figure 6.1, this would correspond to the discounted difference between $Y_0$ and Y(t) between the time of the reform and $t_{Y0}$, i.e. the period in which output reaches pre-reform levels again. In this chapter, we will refer to that value as the adjustment costs, as opposed to gross adjustment costs defined in the previous paragraph.

Net losses such as those depicted in figure 6.1 for the first years following reform, though possible, do not always occur (Bacchetta and Jansen, 2003). Indeed, the adjustment costs such as unemployment and lower output in some sectors may be outweighed by benefits in others. In this case, Y(t) does not fall below $Y_0$. According to the definition used in this chapter, adjustment costs would then be zero, even though gross adjustment costs are positive. Even if net losses occur during the beginning of the adjustment period, the overall benefits from trade liberalization (equal to the surface between Y(t) and $Y_0$) are very likely to be significantly positive, in particular if the period of net losses is short.

In the theoretical literature, another scenario has been discussed quite prominently that has received relatively little attention in empirical work. A number of theoretical studies find that the long-run free trade equilibrium may be affected negatively by the existence of adjustment costs. Graphically this could, for instance, take the form of an adjustment path as the one depicted in the right-hand part of figure 6.1, where the long-run equilibrium after trade liberalization would shift from $Y_T$ to $Y_{T,A}$ in the presence of adjustment costs. Mussa (1978), for instance, finds in a

---

[3] This method of calculating adjustment costs was suggested by Neary (1982) and has also been used by Davidson and Matusz (2004b).

Figure 6.1: Adjustment paths following trade liberalization

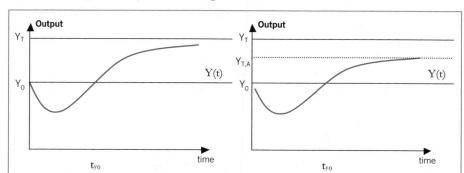

Heckscher-Ohlin framework that the original free trade equilibrium may not be reached in the presence of adjustment costs. In that paper, the adjustment of capital is assumed to be costly, while labour moves smoothly from the shrinking import to the expanding export sector. Davidson and Matusz (2004a), instead, assume that the labour market is characterized by frictions. In particular, they assume that finding new jobs in the exporting sector involves a search process and that this search process is categorized by congestion externalities. In that set-up, a temporary terms-of-trade shock can lead to multiple equilibriums, a "good" steady state with high job-acquisition rates and high output, and a "bad" steady state with lower job-acquisition rates and lower output. Government intervention is warranted in order to guide the economy towards the "good" path.

In theory, trade liberalization may entail a net welfare loss if the gains are sufficiently small relative to the adjustment costs, i.e. if the discounted sum of the annual net gains following $t_{y0}$ is smaller than the discounted sum of the annual net losses in the first years following trade reform and until $t_{y0}$ is reached. However, adjustment costs would have to be very large relative to the standard gains from trade liberalization in order to dominate the latter. Adjustment costs tend to be temporary and must be set against an indefinite stream of future higher incomes. It would therefore take very large costs, or a very short-run perspective (i.e. a high discount rate) in order for the net costs to outweigh the net gains. This is further reinforced by the fact that the (static) gains from trade liberalization tend to grow over time as a result of general economic growth.[4]

Figure 6.1 above provides a graphical representation of the possible adjustment costs to the economy as a whole. Those costs are sometimes referred to as social costs. A substantive amount of literature has looked at individual components of those social adjustment costs, i.e. at the costs occurring to labour, capital or the public sector. Table 6.1 provides an overview of the different possible components.

---

[4] Trade liberalization may under certain circumstances also lead to long-term net losses for some economies, i.e. $Y_T < Y_0$. Peters and Vanzetti (2004) show, for example, that some countries could expect long-term losses from multilateral agricultural trade liberalization, e.g. due to preference erosion.

Table 6.1: Components of adjustment costs[5]

| Social adjustment costs (aggregate) | Private adjustment costs | Labour | Unemployment<br>Lower wage during transition<br>Obsolescence of skills<br>Training costs<br>Personal costs (e.g. mental suffering; not considered here) |
| --- | --- | --- | --- |
| | | Capital | Underutilized capital<br>Obsolete machines or buildings<br>Transition cost of shifting capital to other activities<br>Investments to become an exporter |
| | Public-sector adjustment costs | | Lower tax revenue<br>Social safety net spending<br>Implementation costs of trade reform |

Source: Author's table based on Laird and de Córdoba (2006).

There is a fair amount of empirical evidence that trade liberalization may entail significant losses for some groups. For instance, several studies report that replaced workers may earn substantially less in their new occupations, even several years after replacement. Jacobson, Lalonde and Sullivan (1993a; 1993b) provide examples for the United States. Whether this is a temporary phenomenon, and thus an adjustment cost, or a permanent phenomenon is often difficult to determine. In addition to costs that are borne by workers, capital owners and firms can be adversely affected. Machines may become obsolete, and firms that want to capture new export opportunities may have to invest in order to become an exporter.

One reason why it is important to look at private adjustment costs is that they are typically unevenly distributed, as some factor markets work more smoothly than others to redirect resources that are freed up through liberalization. Adjustment costs may be concentrated in specific sectors, as would be predicted by traditional trade theory, whereby industries with a comparative advantage increase and others decrease; or they may be concentrated among companies of a specific size, as predicted by the so-called new new trade theory that predicts reallocation within industries with larger, more productive firms being more likely to grow and smaller, less productive firms being more likely to shrink. There may also be strong differences in regions or personal characteristics, such as skill levels, that imply that different factor owners

---

[5] Matusz (2001) argues that not all private costs are societal costs. Someone deciding to accept a lower wage before retirement, who continues to be paid according to his productivity, entails a private cost but no societal cost. We focus only on the transition period and, thus, if the worker would continue to receive a lower wage, it would be a permanent change and, therefore, not an adjustment cost.

---

**Box 6-1: Ongoing adjustment pressure**

In open markets, adjustment is a permanent occurrence. One reason is the exposure to external shocks. These shocks may or may not require structural adjustment. There is evidence, for example, that the 2008–09 crisis had in numerous countries the effect of a business cycle dip, where production and trade return to the previous pattern after a limited period.

A second reason is the acceleration of structural change in production processes as well as other areas in open markets. Higher competition and continuously changing production patterns, such as global value chains, put permanent pressure on economies to adjust.

These phenomena are linked to open markets but they are not transitional consequences of a trade policy change, such as a reduction of tariffs, and are thus not the focus of this chapter. The policy conclusion of this chapter, that coherent trade and labour market policies, and generally available social security programmes can contribute to mitigating adjustment costs, though, does also hold for these aspects of ongoing adjustment.

---

experience different adjustment costs. These distribution effects caused by adjustment have to be distinguished from long-term distributional effects where, for example, the skill premium increases as a result of trade reform.

The distributional consequences of adjustment can have two important ramifications. First, they may generally be perceived as being undesirable, and may thus call for some form of government intervention on equity grounds. But the least-cost way of providing this assistance would very rarely be in the form of protection, but more plausibly in the form of retraining, flexible housing markets, income support, and so on (see section 6.4).

Another reason why adjustment costs may be important involves the political economy. Private adjustment costs are significant determinants, together with the long-run effects of trade liberalization, of the identity of winners and losers from trade liberalization. They influence the line-up of interests that might oppose trade liberalization, despite any aggregate gains it may bring. Because individual workers or enterprises often do not know in advance whether they will be among the winners or the losers of trade reform, those opposing trade reform ex-ante may even exceed the number of those who would eventually lose from reform.[6] Individual adjustment costs – real or expected – may therefore have significant consequences for political strategies.


## 6.3 ADJUSTMENT COST: MEASUREMENT AND DETERMINANTS

In this section, approaches to quantify the economic adjustment costs and factors that impact the costs are discussed. A distinction is made between ex-post analyses and ex-ante analyses. Ex-post analyses typically use econometric methods to evaluate

---

[6] This argument has been made by Fernandez and Rodrik (1991), albeit with a view on long-term gains and losses from trade liberalization rather than short-term costs.

the adjustment costs of trade reforms or trade shocks that have taken place in the past. Ex-ante analyses, instead, use simulation methods to evaluate adjustment costs of trade reforms or shocks before the costs have actually materialized. They can therefore represent a useful planning tool for policy-makers. While early studies using ex-post evaluations date back to the 1970s, the inclusion of adjustment costs in ex-ante analyses is a rather recent phenomenon. Costs that are harder to quantify, such as the mental suffering of unemployed workers, are typically ignored in both types of analysis.

## 6.3.1 Factors determining adjustment costs

The magnitude of adjustment costs is a direct reflection of the speed at which the economy manages to redirect resources in response to liberalization. These costs depend on a large number of factors that determine, for instance, the ease with which firms expand or contract, and the likelihood of expansion being accompanied by employment creation and vice versa. In this context, the flexibility of labour markets and credit markets are of particular importance.

If firms in sectors with potential for expansion do not have strong incentives to hire new employees, for instance because of administrative regulations or externally imposed labour market contract requirements, the adjustment will be more costly than otherwise. Likewise, firms will need to invest in order to exploit new opportunities, and this requires access to credit. The possibility of smooth adjustment also depends on the functioning of other markets. For example, the willingness of workers to accept employment in other geographical areas may depend on the housing market. The likelihood of displaced workers finding work in expanding firms may depend on their skills. Their education level and the availability of relevant (re)training opportunities may therefore also affect an economy's capacity to adjust to a trade reform or trade shock.

Adjustment costs are also influenced by the degree of ease with which firms in contracting sectors or with low productivity are able to release factors. For instance, if production in these firms is maintained through government support, the adjustment process might be prolonged. This is not to say, however, that it would be economically desirable that factors are laid off immediately after liberalization. From a purely economic point of view, minimization of adjustment costs requires a careful balance between the speed at which factors are released and the speed at which they can be re-employed. It is sometimes argued that the existence of adjustment costs makes it desirable for the trade liberalization process itself to be gradual, for instance, in order to avoid congestion in labour markets. The question of the appropriate speed of trade liberalization is complex, however, and typically also involves the question of political credibility.

It should be stressed that the literature on adjustment costs has focused on developed countries where the nature and the magnitude of the adjustment costs may be different for several reasons, such as greater diversification or the existence of institutions or social safety nets. Rodrik (2004) argues that such results ought not be extrapolated to developing countries. This is because of the greater role played by the informal sector, sparse social safety nets and the less-diversified nature of developing country economies. OECD (2005b) instead argues that differences between developed and developing countries exist but that key findings of the literature on adjustment costs are broadly applicable across countries, albeit with differing degrees of emphasis.

## 6.3.2 Measuring adjustment costs: Ex-post analysis

The empirical literature on the magnitude of adjustment costs from trade liberalization was rather thin until recently. This is probably a reflection of the perception among researchers during the 1960s and 1970s that adjustment costs were negligible in proportion to the aggregate gross gains, an impression that is supported by the limited number of studies that were undertaken. The interest in the topic increased when evidence suggested that the costs may be significant and new sources of data at the micro level allowed researchers to inquire at a more detailed level of analysis.

### 6.3.2.1 Magnitude of adjustment costs and long-term trade liberalization

Although the evidence about the relationship between long-term gains and temporary adjustment costs is mixed, a majority of studies finds that the benefits outweigh the adjustment costs. The two main contributions to the early literature on this topic (Magee, 1972; Baldwin, Mutti and Richardson, 1980) found adjustment costs of less than 5 per cent of total benefits from trade liberalization.

Both studies assessed the temporary income loss roughly by multiplying an estimate of the average amount of time workers are unemployed by an estimate of their average wages before unemployment.[7] For instance, Magee (1972) calculates the output changes if all import restrictions in the United States were dismantled. The output changes are converted into changes in employment. The average length of unemployment estimated for workers who switch their jobs after trade liberalization is multiplied by the estimated wages of displaced workers. Magee finds a ratio of adjustment costs to total gains from trade of around 4 per cent. He ignores other costs, such as those of moving capital, and thus underestimates the total costs. Baldwin, Mutti and Richardson (1980) include estimated costs for adjustment of firms' capital stocks and find that labour bears nearly 90 per cent of the total adjustment costs. In order to estimate individual wage losses, the authors disaggregate the United States economy into 327 sectors, and calculate the amount by which each sector would contract or expand. They assume that workers in contracting sectors would spend an average period of unemployment that is based on workers' characteristics. The net effect is then multiplied by sector-specific wages to calculate the lost wages due to

---

[7] With the same method, private adjustment costs can be assessed. Bale (1976), for example, from a sample of workers assisted under the United States Trade Expansion Act of 1962, estimated that the average income loss was US$3,370 during 1969–70 for a worker who was displaced because of import competition, before taking into account such factors as trade adjustment assistance and unemployment insurance.

adjustment. According to their estimates, the bulk of adjustment costs occur in their set-up during the first year after liberalization. Net welfare effects, however, are positive even during the first year.

Takacs and Winters (1991) use a similar approach in a sectoral study that evaluates the adjustment costs of the removal of quantitative restrictions in the British footwear industry. One specific aspect of their study is that they take into account the fairly high natural rate of turnover in the industry (almost 17 per cent per year) when estimating the duration of unemployment of trade-displaced workers. The authors find that even under their most pessimistic scenario, the adjustment costs are almost negligible in comparison to the potential gains from trade liberalization – that is, slightly less than £10 million in losses compared to £570 million in gains. Their results point to a ratio of costs to gains from liberalization of 0.5 to 1.5 per cent for the first year after quota elimination.

De Melo and Tarr (1990) use a computable general equilibrium (CGE) model in another sectoral study that quantifies the adjustment costs of the elimination of import quotas on textiles and clothing, steel and cars in the United States. They find that during the first six years after liberalization, adjustment costs represent about 1.5 per cent of the gains from trade liberalization. The result is influenced by the type of liberalization, since gains from quota removal are usually higher than those from tariff reduction.

Another approach that has been used to estimate social adjustment costs is to study outlays in Trade Adjustment Assistance (TAA) schemes in the United States (see section 6.4.4). According to Richardson (1982), total outlays in TAA under the United States Trade Expansion Act of 1962 were approximately US$75 million for the period 1962–75. The corresponding figure for assistance under the United States Trade Act of 1974 for the period 1975–79 was approximately US$870 million, with a sharp increase in 1980–81 due to the auto-centred recession.

More recent work often finds a higher ratio of adjustment costs to total gains from trade. Either the adjustment costs are higher, or the total gains are lower, or both. Davidson and Matusz (2000) find that, in economies with sluggish labour markets, the adjustment costs might offset the gains to a significant extent because of the decrease in output and income associated with unemployment. However, most studies still find that the benefits are higher than the costs, for example, Bradford, Grieco and Hufbauer (2005) find that benefits are seven times the estimated costs. Davidson and Matusz (2004b) explicitly take into account the time and resource costs of retraining and job search in their estimation of adjustment costs. According to their most modest estimates, roughly 30 per cent of gross benefits will be eaten away by adjustment. This share goes up to 80 per cent under different model assumptions.

The amount of literature dealing with developing countries is considerably smaller than that dealing with developed countries. For developing countries, the lack of available data is a limitation. Matusz and Tarr (1999), and Laird and de Córdoba (2006), review several developing-country studies. Some reviewed studies are directly related to trade liberalization and labour markets, such as Milner and Wright (1998) who studied the economy of Mauritius after liberalization; others are about other shocks, such as the experience of downsizing public sectors. Broadly, the empirical studies conclude that the benefits are also higher than the costs even in the short term.

Despite differences in methodological approach and in underlying assumptions, ex-post empirical studies typically convey the message that social adjustment costs are smaller, in aggregate, than the standard gains from trade liberalization. It should be noted, however, that regardless of the method employed, the estimates presented above should be viewed with caution. For instance, since the costs and benefits of liberalization are typically distributed unevenly through time, they are sensitive to the assumed rate of discounting of future gains and losses – an assumption that by its very nature must be quite arbitrary. Even if aggregate adjustment costs are small compared to long-term welfare gains, individual costs can be very significant for those affected. They are the object of the discussion in the following subsections.

### 6.3.2.2 Evidence on employment-related adjustment costs

Workers who are laid off as a result of structural adjustment triggered by trade liberalization bear adjustment costs in the forms of: potential unemployment, generally associated with an income loss during that period; potential lower wages in a new job during a transition period until new skills needed for the new job are obtained; and other costs, such as costs related to finding and taking up a new job.

In our definition of individual adjustment costs, we do not include lower wages that workers may have to accept in a new job unless the lower wage is temporary. The longer-term effect of trade liberalization on wages is discussed in McMillan and Verduzco in Chapter 2 of this volume, where it is shown that trade-displaced workers frequently have to accept lower wages though some find better-paid jobs. This subsection, instead, focuses on adjustment costs measured in terms of changes in the number of unemployed.

Assessments of the adjustment costs of trade reform or shocks in terms of numbers of unemployed have tended to focus on two questions. One strand of literature has analysed whether unemployment may temporarily increase as a consequence of trade reform, while a second strand of literature has analysed whether the nature of unemployment is different for those displaced by trade reform than for those displaced for other reasons. Indeed, it turns out to be quite difficult to measure the incidence of trade-related displacement, since there are so many other factors influencing movement, and the impact depends on the degree of the trade policy change.

Overall, evidence does not seem to confirm labour reallocation across sectors on a large scale after liberalization as it could be expected from traditional trade theory (Hoekman and Porto, 2010). Attanasio, Goldberg and Pavcnik (2004), for instance, analyse household data for Colombia during its trade liberalization and fail to find evidence that industry-level employment is affected by the shock of import liberalization. De Melo and Roland-Holst (1994) build a CGE model of the Uruguayan economy and include rigidities in the labour market. They quantify the relocation of the labour force and find, for one scenario, that 5 per cent of the labour force was removed as a result of the liberalization. This failure to observe significant levels of labour turnover may explain why empirical work has so far not found strong evidence of temporary unemployment surges following trade reform.

A comprehensive World Bank study of trade reform in developing countries, Papageorgiou et al. (1991), found that in eight out of nine countries manufacturing employment was higher during and one year after the liberalization period than before. Only in Chile did manufacturing employment decrease significantly.

Rama (1994) finds a negative effect of trade liberalization on employment in Uruguay in the late 1970s and early 1980s. Milner and Wright (1998) studied the economy of Mauritius after liberalization and show, in contrast, that manufacturing employment increased significantly in the period directly after liberalization.

Harrison and Revenga (1995) track total employment growth for six countries that underwent significant liberalization (cited in Matusz and Tarr, 1999). Employment continued to grow throughout the period prior to, during, and after reform in Costa Rica, Peru and Uruguay. They found, however, the opposite for three countries in transition but argue that these countries undertook reforms that went well beyond trade liberalization.

Two studies on the effects of the Canada-United States free trade agreement (FTA) have estimated the job losses induced by the implementation of a trade agreement that took place in a period in which both Canada and the United States were going through a significant recession. Gaston and Trefler (1997) estimate that 9-14 per cent of the jobs lost in the period following trade reform were induced by the FTA-mandated tariff cuts. In a follow-up paper, Trefler (2004) finds a bigger role for the tariff cuts and estimates that close to 30 per cent of the observed employment losses in manufacturing had been the result of FTA-mandated tariff cuts. That paper also finds that employment levels only recovered their pre-FTA level after a period of seven years.[8]

Studies belonging to the second strand of literature, which analyses the nature of unemployment caused by trade reform or shocks, find that trade-displaced workers are likely to go through significant spells of unemployment. Bale (1976) finds, for example, an average of 31 weeks of unemployment in the United States. Some studies analyse whether the duration of unemployment is higher for job losses related to trade liberalization than those caused by other lay-offs. Kletzer (2001) finds for the United States, and the OECD (2005a) for 14 EU countries, that the share of re-employed workers after two years is only slightly lower in sectors with high import competition. These studies also look at the characteristics of dismissed workers and find that, on average, the groups appear quite similar in terms of education and work experience, though the trade-related unemployed are slightly older, have more tenure and slightly higher earnings related to the lost job. Previous studies found that being older and having less formal education is associated with greater post-displacement difficulties (see OECD, 2005a).

---

[8] Even taking into account that employment typically recovers slower than output after a shock, this is a long period compared with the finding in Davidson and Matusz's (2004b) simulations, that output recovers after 2.5 years or less.

Overall, therefore, the existing empirical literature does not provide strong evidence of trade-induced unemployment being very different from unemployment caused by other economic shocks or changes. There is also no strong evidence of trade reform having a strong negative effect on unemployment rates, although there are some indications that trade reform can add significantly to job displacement if undertaken when the job market is already under stress, such as situations of economic recession or major structural change.

### 6.3.3 Measuring adjustment costs: CGE models

The basic approach to ex-ante assessment (in a developed or developing country context) involves the application of a partial or general equilibrium simulation model (see Francois and Reinert, 1997; Francois, 2004).[9] Francois (2004) offers a range of indices for use in CGE models to track factors that drive adjustment costs. In this section, we expand on these by defining a range of indexes that track various aspects of structural adjustment linked to trade. In particular, some of the indices discussed in this section will explicitly deal with the firm-level dimension of adjustment to trade reform, a dimension emphasized in recent literature on changes in the composition and size of firms within sectors in response to trade-related changes in the business climate (Brulhart, 2000; Schott, 2004; Davis, Faberman and Haltiwanger, 2006). The discussion in this section focuses on adjustment in employment levels. Readers not familiar with statistical formulations may consider to skip the equations and focus instead on the descriptive text. The annex to this chapter provides a related discussion on indices to measure adjustment in output and changes in inequality levels.

CGE-based simulations of the effects of trade reforms usually generate information on sectoral employment levels after adjustment to the reform. Using information on pre-reform employment levels, changes in sectoral employment levels ( $\hat{l}_j$ ) can easily be computed with the use of such models. In order to find out the total change in employment as a result of trade reform, it is enough to take the sum of the changes at sectoral level:

$$m_L = \sum_{j=1}^{n} \lambda_j \hat{l}_j \tag{1}$$

where $\lambda_j$ reflects the share of sector $j$'s employment in total employment, and $n$ represents the number of sectors.

Trade reform will typically induce some sectors to shrink and others to grow. The economy-wide change in employment found may thus turn out to be minor, even if changes in sectoral employment levels are large. This is the case because sectoral gains and losses will (partially) cancel out, with the result that net changes

---

[9] See also Piermartini and Teh (2005) for background information on the functioning of computable general equilibrium models (CGEs) and the effect of different modelling assumptions on the welfare effects generated by CGE simulations.

in total employment may be much smaller than gross movements. In fact, most CGE models assume that, in the long run, employment levels are unchanged. By definition, the economy-wide change of employment levels would therefore be zero.

Looking at the sum of sectoral changes is therefore not useful. Instead, it is necessary to look at a variance-based measure such as the one described in the equation below:

$$s_{L,across}^2 = \sum_{j=1}^{n} \lambda_j \left( \hat{l}_j - m_L \right)^2 \tag{2}$$

Taking the square root of $s_{L,across}^2$ gives us a measure of variation of employment across sectors and thus a measure of the actual number of workers that change jobs by moving across sectors. This index, which can easily be calculated using standard CGE models, thus provides a useful indication for the adjustments taking place in labour markets following trade reform. Unfortunately, they are likely to underestimate the actual amount of job churning that occurs. Indeed, workers who change jobs but do not change sectors are not captured by the above measure. In order to capture those workers, it would be necessary to have information on employment changes at the firm level ($\hat{l}_{i,j}$, where the subscript $i$ describes individual firms), information not available in typical CGE models.

Variation of employment within sector $j$ would be:[10]

$$s_{L,j:within,}^2 = \sum_{i=1}^{f_i} \theta_{ij} \left( \hat{l}_{ij} - m_{L,j} \right)^2 \quad \text{where} \quad m_{L,j} = \sum_{i=1}^{f_j} \theta_{ij} \hat{l}_{ij} \tag{3}$$

A measure for adjustments in the labour market, capturing all worker movements, those within and across sectors, would look as follows:

$$s_{L,Total}^2 = \sum_{j=1}^{n} \sum_{i=1}^{f_i} \lambda_j \theta_{ij} \left( \hat{l}_{ij} - m_{L,j} \right)^2$$

$$= \sum_{j=1}^{n} \lambda_j s_{L,j:within}^2 + s_{L,across}^2 \tag{4}$$

In the absence of information on changes in firm-level employment, it is not possible to compute the within-sectoral variation, i.e. the first of the two terms on the right-hand side of the equation. We are left to working with the second term and thus with an index only based on shifts across sectors. To the extent that changes within individual sectors have been found to be very important in the recent literature mentioned above, indices based on equation (2) – or the second element on the right-hand side of equation (4) – run the risk of grossly misrepresenting the actual extent to which workers are displaced.

---

[10] Where $\theta_{ij}$ is the employment share of firm $i$ in sector $j$, and $j$, and $\sum_{i=1}^{f_j} \theta_{ij} = 1$.

Alternative measures for gross displacement of workers are defined in equations (5) and (6):

$$\Delta_{L,j} = \left(1/2\right) \sum_{i=1}^{f_j} \theta_{ij} \text{ABS}\left(\hat{l}_{ij}\right) \tag{5}$$

$$\Delta_L = \left(1/2\right) \sum_{j=1}^{n} \sum_{i=1}^{f_j} \lambda_j \theta_{ij} \text{ABS}\left(\hat{l}_{ij}\right) = \sum_{j=1}^{n} \lambda_j \Delta_{L,j} \tag{6}$$

Equation (5) provides an approximate gross measure of the total workers displaced within a sector (and an exact measure when net displacement is zero). Equation (6) provides a measure of total, economy-wide displacement of workers. Again, firm-level data would be necessary to compute these measures. A variation of equation (6) has been employed in recent European Commission studies of the social impact of trade agreements; known as sustainability impact assessments (SIAs). They can be calculated for models with representative or identical firms based on weighted industry-level deviations in output  (see ECORYS, 2009a, 2009b).  However, even in this context it is limited to adjustment across sectors, and not adjustment within sectors (i.e. across firms). Indeed, such displacement across firms is widely ignored in this literature.

Given the absence of firm-level information in CGE models, existing studies therefore rely on estimates concerning labour displacement across sectors in order to give an indication of the possible adjustment costs following trade liberalization. In the following, we present a number of those findings. Table 6.2 presents estimates for the cross-sectoral displacement following an EU-Andean trade liberalization agreement and is based on Development Solutions, CEPR and Manchester 1824 (2009). The table presents findings for the short run and the long run where, in the short

Table 6.2: Effect on EU and Andean labour displacement for unskilled and skilled workers (shifts in total employment in per cent)

| Country | Static/short-term effects | | | | Dynamic/long-term effects | | | |
| | Modest liberalization | | Ambitious liberalization | | Modest liberalization | | Ambitious liberalization | |
| | Unskilled | Skilled | Unskilled | Skilled | Unskilled | Skilled | Unskilled | Skilled |
|---|---|---|---|---|---|---|---|---|
| EU27 | 0.0 | 0.0 | 0.03 | 0.0 | 0.0 | 0.0 | 0.0 | 0.0 |
| Bolivia | 1.0 | 1.5 | 1.0 | 1.4 | 2.1 | 3.0 | 2.1 | 2.9 |
| Colombia | 1.3 | 0.9 | 0.9 | 1.3 | 2.0 | 1.8 | 2.0 | 1.8 |
| Ecuador | 2.2 | 1.7 | 1.7 | 2.2 | 2.7 | 2.9 | 2.7 | 2.8 |
| Peru | 0.7 | 0.6 | 0.6 | 0.7 | 1.1 | 1.2 | 1.1 | 1.2 |

Source: Development Solutions, CEPR and Manchester 1824 (2009).

run, capital is assumed to be fixed, while in the long-run capital allocations adjust to the new price signals created by trade liberalization. Labour markets are assumed to adjust smoothly in both scenarios and full employment is assumed. The estimated labour displacement effects are thus purely based on labour shifts across sectors as reflected in equation (2) above. The table indicates that, in the long run, close to 3 per cent of the employed labour force in Bolivia and Ecuador would be involved in inter-sectoral shifts in employment, giving rise to accompanying adjustment costs. This is based on the weighted standard deviation of shifts in employment (weighted by sectoral employment shares). The corresponding numbers for the other Andean countries are lower, and displacement in the EU is negligible.

Table 6.3 presents estimations for the labour displacement effects of an EU-Central American FTA for two different liberalization scenarios.[11] Under both scenarios, labour displacement is significant in Costa Rica, Nicaragua and Panama. This is the case in both the short run and the long run. For Panama, a high standard deviation is predicted even in the short term, which implies that labour-related adjustment costs in Panama can be expected to be high. Combined with the estimations' findings that long-run wage effects in Panama will be negative, the country is likely to experience substantial and negative labour market impacts from an FTA with the EU.

Both the EU-Andean FTA simulations (Development Solutions, CEPR and Manchester 1824, 2009) and the EU-Central American FTA simulations (ECORYS, 2009a) predict small labour adjustment effects in the EU. Also, ECORYS (2009b), which presents findings of simulations for a hypothetical EU-Indian FTA, finds that

Table 6.3: Effect on EU and Central American labour displacement for unskilled and skilled workers, standard deviation of sector changes in employment (expressed as percentage of total employment)

| Country | Static/short-term effects | | | | Dynamic/long-term effects | | | |
| | Comprehensive FTA | | Very comprehensive FTA | | Comprehensive FTA | | Very comprehensive FTA | |
| | Unskilled | Skilled | Unskilled | Skilled | Unskilled | Skilled | Unskilled | Skilled |
|---|---|---|---|---|---|---|---|---|
| EU27 | 0.2 | 0.2 | 0.3 | 0.3 | 0.2 | 0.2 | 0.3 | 0.3 |
| Costa Rica | 6.2 | 6.2 | 10.6 | 10.7 | 6.3 | 6.3 | 11.2 | 11.2 |
| Guatemala | 2.0 | 2.0 | 2.7 | 2.7 | 2.1 | 2.1 | 2.7 | 2.7 |
| Nicaragua | 3.6 | 3.6 | 5.2 | 5.2 | 3.5 | 3.5 | 5.1 | 5.1 |
| Panama | 15.0 | 15.0 | 17.1 | 17.1 | 15.2 | 15.2 | 17.4 | 17.4 |

Source: ECORYS (2009a).

---

[11] The "comprehensive FTA" assumption assumes 90 per cent bilateral tariff reductions in agriculture and manufacturing, a 25 per cent reduction in trade costs to services, and a reduction in trade costs of 1 per cent due to less restrictive non-tariff measures (NTMs). The corresponding values for the "very comprehensive FTA" are 97 per cent, 75 per cent and 3 per cent.

labour market adjustment in the EU is small. The study predicts a mean absolute change in employment by sector of between 0.25 and 0.36 per cent of baseline employment, or between 250 and 360 workers in EU27 per 100,000. The estimated number for India is larger, between 1,830 and 2,650 workers change sector per 100,000.

## 6.4   ADJUSTMENT ASSISTANCE

### 6.4.1   Definition of trade adjustment assistance

As shown in the previous sections, increasing trade and trade liberalization cause adjustment costs as factors of production are reallocated within and between firms and sectors. It is difficult to identify where exactly the costs occur and what the magnitude of the costs is. Until recently, the focus was on industry-level adjustment, i.e. those sectors that have a comparative advantage benefit from liberalization, while others are likely to shrink. New evidence shows that even within industrial sectors, reshuffling occurs. Less efficient companies may shrink or close down while more efficient ones grow.

The details of the adjustment costs are important for policy-makers who have to identify priorities and trade-offs between likely long-term gains and short-term costs from trade liberalization. Knowledge about the adjustment costs is also important with respect to the decision whether to provide trade adjustment assistance (TAA) and, if so, what kind of assistance and how to best target it.

The term "trade adjustment assistance" is commonly used for programmes providing assistance for workers and firms in industries that have suffered from competition with imports or for firms in expanding industries that are not able to fully use new export opportunities.[12]

Few examples of assistance programmes explicitly targeting trade-affected workers or firms exist. The best known one is arguably the United States Trade Adjustment Assistance (US-TAA) that provides support to workers, firms or regions that are adversely affected by increased imports. TAA programmes can also comprise assistance for companies to become an exporter in expanding sectors. In the policy community, such programmes are also often referred to as assistance to overcome supply constraints. For example, Cadot, Dutoit and Olarreaga (2005) estimate for Madagascar that a sunk cost of 120 to 150 per cent of the annual output is necessary to shift out of subsistence farming and to become an exporter. Assistance programmes can help potential exporters to meet the fixed costs or increase their productivity. The Food and Agricultural Organization (FAO), for example, provides technical assistance to potential exporters in countries with a comparative advantage in agriculture to meet the high standards in importing countries (for example, FAO, 2007).

Lower wages for some workers as a result of trade policy changes may not be temporary but permanent. Someone losing his or her job in the car industry and

---

[12] Partly based on *Deardorff's Glossary of International Economics.*

Table 6.4: Categorization of adjustment policies related to labour market issues

| | Labour market and social policies | | Trade policies | |
|---|---|---|---|---|
| | | Examples | | Examples |
| Coherent policies to facilitate adjustment | Passive labour market policy | Unemployment insurance | Gradual liberalization | Transition period in trade agreements |
| | Active labour market policy | Unemployment services; training | Early announcement | Implementation period after conclusion of agreement |
| | Social security | Health care | | |
| Specific trade-adjustment polices | Extending and targeting labour market policies to trade-affected workers | Services in case of mass lay-offs | Safeguard measures | GATT Article XIX |

finding a job in a fast-food restaurant may have to accept a lower wage and may never reach his or her former wage. Since this is not a temporary loss, we do not consider any assistance to compensate for the loss as trade adjustment assistance. Some programmes, however, include such payments.

The consequence of temporary unemployment or wage losses can be very severe for individuals and can have long-lasting negative effects on growth and development. Policy-makers can, to a certain extent, influence the adjustment costs that workers and firms face as a consequence of their trade policies through appropriate policies and assistance programmes. In the following section, those policies and adjustment assistance programmes are discussed.

Two major areas where policy-makers can influence the adjustment cost are distinguished and considered here. First, given a certain trade policy or trade liberalization scheme, adjustment assistance programmes or other domestic policy measures can mitigate the adjustment costs. Second, the trade policy itself can be chosen in a way where adjustment costs are taken into consideration. Other policies, such as exchange rate policies or other macroeconomic policies, could also impact on the adjustment costs, but they are not discussed here.

### 6.4.2 Reasons for adjustment assistance

Motivation for adjustment assistance may arise from efficiency and equity objectives. If markets are absent or are not functioning well, policy interventions to improve functioning of markets can mitigate the frictional costs of reallocations and therefore increase efficiency and, ultimately, the net gains from trade liberalization.[13] For example, if a rigid labour market prevents workers moving from firms that are shrinking due to import competition to other firms that are expanding due to improved export opportunities, programmes that facilitate those moves may be efficiency-increasing.[14] If financial markets are weak, private investors may find it difficult to get the capital to move into expanding sectors. Private adjustment activities that have positive externalities, such as on-the-job learning, which cannot be fully captured by firms that pay for them, may be subsidized to increase efficiency as well. Marcal (2001), for instance, finds some evidence that training under the US-TAA programme increases the re-employment rates, i.e. those trained have a higher probability to find a new job than those not trained.

An argument for adjustment assistance linked to the equity context is the political economy consideration by which losers of trade-policy changes would be compensated in order to reduce opposition against that policy change. In agriculture, for example, the Australian Government provided farmers with special retirement schemes to compensate for losses resulting from its agricultural liberalization. The WTO Agreement on Agriculture (AoA) explicitly exempts such retirement schemes from reduction commitments (AoA Annex II).[15] Compensating opponents may in some cases be the only way to achieve necessary support for policy changes. Aho and Bayard (1984) argue that the alternative to special TAA programmes is increased trade barriers or greater difficulty in reducing existing trade restrictions because of the political power of the potential "losers". Davidson and Matusz (2006) show that an optimal way to compensate those who have to move jobs is to offer a wage subsidy to them.[16] They also show that the optimal way to compensate losers who remain trapped in the import-competing sector is to offer an employment subsidy. In another paper, co-authored with Douglas Nelson (Davidson, Matusz and Nelson, 2007), the authors show that such policies can indeed increase voters' support for trade liberalization.

The public debate and also the economic literature focusing on equity concerns, though, tends to use the concept of compensation as a compensation for both the short-run and long-run losses suffered by individuals. This debate thus goes beyond the concept of "adjustment assistance" as it is used in this chapter.[17]

---

[13] Laird and de Córdoba (2006), p. 63.

[14] See also WTO (2008), p. 154.

[15] A compensation policy for cotton producers in developed countries that is not trade-distorting could perhaps also contribute to overcome difficulties in the current Doha Round.

[16] "Optimal policies" are defined here as policies that fully compensate losers while imposing the smallest distortion on the economy.

[17] Another point worth noting is the one made by Baldwin (2006), who argues that resistance against liberalization decreases as liberalization increases since export-oriented enterprises would grow and intensify lobbying while enterprises in sectors that are affected by import competition shrink and lose political influence. Thus, the political economy argument is stronger for economies with relatively high protection.

### 6.4.3 Labour market policies to facilitate adjustment

Governments decide whether no adjustment assistance, specific programmes for trade-related adjustment, or generally available programmes that facilitate adjustment are desirable. In modern and market-oriented economies, the appearance of new companies and the disappearance of some enterprises, changed skill requirements as well as other changes such as in tastes, are normal and frequent. This constantly causes movements and adjustments independent of trade-policy changes. Rama (2003) argues that it is not desirable to disentangle adjustment costs caused by trade or other factors, since pressure comes from globalization as a whole and not trade agreements in particular. Another argument is that it may not be feasible to identify adversely affected persons or firms for at least two reasons. First, the production process is more and more interlinked, and it would be difficult to decide at what point of the value chain persons or firms are adversely affected due to trade policy changes. Second, as discussed above, new evidence shows that it is not necessarily entire sectors that are positively or negatively affected, which makes the identification of winners and losers difficult.

However, specific TAA may be justified for political economic reasons or if the consequences of trade-related job losses are systematically different from job losses due to other reasons. Yet, the work by Kletzer (2001) on the United States, and by OECD (2005a) discussed above, indicates that there are no significant and systematic differences between the unemployment and re-employment experiences of workers laid off for trade-related reasons and those displaced for other reasons. These findings, together with the fact that it is difficult to identify workers negatively affected by trade, provide strong arguments in favour of general – as opposed to trade-specific – policies that assist workers who lose their jobs. Labour market policies can be designed to address this issue, the challenge being that labour market policies should assist and protect those suffering from trade reform or shocks, while at the same time guaranteeing sufficient flexibility in markets for the economy to be able to benefit from the opportunities provided by globalization.

Labour market policies comprise income replacement, usually labelled passive labour market policy (PLMP), and labour market integration measures available to the unemployed or those threatened by unemployment, usually labelled as active labour market policy (ALMP). There is evidence that a well-designed and country-specific combination of active and passive labour market policies can go a long way in reducing the burden of adjustment for workers, providing protection in times of shocks, while at the same time facilitating the adjustment processes following trade reform.

#### 6.4.3.1 Passive labour market policy

The constant reallocation of capital and labour, as well as employment being a "discrete" event,[18] is part of our modern economic model. Most workers highly value security and insurance against adverse consequences of job losses. Governments use

---

[18] In industrialized urban societies, workers either work or do not work. If they do not work, they are unable to resort to self- or home-production (Vodopivec, 2009).

different tools to bridge this. Those tools include job-security regulation that provides a disincentive for employers to lay off workers and income replacement that provides the unemployed with a certain minimum level of income.

Job security regulation typically consists of a combination of two elements: the obligation of employers to pay dismissed workers a severance payment (often consisting of multiple times the workers' monthly salaries), and the obligation to announce dismissal a stipulated number of months in advance. Both provisions make it costly for employers to lay off workers and have a tendency to increase job stability for workers. Measures that increase lay-off costs in order to provide disincentives to lay off workers have also proven to be a useful tool to deal with temporary fluctuations or demand shocks (Gamberoni et al. 2010). During the economic crisis in 2008–09, short-time working schemes, such as the German *Kurzarbeit* scheme or the French *chômage partiel*, have proved to be particularly effective in protecting viable jobs (OECD, 2010). However, tools preserving jobs are less appropriate in the case of structural changes such as those induced by trade policy changes.

Indeed, if job security legislation impedes workers from moving out of uncompetitive firms or industries into competitive ones, one of the main mechanisms of securing gains from trade is lost. If labour is not mobile across sectors or firms, trade can lead to significant losses for some workers (Saint-Paul, 2007). Ideally, therefore, labour market policies would provide workers with security while maintaining incentives to move jobs. Blanchard (2005) argues that this can be reached by protecting workers rather than jobs, in the sense of providing a certain level of income insurance also during unemployment (protect workers) but while not creating disincentives to lay off workers (do not protect jobs). This approach favours unemployment insurance over job-security regulations and has typically been associated with the term "flexicurity". The flexicurity model is arguably followed in a number of Scandinavian countries that allow for a high degree of flexibility of the factor labour while providing security through relatively generous unemployment benefits. Blanchard (2005) argues that such a system is efficient, since it provides the demanded security, and those countries would be characterized by high employment levels compared to the OECD average.[19]

Many developing countries have relatively restrictive severance pay programmes, (see, for example, figure 6.2) and it has been argued that removing excessive job protection could boost the creation of more and better jobs, and improve job prospects for vulnerable groups (see section 6.4.3.2 below; Heckman and Pages, 2000). Yet reducing job protection is an extremely sensitive task that can have highly undesirable effects for workers if not accompanied by a strengthening of income protection programmes. In other words, introducing flexibility without accompanying security can have significant equity effects. Absence of unemployment insurance can also be counterproductive for the efficiency objective, as it discourages the emergence or expansion of more risky jobs and industries (Acemoglu and Shimer, 2000).

---

[19] See Cazes and Nesperova (2007) for a discussion of the potential role of flexicurity in Central and Eastern Europe.

Figure 6.2: Severance pay in Asia

**A worker with 4-years experience at the firm and dismissed for economic reasons**

Severance pay in no. of monthly wages

Source: Hill and Aswicahyono (2004).

To date, the incidence of unemployment benefit programmes is strongly related to the level of development. Unemployment benefits are common in most developed countries, though with varying degrees of entitlements. About 80 per cent of high-income countries provide unemployment benefits – in general, these are not trade related (ILO, 2010). Few developing countries have any unemployment benefits. Provisions exist in only about 10 per cent of low-income countries and about half of middle-income countries. In developing countries, often only a minority of the labour force is covered. Coverage rates, in terms of the proportion of unemployed who receive benefits, are lowest in Africa, Asia and the Middle East (less than 10 per cent) (ILO, 2010). The low incidence of unemployment benefit schemes in low-income countries can partly be explained by the fact that they are administratively more challenging to handle than, for instance, job security legislation. However, prompted by increased market openness and fearing future global crises, more de-veloping countries – including lower middle-income developing countries, such as the Philippines – are contemplating introducing those systems (Vodopivec, 2009). Such considerations appear to be backed by the prospect of efficiency and distributive advantages of reforming social protection programmes for workers in developing countries. Due to the predominance of the informal economy, in low-income coun-tries social protection is typically confined to the minority of workers. Providing social protection to workers in the informal economy remains, therefore, a major challenge (Jansen and Lee, 2007). Vodopivec (2009) attempts to develop an unem-ployment insurance scheme for developing countries that includes the informal sector.

Another challenge that policy-makers face when designing unemployment ben-efit schemes is setting income replacement rates at such a level that they provide income protection without having negative effects on the reallocation speed, as un-employment benefits may provide a disincentive to take up a new job with a lower wage (see, for example, Boone and von Ours, 2004). Another possible drawback of unemployment benefit schemes is that they are not designed to improve workers' employability in any fundamental sense. Despite those drawbacks, it has been argued that a key strength of unemployment insurance programmes is its good provision of protection, enabling strong consumption-smoothing, for all covered workers (Vodopivec, 2009). This can make it a useful tool to contribute to both the efficiency and the equity objective in the case of trade-related adjustment costs. Furthermore, it appears to perform well under all types of shocks, which is important due to the difficulties in determining trade-related shocks and other causes, including globalization and technological change.

### 6.4.3.2 Active labour market policy

Particularly in OECD countries, there has been an increasing effort to "activate" passive measures in order to enhance the integration of the unemployed and underemployed (Cazes, Verick and Heuer, 2009). The ALMPs include a wide range of activities, intended to increase the quality of labour supply (for example, retraining); to increase labour demand (for example, direct employment creation such as public work schemes); or to improve the matching of workers and jobs (for example, job search assistance) (World Bank, 1999). ALMPs also include promotion of self-employment and employment subsidies to promote the hiring of vulnerable groups, such as new labour force entrants.

"Activation" programmes differ from free public employment services in that participation is obligatory for relevant target groups (OECD, 2005a). Key examples of activation programmes are requirements on unemployed people to attend intensive interviews with employment counsellors, to apply for job vacancies, to accept offers of suitable work, and to participate in training programmes.

The metaphors "safety net" and "trampoline", contrasting the passive and active approaches, suggest that the latter is a successful policy to assist the unemployed. However, as the experience of the past decades has demonstrated, actually implementing an active labour market policy poses many challenges, and the cost-effectiveness of some measures could be low or negative.

Heckman et al. (1999) review several microeconometric evaluation studies. They conclude that active labour market programmes have a modest impact on participants' labour market prospects. The gains from existing programmes are not sufficiently large to lift many economically disadvantaged persons out of poverty, nor to significantly reduce unemployment rates. However, there is considerable heterogeneity in the impact of these programmes; for some groups, the policies are more effective and can generate high rates of return, while for other groups these policies have had no impact and may have been even harmful.

Boone and von Ours (2004) confirm the mixed evidence and show that some ALMPs are more effective than other programmes, using data from 20 OECD countries. An increase in expenditures on both labour market training and public employment services (PESs), such as placement and vocational guidance, cause unemployment to fall. Expenditures on labour market training seem to have a larger impact on the functioning of the labour market than expenditures on PESs have. The authors fail to find significant effects of expenditures on subsidized jobs on unemployment. Betcherman et al. (1999) reviewed several studies and found that training for youth or the long-term unemployed is less cost effective than other measures, such as job-search assistance, and may even have a negative rate of return. Drawbacks of many ALMPs are that positive effects for an individual unemployed worker may not be effective in terms of the aggregate level of unemployment (the "crowding-out" effect) or that they may stimulate workers to reduce their search efforts instead of increasing them (the "locking-in" effect). Sapir (2006), however, finds that active labour market policies that are coupled with measures to increase the incentive and obligation to seek work appear to have the potential to raise the employment rate. Furthermore, crowding out may be relatively less prevalent in the case of structural adjustment, where workers also move between industries as a result of trade liberalization.

Results of the effectiveness of ALMPs appear to depend also on the economic environment. Fay (1996) found no evidence that services in the case of mass lay-offs reduce the unemployment duration during economic downturn. On the other hand, the effectiveness of job-search assistance seems to increase when economic conditions improve and when new jobs are being generated. During the decline in unemployment rates in the Netherlands in the late 1980s, programme participants were more likely to be employed than those in the control group (OECD, 1993). Since trade liberalization can have positive growth effects ALMPs could lead to positive results during the adjustment period.

The general picture that occurs seems to be that the effectiveness depends on the specific type and design of the policy, and that the impact on different groups can vary significantly. Due to the growth and structural change effect accompanying trade liberalization, a well-designed and targeted ALMP can have positive but probably relatively small effects on those unemployed who lost their job due to trade increases.

### 6.4.4 Specific trade adjustment assistance

Two well-known programmes that explicitly serve the purpose of private trade-related adjustment assistance are the US-TAA programme and the European Globalisation Adjustment Fund (EGF).

The US-TAA comprises programmes for workers, firms, farmers and fishermen.[20] The TAA for Workers programme is by far the largest of the three existing programmes. In order to receive assistance, workers must show that they lost their jobs due to any one of the following three eligibility criteria: an increase in imports; laid off from either an upstream or downstream producer; or a shift in production to another country. The criteria must have "contributed importantly" to a firm's decline in production and sales. Covered workers are eligible to receive assistance such as for maintenance payments, training expenses, wage insurance, under which older workers may be eligible to receive half the difference between their old and new wages, and

---

[20] United States Department of Labor; see: http://www.doleta.gov/tradeact/benefits.cfm#2.

parts of costs associated with job-searching and job relocation. The wage subsidy is only available for older workers under the Alternative TAA, for whom retraining may not be appropriate.

The objective of the TAA for Firms programme is to help manufacturers and producers injured by increased imports prepare and implement strategies to guide their economic recovery by providing technical assistance.

The EGF is a significantly more recent programme that provides one-off, time-limited individual support to workers who have suffered redundancies as a result of globalization. The EGF does not finance company costs for modernization or structural adjustment, which is covered by other EU assistance programmes such as the Structural Funds.

The EGF supports workers who lose their jobs as a result of changing global trade patterns so that they can find another job as quickly as possible.[21] When a large enterprise shuts down, or a factory is relocated to a country outside the EU, or a whole sector loses many jobs in a region, EU Member States design active labour market policies for redundant workers, such as job search, occupational guidance, training, upskilling, outplacement and entrepreneurship promotion, and apply for EGF support of up to 65 per cent of the total costs. A maximum amount of €500 million per year is available to the EGF to finance such interventions. Applications were received from a range of countries and sectors from 2007 until 2010. Dominating sectors are textile, automotive, motor industry supplier, printing industry and electronic equipment. The EGF has also been used as part of Europe's response to the global financial crisis.

Adjustment assistance is also discussed as one out of four main areas of the Aid for Trade initiative.[22] The Aid for Trade initiative has emerged during the Doha Round of trade negotiations to address "supply-side" constraints in developing countries. The specific objective of Aid for Trade is to help developing countries, in particular the least developed, to play an active role in the global trading system and to use trade as an instrument for growth and poverty alleviation. Adjustment assistance is provided to help with any transition costs from liberalization, including preference erosion, loss of fiscal revenue or declining terms of trade and, in the context of Aid for Trade, the discussion has so far mostly focused on assistance to overcome supply constraints; albeit, the possibility of using it for labour market-related concerns has been raised (Jansen and Lee, 2007; ILO, OECD, World Bank and WTO, 2010).

A specific reference to labour market adjustment in a trade agreement is made in the (interim) Economic Partnership Agreements (EPAs) between the EU and African, Caribbean and Pacific (ACP) States (see, for example, CARIFORUM EPA Articles 195 and 196). The EPAs are accompanied by development assistance, including to cover adjustment assistance (ODI, ECDPM, CaPRI and EU, 2009).

---

[21] See: http://ec.europa.eu/egf/.

[22] The others are trade policy and regulation, economic infrastructure and productive capacity building.

The labour market-related components of trade-related adjustment assistance programmes usually include passive or active labour market policy components that are discussed above. Given that trade-displaced workers tend not to differ significantly from other displaced workers, the justification for providing different or even privileged (for instance, in the form of longer duration of unemployment benefit coverage) treatment to trade-displaced workers is not easily justifiable.

One possible justification is that trade reform has a higher potential to lead to large-scale structural change, with resulting mass lay-offs as a result of plant closures. As such mass lay-offs are more likely to lead to congestion effects or other negative externalities, targeted intervention may be justified on efficiency grounds. But also in those cases, the evidence on the effects of intervention is mixed.

Betcherman et al. (1999) reviewed 12 studies relating to retraining programmes for workers displaced through mass lay-offs (related to public sector restructuring). They found that some retraining programmes result in a modest increase in re-employment probabilities, though this result is often statistically insignificant. The effect on post-programme earnings is, however, more discouraging since wages of participants, compared to the control-group workers, are rarely higher and, in most cases, even lower.

The results for specific trade-related adjustment assistance training are similar to those of the studies about mass lay-offs. Marcal (2001) also found evidence of a higher re-employment ratio of US-TAA trainees relative to the control group that did not receive training and to those that had exhausted unemployment insurance benefits. Furthermore, both Decker and Corson (1995) and Marcal (2001) fail to find a positive impact on the re-employment wage.

In the context of public sector downsizing in developing countries or economies in transition, Matusz and Tarr (1999) cite similar evidence based on government-sponsored retraining programmes in Hungary and Mexico. In Hungary, evidence suggests that the re-employment rate is slightly higher among participants of programmes than among the control group. The difference is, however, the impact on wages of the re-employed where, in Hungary, evidence suggests a positive impact on the participants that was not found in the other studies cited above. In Mexico, the retraining programme seemed only to increase the re-employment rate and the new wages for trainees who had previous work experience and for adult male participants. Rama (1999) argues that the failure of targeted retraining programmes is partly due to the wrong focus of the programmes, which often concentrate on updating previous skills rather than acquiring entirely new skills.

A major challenge of specific trade-related adjustment assistance programmes is to decide who is eligible to receive assistance. Due to the traditional trade theory, adjustment was expected across sectors as production would increase in the exporting sector and decrease in the import-competing sectors. Adjustment assistance was thus targeted at sectors that lack comparative advantage. Eligibility for assistance under the TAA, for example, was based on an increase in imports of articles of the same nature or directly competitive with articles produced by sectors that subsequently experienced lay-offs (Magee, 2001). The 2002 reform broadened the group of eligible workers to include those laid off in plant relocations, reflecting the concern of foreign direct investment (FDI) abroad, and those laid off in upstream suppliers or downstream customers of firms affected by trade liberalization (WTO, 2008).

Recent theoretical developments and empirical analysis that have emphasized the heterogeneity of firms and adjustment within industries, however, suggest that even such broadening fails to capture all workers that are affected by trade and may prove the impossibility to identify them. Scheve and Slaughter (2004) support this research with a survey on how liberalization affects the felt job security: workers in very different types of industries felt greater insecurity.

Taking into account the difficulties in appropriately targeting specific TAA and the fact that there are not many reasons why trade-affected workers should be dealt with differently than other displaced workers, it is tempting to conclude that strong general labour market policies represent a better tool to deal with workers' adjustment costs triggered by trade reform. By assisting all displaced workers, they are sure to capture all trade-displaced workers and they also treat equally those displaced by trade, migration, FDI, technological change, macroeconomic or other shocks. In an integrated world where it is hard to foresee from where the next shock will hit, and where workers are constantly exposed to changes, broadly targeted labour market policies that provide income to those without jobs and assist the jobless in finding new jobs are likely to perform better than specifically designed trade adjustment programmes.

## 6.4.5 Trade policies addressing adjustment costs

Trade policy itself is another very important instrument to address adjustment costs. Postponing or lowering the degree of trade liberalization would eliminate or reduce the adjustment costs, but this policy would be at the expense of gains from trade liberalization. As discussed above, empirical studies suggest that the benefits of international trade are often large and generally greater than the costs associated with it.

Multilateral as well as regional trade agreements often comprise provisions to mitigate adjustment costs. These provisions include transition periods for phasing-in liberalization, safeguard measures that can be used when imports of a particular product increase and cause injury to the domestic industry, and subsidies of certain kinds to ease the adjustment process (Bacchetta and Jansen, 2003). North-South regional trade agreements (RTAs) are also often linked to development assistance. An example is the European Development Fund for ACP countries.

### 6.4.5.1 Gradual liberalization with early announcement of policy change

Gradual liberalization with early announcement of the policy change and flanking measures may substantially reduce adjustment costs that mostly take place upfront (Laird and de Córdoba, 2006). Reducing protection gradually can above all be useful to avoid congestion problems and in cases where individual actors underestimate adjustment costs. Congestion may, for instance, occur in labour markets in the cases of mass lay-offs. If a drastic change in tariffs leads to mass lay-offs, while a gradual reduction of tariffs leads to a gradual displacement of workers, the latter scenario may be more desirable as it avoids congestion and related costs. Mussa (1986) has analysed this phenomenon in a set-up where trade reform triggers mass lay-offs because of the presence of minimum wages. He confirms that gradual liberalization would lead to gradual adjustment, with lower costs to the economy.

Gradual liberalization can also be a useful tool when individuals underestimate adjustment costs, as may be the case if an industry is a major local, regional or national employer. Shrinkage of the industry would then have serious repercussions and negative spillovers on the surrounding economy. Those repercussions represent externalities, which, if not taken into account, may result in excessive lay-offs (Bacchetta and Jansen, 2003). Gradual liberalization may in these cases manage to soften the adjustment process. Given that developing country economies tend to be characterized by more concentrated production structures than industrialized countries (Imbs and Wacziarg, 2003), the arguments in favour of gradual liberalization are arguably stronger in the case of the former.

Early and credible announcement of policy changes can give companies and workers time to prepare for the change. This can be particularly useful in environments where credit constraints are prevalent. Early announcement then gives firms and workers the opportunity to make the savings necessary to prepare for the policy change or to bridge the costly adjustment period. Levy and van Wijnbergen (1995) argue in favour of gradual agricultural liberalization in the context of the North American Free Trade Agreement (NAFTA) in Mexico together with well-targeted adjustment programmes of investments in land improvements. Early announcements may also play a particularly important role in environments where companies are not used to working in a competitive environment. Examples are companies representing a public monopoly. If such companies have to go simultaneously through a process of privatization and exposure to foreign competition, they are unlikely to survive. If privatization is first conducted behind closed borders and then followed by international liberalization, the industry may, instead, have time to prepare for the competitive environment. Pastor et al. (2000) and Vives (2000), for example, show that the competitiveness of the Spanish banking sector was increased through domestic deregulation before the sector was opened for foreign competitors as part of the EU's Single Market programme.

Typically, trade agreements determine that new commitments, such as tariff reductions or revising domestic legislation, are implemented over a couple of years. The Uruguay Round agreement, for example, allowed developed countries to phase in new tariff commitments over four years and developing countries over six years. Similar provisions are agreed in most RTAs. The EPAs between the EU and several ACP countries, for example, envisage full implementation in some sectors over 25 years (Meyn and Kennan, 2010).

### 6.4.5.2 Safeguards

Transition periods allow countries to address ex-ante anticipated adjustment costs. Safeguards instead offer countries to react ex-post to problems caused by unforeseen

Table 6.5: Overview of safeguard measures in WTO provisions

| Measure | Agreement | Description |
|---|---|---|
| Measures to limit imports that cause or threaten to cause serious injury to domestic industry | GATT Article XIX and Agreement on Safeguards | Measures shall be applied to prevent or remedy injury and to facilitate adjustment |
| Renegotiate bound tariff rates | GATT Article XXVIII | Difficult process; requires compensation |
| Restrictions to safeguard the balance of payment | GATT Article XII and Article XVIII.B | Can be used in reaction to an unsustainable deterioration in a country's external financial position, but not in reaction to sector-specific adjustment problems |
| Infant industry protection in developing countries | GATT Article XVIII.C | Barely used |
| Emergency safeguard in services | GATS Article X | Mandate to negotiate |
| Special agricultural safeguard | Agreement on Agriculture Article 5 | Additional duty possible in case of price decrease or import surge; right to use had to be reserved during Uruguay Round |

Source: WTO agreements, and Bacchetta and Jansen (2003).

events, such as import surges (Bacchetta and Jansen, 2003). The safeguard measures include temporary tariff increases and quantitative restrictions. It is often argued that governments may be reluctant to sign trade agreements that lead to substantial liberalization without the insurance that a safeguard provision would provide.

The WTO Agreement on Safeguards refers explicitly to structural adjustment in its preamble and creates certain mechanisms to address that objective. Remedies, such as quantitative restrictions, can be used temporarily and evidence of adjustment of the industry is necessary to justify extending the measure. Progressive liberalization is intended to facilitate adjustment in cases of measures originally imposed for longer than one year.[23]

Safeguards may be justified from a political economic point of view and helpful in unusual circumstances, but their role as contributing to adjustment has been

---

[23] Safeguard measures may be broader in scope than anti-dumping measures and cover imports from all sources. However, anti-dumping measures have much more often been used than safeguard measures (Bown and McCulloch, 2007). With increasing liberalization and higher exposure to external shocks, safeguards may perhaps be used more frequently in the future.

questioned. Davidson and Matusz (2004a) show that temporary tariffs can be useful in cases where the presence of congestion externalities pushes economies into low-output equilibriums as a result of a temporary trade shock. In such a case, temporary protection impedes the economy adjusting to a temporary shock, as this adjustment may be undesirable.

If changes in trade flows are permanent, though, adjustment is desirable. Bown and McCulloch (2007) argue that most safeguard measures are far from promoting adjustment, and can actually have an anti-adjustment bias. A temporary import-restricting policy, for instance, does nothing to cause an industry to become more internationally competitive but rather allows the industry to continue production in a protected environment. Moreover, since these measures encourage productive inputs to remain in their former use, policies that slow adjustment out of uncompetitive industries would also have the effect of slowing expansion of newly competitive industries. Indeed, safeguard measures such as those in the WTO Agreement on Safeguards appear to be designed for the purpose of helping industries to recover competitiveness and not for the purpose of helping an economy to adjust to the fact that uncompetitive industries shrink (Bacchetta and Jansen, 2003).

A special agricultural safeguard mechanism for developing countries is one of the major sticking points in the current Doha Round of trade negotiations. Most developing countries request a Special Safeguard Mechanism (SSM) to protect their domestic producers from suddenly falling import prices and import surges. They argue that this measure is the only possibility to protect their farmers from volatile world market prices and subsidized imports. Agricultural exporters, however, are concerned about the potential negative implications for market access and predictability. Other elements currently under negotiation are the sensitive and special product provisions where tariffs for some agricultural products (for example, those that are important for rural development, food security and livelihood security) would not have to be reduced or only to a lesser extent. This would eliminate or reduce any adjustment requirements, but also potential benefits from trade liberalization. It has been argued, however, that in the presence of externalities, such as food security and lower rural-urban migration, it might be justifiable from an economic point of view.

## 6.4.6 Other domestic policies

A wide basket of other domestic policies can facilitate adjustment processes. Stable macroeconomic conditions (such as realistic exchange rates), the absence of anti-export bias, adequate infrastructure and secure property rights are all likely to affect the ease and speed of adjustment. Because of the nature of this book, labour adjustment has received quite a lot of attention in this chapter. Capital is another input factor in the private sector that needs to adjust when economic activities shift. Adjustment costs related to capital are opportunity costs of underutilized or obsolete machines, buildings and other physical capital goods. To shift capital from one activity to another causes transition costs. Since financial capital is more mobile than physical capital, the costs of shifting the former are usually lower. When credit markets do not function efficiently, companies may face credit constraints and may not be able to obtain funding for adjustment-related investments (Bacchetta and Jansen, 2003).

Functioning capital and credit markets are important to reduce adjustment costs related to capital movement. Since, in many developing countries, capital mobility may be limited by a lack of capital and credit markets, resulting costs are higher (Laird and de Córdoba, 2006). In agriculture, adjustment costs can be significant because it takes time for new crops to grow. McMillan et al. (2002), for instance, demonstrate the adjustment difficulties in the case of cashews. Adjustment costs are typically expected to be lower for field crops than for tree crops, such as wine, coffee, tea or rubber. Thus, adjustment assistance programmes may be efficiency-increasing but, as in the case of labour markets, the question of special programmes or general policies easing adjustment is to be considered. Hoekman and Javorcik (2004) stress the importance of policies that encourage adjustment by firms to globalization. Barriers that hinder entry and exit of firms should be removed, and policies should be "neutral" towards small enterprises. If externalities exist, subsidies or similar incentives would help expand innovation and risk-taking.

## 6.5. CONCLUSION AND POLICY RECOMMENDATION

Structural adjustment is a necessary condition to benefit from trade liberalization. It implies a reallocation of resources. The shifts of labour and capital are likely to lead to adjustment costs that occur until all factors are in their long-term equilibrium. The costs depend very much on the magnitude of liberalization and the functioning of markets, i.e. the time that is needed to reach the new equilibrium.

Aggregate adjustment costs appear to be significantly smaller than the long-term benefits. Recent analysis shows, however, that the costs can be high, especially in the case of very rigid labour markets. The factor labour appears to bear the bulk of the costs, although it appears that trade reforms do not have strong negative effects on unemployment rates. Costs for unlucky individuals can be substantial. Although trade competition does not appear to target particular types of workers, evidence suggests that trade-displaced workers tend to be slightly older, have more tenure and higher earnings related to the lost job. There is no strong evidence, though, of trade-induced unemployment being very different from unemployment caused by other shocks.

A reason contributing to the observation that the characteristics and duration of unemployment of trade-displaced workers are similar to those losing their job for other reasons could be that trade liberalization does not necessarily cause entire non-comparative sectors to shrink and others to expand, but also that labour churning within sectors occur. We therefore developed indices measuring intra-sectoral employment movements.

Adjustment assistance, i.e. policy measures to mitigate the costs of adjustment from trade, can be designed to redistribute income or to increase efficiency, depending on the political goals. It appears that from an economic perspective, generally available adjustment measures should be preferred over targeted TAA. Apart from moral concerns why those affected by trade liberalization should be treated differently than those affected by other shocks, including those stemming from globalization as a whole, targeted assistance appears to have had rather mixed success in facilitating structural adjustment. It addition, it appears nearly impossible to identify all workers adversely affected by trade liberalization.

The political economy argument – that there is more support for liberalization if adjustment assistance exists – is important, but may be less relevant if a good generally available social protection system is in place. Very concentrated structural changes, such as mass lay-offs or regional concentration, though, may justify specific TAA.

Demand for social protection in developing countries, especially emerging economies, appears to be increasing as the exposure to external shocks is increasing with globalization. Strengths and weaknesses of passive and active labour market policies have been discussed in this chapter. Many of the instruments may presently be beyond reach in many developing countries but important lessons can be learned from experiences in developed countries.

A strong case can be made that it is important that adjustment policy measures focus on supporting the distribution of gains from globalization more equally and to increase efficiency of the adjustment process. Most adjustment costs appear to be borne by workers. In many countries, the majority of workers seem to be very concerned about trade liberalization. Labour market policies can have significant leverage here, as they have the potential to raise support for liberalization among voters if liberalization is expected to bring net benefits for a country.

## REFERENCES

Acemoglu, D.; Shimer, R. 2000. "Productivity gains from unemployment insurance", in *European Economic Review*, Vol. 44, No. 7, pp. 1195-1224.

Aho, C.M.; Bayard, T.O. 1984. "Cost and benefits of trade adjustment assistance", in R.E. Baldwin; A.O. Krueger (eds): *The structure and evolution of recent U.S. trade policy* (University of Chicago Press), pp. 151-193.

Bacchetta, M.; Jansen, M. 2003. "Adjusting to trade liberalization: The role of policy, institutions and WTO disciplines", *WTO Special Study 7* (WTO).

Baldwin, R.E. 1989. "The political economy of trade policy", in *Journal of Economic Perspectives*, Vol. 3, No. 4, pp. 119-135.

Baldwin, R.E. 2006. "Multilateralising regionalism: Spaghetti bowls as building blocks on the path to global free trade", in *The World Economy*, Vol. 29, No. 11, pp. 1451-1518.

Baldwin, R.E.; Francois, J.; Portes, R. 1997. "The costs and benefits of eastern enlargement: The impact on the EU and central Europe", in *Economic Policy*, Vol. 12, No. 24, pp. 125-176.

Baldwin, R.E.; Mutti, J.; Richardson, D. 1980. "Welfare effects on the United States of a significant multilateral tariff reduction", in *Journal of International Economics*, Vol. 10, No. 3, pp. 405-23.

Bale, M.D. 1976. "Estimates of trade-displacement costs for U.S. workers", in *Journal of International Economics* , Vol. 6, No. 3, pp. 245-250.

Beaudry, P.; Green, D.A.; Sand, B.M. 2007. "Spill-overs from good jobs", *NBER Working Paper* No. 13006.

Betcherman, G.; Amit D.; Luinstra, A.; Ogawa, M. 1999. "Active labor market policies: Policy issues for East Asia", mimeo (World Bank).

Blanchard, O. 2005. "European unemployment: The evolution of facts and ideas", *NBER Working Paper* No. 11750.

Boone, J.; van Ours, J.C. 2004. "Effective Active Labour Market Policies", *CEPR Discussion Paper* No. 4707.

Bown, C.P.; McCulloch, R. 2007. "Trade adjustment in the WTO system: Are more safeguards the answer?", in *Oxford Review of Economic Policy*, Vol. 23, No. 3, pp. 415-439.

Bradford, S.C.; Grieco, P.L.E.; Hufbauer, G.C. 2005. "The payoff to America from global integration", in *The United States and the world economy: Foreign economic policy for the next Decade* (Bergsten, C.F. and the Peterson Institute for International Economics).

Brahmbhatt, M. 1997. *Global Economic Prospects and the Developing Countries* (Washington, DC, World Bank).

Brülhart, M. 2000. "Dynamics of intraindustry trade and labor-market adjustment", in *Review of International Economics*, Vol. 8, No. 3, pp. 420-435.

Burda, M.; Dluhosch, B. 2000. "Fragmentation, globalization and labor markets", *GEP Research Paper Series* No. 2001/05.

Cadot, O.; Dutoit, L.; Olarreaga, M. 2005. "Subsistence farming, adjustment costs and agricultural prices: Evidence from madagascar", *ETSG 2005 conference paper*.

Casas, F.R. 1984. "Imperfect factor mobility: A generalization and synthesis of two-sector models of international trade", in *The Canadian Journal of Economics*, Vol. 17, No. 4, Nov.

Cazes, S.; Nesperova, A. 2007. *Flexicurity: A relevant approach in Central and Eastern Europe* (ILO).

Cazes, S.; Verick, S.; Heuer, C. 2009. "Labour market policies in times of crisis", *Employment Working Paper* No. 35.

Davidson, C.; Matusz, S.J. 2000. "Globalization and labour market adjustment: How fast and at what cost?", in *Oxford Review of Economic Policy*, Vol. 16, No. 3, pp. 42- 56.

Davidson, C.; Matusz, S.J. 2004a. "An overlapping-generations model of escape clause protection", in *Review of International Economics*, Vol. 12, No. 5, pp. 749-68, Nov.

Davidson, C.; Matusz, S.J. 2004b. "Should policy makers be concerned about adjustment costs?", in *The Political Economy of Trade, Aid and Foreign Investment* (Emerald Publishing).

Davidson, C.; Matusz, S.J. 2006. "Trade liberalization and compensation", in *International Economic Review*, Vol. 47, No. 3, pp. 723-748.

Davidson, C.; Matusz, S.J. 2010. *International trade with equilibrium unemployment* (Princeton University Press).

Davidson, C.; Matusz, S.J.; Nelson, D.R. 2007. "Can compensation save free trade?", in *Journal of International Economics*, Vol. 71, No. 1, pp. 167-186.

Davis, S.J.; Faberman, R.J.; Haltiwanger, J. 2006. "The flow approach to labor markets: New data sources and micro-macro links", in *Journal of Economic Perspectives*, Vol. 20, No. 3, pp. 3-26.

Davis, D.R.; Harrigan, J. 2007. "Good jobs, bad jobs, and trade liberalization", *NBER Working Paper* No. 13139.

Decker, P.; Corson, W. 1995 "International trade and worker displacement: Evaluation of the trade adjustment assistance program", in *Industrial and Labor Relations Review*, Vol. 48, No. 4, pp. 758-774.

Development Solutions; CEPR; Manchester 1824. 2009. *EU-Andean trade sustainability impact assessment*. Final report for European Commission DG Trade, Oct.

Dluhosch, B. 2000. *Industrial location and economic integration: Centrifugal and centripetal forces in the new Europe* ( Edward Elgar).

ECORYS. 2009a. *Trade sustainability impact assessment: EU-Central America FTA*, report prepared for the European Commission DG Trade.

ECORYS. 2009b. *Trade sustainability impact assessment: EU-India FTA*, report prepared for the European Commission DG Trade.

Ethier, W. 1982. "National and international returns to scale in the modern theory of international trade", in *American Economic Review*, Vol. 72, No. 3, pp. 389-405.

Fernandez, R.; Rodrik, D. 1991. "Resistance to reform: Status quo bias in the presence of individual-specific uncertainty", in *The American Economic Review*, Vol. 81, No. 5, pp. 1146-1155, Dec.

Francois, J.F. 2004. "Assessing the impact of trade policy on labour markets and production", in *Economie Internationale*, Vol. 3Q, pp. 27-47.

Francois, J.F.; Nelson, D.R. 2001. "Victims of progress: Economic integration, specialization and wages for unskilled labour", *CEPR Discussion Paper* No. 2527.

Francois, J.F.; Nelson, D.R. 2002. "A geometry of specialization", in *The Economic Journal*, Vol. 112, No. 481, pp. 649-678.

Francois, J.F.; Grier, K.B.; Nelson, D.R. 2004. "Globalization, roundaboutness and relative wages", *Tinbergen Institute Discussion Paper* No. 04-021/2.

Francois, J.F.; Grier, K.B.; Nelson, D.R. 2008. "Globalization, intermediate specialization, and relative wages", *Johannes Kepler University Working Paper*.

Francois, J.F.; Reinert, K.A. 1997. *Applied methods for trade policy analysis: A handbook* (Cambridge University Press).

Francois, J.; Rojas-Romagosa, H. 2010. "Household inequality, social welfare, and trade", *CEPR Discussion Paper* No. 7998.

Gamberoni, E.; von Uexkull, E.; Weber, S. 2010. "The roles of openness and labour market institutions for employment dynamics during economic crises", *ILO Employment Working Paper* No. 68.

Gaston, N.; Trefler, D. 1997. "The labour market consequences of the Canada-US free trade agreement", in *Canadian Journal of Economics*, Vol. 30, No. 1, pp. 18-41.

Goldberg, P.K.; Pavcnik, N. 2003. "Trade, wages, and the political economy of trade protection: Evidence from the Colombian trade reforms", *CEPR discussion papers* No. 3877.

Greenaway, D.; Hine, R.C.; Wright, P. 1999. "An empirical assessment of the impact of trade on employment in the United Kingdom", in *European Journal of Political Economy*, Vol. 15, No. 3, pp. 485-500, Sept.

Greenaway, D.; Milner, C.R. 1986. *The economics of intra-industry trade* (Basil Blackwell).

Harrison, A.; Revenga, A. 1995. "Factor markets and trade policy reform", mimeo (World Bank).

Heckman, J.J.; Pages, C. 2000. "The cost of job security regulation: Evidence from Latin American labor markets", *NBER Working Paper* No. 7773.

Heckman, J.J.; Lalonde, R.J.; Smith, J.A. 1999. "The economics and econometrics of active labor market programs", Chapter 31 in O.C. Ashenfelter; D. Card (eds): *Handbook of Labor Economics*, (Amsterdam), pp. 1865-2097.

Hill, H.; Aswicahyono, H. 2004. "Survey of recent developments", in *Bulletin of Indonesian Economic Studies*, Vol. 40, No. 3, pp. 277-305, Dec.

Hoekman, B.M.; Porto, G. 2011. *Trade adjustment costs in developing countries: Impacts, determinants and policy responses* (World Bank and CEPR).

Hoekman, B.M.; Javorcik, B.S. 2004 "Policies facilitating firm adjustment to globalization", *World Bank Policy Research Working Paper* No. 3441.

Hertel, T.W.; Ivanic, M.; Preckel, P.V.; Cranfield, J.A.L. 2004. "The earnings effects of multilateral trade liberalization: Implications for Poverty", in *World Bank Economic Review*, Vol. 18, No. 2, pp. 205-236.

ILO. 2010. *World social security report 2010/11. Providing coverage in times of crisis and beyond* (Geneva).

ILO; OECD; World Bank; WTO. 2010. *Seizing the benefits of trade for employment and growth* (OECD).

Imbs, J.; Wacziarg, R. 2003. "Stages of diversification", in *American Economic Review*, Vol. 93, No. 1, pp. 63-86.

Jacobson, L.S.; LaLonde, R.J.; Sullivan, D.G. 1993a. "Earnings losses of displaced workers", in *The American Economic Review*, Vol. 83, No. 4, pp. 685-709, Sep.

Jacobson, L.S.; LaLonde, R.J.; Sullivan, D.G. 1993b. Long-term earnings losses of high-seniority displaced workers", in *Economic Perspectives*, Vol. 17, pp. 2-20, Nov.

Jansen, M.; Lee, E. 2007. *Trade and employment: Challenges for policy research* (ILO/WTO).

Jansen, M.; von Uexkull, E. 2010. *Trade and employment in the global crisis* (ILO).

Kemp, M.C. 1964. *The pure theory of international trade*, Chapter 8 (Prentice-Hall)

Krugman, P.; Venables, A.J. 1995. "Globalization and the inequality of nations", in *Quarterly Journal of Economics*; Vol. 110, No. 4, pp. 857-880.

Laird, S.; de Córdoba, S.F. 2006. *Coping with trade reforms, A developing-country perspective on the WTO industrial tariff negotiations* (Palgrave McMillan).

Levy, S.; van Wijnbergen, S. 1995. "Transition problems in economic reform: Agriculture in the North American free trade agreement", in *American Economic Review*, Vol. 85, No. 4, pp. 738-754, Sep.

Lovely, M.E.; Nelson, D.R. 2000. "Marginal intraindustry trade and labor adjustment", in *Review of International Economics*; Vol. 8, No. 3, pp. 436-447, Aug.

Magee, C. 2001. "Administered protection for workers: An analysis of the trade adjustment assistance program", in *Journal of International Economics*, Vol. 53, No. 1, pp. 105-125, Feb.

Magee, S.P. 1972. "The welfare effects of restriction on U.S. trade", *Brookings Papers on Economy Activity* No. 3, N. 1972-3, pp. 645-708.

Marcal, L.E. 2001. "Does trade adjustment assistance help trade displaced workers?", in *Contemporary Economic Policy*, Vol. 19, No. 1, pp. 59-72.

Markusen, J.R. 1988. "Production, trade, and migration with differentiated, skilled workers", in *Canadian Journal of Economics*; Vol. 21, No. 3, pp. 492-506, Aug.

Markusen, J.R. 1990. "Micro-foundations of external economies", in *Canadian Journal of Economics*, Vol. 23, No. 3, pp. 495-508, Aug.

Markusen, J.R.; Venables, A.J. 1997. "The role of multinational firms in the wage-gap debate", in *Review of International Economics*, Vol. 5, No. 4, pp. 435-451, Nov.

Markusen, J.R.; Venables, A.J. 1999. "Multinational production, skilled labor and real wages", in R. Baldwin; F. Francois (eds): *Dynamic issues in commercial policy analysis* (Cambridge University Press).

Martins, J.O.; Scarpetta, S.; Pilat, D. 1996. "Mark-up pricing, market structure and the business cycle", in *OECD Economic Studies*, No. 27, pp. 71-102.

Matusz, S. 1997. "Adjusting to trade liberalization", mimeo (Michigan State University).

Matusz, S.J. 2001. "Trade policy reform and labor market dynamics, issues and an agenda for future research", *Economic Study Area Working Paper* No. 24 (East-West Center).

Matusz S.J.; Tarr, D.G. 1999. "Adjusting to trade policy reform", *World Bank Working Paper* No. 2142.

McMillan, M.; Rodrik, R.; Horn Welch, K. 2002. "When economic reform goes wrong: Cashews in Mozambique", *NBER Working Paper* No. 9117.

de Melo, J.; Roland-Holst, D. 1994. "Economywide costs of protection and labor market rigidities", in M. Connolly; J. de Melo (eds): *The effects of protectionism on a small country: The case of Uruguay* (World Bank).

de Melo, J.; Tarr, D. 1990. "Welfare costs of U.S. quotas in textiles, steel and autos", in *Review of Economics and Statistics*, Vol. 72, No. 3, pp. 489-497.

Menon, J.; Dixon, P.B. 1997. "Intra-industry versus inter-industry trade: Relevance for adjustment costs", in *Weltwirtschaftliches Archiv*, Vol. 133, No. 1, pp. 164-169.

Meyn, M.; Kennan, J. 2010. "Economic partnership agreements: Comparative analysis of the agriculture provisions (UNCTAD).

Mills, B.F; Sahn, D.E. 1995. "Reducing the size of the public sector workforce: Institutional constraints and human consequences in Guinea", in *Journal of Development Studies*, Vol. 31, No. 4, pp. 505-528.

Milner, C.; Wright, P. 1998. "Modelling labour market adjustment to trade liberalisation in an industrialising economy", in *The Economic Journal*, Vol. 108, No. 447, pp 509-528, Mar.

Mussa, M. 1978. "Dynamic adjustment in the Heckscher-Ohlin-Samuelson Model", in *Journal of Political Economy*, Vol. 86, No. 5, pp. 775-791, Oct.

Mussa, M. 1986. "The adjustment process and the timing of trade liberalization", in A.M. Choksi; D. Papageorgiou (eds): *Economic liberalization in developing countries* (Blackwell Publishing).

Mutti, J. 1978. "Aspects of unilateral trade policy and facto adjustment costs", in *The Review of Economics and Statistics*, Vol. 6, No. 1, pp. 102-110, Feb.

Neary, J.P. 1982. "Intersectoral capital mobility, Wage stickiness, and the case for adjustment assistance", in J.N. Bhagwati (ed.): *Import competition and response* (University of Chicago Press).

OECD. 1993. *Employment Outlook 1993* (Paris).

OECD. 2005a. *Employment Outlook 2005* (Paris).

OECD. 2005b. *Trade and structural adjustment* (Paris).

OECD. 2010. *OECD employment outlook 2010* (Paris).

ODI; ECDPM; CaPRI; EU. 2009. *The CARIFORUM EU-Economic partnership agreement (EPA): The development component*. Report prepared for the European Parliament's Committee on Development.

Papageorgiou, D.; Choksi, A.M.; Michaely, M. 1991. *Liberalizing foreign trade in developing countries: The lessons of experience* (World Bank).

Pastor, J.M.; Pérez, F.; Quesada, J. 2000. "The opening of the Spanish banking system: 1985-98", in S. Claessens; M. Jansen (eds): *The internationalization of financial services: Issues and lessons for developing countries* (Kluwer Law International).

Peters, R.; Vanzetti, D. 2004. "Shifting sands: Searching for a compromise in the WTO negotiations on agriculture", *Policy Issues in International Trade and Commodities Study Series* No. 23 (UNCTAD).

Piermartini, R.; Teh, R. 2005. "Demystifying modelling methods for trade policy", *Discussion Paper* No. 10 (WTO).

Rama, M. 1994. "The labour market and trade reform in manufacturing", in M.B. Connolly; J. de Melo (eds): *Effects of protectionism on a small country: The case of Uruguay* (World Bank).

Rama, M. 1999. "Public sector downsizing: An introduction", in *World Bank Economic Review*, Vol. 13, No. 1, pp. 1-22, Jan.

Rama, M. 2003. "Globalization and workers in developing countries", *Policy Research Working Paper Series* No. 2958 (World Bank).

Richardson, D.J. 1982. "Trade adjustment assistance under the U.S. Trade Act of 1974: An analytical examination and worker survey", in J. Bhagwati (ed.): *Import competition and response* (University of Chicago Press).

Rivera-Batiz, F.L.; Rivera-Batiz, L.A. 1991. "The effects of direct foreign investment in the presence of increasing returns due to specialization", in *Journal of Development Economics*, Vol. 34, No. 1-2, pp. 287-307, Nov.

Rodrik, D. 2004. "Getting institutions right", *CESifo DICE Report* 2/2004.

Saint-Paul, G. 2007. "Making sense of Bolkenstein-bashing: Trade liberalization under segmented labour markets", in *Journal of International Economics*, Vol. 73, No. 1, pp. 152-174.

Sapir, A. 2006. "Globalization and the reform of European social models", in *Journal of Common Market Studies*, Vol. 44, No. 2, pp. 369-390.

Scheve, K.F.; Slaughter, M.J. 2004. "Economic insecurity and the globalization of production", in *American Journal of Political Science*, Vol. 48, No. 4, pp. 662-674, Oct.

Schott, P.K. 2004. "Across-product versus within-product specialization in international trade", in *Quarterly Journal of Economics*, Vol. 119, No. 2, pp. 647-678, Mar.

Takacs, W.E.; Winters, L.A. 1991. "Labour adjustment costs and British footwear protection", *Oxford Economic Papers,* Vol. 43, No. 3, pp. 479-501, July.

Trefler, D. 2004. "The long and short of the Canada-U.S. free trade agreement", in *American Economic Review*, Vol. 94, No. 4, pp. 870-895, Sep.

Vives, X. 2000. "Lessons from European banking liberalization and integration", in S. Claessens; M. Jansen (eds): *The internationalization of financial services: Issues and lessons for developing countries* (Kluwer Law International).

Vodopivec, M. 2009. "Introducing unemployment insurance to developing countries", *IZA Policy Paper* No. 6 (German Institute for the Study of Labour).

Wood, A. 1997. "Openness and wage inequality in developing countries: The Latin American challenge to East Asian conventional wisdom", in *World Bank Economic Review*, Vol. 11, No. 1, pp. 33-57, Jan.

World Bank. 1997. *Global economic prospects and the developing countries.*

WTO. 2008. *World trade report 2008: Trade in a globalizing world.*

Yeaple, S.R. 2005. "A simple model of firm heterogeneity, international trade, and wages", in *Journal of International Economics*, Vol. 65, No. 1, pp. 1-20, Jan

ANNEX 6.A:  MEASURING ADJUSTMENT IN OUTPUT AND
CHANGES IN INEQUALITY LEVELS

### 6.A.1 *Measuring adjustment in terms of output*

The metrics presented in equations (1) to (4) in the main text to capture adjustment in labour markets can also be developed to capture adjustment in terms of output.

The starting point is again information on sectoral-level output generated, for example, with CGE simulations. We will refer to changes in sectoral output as $\hat{q}_j$ where the subscript $j$ represents sectors. Total change in output $m_q$ resulting from trade reform in an economy with $n$ sectors can then be computed using:

$$m_q = \sum_{j=1}^{n} \lambda_j \hat{q}_j \tag{Q1}$$

Where $\lambda_j$ represents the weight of a sector $j$ in the total economy. As in the case of the employment measure in equation (1), the measure $m_q$ is only of limited use to reflect the extent of adjustment processes, as positive and negative output changes will cancel out. It is therefore preferable to use a variance-based measure of the type:

$$s_{q,across}^2 = \sum_{j=1}^{n} \lambda_j \left( \hat{q}_j - m_q \right)^2 \tag{Q2}$$

Taking the square root of $s_{q,across}^2$ provides a useful measure of variation across sectors. This measure can be calculated in a rather straightforward way with standard CGE models.

An important weakness of this measure is that it does not capture output shifts across firms within the same sector. For a given change of output within a sector, Q2 would signal the same extent of adjustment if that change entails proportional shifts in output across firms or if it entails company failures and creation of new companies. Yet, adjustment of the second type is likely to be more costly for an economy, in particular if growing and shrinking firms are located in different regions. The importance of firm-level adjustments has been emphasized in recent trade literature. A more appropriate measure would therefore take into account within-sector adjustment:

$$s_{q,within,j}^2 = \sum_{i=1}^{f_i} \theta_{ij} \left( \hat{q}_{ij} - m_{q,j} \right)^2, \tag{Q3}$$

where $m_{q,j} = \sum_{i=1}^{f_j} \theta_{ij} \hat{q}_{ij}$ and $\theta_{ij}$ weight of firm i sector j

A measure for total adjustment, capturing all changes in output, those within and across sectors, would look as follows:

$$s_{q,Total}^2 = \sum_{j=1}^{n} \sum_{i=1}^{f_i} \lambda_j \theta_{ij} \left( \hat{q}_{ij} - m_q \right)^2$$
$$= \sum_{j=1}^{n} \lambda_j s_{q,j:within}^2 + s_{q,across}^2 \tag{Q4}$$

Given that establishment-level information is typically not available in CGE models, the within variation measure can most of the time not be measured, which leads to a probable underestimation of output adjustment.

## 6.A.2 Changes in the distribution of income

Changes in the distribution of income fall, in principle, outside of the definition of adjustment employed in this chapter. While this chapter is concerned with the short term, i.e. the period immediately following trade reform, changes in income distribution are typically discussed with respect to the long run. Yet the changes of income suffered by trade-displaced workers have often been used as an argument in favour of adjustment assistance, as discussed in the main text. Income changes are also typically regarded as an important determinant of trade policy behaviour (see Baldwin, 1989). We therefore propose in this annex a metric that can be used to measure income inequality in a CGE context, based on information on household income. We propose to use this type of measure to establish a social welfare metric. Such a metric would make it possible to evaluate changes in social welfare resulting from trade reform.

Starting with constant relative risk aversion (CRRA) preferences, it is possible to map the so-called Atkinson inequality index to social welfare. This in turn means we can, in theory, make inequality-related adjustments to measures of social welfare. To the extent that labour market adjustments are manifested in rising or falling inequality, this also gives us a vector for mapping long-term labour market adjustment to social welfare, this time through the income distribution channel. In formal terms, we first need to define the inequality index:

$$I = 1 - \left( \frac{1}{h} \sum_h \left( \frac{y^h}{\bar{y}} \right)^{1-\rho} \right)^{\frac{1}{1-\rho}} \tag{D1}$$

In equation (D1), $h$ indexes households, while the coefficient $\rho$ measures the degree of relative risk aversion. From the macroeconomics literature, this coefficient is estimated to be less than (though close to) 1. The terms $\bar{y}$ and $y^h$ indicate household income and average income across households. From Francois and Rojas-Romagosa (2010), we can rewrite (D1) as follows.

$$I_A = 1 - \left\{ h^{-\rho} \sum_h \left[ h^{-1} + \sum_z \beta_h \left( \omega_z^h - n^{-1} \right) \right]^{1-\rho} \right\}^{\frac{1}{1-\rho}} \tag{D2}$$

In equation (D2), the term $\beta_h$ measures the importance of income to primary factors indexed by $z$ in total national income, while $\omega_z^h$ represents the household ownership share of this factor. From equation (D2), inequality depends on the unequal distribution of sources of factor income (the last set of terms in round brackets in equation (D2)) combined with the importance of factors in total national income. Hence, for a given unequal distribution of land, for example, the greater the importance of land to total income, the greater the inequality index.

Working with CRRA preferences, the corresponding social welfare function is a Sen-type welfare function. This means we have separability between average income and its dispersion at the household level and can generate the following equation:

$$SW = \left[ \left( \frac{\bar{y}}{p_c} \right) (1 - I_A) \right]^{1-\theta} \qquad \text{(D3)}$$

The recent literature has employed household data to measure changes in inequality due to globalization trends. Equation (D3) offers a metric for using these CGE-based estimates to calculate welfare metrics for such changes, though to our knowledge this has not been done to date. While equation (D3) measures impacts on welfare, in a dynamic context (over a period of adjustment) it can also be used to translate inequality-related dynamics into dynamic social welfare-related adjustment costs following from transitional changes in inequality.

# TRADE DIVERSIFICATION: DRIVERS AND IMPACTS

# 7

*By Olivier Cadot, Céline Carrère and Vanessa Strauss-Kahn*

## 7.1   INTRODUCTION

Policy interest in export diversification is not new but, for over two decades, it was mired in an ideologically loaded debate about the role of the State. Old-time industrial policy having died of its own excesses, the debate over what, if anything, the government should do to promote export growth was contained within the fringe of the economics profession. Mainstream economists were happy to believe that whatever market failures were out there, government failures were worse, and that anyway most governments in developing countries lacked the means to do anything. But by an ironic twist of history, years of (Washington-consensus inspired) fiscal and monetary discipline have put a number of developing-country governments back in a position to do something for export promotion, having recovered room to manoeuvre in terms of both external balance and budget position. So the question is back.

With limited guidance from theory, the economics profession's answer to the return of the industrial-policy debate has been to go back to descriptive statistics (as opposed to the investigation of causal chains). The result is a wealth of new stylized facts. For instance, surprising patterns of export entrepreneurship have emerged from the use of increasingly disaggregated data.

One area where theory has proved useful is in the exploration of the linkages between productivity and trade. So-called "new-new" trade models (featuring firm heterogeneity) have highlighted complex relationships between trade diversification and productivity, with causation running one way at the firm level and the other way around (or both ways) at the aggregate level.

Even at the aggregate level, new issues have appeared. First, Imbs and Wacziarg (2003) uncovered a curious pattern of diversification and re-concentration in production, prompting researchers to explore whether the same was true of trade. Second, a wave of recent empirical work has questioned traditional views on the "natural-resource curse", challenging the notion that diversification out of primary resources was a prerequisite for growth.

Thus, our current understanding of the trade diversification/productivity/ growth nexus draws on several theoretical and empirical works, all well developed and growing rapidly. It is easy to get lost in the issues, and the present paper's objective is to sort them out and take stock of elements of answers to the basic questions.

Among those questions, the first are simply factual ones — "how is export diversification measured?" and "what are the basic stylized facts about trade export diversification, across time and countries?", which we explore in sections 7.2 and 7.3, respectively. The third question is about diversification's drivers, among which industrial policy, and is tackled in section 7.7. In section 7.5, we turn to the relationship between trade diversification, growth and employment. Section 7.6 focuses on the import side; we review the evidence on the impact of import diversification on productivity and extend the discussion to labour-market issues. Section 7.7 concludes.

## 7.2   MEASURING DIVERSIFICATION

### 7.2.1  Concentration/diversification indices

While the focus of this chapter is on diversification, quantitative indices measure concentration rather than diversification. These indices are mainly used in the income-distribution literature where they illustrate income dispersion across individuals. We will review these measures, taking the example of export diversification (which has anyway been the focus of most papers) but keeping in mind that they apply equally well to imports. All concentration indices basically measure inequality between export shares; these shares, in turn, can be defined at any level of aggregation. Of course, the finer the disaggregation, the better the measure.

The most frequently used concentration indices are the ones used in the income-distribution literature: Herfindahl, Gini and Theil. These indices are formalized in technical appendix 7.A.1.1. All three indices can be easily programmed but are also available as packages in Stata. Authors have used one or several of these measures. Across the board, results are not dependent on the index chosen.

The Theil (1972) index has decomposability properties that make it especially useful. It can indeed be calculated for groups of individuals (export lines) and decomposed additively into within-groups and between-groups components (that is, the within- and between-groups components add up to the overall index).[1] It is thus possible to distinguish an increased concentration (diversification) that occurs mainly within groups from one that occurred mainly across groups. We will see in the next section a useful application of this property in our context.

---

[1] Technical appendix 7.A.1.2 presents the Theil index decomposition.

## 7.2.2 Trade-expansion margins

Recent research on trade diversification distinguishes evolution at the intensive and extensive margins. In summary, by focusing on the intensive margins one relates to changes in diversification among a set of goods that are commonly traded over the period. In contrast, by looking at the extensive margin one takes account of the effect of newly traded (or disappearing) goods on diversification. More specifically, export concentration measured at the intensive margin reflects inequality between the shares of active export lines.[2] Conversely, diversification at the intensive margin during a period $t_0$ to $t_1$ means convergence in export shares among goods that were exported at $t_0$. Concentration at the extensive margin is a subtler concept. At the simplest, it can be taken to mean a small number of active export lines. Then, diversification at the extensive margin means a rising number of active export lines. This is a widely used notion of the extensive margin (in differential form), and the decomposition of Theil's index can be usefully mapped into the intensive and extensive margins thus defined.

Suppose that, for a given country and year, we partition the 5,000 or so lines making up the HS6 nomenclature into two groups: group "one" is made of active export lines for this country and year, and group "zero" is made of inactive export lines (i.e. export lines for which there are no exports). This partition can be used to construct within-groups and between-groups components of the overall Theil index. As shown in the technical appendix 7.A.2, by distinguishing the Theil sub-index for the group of inactive lines from the Theil sub-index for the group of active lines, changes in concentration/diversification within and between groups can be set apart. More importantly, it can be shown that, given this partition, changes in the within-groups Theil index measure changes at the intensive margin, whereas changes in the between-groups Theil index measure changes at the extensive margin. In sum, Theil's decomposition makes it possible to decompose changes in overall concentration into extensive-margin and intensive-margin changes.[3] This is a particularly important feature, as changes at the intensive margin or extensive margin reflect very different evolution of a country's productive activities and policies aiming at enhancing diversification in either margin entail distinct recommendations.

The extensive margin defined this way (by simply counting the number of active export lines) leaves out, however, important information. To see why, observe that a country can raise its number of active export lines in many different ways. For instance, it could add "embroidery in the piece, in strips or in motifs" (HS 5810); or it could add "compression-ignition internal combustion piston engines" (HS 8408, i.e. diesel engines). Clearly, these two items are not of the same significance economically, although a mere count of active lines would treat them alike. Hummels

---

[2] An active line corresponds to a non-zero export line of the HS6 nomenclature (about 5,000 lines) for a given year.

[3] This mapping between the Theil decomposition and the margins was first proposed by Cadot, Carrère and Strauss-Kahn (2011).

and Klenow (2005) proposed an alternative definition of the intensive and extensive margins that takes this information into account. They define the intensive margin as the share of country *i*'s exports value of good *k* in the world's exports of that good. That is, country *i*'s intensive margin is its market share in what it exports. The extensive margin is defined as the share, in world exports, of those goods that country *i* exports (irrespective of how much *i* itself exports of those goods). That is, it indicates how much the goods that *i* exports count in world trade.[4]

### 7.2.3 Alternative margins

Although the intensive and extensive product margins as defined above are the most widely studied in the literature on diversification, several other margins bring further understanding on trade and diversification patterns. Brenton and Newfarmer (2007) proposed an alternative definition of the extensive margin based on bilateral flows. The index measures how many of destination country *j*'s imports are covered (completely or partly, the index does not use information on the value of trade flows) by exports from country *i*. The numerator of Brenton and Newfarmer's index for country *i* is the number of products that *i* exports to *j*, while its denominator is the number of products that (a) *j* imports from anywhere and (b) *i* exports to anywhere (see technical appendix 7.A.3). It is thus the sum of actual and potential bilateral trade flows (for which there is a demand in *j* and a supply in *i*), and the fraction indicates how many of those potential trade flows actually take place.

The survival of trade flows (export sustainability), analysed for the first time in the seminal work by Besedes and Prusa (2006), provides another margin of export expansion. The length of time during which bilateral exports of a given good take place without interruption is a dimension along which exports vary and which may

Figure 7.1: Margins of export growth

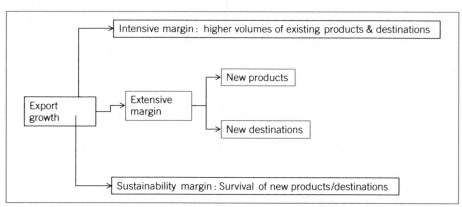

---

[4] See technical appendix 7.A.2.2 for a formalization of the Hummels and Klenow index.

also be a margin for export promotion. Figure 7.1 summarizes our decomposition of export growth.

Theil's,[5] Hummels and Klenow's, and Brenton and Newfarmer's indices provide different pieces of information and should be used accordingly. The former index measures the concentration in products. It thus informs policy-makers on the distribution of economic activity across existing products/sectors (intervention at the intensive margin) and the potential for broadening the country's export portfolio to new sectors (intervention at the extensive margin). Brenton and Newfarmer's index gives information about geographic diversification at the extensive margin. For existing products, it shows how many markets are reached and informs on the potentiality of extending production to new markets. Policies aimed at increasing the scope of exports in terms of products or destination markets are obviously very different. It is therefore important for policy-makers to use the right tool for the right policy question. Finally, Hummels and Klenow's index gives an idea of whether national exporters are "big fish in a small pond" (large intensive margin, small extensive margin) or "small fish in a big pond" (small intensive margin, large extensive margin).

As an illustration of how these concepts can be put to work for policy analysis, figure 7.2 shows the evolution of the intensive and extensive margins defined as in

Figure 7.2: Evolution of the intensive and extensive margins, selected countries, 1998–2008

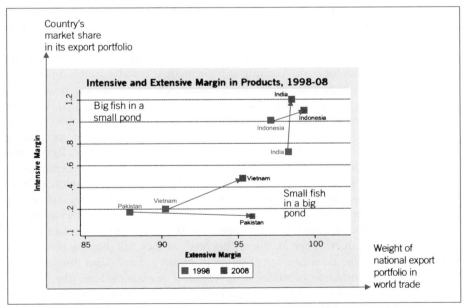

Source: Comtrade. The authors are grateful to Swarnim Wagle, of the World Bank's Trade Division, for sharing this graph.

---

[5] The interpretation for Herfindhal or Gini indices is obviously similar.

Hummels and Klenow for selected countries over the decade preceding the global financial crisis. It can be seen, for instance, that Pakistan's extensive margin has been rising, suggesting active export entrepreneurship. By contrast, its intensive margin has slightly shrunk, suggesting that existing Pakistani exporters are finding it difficult to maintain competitiveness. This type of broad-brush observation is useful to get a first shot at potential constraints on growth – for example, the problem may be declining competitiveness in the textile and clothing sector due to the elimination of Multi-Fibre Arrangement (MFA) quotas. By contrast, India has grown almost only at the intensive margin, which is to be expected given that it is already fully diversified (as the products that belong to its export portfolio account for close to 100 per cent of world trade). Overall, countries can be expected to walk a crescent-shaped trail, first eastward as they broaden their portfolio, then full north as they consolidate positions.

## 7.3    WHAT DO WE LEARN FROM THESE MEASURES?

### 7.3.1   Trends in diversification

The seminal work by Imbs and Wacziarg (2003) uncovered an unexpected non-monotonic relationship between production diversification and gross domestic product (GDP) per capita. Past a certain level of income ($9,000 in 1985 purchasing power parity (PPP) dollars), countries re-concentrate their production structure, whether measured by employment or value added. Using different data, Koren and Tenreyro (2007) confirmed the existence of a U-shaped relationship between the concentration of production and the level of development.

Following their work, several papers have looked at whether a similar non-monotone pattern holds for trade. Looking at trade made it possible to reformulate the question at a much higher degree of disaggregation, since trade data is available for the 5,000 or so lines of the six-digit harmonized system (henceforth HS6). In terms of concentration levels, exports are typically much more concentrated than production. This concentration, which was observed initially by Hausmann and Rodrik (2006), is documented in detail for manufacturing exports in Easterly, Reshef and Schwenkenberg (2009). A striking (but not unique) example of this concentration is the case of Egypt, which, "[out] of 2,985 possible manufacturing products in [the] dataset and 217 possible destinations, [...] gets 23 per cent of its total manufacturing exports from exporting one product – "ceramic bathroom kitchen sanitary items not porcelain" – to one destination, Italy, capturing 94 per cent of the Italian import market for that product" (page 3). These "big hits", as they call them, account for a substantial part of the cross-country variation in export volumes. But they also document that the distribution of values at the export × destination level (their unit of analysis) closely follows a power law; that is, the probability of a big hit decreases exponentially with its size.

Klinger and Lederman (2006), as well as Cadot, Carrère and Strauss-Kahn (2011), analyse the evolution of trade diversification. The former study uses a panel of 73 countries between 1992 and 2003, while the latter focuses on a larger one, with 156 countries representing all regions and all levels of development between 1988 and 2006. In both cases, concentration measures obtained with trade data turned out to be much higher than those obtained with production and employment data.[6] But the U-shaped pattern showed up again, albeit with a turning point at much higher income levels ($22,500 in constant 2000 PPP dollars for Klinger and Lederman, and $25,000 in constant 2005 PPP dollars for Cadot, Carrère and Strauss-Kahn). Note that, as the turning point occurs quite late, the level of export concentration of the richest countries in the sample is much lower than that of the poorest.

## 7.3.2 Which margin matters?

The literature so far shows that growth at the intensive margin is the main component of export growth. The early work by Evenett and Venables (2002) used three-digit trade data for 23 exporters over the period 1970–97 and found that about 60 per cent of total export growth is at the intensive margin, i.e. comes from larger exports of products traded since 1970 to long-standing trading partners. Of the rest, most of which was the destination-wise extensive margin, as the product-wise extensive margin accounted for a small fraction (about 10 per cent) of export growth. Brenton and Newfarmer (2007), using Standard International Trade Classification (SITC) data at the five-digit level over 99 countries and 20 years, also found that intensive-margin growth accounts for the biggest part of trade growth (80.4 per cent), and that growth at the extensive margin was essentially destination-wise (18 per cent). Amurgo-Pacheco and Pierola (2008) found that extensive-margin growth accounts for only 14 per cent of export at the HS6 level for a panel of 24 countries over the period 1990–2005.

The observation that the product-wise extensive margin accounts for little of the growth of exports may seem puzzling, as Cadot et al. (2011) found precisely that margin to be very active, especially at low levels of income. Thus, export entrepreneurship is not lacking. Why then does it not generate export growth? There are two answers, one technical and one of substance. The technical answer is that when a new export appears in statistics, it typically appears at a small scale and can only contribute marginally to growth. But the following year, it is already in the intensive margin. Thus, by construction, the extensive margin can only be small. But there is a deeper reason. In work already cited, Besedes and Prusa (2006) showed that the churning rate is very high in all countries' exports, and especially so for developing

---

[6] The reason has to do with the level of disaggregation rather than with any conceptual difference between trade, production and employment shares. Whereas Imbs and Wacziarg calculated their indices at a relatively high degree of aggregation (ILO, one digit; UNIDO, three digits; and OECD, two digits), Cadot, Carrère and Strauss-Kahn (2011) use very disaggregated trade nomenclature. At that level, there is a large number of product lines with small trade values, while a relatively limited number of them account for the bulk of all countries' trade (especially so of course for developing countries, but even for industrial ones). The reason for this pattern is that the harmonized system used by Comtrade is derived from nomenclatures originally designed for tariff-collection purposes rather than to generate meaningful economic statistics. Thus, it has a large number of economically irrelevant categories, e.g. in the textile-clothing sector, while economically important categories in machinery, vehicles, computer equipment, etc. are grouped together in "mammoth" lines.

ones. That is, many new export products are tried, but many also fail. Raising the contribution of the extensive margin to export growth requires also improving the "sustainability" margin.

Although not predominant quantitatively as a driver of export growth, the extensive margin can react strongly to changes in trade costs, an issue discussed later in this chapter. For instance, Kehoe and Ruhl (2009) found that the set of least-traded goods, which accounted for only 10 per cent of trade before trade liberalization, may grow to account for 30 per cent of trade or more after liberalization. Activity at the extensive margin also varies greatly along the economic development process. Klinger and Lederman (2006) and Cadot, Carrère and Strauss-Kahn (2011) show that the number of new exports falls rapidly as countries develop, after peaking at the lower-middle income level. The poorest countries, which have the greatest scope for new-product introduction because of their very undiversified trade structures, unsurprisingly have the strongest extensive-margin activity.[7]

Figure 7.3 depicts the contribution of the between-groups and within-groups components to Theil's overall index, using the formulae derived in the previous section.

Figure 7.3: Contributions of within- and between-groups to overall concentration, all countries

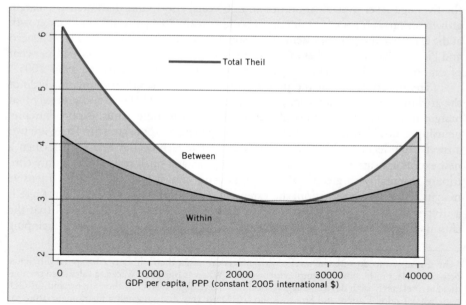

Source: Cadot, Carrère and Strauss-Kahn (2011).

---

[7] The average number of active export lines is generally low at a sample average of 2,062 per country per year (using Cadot, Carrère and Strauss-Kahn's sample), i.e. a little less than half the total, with a minimum of eight for Kiribati in 1993 and a maximum of 4,988 for Germany in 1994 and the United States in 1995.

It can be seen that the within component dominates the index while the between component accounts for most of the evolution. Put differently, most of the concentration in levels occurs at the intensive margin (in goods that are long-standing exports) while changes in concentration are at the extensive margin (for example the decreased concentration for lower-income countries results mainly from a rise in the number of exported goods).

Whereas the extensive margin in figure 7.3 is measured only by the number of exports, using their alternative definition (see Appendix 7.A.2) Hummels and Klenow (2005) performed a cross-sectional analysis of exports for 126 countries decomposing exports into extensive and intensive margins. Interestingly, they found that 62 per cent of the higher trade of larger economies is driven by the extensive margin, while only 38 per cent is driven by the intensive margin. Thus, once the extensive margin is corrected for the importance of the new exports introduced (Hummels-Klenow's version), it dominates the intensive margin in explaining exports growth.

## 7.4    DRIVERS OF DIVERSIFICATION

### 7.4.1  Quantitative insights

What does the theoretical trade literature have to say on the potential determinants of export diversification? In traditional Ricardian models, productivity affects trade patterns. In the specification proposed by Melitz (2003) – "new-new trade theory" – firms are heterogeneous in productivity levels, and only a subset of them – the most productive – become exporters. Thus, exporting status and productivity are correlated at the firm level, although this comes essentially from a selection effect.

Several papers have studied the impact of productivity/income on diversification by putting export diversification on the left-hand side of the equation and income on the right-hand side. As we already saw, Klinger and Lederman (2006) as well as Cadot, Carrère and Strauss-Kahn (2011) found a U-shaped relationship between export concentration and GDP per capita by regressing the former on the latter, hence providing evidence of a non-linear effect of income on export diversification.

We now consider some of its non-income determinants. In a symmetric (representative-firm) monopolistic-competition model, the volume of trade, the number of exporting firms and the number of varieties marketed are all proportional. In a heterogeneous-firms model, the relationship is more complex, but the ratio of export to domestic varieties is also directly related to the ratio of export to domestic sales. Thus, it is no surprise that gravity determinants of trade volumes also affect the diversity of traded goods. For instance, Amurgo-Pacheco and Pierola (2008) find that the distance and size of destination markets is related to the diversity of bilateral trade.

Parteka and Tamberi (2008) apply a two-step estimation strategy to uncover some of the systematic (permanent) cross-country differences in export diversification. To do so, they break down country effects into a wide range of country-specific characteristics, such as size, geographical conditions, endowments, human capital and institutional setting. Using a panel data set for 60 countries and 20 years (1985–2004), they show that distance from major markets and country size are the most relevant and robust determinants of export diversity, once GDP per capita is controlled for. These results are consistent with those of Dutt, Mihov and van Zandt (2009), who show that distance to trading centres and market access (proxied by a host of bilateral and multilateral trading arrangements) are key determinants of diversification.

We take account of the main variables used in the above cited empirical studies and propose a quantitative assessment of the main determinants of export diversification. We then go a step further and extend the discussion by assessing whether determinants mainly affect the extensive or intensive margins of diversification.[8]

As theoretical background stays silent on the potential form of the relationship between export diversification and its determinants, we start by showing non-parametric "smoother" regressions.[9] Such regressions do not impose any functional form and are therefore well suited to a first exploration of data with no ad-hoc pre-defined relationships between variables.

In addition to per capita GDP (specified with a quadratic term to capture the hump-shaped relationship described in section 7.2.2), we introduce the following variables in our analysis:[10]

- Size of the economy, proxied by population. We expect larger countries to be more diversified due to larger internal markets and higher degree of product differentiation.

- Market access, proxied by the country membership in preferential trade agreements. Preferential market access should help both export volumes and export of new products.

- Transport costs, proxied by both a remoteness index (as in Rose, 2004) and the quality of infrastructures (captured by the density of railway, paved road and telephone lines). The more remote a country, the lower its exports both in volume and number of products; in contrast, better infrastructures should boost export diversification.

- Human capital, proxied by the number of years of schooling (from Barro and Lee, 2010) and the percentage of GDP invested in research and development (R&D). We expect both variables to have a positive impact on export diversification, in particular through the extensive margin, i.e. through the development and export of new products.

- The quality of institution may also have a positive impact on diversification. This is proxied by two variables, the International Country Risk Guide (ICRG) Indicator of Quality of Government (QoG) and the Revised Combined Polity Score, both provided by the QoG institute.

---

[8] As a measure of diversification, we use Theil indices computed at the HS6 level by Cadot, Carrère and Strauss-Kahn (2011) for 1988-2006.

[9] Non-parametric "smoother" regression (also called "lowess" regression) consists of re-estimating regression for overlapping samples centred on each observation.

[10] A detailed description of these variables is available in technical appendix 7.A.4.

- Finally, we expect foreign direct investment (FDI) to also impact export structure. We thus introduce FDI in the analysis.

Figure 7.4 presents the scatter plots of export diversification measured by the 2006 Theil index versus the variables listed above. Scatter plots show correlations between the variables, whereas curves correspond to "smoother" non-parametric regression. In all scatter plots, a "full diamond" represents a developing country (i.e. low- and middle-income countries) and a "hollow circle" represents a developed country (i.e. high-income OECD and non-OECD countries). The sample includes 129 to 150 countries depending on data availability.

Figure 7.4: Average Theil indices in 2006 on each of the ten explanatory variables in 2005

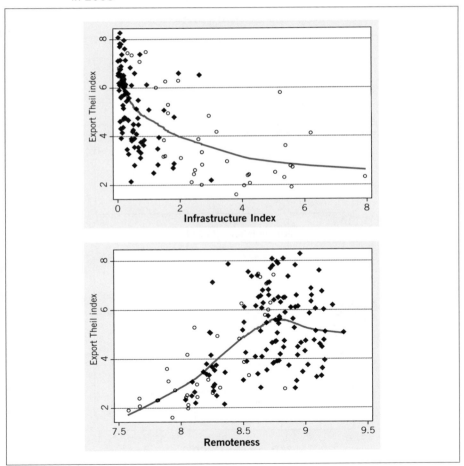

Figure 7.4: Average Theil indices in 2006 on each of the ten explanatory variables in 2005 *(Continued)*

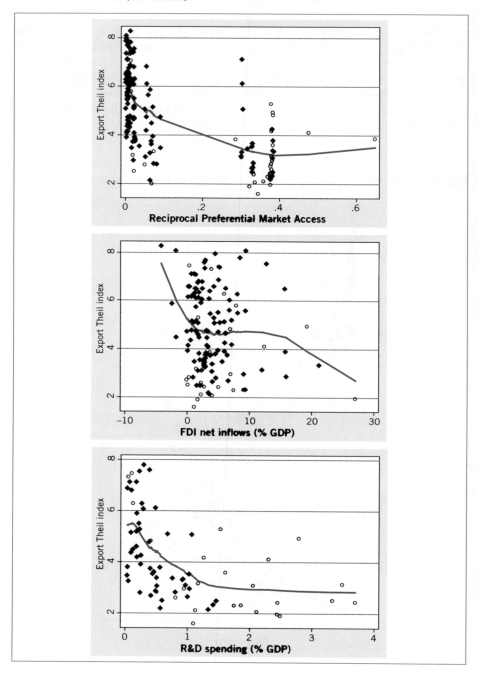

Figure 7.4: Average Theil indices in 2006 on each of the ten explanatory variables in 2005 *(Continued)*

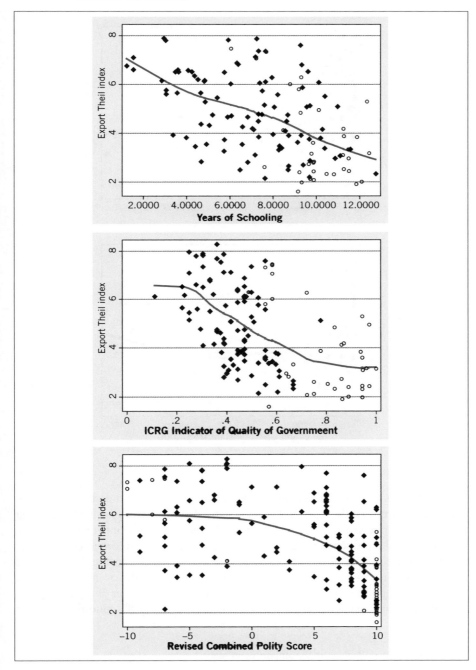

Figure 7.4: Average Theil indices in 2006 on each of the ten explanatory variables in 2005 *(Continued)*

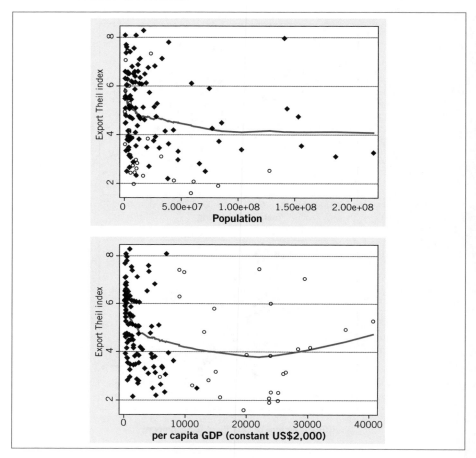

These figures reveal links between export diversification and each of these variables, which, importantly, have the expected signs. A similar test run using the number of exported products instead of the Theil index provides very similar figures, suggesting that our variables influence essentially the extensive margin.[11] In order to get further insights on the impact of the set of variables described above on the extensive and intensive margins, we turn to a regression analysis. We regress the overall Theil index, the within-groups Theil, the between-groups Theil and the number of exported products on the ten variables using a panel database, including 87 countries over the

---

[11] These figures are available from the authors upon request.

Table 7.1: Diversification drivers in a panel data set, 1990–2004, 87 countries

| | ln (Theil) | | | | ln (Theil_between) | | ln (Nber) | |
|---|---|---|---|---|---|---|---|---|
| | **Coef.** *Std. Err.* | | **Coef.** *Std. Err.* | | **Coef.** *Std. Err.* | | **Coef.** *Std. Err.* | |
| ln (per capita GDP) | -0.505 | *0.09* *** | -0.193 | *0.13* * | -1.054 | *0.32* *** | 1.055 | *0.38* *** |
| ln (per capita GDP) squared | 0.040 | *0.01* *** | 0.009 | *0.01* | 0.054 | *0.02* ** | -0.106 | *0.02* *** |
| ln (Infrastructure) | -0.072 | *0.03* *** | -0.122 | *0.04* *** | -0.303 | *0.08* *** | 0.119 | *0.07* * |
| ln (Remoteness) | 1.092 | *0.46* ** | -0.439 | *0.50* | 3.753 | *2.14* * | -3.533 | *1.51* ** |
| Trade liberalization | -0.009 | *0.01* | 0.017 | *0.02* | 0.031 | *0.05* | 0.108 | *0.06* * |
| Pref. Market Access | -0.179 | *0.04* *** | -0.244 | *0.05* *** | -1.031 | *0.21* *** | 0.316 | *0.11* *** |
| FDI (% GDP) | 0.001 | *0.00* ** | 0.001 | *0.00* * | 0.002 | *0.00* | 0.000 | *0.00* |
| ln (Years of Schooling) | -0.114 | *0.06* * | 0.017 | *0.07* | -0.625 | *0.26* ** | 0.619 | *0.21* *** |
| ICRG | -0.047 | *0.04* * | 0.086 | *0.04* ** | -0.584 | *0.14* *** | 0.416 | *0.12* *** |
| Polity Score | -0.002 | *0.00* * | 0.002 | *0.00* | -0.003 | *0.00* | 0.019 | *0.00* *** |
| ln (population) | -0.187 | *0.07* *** | 0.041 | *0.08* | -0.642 | *0.27* ** | 1.582 | *0.27* *** |
| Country fixed effects | yes | | yes | | yes | | yes | |
| Year fixed effects | yes | | yes | | yes | | yes | |
| Observations | 1195 | | 1257 | | 1257 | | 1257 | |
| Ajusted R-squared | 0.97 | | 0.92 | | 0.98 | | 0.95 | |

Notes: Robust standard errors in italics, with * meaning that the correspondent coefficient is significantly different from zero at 10 per cent; ** significant at 5 per cent; *** significant at 1 per cent.

1990–2004 period.[12] Country and year fixed-effects control for unobservable characteristics in all regressions. The regression analysis, reported in table 7.1, confirms our results from the scatter plots.

Table 7.1 shows a negative significant coefficient on GDP per capita and a positive significant one on GDP per capita squared. We thus retrieve the main result of Cadot, Carrère and Strauss-Kahn (2011) which reveals a quadratic relationship between the Theil index and GDP per capita, mainly driven by the extensive margin (the between component of the Theil index). Once controlled for GDP per capita, infrastructure still appears as an important driver of diversification: a 10 per cent increase in the infrastructure index decreases the Theil's index by about 0.7 per cent.[13] Better infrastructure increases diversification on both margins. Remoteness also has the expected sign: the more remote the country, the lower its export diversification (i.e. the higher its Theil index), essentially in terms of the extensive margin and number of products. Our analysis thus confirms the result that high distance to importers increases the export fixed cost and, consequently, drastically reduces export diversification. Preferential market access is clearly an important factor of diversification at both margins and this result is consistent with other studies (for example,

---

[12] As seen in section 7.2.2, the within-groups Theil index corresponds to the intensive margin, whereas the between-groups Theil index corresponds to the extensive margin.

[13] Note that the log-log specification allows an interpretation of the results in terms of elasticity, which is easily understandable.

Amurgo-Pacheco, 2006; Gamberoni, 2007; Feenstra and Kee, 2007; or Dutt, Mihov and van Zandt, 2009). In contrast, net inflows of FDI (as a percentage of GDP) seem to concentrate exports value on some products and thereby increases concentration at the intensive margin. This result could be expected as multinational corporations specialize in specific products, which they produce in high volumes. We also find a significant impact of education on export diversification. A 10 per cent increase in the years of schooling reduces the Theil index by 1.1 per cent and increases the numbers of exported products by 6.2 per cent. Similarly, the quality of institution appears clearly significant, with a positive impact on diversification. As expected, the larger the population, the more diversified the economy.[14]

Note that the above results should be understood with caution. Regressions in table 7.1 are informative of the factors that have a significant impact on diversification and of the sign of this impact once controlled for others factors. It is difficult however to rank these factors and clearly isolate a single impact due to potential multicolinearity issues existing between these variables.

As shown in table 7.1, we also account for a potential factor of diversification largely ignored in empirical literature: the unilateral trade liberalization. We use the dummy variable as defined by Wacziarg and Welch (2008) (see section 7.2.2 for further indications on this variable). This factor appears non-significant except in column (4): import liberalization increases the diversification through a larger number of exported lines. Further investigations reveal that the non-significance of the trade liberalization variable in columns (1)-(3) is mainly due to the "year of schooling" variables. If we drop the latter from the regression, the trade liberalization dummy becomes negative and significant at the 1 per cent level in the three first columns. Strikingly, if we introduce an interactive variable between unilateral trade liberalization and years of schooling, the trade liberalization dummies and the interactive variables are significant, whereas schooling is not. That is: years of schooling matter for export diversification *only in a liberalized regime*. Similar conclusions hold for some other drivers of export diversification of Table 7.1 such as infrastructure. Thus, unilateral trade liberalization appears to be an important underlying driver of export diversification. We now explore this feature in more detail.

### 7.4.2   Trade liberalization as a driver of diversification

Although preferential trade liberalization has received considerable attention in the empirical literature as a driver of product diversification (for example, Amurgo-Pacheco, 2006; Gamberoni, 2007; Feenstra and Kee, 2007; or Dutt, Mihov and van Zandt, 2009), unilateral trade reforms have not. Yet we will see in section 7.5 that the link between import diversification and total factor productivity (TFP) is strongly

---

[14] The variable on R&D spending is not included in the regression analysis as it covers only a small number of countries and years, and consequently reduces the sample drastically. The "years of schooling" variable, available every five years in the Barro and Lee database, is considered as constant within the five-year period.

established at the firm level. Thus, import liberalization can be taken as a positive shock on TFP, which should, according to the Melitz (2003) argument, raise the number of industries with an upper tail of firms capable of exporting – and thus raise overall export diversification.[15] Indeed, arguments running roughly along this line can be found in, for example, Bernard, Jensen and Schott (2006) or in Broda, Greenfield and Weinstein (2006). This section presents a brief statistical analysis of this relationship.

To do so, we combine the Theil index of export concentration computed at the HS6 level by Cadot, Carrère and Strauss-Kahn (2011) for the period 1988–2006 with the trade liberalization date of Wacziarg and Welch (2008). The sample used includes 100 countries, 62 middle-income and 38 low-income countries over the period 1988–2006, with respectively 68 per cent and 49 per cent of country-year observations occurring in liberalized regimes (see technical appendix table 4.A.1). We exclude from the sample 34 high-income countries, as 95 per cent of the observations of this group occurs in liberalized regimes throughout the period (Estonia and Iceland are the only countries considered as non-liberalized and they do not change regime over the period – see technical appendix table 7.A.1).

Wacziarg and Welch (2008) propose an update covering the late 1990s of Sachs and Warner (1995)'s trade liberalization dates. Such data were first collected from a comprehensive survey of broad country-specific case studies. More precisely, Sachs and Warner determined trade liberalization dates based on primary-source data on annual tariffs, non-tariff barriers and black market premium. A variety of secondary sources was also used, particularly to identify when export marketing boards were abolished and multi-party governance systems replaced Communist Party rule.[16]

As shown in figure 7.5, the conditional mean of Theil's concentration index is 4.8 in a liberalized regime versus 5.9 in a non-liberalized one, while the number of exported products is clearly higher when the trade regime is liberalized (1,893 products versus 1,178 in a non-liberalized trade regime). The difference in Theil indices means is higher for middle-income than for low-income countries, although it is still statistically significant for low-income countries. This suggests a stronger dynamic between trade liberalization and diversification of exports in developing countries with better infrastructure and higher skill levels.

---

[15] This mechanism is further described in section 7.5.1.

[16] Rodriguez and Rodrik (2000) criticized the Sachs-Warner (1995) openness variable, showing that its explanatory power on growth was driven by only two of its five components: the black market premium on foreign exchange (a measure of overvalued exchange rates rather than trade openness) and the presence of export marketing boards. By contrast, tariffs and non-tariff barriers correlated poorly with growth. As export marketing boards essentially characterized sub-Saharan Africa and overvalued exchange rate Latin America, the Sachs-Warner measure was indistinguishable from African and Latin American "dummy variables". Wacziarg and Welch (2008) improved the methodology by better identifying export marketing boards and trade liberalization dates. Using their improved openness definition and panel data over a long period, they confirmed that openness correlates with faster growth, delivering on average 2 percentage points of additional growth (largely driven by additional investment).

Figure 7.5: Differential of means in liberalized versus non-liberalized regimes (100 middle- and low-income countries, 1988–2006)

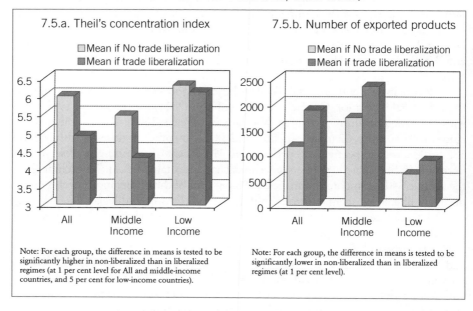

7.5.a. Theil's concentration index

☐ Mean if No trade liberalization
■ Mean if trade liberalization

7.5.b. Number of exported products

☐ Mean if No trade liberalization
■ Mean if trade liberalization

Note: For each group, the difference in means is tested to be significantly higher in non-liberalized than in liberalized regimes (at 1 per cent level for All and middle-income countries, and 5 per cent for low-income countries).

Note: For each group, the difference in means is tested to be significantly lower in non-liberalized than in liberalized regimes (at 1 per cent level).

We then run fixed-effects regressions of the Theil index on a binary liberalization indicator defined by the dates of liberalization (equal to 1 when liberalized) to assess the within-country effect of trade liberalization on the diversification of exports. We use a difference-in-difference specification similar to the one used by Wacziarg and Welch (2008):

$$Theil_{it} = \lambda_i + \delta_t + \phi LIB_{it} + \varepsilon_{it} \tag{1}$$

where $Theil_{it}$ is the Theil index of country $i$ exports in year $t$; $LIB_{it}$ a dummy equal to 1 if $t$ is greater than the year of liberalization (defined by Wacziarg and Welch); and 0 otherwise. We introduce both country and year fixed-effects ( $\lambda_i$ and $\delta_t$, respectively). The sample is not restricted to countries that underwent reforms.

The regression for the period 1988–2006 shows a highly significant within-country difference in export diversification between a liberalized and a non-liberalized regime ($\phi$ reported in table 7.2, column 1), with a coefficient twice higher for middle- than for low-income countries, confirming the pattern observed in figure 7.5. We also regress equation (1) using the Theil index's decomposition (within-groups versus between-groups, see section 7.2). Results are reported in table 7.2, columns 3-6. Controlling for country and year effects, the results suggest that middle-income countries that undertook trade liberalization reforms have a significantly more diversified structure of exports along the intensive margin. By contrast, low-income countries diversify mostly along the extensive margin. Thus, trade liberalization helps middle-income countries to consolidate their positions in goods they are already exporting while it helps low-income countries to develop new exports. As the poorest countries are often the most concentrated (see figure 7.3 and section 7.5.2), it is indeed likely that trade liberalization do not increase exports in sectors (often natural resources) in which they already specialize.

Table 7.2: Fixed-effects regressions of diversification index on liberalization status

| | Theil | | Theil-within | | Theil-between | |
|---|---|---|---|---|---|---|
| | **(1)** | **(2)** | **(3)** | **(4)** | **(5)** | **(6)** |
| Liberalization (LIB) | −0.190* | | −0.075 | | −0.100* | |
| | (2.0) | | (0.8) | | (2.8) | |
| LIB - Middle-Income | | −0.241* | | −0.271* | | 0.067 |
| | | (2.0) | | (2.0) | | (0.5) |
| LIB - Low-Income | | −0.138* | | 0.053 | | −0.209* |
| | | (1.6) | | (0.5) | | (2.0) |
| Number of Obs. | 1794 | | 1394 | | 1394 | |
| Number of countries | 100 | | 100 | | 100 | |
| Period | 1988-2006 | | 1990-2004 | | 1990-2004 | |
| Country fixed effects | Yes | | Yes | | Yes | |
| Year fixed effects | Yes | | Yes | | Yes | |
| R² within | 0.39 | 0.39 | 0.28 | 0.29 | 0.75 | 0.75 |

Note: * means a significant coefficient (at 10 per cent level) standard errors in parentheses, heteroscedasticity consistent and adjusted for country clustering.

Figure 7.6 shows the time path of export diversification for an average country before and after liberalization for middle- and low-income countries, respectively. The plain curve shows the Theil index (left-hand scale) and the dotted one shows the number of exported products at the HS6 level (right-hand scale) over a window of ten years before and after liberalization. The sample is made of countries that underwent permanent (non-reversed) liberalizations. For middle-income countries, a strong diversification trend (shrinking Theil index) is apparent over the entire post-liberalization windows, and particularly strong in the five years following liberalization. The figure also suggests an anticipation effect in the three years preceding liberalization. Patterns are less clear in the low-income countries figure.

In order to further examine the timing of export diversification, we follow Wacziarg and Welch (2008) and replace the *LIB* variable with five dummies, each capturing a two-year period immediately before and after the trade-liberalization date *T*. Coefficients on these dummies capture the average difference in the Theil index (and number of exported lines) between the period in question and a baseline period running from sample start to *T*−3.[17] Estimated coefficients (in absolute value) are reported in figure 7.7.

---

[17] We also run the regression on a larger sample starting at T-5, but coefficients on [T-5] to [T-3] were not significant and did not affect coefficients on other periods.

Figure 7.6: Time pattern of export diversification pre- and post-liberalization

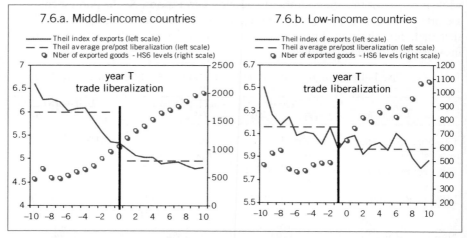

Source: Authors' computation. Trade liberalization dates are from Wacziarg and Welch (2008) and Theil index of exports and the number of exported goods from Cadot, Carrère and Strauss-Kahn (2011).

Figure 7.7 shows that the anticipation effect apparent in figure 7.6 disappears in formal tests using the fixed-effects regression, i.e. in the presence of country and year effects. Diversification starts at the date of trade liberalization and proceeds steadily thereafter, as shown by the rising coefficients (in absolute value) on the period dummies.

Figure 7.7: Estimated marginal increase in the export diversification around a trade Liberalization event

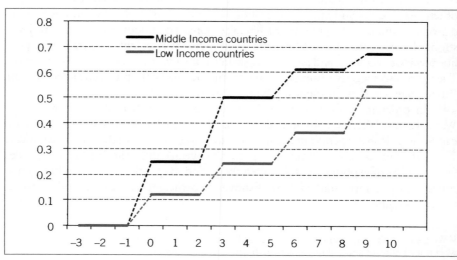

## 7.4.3 Diversification, spillovers and industrial policy

The graphs in figure 7.4 highlight a clear statistical association between government supply-side policies, notably the provision of education and infrastructure, and export diversification.

Government provision of infrastructure and education reflects the presence of market failures. As for education, the willingness of employers to provide it is limited, even for vocational training.[18] Reasons include the public-good character of education, the difficulty to retain trained workers, and the footloose nature of many employers in developing countries, which does not encourage social responsibility.

As for road infrastructure, building costs are largely beyond what private-sector users are willing to invest given their public-good nature. Only mining companies are sometimes willing to invest in road infrastructure directly serving their needs, or large plantations in local networks of rural roads. Where governments are unable or unwilling to invest in road infrastructure, transportation costs choke commercial activities, both domestic and international, as Gollin and Rogerson (2010) document in the case of Uganda.[19] As a consequence, only a tiny proportion of crops make it to urban markets and even fewer to international markets, resulting in very concentrated export structures.

Even where roads exist, sometimes transportation services are too expensive for the private sector to provide, in particular in low-density areas. A recent paper by Raballand et al. (2011) reports the results of a randomized experiment in rural Malawi aimed at understanding why rural transportation services are not provided even when rural roads exist. By randomly varying bus fares, they show that bus use is strongly price-sensitive but, most strikingly, that there is no price with positive demand at which costs are covered.[20] In the absence of a rural bus service, it is virtually impossible to transport goods (handicrafts, spices and other low-volume items) to the market, reducing the scope of marketable products and income-earning opportunities (in particular for women). Citing other studies that point in the same direction, Raballand et al. (2011) conclude that building roads – a favourite donor activity – does not

---

[18] As an illustration, the World Bank's Private Sector Competitiveness and Economic Diversification Project in Lesotho has aimed at building workforce skills through the establishment of two worker-training centres in Maseru and Maputsoe. The initiative had both public- and private-sector participation, the management councils in both centres being led by the private sector. But obtaining government funding for the centres has proved a challenge, since only three employers (from Lesotho, South Africa and Malaysia) have expressed interest in participating in their financing.

[19] Gollin and Rogerson (2010) observe that the density of paved roads in Uganda today (16,300 km for a land area of 200,000 km2) is comparable to what the Romans left behind when they evacuated Britain in AD 350 (between 12,000 and 15,000 km of paved roads for a land area of 242,000 km²). As a result, the prices of agricultural products when they reach markets are often more than double the farmgate prices.

[20] Raballand et al. (2011) refrain from estimating a price elasticity of demand, but instead regress the probability that an individual took the bus over the investigation period (July-December 2009) for a fare, which was randomly assigned using a voucher system. When the bus service was free, 47 per cent of the surveyed individuals took the bus at least once. The proportion declined smoothly to reach zero at 500 kwacha (US$3.57) per ride. Similar results were obtained using the number of rides as the dependent variable.

appear to be enough, by itself, to get farmers to the market. In order to promote diversification at the country and household levels, governments may need to intervene directly in the provision of transportation services, a notion that goes against a philosophy of government retrenchment that has dominated development thinking over the last 30 years.

Other sources of market failure can hamper export diversification. Conceptually, the argument is shown in figure 7.8, where the production-possibility frontier (PPF) between two goods is shown with a convex part, reflecting economies of scale in the production of "good 2" in a certain range (at low levels of production).[21] This is a classic infant-industry argument. At the relative prices shown by the dotted lines, the economy can find itself stuck at corner equilibrium $E_1$ where it produces only "good 1" because the curvature of the PPF makes it locally unprofitable to move resources to good 2, even though the economy would be better off at the diversified equilibrium $E_2$. In such circumstances, sectorally-targeted industrial policy can have a socially beneficial role to play.

The argument is crucially dependent on the presence of some sort of increasing returns at the industry or cross-industry level. Do these externalities exist outside of development-economics textbooks? Rosenthal and Strange (2004) present a substantial body of evidence in favour of spatial agglomeration externalities. More recently, Alfaro and Chen (2009) show evidence that the location of establishments by multinational companies follows not only "first-nature" determinants (proximity to markets

Figure 7.8: Externalities in a two-good economy

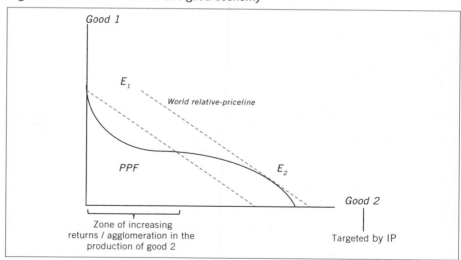

---

[21] On this, see Harrison and Rodríguez-Clare (2010), who provide an excellent overview of the literature on industrial policy.

and low production costs) but also "second-nature" ones – pure agglomeration forces.[22] Among those, Alfaro and Chen examine the role of labour-market pooling (a larger pool reduces unemployment risk for workers and, therefore, wage premia), capital-equipment linkages (larger pools of capital-intensive industries attract support services), input-output (IO) linkages, and knowledge spillovers between industries measured by cross-citations in patents. They find very strong evidence of capital-equipment linkages and knowledge spillovers in the location of subsidiaries. IO linkages are significant, although weaker. By contrast, evidence of labour-market pooling is weak.

Inter-industry spillovers are also identified empirically by Shakurova (2010), who estimates how the probability of exporting a good depends on previous experience in exporting either similar goods ("horizontal" spillovers) or upstream ones ("vertical" spillovers). Cross-country regressions at the industry level show that the size of those spillovers varies across industries but is, in most cases, statistically significant. Figure 7.9 shows those spillovers in the form of marginal effects for each industry.

Figure 7.9: Vertical and horizontal export spillovers

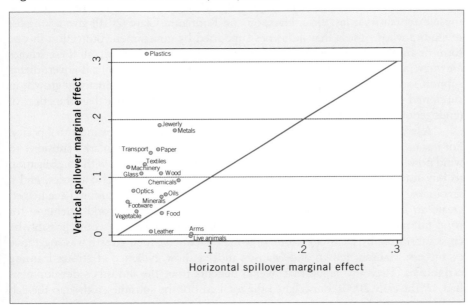

Source: Adapted from Shakurova (2010).

Note: Marginal effects from a probit regression of export status in product i on export status in product j at t-1 on a cross-section of countries. Those shown were significant at 5 per cent or more.

---

[22] Alfaro and Chen (2009) combine geocode software with Dunn and Bradstreet's worldbase data set, which contains detailed location information on over 41 million establishments, to calculate distances between establishments belonging to different industries (as Alfaro and Chen focus on between-industry agglomeration). Distances are used to estimate actual and counterfactual densities, the difference between the two being the agglomeration index.

Other externalities include information spillovers leading to underinvestment in export entrepreneurship at the extensive margin (Hausmann and Rodrik, 2003). That is, export expansion at the extensive margin reflects a "self-discovery" process whereby export entrepreneurs test the viability of new products on foreign markets. Once they succeed, imitators follow, creating a public-good problem. Spillovers at the extensive margin among exporters of the same country are documented using firm-level data from four African countries by Cadot et al. (2011), who find that the probability of survival of an exporter of good $k$ to country $d$ past the first year rises with the number of exporters of $k$ to $d$ from the same country. Strikingly, the number of exporters of $k$ to $d$ from *other* countries is insignificant, suggesting that the externality is essentially within-country. Interacting this network effect with various measures of dependence on finance suggests that the information spillover may go through domestic credit markets (using competitor performance as a substitute for direct information on export risk) rather than through the direct firm-to-firm imitation effect postulated by Hausmann and Rodrik, although the implications are similar.

If the case for externalities across exporters and industries seems fairly well-established both conceptually and empirically, what governments can do to leverage those externalities is less clear. Harrison and Rodriguez-Clare (2010) give a long list of studies whose gist is that industries supported by government protection in one form or another do not enjoy faster productivity growth. However, all these studies are vulnerable to the endogeneity critique of Rodrik (2007). Namely, if governments support industries to compensate for market failures, slower productivity growth in supported industries may reflect the underlying constraints rather than the effect of (endogenous) industrial policies.

A few case studies identify industries successfully supported by industrial policy. For instance, Hansen, Jensen and Madsen (2003) show how Denmark's subsidies to wind power (a guaranteed-price scheme for wind power combined with an obligation to buy for power companies that was also adopted in other EU countries, and a favourable tax treatment of investments in wind-turbine manufacturing) have helped create an industry that, by the early 2000s, supplied half the world's demand for wind turbines. As export sales were not subsidized (although they could possibly be cross-subsidized by Denmark's four large manufacturers), their growth was suggestive of success. Hansen, Jensen and Madsen indeed show evidence of strong learning economies. They also argue that overall benefits from the industry's development had, by the early 2000s, outweighed the total cost of the subsidies, although the calculation is complex.

Export promotion has a more uneven record. After reviewing the mixed evidence so far, Lederman, Olarreaga and Payton (2006, 2009) find, on the basis of cross-country evidence, extremely high rates of return on public money invested in export-promotion agencies (EPAs). Some conditions, however, must be fulfilled, including private-sector involvement in agency management. They also find strongly diminishing returns; that is, a little money does a lot of good, but a lot of money does not. A recent impact evaluation of Tunisia's export-promotion agency by Gourdon et al. (2011) sheds some light on whether export promotion promotes growth at the intensive or extensive margin. Compared to a control group of firms that did not benefit from export promotion, beneficiary firms expanded at the extensive margin in terms of products and markets. However, overall, their export sales grew faster than those of control-group firms only during the year of the treatment. After one year, they were back to a parallel trajectory. Thus, export promotion seems to foster diversification, but might in the end lead firms to spread themselves too thinly.[23]

By and large, it is fair to say that, given the strong empirical evidence in support of the existence of externalities, the case for industrial policy is less easily brushed aside than it was one or two decades ago. But, as Harrison and Rodriguez-Clare (2010) put it, "the key question is whether [industrial policy] has worked in practice". In this regard, they cite countless studies showing that infant-industry promotion through trade-restricting measures does not pass the classic tests of industrial policy's worthiness.[24] As for trade-promoting measures, such as tax breaks for multinational investors, they are costly to public budgets and raise fairness issues. For instance, the list of concessions offered by Costa Rica to Intel in the late 1990s strikes one as transfers from taxpayers in a poor country to shareholders in a rich one – a proposition of dubious ethical appeal even if it passes the Mill and Bastable tests. Moreover, competition between potential host countries for attracting multinational subsidiaries makes tax breaks a negative-sum game between developing countries, even if those tax breaks are trade-enhancing and pass the Mill and Bastable tests at the national level.

## 7.5    EXPORT DIVERSIFICATION, GROWTH AND EMPLOYMENT

We now look at export diversification as a potential determinant of growth – diversification measures become explanatory rather than a dependent variable. We first briefly discuss the causality between export diversification and productivity. We then review the existing evidence on the relationship between initial diversification and subsequent growth, starting with the widely discussed "natural resource curse". We then focus on the link between export diversification and employment.

### 7.5.1 Diversification and productivity: An issue of causality

As seen earlier, Ricardian theory posits that causation runs from productivity to trade patterns and not the other way around. In Melitz (2003) models, causation may run both ways depending on whether we look at the firm or aggregate level. Firms are

---

[23] Volpe and Carballo (2008) also found benefits to be stronger at the extensive margin in a rigorous impact evaluation of export promotion in Peru.

[24] An industrial policy passes the "Mill test" if the beneficiary industry becomes profitable without support after some period of time. It passes the "Bastable test" if the societal benefits of industrial support outweigh its costs (fiscal and other).

heterogeneous in productivity levels, and only the most productive export. At the firm level, causation thus runs only one way, from productivity to export status, like in Ricardian models, as productivity draw is distributed across firms as an i.i.d. random variable and is not affected by the decision to export, be it through learning or any other mechanism.

At the aggregate level, however, causation can run either way in a Melitz model, depending on the nature of the shock. To see this, suppose first that the initial shock is a decrease in trade costs. Melitz's model and recent variants of it (for example, Chaney, 2008; Feenstra and Kee, 2008) show that more firms will export, which will raise export diversification since in a monopolistic-competition model each firm sells a different variety. But low-productivity firms will exit the market altogether, pushing up aggregate industry productivity – albeit, again, by a selection effect. In this case, trade drives aggregate productivity.

Suppose now that the shock is an exogenous – for example, technology-driven – increase in firm productivity across the board, i.e. affecting equally all firms and all sectors. For a given trade cost, only those firms with high productivity draw can bear the cost of exporting. Ceteris paribus, the productivity shock will raise the number of firms with high enough productivity, and thus the number of active export lines. In this case, productivity will drive trade.

The pre-Melitz empirical literature on the productivity-export linkage at the firm level was predicated on the idea that firms learn by exporting (see, for example, Haddad, 1993; Aw and Hwang, 1995; Tybout and Westbrook, 1995). However, Clerides, Lach and Tybout (1998) argued theoretically that the productivity differential between exporting and non-exporting firms was a selection effect, not a learning one, and found support for this interpretation using plant-level data in Colombia, Mexico and Morocco. Subsequent studies (Bernard and Jensen, 1999; Eaton, Kortum and Kramarz, 2004, 2007; Helpman, Melitz and Yeaple, 2004; Demidova, Kee and Krishna, 2006) confirmed the importance of selection effects at the firm level. The most recent literature extends the source of heterogeneity to characteristics other than just productivity; for instance, several recent papers consider the ability to deliver quality (Johnson, 2008; Verhoogen, 2008; or Kugler and Verhoogen, 2008). Hallak and Sivadasan (2009) combine the two in a model with multidimensional heterogeneity where firms differ both in their productivity and in their ability to deliver quality. They find, in conformity with their model, that the empirical firm-level determinants of export performance are more complex than just the level of productivity.

At the aggregate level, most of the literature so far (for example, Klinger and Lederman, 2006; or Cadot, Carrère and Strauss-Kahn, 2011) has regressed export diversification (i.e. left-hand side of the equation) on income (i.e. the right-hand side) and found a U-shaped relationship between export concentration and GDP per capita. This can be interpreted as supporting the income-drives-export-diversification conjecture, as the hypothetical reverse mapping, from diversification to income, would, in a certain range, assign two levels of income (a low one and a high one) to the same level of diversification. While multiple equilibria are common in economics, the rationale for this particular one would be difficult to understand. Feenstra and

Kee (2008) were the first to test empirically the importance of the reverse mechanism – from export diversification to productivity. They do so by estimating simultaneously a GDP function derived from a heterogeneous-firm model and a TFP equation where the number of export varieties (i.e. of exporting firms) is correlated with aggregate productivity through the usual selection effect. On a sample of 48 countries, they find that the doubling of product varieties observed over 1980–2000 explains a 3.3 per cent cumulated increase in country-level TFP. Put differently, changes in export variety explain 1 per cent of the variation in TFP across time and countries. The explanatory power of product variety is particularly weak in the between-country dimension (0.3 per cent). Thus, product variety does not seem to explain much of the permanent TFP differences across countries, but an increase in export diversification – for example, due to a decrease in tariffs – seems to trigger non-negligible selection effects. To recall, this selection effect means that the least efficient firms exit the domestic market when trade expands, raising the average productivity of remaining firms. Still, even in the within-country dimension, two-thirds of the variation in productivity is explained by factors other than trade expansion.

While the determinants of diversification have been studied in the previous section, we now turn to the other side of the causality and investigate the effect of export diversification on growth, starting with the well-known "natural resource curse".

### 7.5.2 The "natural-resource curse"

The "natural resource curse" hypothesis found support with Sachs and Warner (1997) empirical findings that a large share of natural-resource exports in GDP is statistically associated, ceteris paribus, with slow growth. Since then the discussion on the existence of such a curse has been fierce. Building on Sachs and Warner (1997), Auty (2000, 2001) also found a negative correlation between growth and natural-resource exports concentration. Prebisch (1950) provides a set of possible explanations for this phenomenon: deteriorating terms of trade, excess volatility, and low productivity growth. A host of other growth-inhibiting syndromes associated with natural-resource economies are discussed in Gylfason (2008). As we will see, each potential channel has been a subject of controversy; moreover, the very conjecture holds only when looking at natural-resource dependence, which is endogenous to a host of influences. Endowments of natural resources, by contrast, do not seem to correlate negatively with growth. In this section, we thus review the main arguments for and against the conjecture that concentrating on a few natural resources leads to lower growth.

The notion that the relative price of primary products has a downward trend is known as the Prebisch-Singer Hypothesis. Verification of the Prebisch-Singer hypothesis was long hampered by a (surprising) lack of consistent price data for primary commodities, but Grilli and Yang (1988) constructed a reliable price index for 24 internationally traded commodities between 1900 and 1986. The index has later been updated by the IMF to 1998. The relative price of commodities, calculated as the ratio of this index to manufacturing unit-value index, indeed showed a downward log-linear trend of -0.6 per cent per year, confirming the Prebisch-Singer hypothesis.

However, Cuddington, Ludema and Jayasuriya (2007) showed that the relative price of commodities has a unit root, so that the Prebisch-Singer hypothesis would be supported by a negative drift coefficient in a regression in first differences, not in levels (possibly allowing for a structural break in 1921). But when the regression equation is first-differenced, there is no downward drift anymore. Thus, in their words, "[d]espite 50 years of empirical testing of the Prebisch-Singer hypothesis, a long-run downward trend in real commodity prices remains elusive" (page 134).

The second argument in support of the natural resource curse has to do with the second moment of the price distribution. Easterly and Kraay (2000) regressed income volatility on terms-of-trade volatility and dummy variables marking exporters of primary products. The dummy variables were significant contributors to income volatility over and above the volatility of the terms of trade. Jansen (2004) confirms those results with variables defined in a slightly different way. Combining these results with those of Ramey and Ramey (1995), who showed that income volatility is statistically associated with low growth, suggests that the dominance of primary-product exports is a factor of growth-inhibiting volatility. Similarly, Collier and Gunning (1999), Dehn (2000) and Collier and Dehn (2001) found significant effects of commodity price shocks on growth.

However, these results must be nuanced. Using vector autoregressive (VAR) models, Deaton and Miller (1996) and Raddatz (2007) showed that although external shocks have significant effects on the growth of low-income countries, together they can explain only a small part of the overall variance of their real per-capita GDP. For instance, in Raddatz (2007), changes in commodity prices account for a little more than 4 per cent of it, shocks in foreign aid about 3 per cent, and climatic and humanitarian disasters about 1.5 per cent each, leaving an enormous 89 per cent to be explained. Raddatz's interpretation is that the bulk of the instability is home-grown, through internal conflicts and economic mismanagement. Although this conclusion may be a bit quick (it is nothing more than a conjecture on a residual), together with those of Deaton and Miller, Raddatz's results suggest that the effect of commodity-price volatility on growth suffers from a missing link: although it is a statistically significant causal factor for GDP volatility and slow growth, it has not been shown yet to be quantitatively important.

A third line of arguments runs as follows. Suppose that goods can be arranged along a spectrum of something that we may loosely think of as technological sophistication, quality or productivity. Hausmann, Hwang and Rodrik (2005) proxy this notion by an index they call PRODY. For each good, this index is the weighted average of the income of countries that export that good where the weight corresponds to a Balassa's index of revealed comparative advantage for each good-country pair. The central idea is that a good mainly exported by highly developed countries has higher technology or quality content. They show that countries with a higher average initial PRODY (across their export portfolio) have subsequently stronger growth, suggesting, as they put it in the paper's title, that "what you export matters". As primary products typically figure in the laggards of the PRODY scale, diversifying out of them may accelerate subsequent growth. In addition, according to the so-called

"Dutch disease" hypothesis (see references in Sachs and Warner, 1997; or Arezki and van der Ploeg, 2007) an expanding primary-product sector may well cannibalize other tradable sectors through cost inflation and exchange-rate appreciation. Thus, natural resources might by themselves prevent the needed diversification out of them. Dutch-disease effects can, in turn, be aggravated by unsustainable policies such as excessive borrowing (Manzano and Rigobon, 2001, in fact argue that excessive borrowing is more of a cause for slow growth than natural resources – more on this below).

However, Hausmann, Hwang and Rodrik's empirical exercise must be interpreted with caution before jumping to the conclusion that public policy should aim at structural adjustment away from natural resources. Using a panel of 50 countries between 1967 and 1992, Martin and Mitra (2006) found evidence of strong productivity (TFP) growth in agriculture – in fact, higher in many instances than that of manufacturing. For low-income countries, for instance, average TFP growth per year was 1.44 per cent to 1.80 per cent per year (depending on the production function's functional form) against 0.22 per cent to 0.93 per cent per year in manufacturing. Results were similar for other country groupings. Thus, a high share of agricultural products in GDP and exports is not necessarily by itself (i.e. through a composition effect) a drag on growth.

Other conjectures for why heavy dependence on primary products can inhibit growth emphasize bad governance and conflict. Tornell and Lane (1999), among many others, argued that deficient protection of property rights would lead, through a common-pool problem, to over-depletion of natural resources. Many others, referenced in Arezki and van der Ploeg (2007) and Gylfason (2008) put forward various political-economy mechanisms through which natural resources would interact with institutional deficiencies to hamper growth. In a series of papers, Collier and Hoeffler (2004; 2005) argued that natural resources can also provide a motive for armed rebellions and found, indeed, a statistical association between the importance of natural resources and the probability of internal conflicts.

However, recent research has questioned not just the relevance of the channels through which natural-resource dependence is supposed to inhibit growth, but the very existence of a resource curse. The first blow came from Manzano and Rigobon (2001) who showed that, once excess borrowing during booms is accounted for, the negative correlation between natural-resource dependence and growth disappears. However, this could simply mean that natural-resource dependence breeds bad policies, which is not inconsistent with the natural-resource curse hypothesis.

More recently, Brunnschweiler and Bulte (2007) argued that measuring natural-resource dependence by either the share of primary products in total exports or that of primary-product exports in GDP makes it endogenous to bad policies and institutional breakdowns, and thus unsuitable as a regressor in a growth equation. To see why, assume that mining is an "activity of last resort"; that is, when institutions break down, manufacturing collapses but well-protected mining enclaves remain relatively sheltered. Then, institutional breakdowns will mechanically result in a higher ratio of natural resources in exports (or natural-resource exports in GDP), while being also associated with lower subsequent growth. The correlation between natural-resource dependence and lower subsequent growth will then be spurious and certainly not reflect causation. In order to avoid endogeneity bias, growth should be regressed on (exogenous) natural-resource abundance. The stock of subsoil resources, on which the World Bank collected data for two years (1994 and 2000), provides just one such measure. But then instrumental-variable techniques yield no evidence of a resource curse; on the contrary, natural-resource abundance seems to bear a positive correlation with growth. Similarly, Brunnschweiler and Bulte (2009) find no evidence of a correlation between natural-resource abundance and the probability of civil war.[25] Thus, it is fair to say that at this stage the evidence in favour of a resource curse is far from clear-cut.

### 7.5.3   A "concentration curse"?

Notwithstanding the role of natural resources, it is possible that export concentration per se has a negative effect on subsequent growth. Lederman and Maloney (2007) found a robust negative association between the initial level of a Herfindahl index of export concentration and subsequent growth. Dutt, Mihov and van Zandt (2009) also found that export diversification correlates with subsequent GDP growth, especially if the initial pattern of export specialization is close to that of the United States.

The idea that all countries should strive to imitate the US export pattern as a recipe for growth sounds slightly far-fetched and would probably not be well received as policy advice in developing countries. But there are additional difficulties with the notion of a "curse of concentration". First, if there is one, we still do not know why, as many of the arguments that could support it were questioned in the debate on the natural-resource curse (for example, the transmission of terms-of-trade volatility to income volatility). Second, we already saw in our discussion of Easterly, Reshef and Schwenkenberg (2009) in section7.3 that export concentration is a fact of life. More than that: as they argued, concentration may well be the result of success, when export growth is achieved by what they call a "big hit". Costa Rica is an example. Thanks to a generally favourable investment climate (in addition to the specific tax breaks it extended), it was able to attract Intel in the late 1990s and became one of the world's major exporters of micro-processors. But, as a result, microprocessors now dwarf all the rest – including bananas – in Costa Rica's exports, and concentration has gone up, not down.

### 7.5.4   Export processing zones (EPZs), export diversification and employment

Notwithstanding the caveats above, export diversification is widely seen by governments not just as insurance against the risks associated with excessive concentration,

---

[25] However, Arezki and van der Ploeg (2007) still found evidence of a resource curse for relatively closed economies when instrumenting for trade à la Frankel and Romer (1999) and for institutions à la Acemoglu, Johnson and Robinson (2001). The debate is thus not quite closed.

but also as a way of fostering manufacturing employment growth. One of the main policy tools used for this objective is the creation of export processing zones (EPZs).[26]

EPZs have spread rapidly over the last two decades. The ILO's EPZ database counted 176 of them in 47 countries in 1986; by 2006, there were 3,500 in 130 countries. Overall, they account for 68 million jobs worldwide, a sizeable figure which, however, represents only a very small share of global employment.

Table 7.3 shows that the share of national workforces employed in EPZs is above 1 per cent only in the Asia and the Pacific region (which accounts for 61 million of the 68 million worldwide in EPZ employment), in the Americas, and in the Middle East and North Africa (MENA) region.

Table 7.3:   Direct employment in EPZs, 2007

|  | Direct employment (millions) | % of nat. employment |
|---|---|---|
| Global | 68.441 | 0.21 |
| Asia & Pacific | 61.089 | 2.30 |
| Americas | 3.084 | 1.15 |
| Western Europe | 0.179 | 0.00 |
| CEECs & Central Asia | 1.590 | 0.00 |
| MENA | 1.458 | 1.59 |
| Sub-Saharan Africa | 1.040 | 0.20 |

Source: World Bank (2008), table 15.

Outliers include Mauritius, whose EPZ accounts for 24 per cent of its workforce, the United Arab Emirates (UAE) (25 per cent) and Tunisia (8 per cent). In addition to generating relatively modest increases in employment, EPZs have sometimes been criticized for relying on anti-union regulations and lax labour standards to attract investors (see, for example, ILO, 2003; or ICFTU, 2003). For instance, collective bargaining and freedom of association are restricted in EPZs in the Dominican Republic (a highly successful one in terms of employment), as well as Bangladesh, Egypt, Nigeria, Pakistan, Panama and Sri Lanka. Strikes are banned in the EPZs of Bangladesh, Namibia, Nigeria, Panama, Turkey and Zimbabwe (World Bank, 2008). Other EPZs, however, show a less labour-hostile set up; for instance, those of the Philippines, Singapore, and Trinidad and Tobago have labour representatives on their boards. In terms of wages, fragmentary evidence suggests that they tend to be higher inside EPZs than outside (Kusago and Tzannatos, 1998).

---

[26] Export processing zones (EPZs) are also known under various other names, such as "free zones", "special economic zones", etc. For simplicity, this chapter uses "EPZ" throughout to designate all such zones, irrespective of their precise legal form.

Beyond their record on employment creation and labour relations, Farole (2010) notes that EPZs have a highly uneven record as tools of industrial policy. Few of them have led to substantial skill development, the most notable exception being Malaysia's Penang Skills Development Centre. In Africa, in particular, EPZs do not seem to have played the role of catalyst for foreign investment that authorities hoped for them. In essence, EPZs were viewed by governments – and sometimes donors – as ways of cutting through "impossible reforms". When reforms aimed at the elimination of red tape, high tariff or non-tariff barriers on intermediate products, or predatory taxes seemed impossible, it was hoped that fencing exporters in a sort of good-governance enclave could offer an attractive alternative. But, as Farole notes, EPZs have tended to flourish in countries that were otherwise improving governance and moving forward with reforms. In countries plagued by bad governance and political instability – in particular, in sub-Saharan Africa – EPZs failed to shelter investors and consequently never really took off.

Farole's cross-country regression of EPZ export performance on EPZ characteristics showed little correlation with labour costs (suggesting that "social dumping" was a poor way of luring investors) and even with the size of fiscal incentives; instead, performance seemed to correlate with the EPZs' infrastructure and logistics quality.

The main lesson from Farole's study (whether from the econometrics or from the narrative based on case studies) is that EPZs are no substitute for domestic reforms. Far from being sheltered enclaves, they reflect the general quality of the host country's business environment. Thus, countries whose export portfolios are dominated by a few primary products can hardly count on EPZs alone to generate export diversification. Ironically, the failure of Africa's EPZs to generate sizeable employment in the garment sector prompts Farole to recommend targeting natural-resource based sectors for EPZ development in Africa, thus eliminating the possibility of export diversification.


## 7.6 IMPORT DIVERSIFICATION, EMPLOYMENT AND INDUSTRIAL POLICIES

Trade diversification concerns imports at least as much as exports. With trade liberalization, countries increase their imports at the intensive margin (i.e., an increase in the size of already existing imports) but they also import new goods/varieties. This leads to a higher import diversification, which has important implications for aggregate welfare, productivity, employment and inequality. The next sections focus on these areas.

### 7.6.1 Gains from diversity and "import competition"

Following Krugman's (1979) seminal paper, several theoretical papers include a "love-for-variety" element capturing the gains from trade resulting from the imports of new varieties (i.e. an increase in import diversification). Empirical work assessing these gains remains scarce, however. Broda and Weinstein (2006) do just this, showing that, over the 1972–2001 period, the number of varieties (products × origin countries) imported by the United States has more than trebled. Half of the increase is caused by an increase in the number of products, the other half resulting from an increase in origin countries. The authors find that although consumers have a low elasticity of substitution across similar goods produced in different countries, the welfare gains due to increased product diversity is small. They show that consumers are willing to spend only 2.6 per cent of their income to have access to these extra varieties; put differently, US welfare is 2.6 per cent higher than otherwise due to the import of new varieties. Using Indian data over the 1989–2003 period, Goldberg et al. (2010) also find that lowering input tariffs increases welfare through a rise in the number of imported varieties. Thanks to the new varieties, the price index is on average 4.7 per cent lower per year than it would be otherwise.

A rise in diversification of imports may also lead to productivity gains through "import competition". As a country imports new products from abroad, local producers of close substitute have to improve in order to stay competitive. Productivity increases through this competitive effect but also though rationalization as less productive firms are forced to exit. For example, using Chilean data for 1979–86, Pavcnik (2002) shows that following trade liberalization productivity of plants in the import competing sector increased by 3 to 10 per cent more than in other sectors of the economy. Pavcnik finds evidence of both an increase in productivity within plants and a reallocation of resources from the less to the most efficient producers. Other studies on developing countries include Levinsohn (1993) for Turkey; Harrison (1994) for the Ivory Coast; Tybout and Westbrook (1995) for Mexico; Krishna and Mitra (1998) for India; and Fernandes (2007) for Colombia. All these papers find a positive effect of increased import competition on domestic productivity. Trefler (2004) shows that Canadian plants' labour productivity increased by 14 per cent following the Canada-US free trade agreement. It also provides industry level evidence for those industries that experience the biggest decline in tariffs. Productivity increases by 15 per cent (half of this coming from rationalization) while employment decreases by 12 per cent (5 per cent for manufacturing as a whole). Trefler's paper is one of the few to consider both the impact on productivity and on employment of lower tariffs through more diversified imports. The paper points out the issue of adjustment costs, which encompasses unemployment and displaced workers in the short run.[27] It is worth mentioning that Trefler finds a rise in aggregate welfare.

Another strand of literature focuses on productivity gains from increasing varieties of imported inputs. In such cases, most gain is measured in terms of productivity growth realized through lower input prices, access to higher quality of inputs and access to new technologies embodied in the imported varieties. Early models from Ethier (1982), Markusen (1989) or Grossman and Helpman (1991) provide such evidence. Increased import of input may also impact the labour market as varieties produced abroad may substitute for local labour and/or may require specific labour

---

[27] See the discussion in chapter 6 of this volume.

skills in order to be processed. The next sections provide empirical findings on these features, studying in turn the effect of increased import diversification on productivity, employment and inequalities.

### 7.6.2 Impacts of imported inputs on productivity and employment

As evidenced in Hummels, Ishii and Yi (2001), Yi (2003) or Strauss-Kahn (2004) the share of imported inputs in production has increased drastically over the past 30 years (e.g. Hummels Ishii and Yi find an increase of 40 per cent between 1970 and 1995). Amador and Cabral (2009) show that this phenomenon is not specific to developed countries but also concerns developing countries such as Malaysia, Singapore or China. This recent pattern of trade reflects the increased ability of firms to "slice the value chain" and locate different stages of production in different countries thanks to reduced transportation and communication costs. Micro-level studies, such as the one listed below, also provide evidence of such an increase in the use of imported intermediate goods and therefore of an increased diversification in imported inputs. For example, Goldberg et al. (2008) find that imported inputs increased by 227 per cent from 1987 to 2000 in India while imported final goods rose by 90 per cent over the period. How does this increased diversification impact the domestic economy? Does it entail technological transfer and productivity growth? What is its impact on employment and exports? These are the questions we now address.

Halpern, Koren and Szeidl (2009) suggest two mechanisms by which intermediate goods affect productivity: access to higher quality and better complementarity of inputs. The complementarity channel encompasses elements of gains from variety and of learning spillovers between foreign and domestic goods. Variety gains come from imperfect substitution across goods, as in the love-of-variety setting of Krugman (1979) and Ethier (1982) and as evidenced by Broda and Weinstein (2006). Keller (2004) states that technological spillovers occur as producers of final goods learn from the technology embodied in the intermediate goods through careful study of the imported product (the blueprint).

Empirical studies analysing the effect of an increase in imported inputs on productivity started in the early 1990s and are still ongoing with new econometric techniques and firm-level data. The early works of Coe and Helpman (1995) and Coe, Helpman and Hoffmaister (1997) find that foreign knowledge embodied in imported inputs from countries with larger R&D stocks has a positive effect on aggregate total factor productivity. Keller (2002) shows that trade in differentiated intermediate goods is a significant channel of technology diffusion. He finds that about 20 per cent of the productivity of a domestic industry can be attributed to foreign R&D, accessed through imports of intermediate goods. Using plant-level data for Indonesia for 1991 to 2001, Amiti and Konings (2007) disentangle the impact of a fall in tariff on output from a fall in tariff on input. They find that a decrease in input tariffs of 10 percentage points increases productivity by 12 per cent in importing firms, whereas non-importing firms benefit by only 3 per cent, suggesting productivity gains through technology effects embodied in the imported inputs rather than through import price effects.[28] Kasahara, and Rodrigue (2008) use Chilean manufacturing plant data from 1979 to 1996 and find a positive and immediate impact of increased use of imported inputs on importers' productivity. They also provide some evidence of learning by importing (i.e. past imports positively impacting current productivity). Muendler (2004), however, does not find a substantial impact of increased use of imported inputs on productivity for Brazil in the early 1990s. Loof and Anderson (2008) use a database of Swedish manufacturing firms over an eight-year period (1997-2004) and find that the distribution of imports across different origin countries matters (i.e. productivity is increasing in the G7-fraction of total import). Bas and Strauss-Kahn (2011) distinguish varieties imported from developed and developing countries and find a similar result. By and large, empirical studies thus evidence that diversification of imported inputs increases the productivity of domestic firms.

Although productivity gains may occur through different channels: increased quality and/or complementarity, very few papers to date analyse the relative contribution of these mechanisms. Halpern, Koren and Szeidl (2009) stands as an exception. The authors use a panel of Hungarian firms from 1992 to 2003 to examine the quality and variety channel (imported inputs are assumed to be imperfect substitutes for domestic inputs), through which imports can affect firm productivity.[29] They find that imports lead to significant productivity gains, of which two-thirds are attributed to the complementarity argument and the remainder to the quality argument. Obviously, these two mechanisms have different implications on the economy. When quality is important, an increase in imported inputs entails large import substitution, hurting domestic intermediate goods producers and thereby employment. By contrast, when complementarities matter, an increase in imported inputs affects the demand for domestic goods much less, because they must be combined with foreign goods to maximize output. Thus, employment is barely impacted.

Diversification in imports of intermediate goods may also affect the number of goods produced domestically (diversification in production) and exported (diversification in exports). Kasahara and Lapham (2006) extend the Melitz model to incorporate imported intermediate goods. In their model, productivity gains from importing intermediates (through the increasing returns to variety in production) may allow some importers to start exporting. Importantly, because imports and exports are complementary, import protection acts as export destruction. Goldberg et al. (2010) show that imports of new varieties of inputs lead to a substantial increase in the number of domestic varieties produced. The paper provides evidence that the growth in product scope results from the access to new varieties of imported inputs rather than the decrease in the import price index for intermediate products. Finally, Bas and Strauss-Kahn (2011) provide robust evidence of the role of an increase in

---

[28] Interestingly, the effect of a decrease in input tariffs is much larger (more than twice as large) than the one found with a decrease in output tariffs.

[29] Their model includes a term related to the number of intermediate imported goods in the production function, which reflects the complementarity channel.

imported intermediate inputs on the number of varieties exported. The effect occurs through an increase in firms' TFP.

Empirical works to date thus confirm that an increase in imported input diversification raises productivity. The increase in productivity results from better complementarity of imported inputs with domestic varieties and learning effects of foreign technology. The increased diversification in imported inputs also entails an increase in the number of domestic varieties produced and exported. It therefore impacts greatly the economic activity. Concerning the effect of increased diversification on employment, the evidence is scarce. As far as we know, no study analyses the impact of imported input diversification on the labour market. Productivity in most studies is measured as total factor productivity and is therefore X-neutral (no impact on employment through variation of the input mix).

More generally, one may wonder how productivity gains affect employment. Unfortunately, and as is common in the literature, there is no clear-cut answer to this question. The seminal work by Gali (1999) finds that productivity gains resulting from positive technology shocks reduced hours worked for the United States and several other G7 countries, except for Japan. While these findings were reinforced by consecutive studies (for example, Gali, 2004; Basu, Fernald and Kimball, 2006; or Francis and Ramey, 2005), other studies have challenged these views, primarily on methodological grounds, finding positive correlations of hours worked with technology shocks. These studies include Christiano, Eichenbaum and Vigfusson (2003), Uhlig (2004) and Chang and Hong (2006). In a nutshell, and apart from the different specifications used in the papers, the impact on employment seems to depend on whether labour productivity or TFP is considered, and on the time lag (i.e. short-run and long-run effects differ). It also varies widely across industries (see Chang and Hong, 2006). In the long run the positive effect of productivity gains on employment seems predominant (for example, this result is also found in the pro-contractionary paper of Basu, Fernald and Kimball, 2006). Concerning the measure of productivity, a negative correlation between increased labour productivity and hours worked is common to most studies. As explained in Chang and Hong (2006), labour productivity reflects change in input mix as well as improved efficiency. Thus, changes in input prices affecting the material-labour ratio increase labour productivity, whereas TFP is unchanged. How can we use this information in our context? As seen above, the increased diversification of imports affects productivity mostly through the channels of better complementarity and learning spillovers. The channel of decreased intermediate input prices leading to increased labour productivity, and consequently decreased employment, is far less important.

## 7.6.3 Productivity gains and absorptive capacities

The effect of an increase in imported input diversity on productivity is likely to depend on the level of the absorptive capacities of the importing country. Human capital and spending in R&D stand out as the main absorptive capacities in term of adoption and integration of foreign technologies into domestic production process (see Keller, 2004; or Eaton and Kortum, 1996, for early work on the topic). Using a database of 22 manufacturing industries in 17 countries for the 1973–2002 period, Acharya and Keller (2007) find that imports are a major channel of international technology transfer. They show that some countries benefit more from foreign technology than others and assert that this suggests an important difference in absorptive capacity. Similarly, Serti and Tomasi (2008) find that importers sourcing from developed countries are more capital-intensive and skill-intensive than firms buying only from developing countries. This may reflect the importance of absorptive capacities, or may be a consequence of "learning by importing".

One important paper on the topic is Augier, Cadot and Dovis (2009). The paper not only evaluates the impact of increased imports on firms' productivity, but it also explores the importance of firms' absorptive capacity in terms of their ability to capture technologies embodied in foreign imports. Importantly, the paper considers imported inputs but also imports in capital equipment, which represents another channel through which technology may spill. Augier, Cadot and Dovis (2009) use a panel of Spanish firms from 1991 to 2002, which includes information on the proportion of skilled labour per firm. As mentioned above, such variables may proxy for absorptive capacities. Firms with a share of skilled labour that is 10 per cent above the average experience a productivity gain of 9 percentage points in the first two years after they start importing and of 7 percentage points in the following year. As these results are much higher than those found with lower-skilled labour-intensive firms, firms' heterogeneity in absorptive capacity seems to affect greatly the contribution of imported input and equipment in increasing productivity.

Further research exploring the role of absorptive capacity in capturing technology embodied in new imported varieties is needed (looking, for example, at the role of R&D spending, the quality of infrastructures or institutions). The evidence so far, however, points out the importance of country/industry absorptive capacities in capturing the positive impact of imported input diversification on productivity.

## 7.6.4 Offshoring and wages

Rising intermediate imports may impact income inequality between skilled and unskilled workers if it reflects a substitution of domestic labour by foreign labour for cost purposes. A first wave of studies considering this issue focused on manufacturing firms. It included: Feenstra and Hanson (1996, 1999) for the United States; Egger and Egger (2003) for Austria; Hijzen, Görg and Hine (2005) for the United Kingdom; or Strauss-Kahn (2004) for France. These papers investigate the impact of rising intermediate imports on the relative demand for skilled versus unskilled workers, and the skill premium. All evidenced that international sourcing had a large and significant impact on relative wages and/or employment, the growth in imported inputs accounting for 11 per cent to 30 per cent of the observed increase in the skill premium.

More recent literature has looked at service offshoring, a new feature of international trade. Amiti and Wei (2006) show that imported service inputs from United States manufacturing firms have grown at an annual rate of 6 per cent over the period

1992–2000, but they find little impact on employment. This might be because: (i) their measure of employment is too broad, as sourcing in services may affect the less-skilled workers among the skilled; and (ii) in countries with relatively flexible labour markets, such as the United States or United Kingdom, the bulk of the adjustment is on wages rather than employment. Indeed, using household-level panel data combined with industry-level data on imported services inputs over 1992–2004, Geishecker and Gorg (2008) found a positive impact of service outsourcing on the skill premium.

How does the increase in imported inputs by developed countries affect inequalities in the developing world? Traditional Heckscher-Ohlin trade theory and its corollary (the Stolper-Samuelson theorem) posits that developed countries import goods that are relatively intensive in factors they do not have abundantly (i.e. imports are relatively unskilled-labour intensive). This should benefit unskilled workers in the exporting developing country relative to skilled workers. Thus, inequalities in developing countries should decrease. However, most of the empirical evidence goes the other way (see, for example, Arbache, Dickerson and Green, 2004, for Brazil; Attanasio, Goldberg and Pavcnik, 2004, for Colombia; Berman and Machin, 2000, for 14 low- and middle-income countries; Gorg and Strobl, 2002, for Ghana; Hanson and Harrison, 1999, for Mexico; or Robbins and Gindling, 1999, for Costa Rica). Several channels have been proposed to explain the increased wage gap in developing countries. Feenstra and Hanson (1996; 1997), as well as Zhu and Trefler (2005), explain that products characterized as unskilled-labour intensive by developed countries may appear skilled-labour intensive from a developing country's perspective, hence increasing the relative demand for skilled labour. Similarly, Xu (2003) shows that, by expanding a developing country's export set, trade can raise wage inequality. Other studies (for example, Yeaple, 2005; or Verhoogen, 2008) argue that exporting to developed countries entails quality upgrading and adoption of new technologies that could explain the increased demand in skilled labour and increased wage inequality in developing countries. Thus, by and large, the increased diversification in imported inputs by developed countries entails an increase in inequality between skilled and unskilled workers in the developing world. One comment and a policy recommendation still have to be made. First, the increased inequality in developing countries can also be widely attributed to skill-biased technological change (for example, personal computers, automated assembly lines, and so on) that touches developed as well as developing countries (although mainly through international transfer of technology for the latter) and allows important productivity gains. In terms of policy, investment in education seems primordial in order to supply sufficient skilled labour and thereby reduce the wage gap between skilled and unskilled workers.

## 7.7    CONCLUSIONS

To sum up: poor countries have, on average, undiversified exports. As they grow, they diversify, then re-concentrate at higher income levels. The extensive margin (new products) dominates the action in terms of diversification, but the intensive margin (higher volumes) dominates the action in terms of export growth. Thus, if governments are ultimately interested in export (and employment) growth, the intensive margin appears to be a better bet. The reason for this is that there is enormous churning, so that many of today's new products are tomorrow's failed products.

The direction of causation between income and diversification is unclear, perhaps because of the observation just outlined – namely, that diversification is driven by the extensive margin, whereas growth is driven by the intensive margin. Even seemingly well-established "stylized facts" linking concentration to growth, such as the natural-resource curse (a negative correlation between the importance of natural resources in a country's wealth and its subsequent growth), do not appear very robust. Thus, diversification and growth are not equivalent objectives.

In spite of the many open questions, a few remarks emerge from the literature as it stands today. First, we find that trade liberalization, which might have been expected to lead to concentration on a country's comparative-advantage sectors, statistically correlates with export diversification at both the intensive and extensive margins.

As for targeted industrial policy, as Easterly, Resheff and Schwenkenberg (2009) show, the probability of a big hit decreases exponentially with its size, making "picking winners" a lottery. What industrial planner would have dreamt of advising the Egyptian Government to target the Italian market for "ceramic bathroom kitchen sanitary items, not porcelain"? We know very little about the channels by which producers of that product became informed of the market opportunities.

Who is best positioned, of the market or government, to identify potential "big hits"? One traditional argument in favour of industrial policy is that the government is better placed than the market to overcome market failures (for example, in the search for information). But the market compensates for this by its ability to generate an endless stream of gamblers, each trying his or her luck in a particular niche. Besedes and Prusa's work (see, for example, Besedes and Prusa (forthcoming) and references therein) shows the importance of this trial-and-error process by the very low survival rate of "export spells" (by which they mean periods of uninterrupted exports in one product between two countries).

Recent work on African exports using firm-level data (Cadot et al. 2011) provides empirical support to the idea that there are agglomeration externalities in export. This suggests that export promotion by the government may be useful to overcome collective-action problems. Indeed, Volpe and Carballo (2008; 2010) find that export promotion has a statistically traceable effect on the export performance of targeted firms. Thus, the new firm-level evidence seems rather supportive of the idea that government intervention can help – although with three caveats. First, the evidence suggests that export promotion works better at the intensive margin than at the extensive one. That is, the rate of growth of the exports of "assisted" firms is higher than that of non-assisted firms (although by a small margin), but the rate at which new products are introduced is unaffected. This does not square well with the conjecture that government intervention can mitigate market failures in "export entrepreneurship". Second, the intervention studied by Volpe and Carballo is more

291

like a "little push" than a big one and the idea that, in export promotion, small is beautiful is also supported by the cross-country evidence in Lederman, Olarreaga and Payton (2010).

Third, the export-diversification literature has focused largely on what is produced rather than on how it is produced. Yet Acemoglu and Zilibotti (2000) developed a model highlighting differences in production methods, themselves driven by differences in the availability of skilled labour. Their work highlights that technologies developed in the North are typically tailored to the needs of a skilled workforce and therefore inappropriate for skill-scarce countries. If countries do not have the capabilities to master the tacit knowledge needed to produce sophisticated goods, no industrial policy will make them successful exporters. The most sensible policies are then supply-side ones, in particular in education (think, for instance, of India's gradual build-up of a world-class network of technology institutes).

As a last remark, although one aim of the export-diversification literature is, ultimately, to generate useful policy advice for developing countries, it sweeps under the carpet an important historical regularity. Practically all latecomers in the industrial revolution, in particular the big ones – France in the early nineteenth century, Japan during the Meiji era, Germany at the turn of the twentieth century, China today, to name but a few – have been aggressive imitators of the technology of more advanced economic powers. All those countries expanded their basket of exports by plundering technology, sometimes (often) with government assistance and with little regard for intellectual property. This process was badly received in advanced countries, but it was a major driver of the diffusion of the Industrial Revolution. We do not know much about the policies that were put in place in the catching-up countries, and the literature has been largely silent on this. No wonder: intellectual-property enforcement is now widely taken as one of the basic good-governance prerequisites for development, and encroachments on the intellectual property of advanced countries are now fought more vigorously than ever before. But for countries that were yesterday's imitators, this might well be a modern version of Friedrich List's famous expression, "kicking away the ladder".

# REFERENCES

Acemoglu, D.; Zilibotti, F. 2000. "Technology differences", mimeo.

Acharya, R.; Keller, W. 2007. "Technology transfer through imports", *NBER Working Paper* No. 13086.

Alfaro, L.; Chen, M. 2009. "The global agglomeration of multinational firms", *NBER Working Paper* No. 15576.

Amador, J.; Cabral, S. 2009. "Vertical specialization across the world: A relative measure", in *North American Journal of Economics and Finance*, Vol. 20, No. 3, pp. 267-280, Dec.

Amiti, M.; Konings, J. 2007. "Trade liberalization, intermediate inputs and productivity: Evidence from Indonesia", in *American Economic Review*, Vol. 97, No. 5, pp. 1611-1638.

Amiti, M.; Wei, S.J. 2006. "Service offshoring, productivity and employment: Evidence from the US", *CEPR Discussion Papers* No. 5475.

Amurgo-Pacheco, A. 2006. "Preferential trade liberalization and the range of exported products: The case of the Euro-Mediterranean FTA", *HEI Working Paper* No. 18/2006.

Amurgo-Pacheco, A.; Pierola, M.D. 2008. "Patterns of export diversification in developing countries: Intensive and extensive margins", *World Bank Policy Research Working Paper* No. 4473.

Arbache, J.; Dickerson, A.; Green, F. 2004. "Trade liberalization and wages in developing countries", in *The Economic Journal*, Vol. 114, pp. 93-96.

Arezki, R.; van der Ploeg, F. 2007. "Can the natural resource curse be turned into a blessing? The role of trade policies and institutions", *IMF Working Paper* No. 07/55.

Attanasio, O.; Goldberg, P.K.; Pavcnik, N. 2004. "Trade reforms and wage inequality in Colombia", in *Journal of Development Economics*, Vol. 74, pp. 331-366.

Augier, P.; Cadot, O.; Dovis, M. 2009. "Imports and TFP at the firm level: The role of absorptive capacity", *CEPR Working Paper* No. 7218.

Auty, R. 2000. "How natural resources affect economic development", in *Development Policy Review*, Vol. 18, No. 4, pp. 347-364.

Auty, R. 2001. "The political economy of resource-driven growth", in *European Economic Review*, Vol. 45, No. 4-6, pp. 839-846.

Aw, B.Y.; Hwang, A.R. 1995. "Productivity and the export market: A firm-level analysis", in *Journal of Development Economics*, No. 47, pp. 313-332.

Barro, R.; Lee, J.W. 2010. "A new data set of educational attainment in the world, 1950–2010", *NBER Working Paper* No. 15902.

Bas, M; Strauss-Kahn, V. 2011. "Does importing more inputs raise exports? Firm-level evidence from France", CEPII Working Paper, No. 2011-15, June.

Basu, S.; Fernald, J.; Kimball, M. 2006. "Are technology improvements contractionary?", in *American Economic Review*, Vol. 96, No. 5, pp. 1418-1448, Dec.

Berman, E.; Machin, S. 2000. "Skill-biased technological transfer around the world", in *Oxford Review of Economic Policy*, Vol. 16, No. 3, pp. 12-22.

Bernard, A.B.; Jensen, J.B. 1999. "Exceptional exporter performance: cause, effect, or both?", in *Journal of International Economics*, Vol. 47, No. 1, pp. 1-25.

Bernard, A.B.; Jensen, J.B.; Schott, P.K. 2006. "Survival of the best fit: Exposure to low-wage countries and the (uneven) growth of U.S. manufacturing plants", in *Journal of International Economics*, Vol. 68, No. 1, pp. 219-237.

Bernard, A.B.; Redding, S.J.; Schott, P.K. 2007. "Comparative advantage and heterogeneous firms", in *Review of Economic Studies*, Vol. 74, No. 1, pp. 31-66, Jan.

Besedes, T.; Prusa, T.J. 2006. "Ins, outs, and the duration of trade", in *Canadian Journal of Economics*, Vol. 39, No. 1, pp. 266-295, Feb.

Besedes, T.; Prusa, T.J. Forthcoming. "The role of extensive and intensive margins and export growth", in *Journal of Development Economics*.

Brenton, P.; Newfarmer, R. 2007. "Watching more than the Discovery channel: Export cycles and diversification in development", *World Bank Policy Research Working Paper* No. 4302 (World Bank).

Broda, C.; Greenfield, J.; Weinstein, D.E. 2006. "From groundnuts to globalization: A structural estimate of trade and growth", *NBER Working Paper* No. 12512.

Broda, C.; Weinstein, D.E. 2006. "Globalization and the gains from variety", in *Quarterly Journal of Economics*, Vol. 121, No. 2, pp. 541-585, May.

Brunnschweiler, C.N.; Bulte, E.H. 2007. "The resource curse revisited and revised: A tale of paradoxes and red herrings", in *Journal of Environmental Economics and Management*, Vol. 55, No. 3, pp. 248-264, May.

Brunnschweiler, C.N.; Bulte, E.H. 2009. "Natural resources and violent conflict: Resource abundance, dependence and the onset of civil wars", in *Oxford Economic Papers*, Vol. 61, No. 4, pp. 651-674, Oct.

Cadot, O.; Carrère, C.; Strauss-Kahn, V. 2011 "Export diversification: What's behind the hump?", in *The Review of Economics and Statistics*, Vol. 93, No. 2, pp. 590-605, May.

Cadot, O.; Carrère, C.; Kukenova, M.; Strauss-Kahn, V. 2010. "OECD imports: Diversification and quality search", *World Bank Policy Research Working Paper* No. 5285.

Cadot, O.; Iacovone, L.; Pierola, M.D.; Rauch, F. 2011. "Success and failure of African exporters", mimeo (World Bank).

Canning, D.; 1998. "A database of world stocks of infrastructure: 1950-1995", in *World Bank Economic Review*, Vol. 12, pp. 529-548.

Carrère, C.; de Melo, J.; Wilson, J. 2011. "The distance effect and the regionalization of the trade of low-income countries", *Etudes et Documents* No 2009-8 (Université d'Auvergne).

Chaney, T. 2008. "Distorted Gravity: The intensive and extensive margins of international trade", in *American Economic Review*, Vol. 98, No. 4, pp. 1707-1721.

Chang, Y.; Hong, J.H. 2006. "Do technological improvements in the manufacturing sector raise or lower employment?", in *American Economic Review*, Vol. 96, No. 1, pp. 352-368.

Cimoli, M.; Dosi, G.; Stiglitz, J.E. 2009. Industrial policy and development: The political economy of capabilities accumulation (Oxford University Press).

Clerides, S.K.; Lach, S.; Tybout, J.R. 1998. "Is learning by exporting important? Micro-dynamic evidence from Colombia, Mexico, And Morocco", in *The Quarterly Journal of Economics*, Vol. 113, No. 3, pp. 903-947.

Coe, D.; Helpman, E. 1995. "International R&D spillovers", in *European Economic Review*, Vol. 39, No. 5, pp. 859-887.

Coe, D.; Helpman, E.; Hoffmaister, W. 1997. "North-south R&D spillovers", in *Economic Journal*, Vol. 107, pp. 134-149, Jan.

Collier, P.; Gunning, J. 1999. "Trade shocks in developing countries", in P. Collier et al. (eds): *Africa, Vol. 1*.

Collier, P.; Dehn, J. 2001. "Aid, shocks, and growth", *World Bank Policy Research Working Paper* No. 2688.

Collier, P.; Hoeffler, A. 2004. "Greed and grievance in civil war", in *Oxford Economic Papers*, Vol. 56, No. 4, pp. 563-595.

Collier, P.; Hoeffler, A. 2005. "Resource rents, governance, and conflict", in *Journal of Conflict Resolution*, Vol. 49, No. 4, pp. 625-633.

Christiano, L.J.; Eichenbaum, M.; Vigfusson R. 2003. "What happens after a technology shock?", *NBER Working Paper* No. 9819.

Cuddington, J.T.; Ludema R.; Jayasuriya, S.A. 2007. "Prebisch-Singer redux", in *Natural resources: Neither curse nor destiny*, pp. 103-140 (Stanford University Press and World Bank).

Daron, A.; Johnson, S.; Robinson, J.A. 2001. "The colonial origins of comparative development: An empirical investigation", in *American Economic Review*, Vol. 91, No. 5, pp. 1369-1401, Dec.

Deaton, A.; Miller, R. 1996. "International commodity prices, macroeconomic performance and politics in Sub-Saharan Africa", in *Journal of African Economies*, Vol. 5, No. 3, pp. 99-191.

Dehn, J. 2000. "The effects on growth of commodity price uncertainty and shocks", *World Bank Policy Research Working Paper* No. 2455.

Demidova, S.; Kee, H.L.; Krishna, K. 2006. "Do trade policy differences induce sorting? Theory and evidence from Bangladeshi apparel exporters", *NBER Working Paper* No. 12725.

Dutt, P.; Mihov, I.; Van Zandt, T. 2009. "Trade diversification and economic development", mimeo (INSEAD).

Easterly, W.; Kraay, A. 2000. "Small states, small problems? Income, growth, and volatility in small states", in *World Development*, Vol. 28, No. 11, pp. 2013-2027.

Easterly, W.; Resheff, A.; Schwenkenberg, J.M. 2009. "The power of exports", *World Bank Policy Research Working Paper* No. 5081.

Eaton, J.; Kortum, S. 1996. "Trade in ideas patenting and productivity in the OECD", in *Journal of International Economics*, Vol. 40, No. 3-4, pp. 251-278.

Eaton, J.; Kortum, S.; Kramarz, F. 2004. "Dissecting trade: Firms, industries, and export destinations", in *American Economic Review*, Vol. 94, pp. 150-154, May.

Eaton, J.; Kortum, S.; Kramarz, F. 2007. "An anatomy of international trade: Evidence from French firms", *NBER Working Paper* No. 14610.

Egger, H., Egger, P. 2003. "Outsourcing and skill-specific employment in a small country: Austria after the fall of the iron curtain", in *Oxford Economic Papers*, Vol. 55, No. 4, pp. 625-643.

Ethier, W. 1982. "National and international returns to scale in the modern theory of international trade", in *American Economic Review*, Vol. 72, No. 3, pp. 389-405.

Evenett, S.J.; Venables, A.J. 2002. "Export growth in developing countries: Market entry and bilateral trade flows", mimeo (University of Bern).

Farole, T. 2010. Special economic zones in Africa: Comparing performance and learning from global experience (World Bank).

Feenstra, R.C.; Hanson, G.H. 1996. "Globalization, outsourcing, and wage inequality", in *American Economic Review*, Vol. 86, No. 2, pp. 240-245.

Feenstra, R.C.; Hanson, G.H. 1997. "Foreign direct investment and relative wages: Evidence from Mexico's Maquiladoras", in *Journal of International Economics*, Vol. 42, No. 3-4, pp. 371-394.

Feenstra, R.C.; Hanson, G.H. 1999. "The impact of outsourcing and high-technology capital on wages: Estimates for the United States, 1979-1990", in *The Quarterly Journal of Economics*, Vol. 114, No. 3, pp. 907-941.

Feenstra, R.C.; Kee, H.L. 2007. "Trade liberalisation and export variety: A comparison of Mexico and China", in *World Economy*, Vol. 30, No. 1, pp. 5-21.

Feenstra, R.C.; Kee, H.L. 2008. "Export variety and country productivity: Estimating the monopolistic competition model with endogenous productivity", in *Journal of International Economics*, Vol. 74, No. 2, pp. 500-518.

Fernandes, A. 2007. "Trade policy, trade volumes and plant-level productivity in Columbian manufacturing industries", in *Journal of International Economics*, Vol. 71, No. 1, pp. 52-71, March.

Francis, N.; Ramey, V. 2005. "Is the technology-driven real business cycle hypothesis dead? Shocks and aggregate fluctuations revised", in *Journal of Monetary Economics*, Vol. 52, No. 8, pp. 1379-1399, Nov.

Frankel, J.A.; Romer D.H. 1999. "Does Trade Cause Growth?", in *American Economic Review*, Vol. 89, No. 3, pp. 379-399, June.

Gali, J. 1999. "Technology, employment and the business cycle: Do technology shocks explain aggregate fluctuations?", in *The American Economic Review*, Vol. 89, No. 1, pp. 249-271.

Gali, J. 2004. "On the role of technology shocks as a source of business cycles: Some new evidence", in *Journal of the European Economic Association*, Vol. 2, No. 2-3, pp. 372-380.

Gamberoni, E. 2007. "Do unilateral trade preferences help export diversification? An investigation of the impact of European unilateral trade preferences on the extensive and intensive margin of trade", *IHEID Working Paper* No. 17/2007.

Geishecker, I.; Gorg, H. 2008. "Services offshoring and wages: Evidence from micro data", *Working Paper* No. 1434 (Kiel Institute for the World Economy).

Goldberg, P.K.; Khandelwal, A.; Pavcnik, N.; Topalova, P. 2010. "Imported intermediate inputs and domestic product growth: Evidence from India", *in Quarterly Journal of Economics*, Vol. 125, No. 4, pp. 1727–1767.

Gollin, D.; Rogerson, R. 2010. "Agriculture, roads, and economic development in Uganda", *NBER Working Paper* No. 15863.

Gorg, H.; Strobl, E.A. 2002. "Relative wages, openness and skilled-biased technological change", *IZA Discussion Papers* No. 596 (Institute for the Study of Labor).

Gourdon, J. et al. 2011. "Pushing firms to spread themselves too thin? An evaluation of Tunisia's export promotion program", mimeo (World Bank).

Grilli, E.R.; Yang, M.C. 1988. "Primary commodity prices, manufactured goods prices, and the terms of trade of developing countries: What the long run shows", in *World Bank Economic Review*, Vol. 2, No. 1, pp. 1-47.

Grossman, G.M.; Helpman, E. 1991. *Innovation and growth in the global economy* (Cambridge, MIT Press).

Gylfason, T. 2004. "Natural resources and economic growth: From dependence to diversification", *CEPR Discussion Paper* No. 4804.

Gylfason, T. 2008. "Development and growth in mineral-rich countries", *CEPR Discussion Paper* No. 7031.

Haddad, M. 1993. "How trade liberalization affected productivity in Morocco", *World Bank Policy Research Working Paper* No. 1096.

Hallak, J.C.; Sivadasan, J. 2009. "Firms' exporting behavior under quality constraints", *NBER Working Paper* No. 14928.

Halpern, L.; Koren, M.; Szeidl A. 2009. "Imported inputs and productivity", *CeFiG Working Paper* (Central European University).

Hansen, J.; Jensen, D.; Madsen, E. 2003. "The establishment of the Danish windmill industry – Was it worthwhile?", in *Review of World Economics*, Vol. 139, No. 2, pp. 324-347, June.

Hanson, G.; Harisson, A.V.E. 1999. "Trade and wage inequality in Mexico", in *Industrial and Labour Relations Review*, Vol. 52, No. 2, pp. 271-288.

Harrison, A.E. 1994. "Productivity, imperfect competition and trade reform: Theory and evidence", in *Journal of International Economics*, Vol. 36, No. 1-2, pp. 53-73.

Harrison, A.E.; Rodríguez-Clare, A. 2010. "Trade, foreign investment, and industrial policy for developing countries", in D. Rodrik; M. Rosenzweig (eds): *Handbook of development Economics*, Vol. 5, pp. 4039-4214.

Hausmann, R.; Rodrik, D. 2003. "Economic development as self-discovery", in *Journal of Development Economics*, Vol. 72, No. 2, pp. 603-633.

Hausmann, R.; Hwang, J.; Rodrik D. 2005. "What you export matters", *NBER Working Paper* No. 11905.

Hausmann, R.; Rodrik, D. 2006. "Doomed to choose: Industrial policy as a predicament", mimeo.

Helpman, E.; Melitz, M.J.; Yeaple, S.R. 2004. "Export versus FDI with heterogeneous firms", in *American Economic Review*, Vol. 94, No. 1, pp. 300-16, Mar.

Hijzen, A.; Gorg, H.; Hine, R.C. 2005. "International outsourcing and the skill structure of labour demand in the United Kingdom", in *The Economic Journal*, Vol. 115, No. 506, pp. 860-878.

Hummels, D.; Ishii, J.; Yi, K.M. 2001. "The nature and growth of vertical specialization in world trade", in *Journal of International Economics*, Vol. 54(1), No. 1, pp. 75-96.

Hummels, D.; Klenow, P.J. 2005. "The variety and quality of a nation's exports", in *American Economic Review*, Vol. 95, No. 3, pp. 704-723, June.

Imbs, J.; Wacziarg, R. 2003. "Stages of diversification", in *American Economic Review*, Vol. 93, No. 1, pp. 63-86.

International Confederation of Free Trade Unions (ICFTU). 2003. Export processing zones – Symbols of exploitation and a development dead-end.

ILO. 2003. ILO database on export processing zones (Geneva).

Jansen, M. 2004. "Income volatility in small and developing countries: Export concentration matters", *WTO Discussion Paper* No. 3.

Johnson, R.C. 2008. "Trade and prices with heterogeneous firms", mimeo (UC Berkeley).

Kasahara, H.; Lapham, B. 2006. "Import protection as export destruction", *Working Papers* No. 1064 (Department of Economics, Queen's University).

Kasahara, H.; Rodrigue, J. 2008. "Does the use of imported intermediates increase productivity? Plant-level evidence", in *Journal of Development Economics*, Vol. 87, No. 1, pp. 106-118.

Kehoe, T.J.; Ruhl, K.J. 2009. "How important is the new goods margin in international trade", *Research Department Staff Report* No. 324 (Federal Reserve Bank of Minneapolis).

Keller, W. 2002. "Geographic localization of international technology diffusion", in *The American Economic Review*, Vol. 92, No. 1, pp. 120-142, Mar.

Keller, W. 2004. "International technology diffusion", in *Journal of Economic Literature*, Vol. 42, No. 3, pp. 752-782.

Klinger, B.; Lederman, D. 2006. "Diversification, innovation, and imitation inside the global technology frontier", *World Bank Policy Research Working Paper* No. 3872.

Koren, M.; Tenreyro, S. 2007. "Volatility and development", in *Quarterly Journal of Economics*, Vol. 122, No. 1, pp. 243-287, Feb.

Krishna, P.; Mitra, D. 1998. "Trade liberalization, market discipline and productivity growth: New evidence from India", in *Journal of Development Economics*, Vol. 56, No. 2, pp. 447-462, Aug.

Krugman, P.R. 1979. "Increasing returns, monopolistic competition, and international trade", in *Journal of International Economics*, Vol. 9, No. 4, pp. 469-479, Nov.

Krugman, P.R. 1980. "Scale economies, product differentiation, and the pattern of trade", in *The American Economic Review*, Vol. 70, No. 5, pp. 950-959, Dec.

Kugler, M.; Verhoogen, E.A. 2008. "Product quality at the plant level: Plant size, exports, output prices and input prices in Columbia", *Columbia University Discussion Papers* No. 0708-12.

Kusago, T.; Tzannatos, Z. 1998. "Export processing zones: A review in need of update", *World Bank Social Protection Discussion Papers* No. 9802.

Lederman, D.; Olarreaga, M.; Payton, L. 2006. "Export promotion agencies: What works and what doesn't", *World Bank Policy Research Working Paper* No. 4044.

Lederman, D.; Olarreaga, M.; Payton, L. 2009. "Export-promotion agencies revisited", *World Bank Policy Research Working Paper* No. 5125.

Lederman, D.; Maloney, W.F. 2007. "Trade structure and growth", in D. Lederman; W.F. Maloney (eds): *Natural resources: Neither curse nor destiny* (World Bank).

Levinsohn, J. 1993. "Testing the imports-as-market-discipline hypothesis", in *Journal of International Economics*, Vol. 35, No. 1-2, pp. 1-22.

Loof, H.; Anderson, M. 2008. "Imports, productivity and the origin markets – The role of knowledge-intensive economies", *CESIS Electronic Working Paper* No. 146 (Royal Institute of Technology).

Manzano, O.; Rigobon, R. 2001. "Resource curse or debt overhang?", *NBER Working Paper* No. 8390.

Markusen, J.R. 1989. "Trade in producer services and in other specialized intermediate inputs", in *The American Economic Review*, Vol. 79, No. 1, pp. 85-95, Mar.

Marshall, M.G.; Jaggers, K. 2002. Polity IV project: Political regime characteristics and transitions, 1800-2002: Dataset users' manual (University of Maryland).

Martin, W.; Mitra, D. 2006. "Productivity growth and convergence in agriculture and manufacturing", mimeo (World Bank).

Melitz, M.J. 2003. "The impact of trade on intra-industry reallocations and aggregate industry productivity", in *Econometrica*, Vol. 71, No. 6, pp. 1695-1725, Nov.

Muendler, M. 2004. "Trade, technology, and productivity: A study of Brazilian manufactures, 1986-1998", *Economics Working Paper* No. 28149 (University of California at San Diego).

Parteka, A.; Tamberi, M. 2008. "Determinants of export diversification: An empirical investigation", *Working Paper* No. 327 (Universita Politecnica delle Marche).

Pavcnik, N. 2002. "Trade liberalization, exit, and productivity improvement: Evidence from Chilean plants", in *Review of Economic Studies*, Vol. 69, No. 1, pp. 245-276, Jan.

Prebisch, R. 1950. "The economic development of Latin America and its principal problems", reprinted in *Economic Bulletin for Latin America*, Vol. 7, 1962, pp. 11-22.

Raballand, G.; Thornton, R.; Yang, D.; Goldberg, J.; Keleher, N. 2011. "Are rural road investments alone sufficient to generate transport flows? Lessons from a randomized experiment in rural Malawi and policy implications", *Policy Research Working Paper* No. 5535 (World Bank).

Raddatz, C. 2007. "Are external shocks responsible for the instability of output in low income countries?", in *Journal of Development Economics*, Vol. 84, No. 1, pp. 155-187, Sep.

Ramey, G.; Ramey, V.A. 1995. "Cross-country evidence on the link between volatility and growth", in *American Economic Review*, Vol. 85, pp. 1138-1151, Dec.

Robbins, D.; Gindling, T.H. 1999. "Trade liberalization and the relative wages for more-skilled workers in Costa Rica", in *Review of Development Economics*, Vol. 3, No. 2, pp. 140-154.

Rodriguez, F.; Rodrik, D. 2000. "Trade policy and economic growth: A skeptic's guide to the cross-national evidence", in B. Bernanke; K.S. Rogoff (eds): *NBER Macroeconomics Annual 2000*, Vol. 15 (MIT Press).

Rodrik, D. 2007. "Industrial development: some stylized facts and policy directions", in D. O'Connor; M. Kjollerstrom (eds): *Industrial development for the 21st century: Sustainable development perspectives* (UNDESA).

Rose, A.K. 2004. "Do WTO members have more liberal trade policy?", in *Journal of International Economics*, Vol. 63, No. 2, pp. 209-235, July.

Rosenthal, S.S.; Strange, W.C. 2004. "Evidence on the nature and sources of agglomeration economies" in J.V. Henderson; J.F. Thisse (eds): *Handbook of regional and urban economics*, Vol. 4, pp. 2119-2171.

Sachs, J.D.; Warner, A. 1995. "Economic reform and the process of global integration", in *Brookings Papers on Economic Activity*, Vol. 1, pp. 1-118.

Sachs, J.D.; Warner, A. 1997. "Natural resource abundance and economic growth", *NBER Working Paper* No. 5398.

Serti, F.; Tomasi, C. 2008. "Firm heterogeneity: Do destinations of exports and origins of imports matter?", *LEM Papers Series* No. 2008/14.

Shakurova, Y. 2010. "Horizontal and vertical export diversification: Propagation effects in the export decisions", mimeo (University of Lausanne).

Strauss-Kahn, V. 2004. "The role of globalization in the within-industry shift away from unskilled workers in France", in R. Baldwin; A. Winters (eds): *Challenges to globalization: Analyzing the economics* (University of Chicago Press).

Teorell, J.; Charron, N.; Samanni, M.; Holmberg, S.; Rothstein, B. 2009. *The quality of government dataset (version 17June09)* (The Quality of Government Institute, University of Gothenburg).

Tornell, A.; Lane, P. 1999. "Are windfalls a curse? A non-representative agent model of the current account and fiscal policy", *NBER Working Paper* No. 4839.

Theil, H. 1972. *Statistical decomposition analysis* (North Holland Publishing Company).

Trefler, D. 2004. "The long and short of the Canada-U.S. free trade agreement", in *American Economic Review*, Vol. 94, No. 4, pp. 870-895, Sep.

Tybout, J.R.; Westbrook, M.D. 1995. "Trade liberalization and the dimensions of efficiency change in Mexican manufacturing industries", in *Journal of International Economics*, Vol. 39, No. 1-2, pp. 53-78.

Uhlig, H. 2004. "Do technology shocks lead to a fall in total hours worked?", in *Journal of the European Economic Association*, Vol. 2, No. 2/3, pp. 361-371, Apr.-May.

Verhoogen, E.A. 2008. "Trade, quality upgrading, and wage inequality in the Mexican manufacturing sector", in *The Quarterly Journal of Economics*, Vol. 123, No. 2, pp. 489-530.

Volpe Martincus, C.; Carballo, J. 2008. "Is export promotion effective in developing countries? Firm-level evidence on the intensive and the extensive margins of exports", in *The Journal of International Economics*, Vol. 76, No. 1, pp. 89-106, Sep.

Volpe Martincus, C.; Carballo, J. 2010. "Beyond the average effects: The distributional impacts of export promotion programs in developing countries", in *Journal of Development Economics*, Vol. 92, No. 2, pp. 201-214.

Wacziarg, R.; Welch, K.H. 2008. "Trade liberalization and growth: New evidence", in *World Bank Economic Review*, Vol. 22, No. 2, pp. 187-231, June.

World Bank. 2008. "Special economic zones: Performance, lessons learned, and implications for zone development", *FIAS Report* No. 45869.

World Bank. 2009a. "Déterminer la priorité des investissements dans l'infrastructure: Une approche spatiale", mimeo.

Xu, B. 2003. "Trade liberalization, wage inequality, and endogenously determined nontraded goods", in *Journal of International Economics*, Vol. 60, No. 2, pp. 417-431, Aug.

Yeaple, S.R. 2005. "A simple model of firm heterogeneity, international trade, and wages", in *Journal of International Economics*, Vol. 65, No. 1, pp. 1-20, Jan.

Yi, K.M. 2003. "Can vertical specialization explain the growth of world trade?", in *Journal of Political Economy*, Vol. 111, No. 1, pp. 52-102, Feb.

Zhu, S.C.; Trefler, D. 2005. "Trade and inequality in developing countries: A general equilibrium analysis", in *Journal of International Economics*, Vol. 65, No. 1, pp. 21-24, Jan.

## TECHNICAL APPENDIX 7.A

### 7.A.1 Overall indices

#### 7.A.1.1 Herfindhal, Gini and Theil

For a given country and year (but omitting country and time subscripts), the Herfindahl index of export concentration, normalized to a range between zero and one, is given by the following formula:

$$H = \frac{\sum_{k=1}^{n} (s_k)^2 - 1/n}{1 - 1/n}$$

where $s_k = x_k / \sum_{k=1}^{n} x_k$ is the share of export line $k$ (with amount exported $x_k$) in total exports and $n$ is the number of export lines.

As for the Gini index, several equivalent definitions have been used in the literature, among which one of the simplest can be calculated by first ordering export items (at the appropriate level of aggregation) by increasing size (or share) and calculating cumulative export shares.

$X_k = \sum_{l=1}^{k} s_l$ . The Gini coefficient is then

$$G = 1 - \sum_{k=1}^{n} (X_k - X_{k-1})/n \quad .$$

Finally, Theil's entropy index (Theil, 1972) is given by

$$T = \frac{1}{n}\sum_{k=1}^{n} \frac{x_k}{\mu} \ln\left(\frac{x_k}{\mu}\right) \quad where \quad \mu = \frac{\sum_{k=1}^{n} x_k}{n} \quad .$$

#### 7.A.1.2 Theil decomposition

Let $n$ be the notional number of export products (the 5,016 lines of the HS6 nomenclature), $n_j$ the number of export lines in group $j$, $\mu$ the average dollar export value, $\mu_j$ group $j$'s average dollar export value, and $x_k$ the dollar value of export line $k$. The between-groups component is

$$T^B = \sum_{j=0}^{1} \frac{n_j}{n}\frac{\mu_j}{\mu} \ln\left(\frac{\mu_j}{\mu}\right) \tag{2}$$

and the within-groups component is

$$T^W = \sum_{j=0}^{1} \frac{n_j}{n} \frac{\mu_j}{\mu} T^j$$

$$= \sum_{j=0}^{1} \frac{n_j}{n} \frac{\mu_j}{\mu} \left[ \frac{1}{n_j} \sum_{k \in j} \frac{x_k}{\mu_j} \ln\left( \frac{x_k}{\mu_j} \right) \right]$$

(3)

where $T^j$ stands for Theil's sub-index for group $j = 0,1$. It is easily verified that $T^W + T^B = T$.

## 7.A.2 The intensive and extensive margins

### 7.A.2.1 Theil decomposition

Let the $n$ lines of the HS6 nomenclature be partitioned into two groups $i = 0,1$ where group "one" is made of active export lines for this country and year, and group "zero" is made of inactive export lines. The Theil index is then decomposed as in section 7.A.1.2. Note, however, that the between-groups sub-index is not defined, since $\mu_0 = 0$ and expression (1) contains a logarithm. Thus, we have to take a limit. By L'Hôpital's rule,

$$\lim_{\mu_0 \to 0} \left[ \frac{\mu_0}{\mu} \ln\left( \frac{\mu_0}{\mu} \right) \right] = 0$$

(4)

so, based on our partition

$$\lim_{\mu_0 \to 0} T^B = \frac{n_1}{n} \frac{\mu_1}{\mu} \ln\left( \frac{\mu_1}{\mu} \right).$$

(5)

As $\mu_1 = (1/n_1) \sum_{k \in G_1} x_k$, $\mu = (1/n) \sum_k x_k$ and, by construction, $\sum_{k \in G_1} x_k = \sum_k x_k$ it follows that

$$\lim_{\mu_0 \to 0} T^B = \ln\left( \frac{n}{n_1} \right).$$

(6)

and, as $n$ is fixed,

$$\lim_{\mu_0 \to 0} \Delta T^B = \Delta n_1 \qquad\qquad (7)$$

where $\Delta$ denote a period-to-period change. That is, given our partition, the be-tween-groups component measures changes at the extensive margin.

As for the "within-groups" component, it is a weighted average of terms combining group-specific means and group-specific Theil indices $T^j$. In group $G_0$ (inactive lines), again $\mu_0 = T^0 = 0$; so, in our case, $T^W$ reduces to $T^1$, the group Theil index for active lines. Thus, given our partition, changes in the within-groups Theil index measure changes at the intensive margin.

### 7.A.2.2 Hummels and Klenow margins

Let $x_k^i$ be the value of country $i$'s exports of good $k$, and $x_k^W$ the world's exports of that good; let also $G_1^i$ stand for the group of country $i$'s active export lines. The intensive margin $(IM^i)$ and extensive margin $(EM^i)$, for country $i$, are defined as

$$IM^i = \frac{\sum_{k \in G_1^i} x_k^i}{\sum_{k \in G_1^i} x_k^W} \; ; \qquad EM^i = \frac{\sum_{k \in G_1^i} x_k^W}{\sum_{k=1}^m x_k^W} .$$

### 7.A.3 Brenton and Newfarmer margins

Let again $G_1^i$ be the set of goods exported by country $i$ to any destination, $G_1^{ij}$ be the set of goods exported by $i$ to destination country $j$, and $M_1^j$ the set of goods imported by destination country $j$ from any origin. Based on these groups, define binary variables

$$g_k^{ij} = \begin{cases} 1 & \text{if } k \in G_1^{ij} \\ 0 & \text{otherwise} \end{cases}$$

and

$$m_k^j = \begin{cases} 1 & \text{if } k \in M_1^j \\ 0 & \text{otherwise.} \end{cases}$$

Brenton and Newfarmer's index for country $i$ is then

$$IEMP_i = \frac{\sum_{k \in G_1^i} g_k^{ij}}{\sum_{k \in G_1^i} m_k^j} .$$

## 7.A.4 Description of the drivers of diversification

**Market access:**

Countries belonging to free trade areas and customs unions obtain privileged access to each other's markets that do not have to be granted to non-members. To capture this aspect of market access we compute, for each country $i$, a weighted sum of all the preferential trade agreements (PTAs) it participates in. The weights correspond to partner's market size (as measured by GDP).

$$PTA_{it} = \left[ \sum_k \frac{GDP_{kt}}{GDP_{wt}} PTA_{ikt} \right],$$

where $i$ is the exporter country, $k$ the importer one, $t$ the year and $w$ the world. This variable is computed by the authors following Dutt, Mihov and van Zandt (2009). PTAs come from Jeffrey Bergstrand's database, available at: http://www.nd.edu/~jbergstr/. For each country pair and year, we define PTA=1 if the exporter benefits from a reciprocal preferential access to the importer's market.[30]

**Remoteness:**

The remoteness index, also called "multilateral resistance" term , is defined as:

$$R_{it} = \left[ \sum_k \frac{GDP_{kt}}{GDP_{wt}} \ln(D_{ik}) \right],$$

where $i$ is the exporter country, $k$ the importer one, $t$ the year and $w$ the world. This variable was computed by Carrère, de Melo and Wilson (2011) on the basis of Rose (2004).

**Infrastructure index:**

This variable was computed by Carrère, de Melo and Wilson (2011), using data from the telecommunication sector (number of main telephone lines per 1000 workers), the transportation sector (the length of the road and railway network −in km per km² of land area) and an index of quality in the service of transport (the share of paved roads in total roads). These raw data come from Canning (1998) and the World Development Indicators (WDI) database (see Carrère, de Melo and Wilson, 2011, appendix A2 for more details).

**Politics variables:**

We use two variables reflecting the political regime and quality of government. Both variables come from the QoG database built up by Teorell et al. (2009). This database

---

[30] This database records the economic integration of bilateral country pairings for 195 countries annually from 1960 through 2005. Depending on the level of economic integration, a country pairing was assigned a code varying from 0 to 6. We convert this code into a 0/1 dummy.

regroups several political variables issued by international institutions and researchers' studies.

The Revised Combined Polity Score assesses the degree of democracy of a country (see Marshall and Jaggers, 2002). It ranges from +10 (strongly democratic) to -10 (strongly autocratic).

The ICRG indicator of Quality of Government is part of the International Country Risk Guide provided by the PRS Group.[31] The ICRG indicator of Quality of Government is a mean value of the ICRG variables "Corruption", "Law and Order" and "Bureaucracy Quality".[32] It scales from 0 to 1 with higher values indicating a higher quality of government.

**Other variables:**
Population, R&D spending and FDI come from the WDI database provided by the World Bank.

---

[31] Available at: http://www.prsgroup.com/ICRG.aspx.
[32] These component variables can be purchased at: http://www.countrydata.com.

Table 7.A.1: Countries in the sample

| Countries (134) | Date of trade Liberalization (1950-2001) | Export Theil index (1988-2006) | Countries (134) | Date of trade Liberalization (1950-2001) | Export Theil index (1988-2006) |
|---|---|---|---|---|---|
| Albania | 1992 | 4.60 | Dominican Republic | 1992 | 4.65 |
| Algeria | closed | 6.98 | Ecuador | 1991 | 6.02 |
| Angola | closed | 8.18 | Egypt | 1995 | 4.69 |
| Argentina | 1991 | 3.58 | El Salvador | 1989 | 4.72 |
| Armenia | 1995 | 5.43 | Estonia | closed | 3.24 |
| Australia | 1964 | 3.60 | Ethiopia | 1996 | 6.33 |
| Austria | 1960 | 1.88 | Finland | 1960 | 3.00 |
| Azerbaijan | 1995 | 6.28 | France | 1959 | 1.95 |
| Bangladesh | 1996 | 4.68 | Gabon | closed | 7.56 |
| Belarus | closed | 4.01 | Gambia, The | 1985 | 6.26 |
| Belgium | 1959 | 2.20 | Georgia | 1996 | 4.74 |
| Benin | 1990 | 6.90 | Germany | 1959 | 1.71 |
| Bolivia | 1985 | 5.21 | Ghana | 1985 | 5.73 |
| Botswana | 1979 | 7.34 | Greece | 1959 | 2.89 |
| Brazil | 1991 | 3.11 | Guatemala | 1988 | 4.45 |
| Bulgaria | 1991 | 2.76 | Guinea | 1986 | 6.97 |
| Burkina Faso | 1998 | 6.87 | Guinea-Bissau | 1987 | 6.98 |
| Burundi | 1999 | 7.36 | Guyana | 1988 | 6.10 |
| Cameroon | 1993 | 6.22 | Haiti | closed | 5.08 |
| Canada | 1952 | 3.15 | Honduras | 1991 | 4.84 |
| Cape Verde | 1991 | 5.77 | Hong Kong (China) | Always | 2.56 |
| Central African Republic | closed | 6.66 | Hungary | 1990 | 2.55 |
| Chad | closed | 7.83 | Iceland | closed | 5.12 |
| Chile | 1976 | 4.57 | India | closed | 2.98 |
| China | closed | 2.17 | Indonesia | 1970 | 3.71 |
| Colombia | 1986 | 4.88 | Iran, Islamic Rep. | closed | 7.45 |
| Dem. Rep. of Congo | closed | 6.43 | Ireland | 1966 | 3.63 |
| Congo | closed | 7.45 | Israel | 1985 | 3.78 |
| Costa Rica | 1986 | 4.97 | Italy | 1959 | 1.56 |
| Côte d'Ivoire | 1994 | 5.63 | Jamaica | 1989 | 5.92 |
| Croatia | closed | 2.74 | Japan | 1964 | 2.47 |
| Cyprus | 1960 | 3.71 | Jordan | 1965 | 4.85 |
| Czech Republic | 1991 | 2.04 | Kazakhstan | closed | 5.16 |
| Denmark | 1959 | 2.22 | | | |

306

Table 7.A.1: Countries in the sample (continued)

| Countries (134) | Date of trade Liberalization (1950-2001) | Export Theil index (1988-2006) | Countries (134) | Date of trade Liberalization (1950-2001) | Export Theil index (1988-2006) |
|---|---|---|---|---|---|
| Kenya | 1993 | 4.73 | Russian Federation | closed | 4.34 |
| Korea, Rep. | 1968 | 2.71 | Rwanda | closed | 7.26 |
| Kyrgyzstan | 1994 | 4.81 | Senegal | closed | 5.07 |
| Latvia | 1993 | 3.99 | Sierra Leone | 2001 | 5.98 |
| Lesotho | closed | 6.10 | Singapore | 1965 | 3.66 |
| Liberia | closed | 6.72 | Slovakia | 1991 | 2.67 |
| Lituania | 1993 | 3.37 | Slovenia | 1991 | 2.39 |
| Luxembourg | 1959 | 3.20 | South Africa | 1991 | 3.41 |
| Macedonia, FYR | 1994 | 3.43 | Spain | 1959 | 2.13 |
| Madagascar | 1996 | 5.11 | Sri Lanka | 1991 | 3.58 |
| Malawi | closed | 6.68 | Swaziland | closed | 4.64 |
| Malaysia | 1963 | 3.64 | Sweden | 1960 | 2.39 |
| Mali | 1988 | 7.22 | Switzerland | Always | 2.32 |
| Mauritania | 1995 | 6.73 | Syrian Arab Republic | closed | 6.57 |
| Mauritius | 1968 | 4.93 | Tajikistan | 1996 | 6.29 |
| Mexico | 1986 | 3.51 | United Rep. of Tanzania | 1995 | 5.09 |
| Republic of Moldova | 1994 | 4.08 | Thailand | Always | 2.91 |
| Morocco | 1984 | 3.82 | Togo | closed | 6.00 |
| Mozambique | 1995 | 5.74 | Trinidad and Tobago | 1992 | 5.72 |
| Nepal | 1991 | 5.27 | Tunisia | 1989 | 3.83 |
| Netherlands | 1959 | 2.00 | Turkey | 1989 | 2.73 |
| New Zealand | 1986 | 3.26 | Turkmenistan | closed | 7.23 |
| Nicaragua | 1991 | 5.20 | Uganda | 1988 | 6.74 |
| Niger | 1994 | 6.64 | Ukraine | closed | 3.16 |
| Nigeria | closed | 7.99 | United Kingdom | Always | 2.15 |
| Norway | Always | 4.60 | United States | Always | 1.97 |
| Pakistan | 2001 | 3.81 | Uruguay | 1990 | 3.73 |
| Panama | 1996 | 4.25 | Uzbekistan | closed | 5.98 |
| Papua New Guinea | closed | 6.33 | Bolivarian Rep. of Venezuela | 1996 | 6.27 |
| Paraguay | 1989 | 5.70 | Yemen | Always | 7.91 |
| Peru | 1991 | 4.60 | Zambia | 1993 | 6.58 |
| Philippines | 1988 | 4.06 | Zimbabwe | closed | 4.80 |
| Poland | 1990 | 2.36 | | | |
| Portugal | Always | 2.73 | | | |
| Romania | 1992 | 2.93 | | | |